PARISH TO PLANET

HOW FOOTBALL CAME TO RULE THE WORLD

PARISH TO PLANET

HOW FOOTBALL CAME TO RULE THE WORLD

Eric Midwinter

Know The Score Books Publications

CULT HEROES	Author	ISBN
CHELSEA	Leo Moynihan	1905449003
MANCHESTER CITY	David Clayton	9781905449057
NEWCASTLE	Dylan Younger	1905449038
SOUTHAMPTON	Jeremy Wilson	1905449011
WEST BROM	Simon Wright	190544902X

MATCH OF MY LIFE	Editor	ISBN
ENGLAND WORLD CUP	Massarella & Moynihan	1905449526
EUROPEAN CUP FINALS	Ben Lyttleton	1905449577
FA CUP FINALS 1953-69	David Saffer	9781905449538
FULHAM	Michael Heatley	1905449518
LEEDS	David Saffer	1905449542
LIVERPOOL	Leo Moynihan	190544950X
MANCHESTER UNITED	Ivan Ponting	9781905449590
SHEFFIELD UNITED	Nick Johnson	1905449623
STOKE CITY	Simon Lowe	9781905449552
SUNDERLAND	Rob Mason	1905449607
SPURS	Allen & Massarella	9781905449583
WOLVES	Simon Lowe	1905449569

GENERAL FOOTBALL	Author	ISBN
2007/8 CHAMPIONS LEAGUE YEARBOOK		9781905449934
BURKSEY The Autobiography of a Football God	Peter Morfoot	1905449496
HOLD THE BACK PAGE	Harry Harris	1905449917
MY PREMIERSHIP DIARY Reading's First Season in the Premiership	Marcus Hahnemann	9781905449330
OUTCASTS The Lands That FIFA Forgot	Steve Menary	9781905449316
PARISH TO PLANET How Football Came To Rule The World	Dr Eric Midwinter	9781905449309
2006 WORLD CUP DIARY	Harry Harris	1905449909

AUTOBIOGRAPHY	Author	ISBN
TACKLES LIKE A FERRET (England Cover)	Paul Parker	190544947X
TACKLES LIKE A FERRET (Manchester United Cover)	Paul Parker	1905449461

CRICKET	Author	ISBN
GROVEL!	David Tossell	9781905449439
The Story & Legacy of the Summer of 1976		
MOML: THE ASHES	Pilger & Wightman	1905449631
MY TURN TO SPIN	Shaun Udal	9781905449422
WASTED?	Paul Smith	9781905449453
LEAGUE CRICKET YEARBOOK		
Midlands edition	Andy Searle	9781905449729
North West edition	Andy Searle	9781905449705

RUGBY LEAGUE	Author	ISBN
MOML Wigan Warriors	David Kuzio	9781905449668

Forthcoming Publications in 2007

CULT HEROES	Author	ISBN
CARLISLE UNITED	Paul Harrison	9781905449095
CELTIC	David Potter	9781905449088
NOTTINGHAM FOREST	David McVay	9781905449064
RANGERS	Paul Smith	9781905449071

MATCH OF MY LIFE	Editor	ISBN
ASTON VILLA	Neil Moxley	9781905449651
BOLTON WANDERERS	David Saffer	9781905449644
DERBY COUNTY	Johnson & Matthews	9781905449682

GENERAL FOOTBALL	Author	ISBN
MARTIN JOL: DUTCH MASTER		
	Harry Harris	9781905449774

Know The Score Books Limited
118 Alcester Road, Studley, Warwickshire, B80 7NT
Tel: 01527 454482 Fax: 01527 452183
info@knowthescorebooks.com
www.knowthescorebooks.com

A CIP catalogue record is available for this book from the British Library

ISBN: 978-1-905449-30-9

Jacket Design by Lisa David
Book Designed and Edited by Andy Searle

Printed and bound in Great Britain
by Cromwell Press, Trowbridge, Wiltshire

Mixed Sources
Product group from well-managed
forests and other controlled sources
www.fsc.org Cert no. TT-COC-2082
© 1996 Forest Stewardship Council
FSC

CONTENTS

PREFACE AND ACKNOWLEDGEMENTS

150 YEARS AGO there was no such thing as organised football. In 2006 half the world's population watched the World Cup Final on television. This was, for reasons both qualitative and quantitative, the largest simultaneously enjoyed experience in the history of humankind. This book is an intrepid attempt to describe and explain not only that sporting miracle, but also the social and cultural phenomenon of which it is an essential part.

The text is divided into three sections. The first 'local' part looks at the origins of sporting 'play' in pre-industrial Britain and at the precursors of formal football in its townships and villages, paying proper attention to the role of the public schools in this regard. It ends with the millennial year of 1863 and the seminal foundation of the Football Association, bringing focus and codification to the nascent game of 'association' football.

The second 'national' part examines the growth of football in Britain, demonstrating the influence of the FA Cup and the powerful effects of professionalism, the Football League and the rise of football as a mainstream spectator sport. This involves a pertinent analysis of the urban and industrial environment in which football developed and expanded. It also describes the main events in British football up until the First World War.

The third 'global' part scrutinises the dramatic spread of football on a worldwide basis, again linking this to social, economic and political factors. This section alternates between the progress of global football and the related condition of the game in Britain, in the belief that this method will best satisfy the interests of most readers. The book ends with some thoughts about the current state of world football and its likely future prospects.

A study that tries to encompass such astounding sporting happenings, within their social and cultural context and over such a wide area, is naturally and heavily reliant on secondary sources. However, in aiming the book at the general rather than the academic reader, it was decided to avoid the possible distraction of an elaborate scholastic apparatus of footnotes and references, although there is, within the text, considerable and appropriate mention of authors and commentators whose work has been utilised. There also now follows a note of the chief sources for the facts and evidence upon which the interpretations offered in Parish to Planet are founded, itself provided as a brief guide to further reading.

For the pre-history of football, Dennis Brailsford, *British Sport; a Social History*, Lutterworth (1992) and Robert W. Malcolmson, *Popular Recreations in English Society, 1700-1850*, CUP (1973) were of particular and enlightening value, while Richard Holt, *Sport and the British; a Modern History*, OUP (1989) was useful for both this and later stages of football's development.

Helpful sources for the growth of British football included Geoffrey Green, *The Official History of the FA Cup*, Sportsman's Book Club (1960); Keith Booth, *The Father of Modern Sport; the Life and Times of Charles W. Alcock*, Parrs Wood Press (2002); James Walvin, *The People's Game; the History of Football Revisited*, Mainstream (1994) and James Walvin, *The Only Game; Football in Our Times*, Pearson Education Ltd (2001), the last two books being also of assistance with the third part of the book. Tony Mason's *Association Football and English Society 1863-1915*, Harvester (1980) remains an excellently crafted standard monograph on this important phase in football's history.

For the spread of football on a global scale, the recent, encyclopaedic and perceptive volume by David Goldblatt, *The Ball is Round; a Global History of Football*, Penguin Viking (2006), has proved of immense value, while my friend Peter Hartland's astute and insightful *Patterns in World Football 1863-2004*, Field Publishing (2005) has been of enormous assistance throughout both the 'national' and 'global' sections of the text. This author is indebted to these authors, and to many others over many years of reading, who have helped in the preparation of this book.

Geoff Wilde, a legendary figure among cricket and other sports statisticians for his eagle-eyed textual analysis, kindly agreed to look through the draft of Parish to Planet, and I am indebted to him for his gentle pointing out of many infelicities in the text. He will understand, as a fellow comedy buff, when I borrow the catchphrase, derived from the cry of a cockney bus conductor, of a diminutive Merseyside apiary-fantasist, and offer him a heartfelt, 'Aythangyew'.

A final tribute to my judicious publisher, Simon Lowe, an estimable source of constant encouragement and of the fine illustrations that lend such support

PREFACE AND ACKNOWLEDGEMENTS

to the text, and to his colleague, the energetic Andy Searle for his most careful editing of these pages and for his valued provision of a detailed index. By and with all these streams of assistance, I could not have hoped for a pleasanter involvement in this interesting project.

Eric Midwinter, June 2007

PART ONE

LOCAL

CHAPTER ONE

PRELUDE; FOOTBALL AND THE CONCEPT OF 'PLAY'

Football; the Global Game

ON 9 JULY 2006 television sets switched on for the football World Cup final. They were tuned in across all of the world's time-zones, so that, quite literally, someone was watching every minute of the day. Teams drawn from 198 of FIFA's 207 member states had been whittled down to the 32 competitors for these last stages in Germany, After three years of qualifying matches came, ultimately, the concluding and decisive drama.

All over the globe they watched in the bright gleam of day and in the dark watches of night. Some watched at the height of sultry summer and some in the depths of chilly winter. It was the largest audience ever for a single television programme. Something over 3 billion people are calculated to have watched as Italy beat France and Zidane chest-butt Materazzi, that is, close to a half of the world's population. The generally accepted estimate for the number of live births the human race has delivered in its 2 million years or so of existence is 60 billion. This means that roughly 5% of the human beings who have ever drawn breath watched the 2006 World Cup Final - a bewildering statistic.

Association Football is unquestionably the first and, so far, only specific cultural formula to have conquered the world. Sport, music and the arts are and have always been, of course, aspects of practically all civilisations, but football is the one prototype of any of these general areas of cultural reference that has become ubiquitous. Types of the arts, including film, literature, and theatre, have been restricted in spread by language and other cultural signifiers, but none have enjoyed, for all their critical or classical endorsement, the wholehearted appeal of football.

Popular music may feel it has a case. John Lennon notoriously asserted, not without some arithmetical justification, that more people living had heard of the Beatles than had of Jesus. Certainly Elvis Presley has some claim to being regarded as an all-pervading icon. Nonetheless, if only because his magnetism was focused on younger people in specified cultural milieux, it is doubtful whether his conquest of the world was so total.

There are, plainly, religious beliefs and political creeds in every part of the world, but their very dissonance means they could never be universal in influence and attraction. The theological and ideological divisions are such that no one doctrine is unanimously acknowledged. Neither Mohammed nor Marx could honestly make that claim. If one were to search for a comprehensively iconic name for the late 20th and the early years of the 21st centuries, an idol that found some resonance in every community, it must be Pelé.

It has largely been a pragmatic process. The global village, with the planet shrinking under the impact of the communications revolution, notably the phenomena of flight and television, means that, for the first time, an omnipresent cultural form is feasible. Football has made real that possibility.

How did football develop from a homely pastime to a planetary marvel? The story is a complex one and it may be traced back, through football's coming of age as a national sport in the 19th century, to its very localised roots in the townships and villages of olden times.

Kicking

Someone, somewhere, sometime, must have been the first to kick something or somebody. Kicking does appear to be a natural and proactive gesture. The youngsters are playing soccer in the park. The ball strays toward the path of the antiquated pensioner escorting his ageing dog on a morning walk - here let the author and his ancient lurcher serve as poignant example - and immediately the instinctive urge arises to take a smart step or two and flight it cleverly back into the melée of juvenile players. Given the indoctrination of nearly four score years of desultory playing and avid watching, it is difficult to differentiate the inherent from the learnt reaction, but the sense is of an organic impulse. The chasm between such an atavistic yearning and the competence of its personal execution is not, thankfully, the present issue. Rather is it the sheer spontaneity of kicking as a human bent.

PRELUDE

The substantial exception of locomotion apart, the legs and feet play a less notable role in sport, as in many other human activities, than the arms and hands. Excluding the self-evident instance of athletics and the not hugely followed sport of kick-boxing, football is the one major sport that depends almost entirely on the feet. Its 'sister' football codes, such as the rugby family of games, rely much more on handling, while related field sports, like hockey and lacrosse, obviously involve holding and wielding an implement. Indeed, a whole series of popular games depend on hand-held or propelled objects, from the net or basket ball, the bowl or the dart to the tennis, badminton or squash rackets, the golf club, the billiard cue and the cricket and baseball bats and balls.

At first sight, then, it might seem curious, even paradoxical, that the only sport to effect a truly global conquest should be based on the uncomplicated foot, not the more flexible hand. Possibly it is this very minimalism that is the secret. One cannot hold a range of sportive tools with the toes. The potential flourishes are meagre in number. Backwards or forwards, left or right, short or long, up or down; that's about all there is to it. The plainness of the act probably contributes to a significant aspect of football that will recur throughout this text, namely, its essential simplicity. Very importantly, in the modern context, it is the ease of watching, no less the ease of playing, that has made it so enduring and all-encompassing.

Because Britain was the cockpit for football's exploration of the sporting world, it has been relatively easy to demonstrate how, before the formal systemisation of the game, there were scores of examples of primitive football being played locally and how these quickly adapted to the nationally codified version. It is important to stress that this pre-history of football, as it is sometimes termed, was equally abundant in incidence throughout other parts of the world. It would be difficult to account for the runaway, worldwide success of football without some presumption of a willingness on the part of other populations to adopt the football format with such affection and urgency.

Human beings resemble one another more than they differ and it would be misleading to suggest that there was something about the British genetic make-up that led games playing to be more typical in these islands than in other environs. It was, as will be explained, the primary industrial and urbanised character of Britain that caused games-playing to be formalised and the resultant formulae to be exported, but that is a different and later dimension. What is apparent is that people everywhere were ready and eager to leap on the

5

footballing bandwagon, precisely because they were already geared up to the prospect by dint of ongoing localised diversions, many of which may have involved an element of kicking at a rounded object of some sort.

The Plainness of Play

The whole apparatus of games in life and society, not least in animal life and society, is the intense subject of arcane and controversial academic consideration. There is apparently an innate desire in some of these scholastic quarters to attach the highest degree of symbolic significance to the games of past societies. The ritualistic, even supernatural, origins of games are asserted, with fertility and rain-making rites common among these theories. Whether it was the Inuit playing cup and ball, in an understandable anxiety magically to entrap the sun, or the Assamese, with their tug of war across the river, attempting to thwart demons, or the Wichita Indian of what would become Oklahoma celebrating the triumph of spring over winter with a mazy form of field-hockey, the anthropologists have been keen to make these esoteric connections. Hittite archery was given a supernatural twist, with a somewhat obscure reference to homosexuality. Even the suburban niceties of genteel badminton have been labelled as initially a mode of divination.

Let us, for instance, examine a couple of hypotheses about football extant in the 1970s and 1980s. The German left-wing theoretician, Gerhard Vinnal, argued that 'the pseudo-activity of football canalises the energies which could shatter the existing power-structures.' This is a tad advanced from the commonplace notion of Victorian employers sweetening the work-force with sops, like funding the football team or, another notable example, the brass band. In Vinnal's view, football not only quells the revolutionary appetite, it also promotes the capitalist ethic by covertly indoctrinating, for example, the values of work-rate, so much admired by the grasping factory-owner.

In 1981 Desmond Morris published *The Soccer Tribe*. He claimed that football was 'the perfect parallel' for the hunt and that the 'survival hunters' of prehistoric times lost the purpose, but not the urge, to hunt with the coming of agriculture. First the 'Arena Blood-sportsmen' of the Roman Collosseum or the bullfight supplied the necessary and vicarious outlet for this desire. Now the 'Arena Ball-sportsmen' made 'their symbolic kill by shooting at the goalmouth', with the goalkeeper 'the claws of the cornered prey'.

PRELUDE

Football is at once a complex of bourgeois conspiracy and replacement therapy. The former thesis depends on thousands of businessmen and entrepreneurs sustaining an elaborate and secretive regime of manipulation. The latter concept fails to explain why there are two goalmouths and two sets of 'claws of the cornered prey'. One suspects that such theorising is too sophisticated for its own good.

Unluckily, sports historians have also relished antiquarian hints that might suggest their game of choice has a superior and long-established vintage. Egyptians at ninepins; Athenians at hockey; the Crusaders at polo; St Cuthbert at hurling; the Romans at fives - it only requires the sighting of a club or circular object on some stone relief, and the cry goes up claiming it for this or that sport. An illuminated Decretal of Pope Gregory IX, circa 1300, picturing a boy with a stick and a ball and a man with a stick, and, *voila*, we have the beginnings of cricket. Misty legends of pre-Christian rituals, aimed at securing magical forces to boost fertility, have led to musings about the origins of football. It is suggested that it might be a sanitised rendering of some gory fertility rite involving the head of an animal or even a human.

What is uncertain, even accepting the tentative nature of much of this ancient testimony, is the sequence of events. Could the pundits be putting the symbolic cart before the authentic horse? If one examines the anthropology of sport in recent generations, one discerns that the game normally came before the encrustation of portentous justification. There is no doubt that football, like some other sports, has been politicised. Football is, so to say, a political football. It has increasingly become the emblem of nationalistic ambition and pride. In truth, it has not yet touched the gruesome depths of the Olympic Games, which is so suffused in an orgy of national rivalries and ideological conflicts as to make it all but unwatchable by the genuine sports lover. It is worth recalling that the ancient Greeks had the sense and the courage to abandon the original games, after a mere thousand years, when they became tainted with similar blotches that, almost from the outset, have disgraced the modern Olympic flag. In so doing, incidentally, they provided further testimony to the earthy notion that sport comes before the flag.

Both sets of Olympic Games, ancient and modern, as well as modern football, indicate that the beginnings were innocent enough. They were no more than the friendly wish to participate in and enjoy sport. The religious and political rationales were added later. Could it have been that, initially, the

Wichita Indian modestly enjoyed his version of field-hockey, only for interfering authority to adopt it for politico-religious purposes in respect of controlling the weather?

For those who prefer an unvarnished account of the origin and value of games and sports there is solace to be found in the work of the Dutch polymathic thinker, Johan Huizinga, and, in particular, in his seminal study, published in 1938, *Homo Ludens; a Study of the Play Element in Culture*. He propagated the idea that, as well as 'homo sapiens' or 'thinking man' and 'homo faber' or creative man, there was 'homo ludens', that is, 'playing man'. Many will spot the linkage with the child's game of Ludo in the coinage. 'Playing man', including, of course, woman and child, signalled, for Johan Huizinga, a discreet aspect of the human condition. 'Play is a uniquely adaptive act,' he wrote, 'not subordinate to some other adaptive act, but with a special function of its own in human experience.' He went on sagely to comment that, 'play...is of a higher order than seriousness. For seriousness seeks to exclude play, which can very well include seriousness.'

Huizinga insisted that 'play' is 'a thing in itself', not explicable by sociological, biological, physiological or other rationalisations, but a human trait in its own right, characterised by its aesthetic quality and the sense of fun it generates in its participants. He saw 'play', in all civilisations, as a voluntary and disinterested 'interlude' between bouts of work and other responsibilities. This magisterial emphasis on 'play' as valuable in itself, unencumbered by the baggage with which some experts have sought to burden it, is music to the ears of those who believe that football, as well as most other sports, have no need of mythological or other explanation.

When, at the end of the crucial and historic Old Trafford Test match in 1902, Fred Tate, having dropped the critical catch and been clean bowled with four runs required, wept alone in the dressing room, he was approached by the cheerily philosophic Somerset cricketer, Len Braund. 'Go upstairs and get your money,' he strongly advised, 'it's only a game.' He might have been playing John the Baptist to Johan Huizinga's Messiah. Yet Samuel Johnson preceded him, for, in his famed dictionary, produced in 1795, he defined 'diversion' in terms of that which 'unbends the mind by turning it off from care.'

It is encouraging to be told that the commonplace aphorism 'a change is as good as a rest', has such scholarly provenance and support. It persuasively answers the question of why football originated and why it eventually became globally popular. For participant and, in time, spectator, it was and remains a necessary - an important adjective - diversion from the workaday cares of the common round. It is, then, fundamentally, a matter of amusement or 'disportment', the base, of course, for the word 'sport'. It is of interest to learn that the word 'sport' used to describe 'participation in games or exercise, especially those pursued in the open air; such games collectively' is dated as late as 1863 - the year the Football Association was established and issued the game's first rules. Disportment or diversion: this was the fulcrum for football - the trappings, not all of them welcome, came later.

Most of the experts, including many of those who have studied 'play' among animals other than the human species, accept that play is marked by its lack of utilitarian purpose in terms of what are usually regarded as basic needs. There may be argument as to whether the kitten playing skittishly with the cotton-reel is rehearsing for future forays in respect of mice or merely enjoying the diversion - what is agreed is that there is no end product; the kitten does not eat the cotton-reel. There is a wide belief that human 'play' is clearly limited by time, space and law, however rudimentary these restraints may be. It is rather like the creation of a fiction, entirely separate from the rigours of work and family raising. That image of a self-contained piece of theatre is plainly illustrated by the great football stadia of the 20th and 21st centuries.

It is sometimes urged that sport, including football, is utilised for specific purposes. The games of both ancient Greece and Rome, no less the archery contests and tournaments of medieval Europe, had overt connection with military skills. However, they offered a second, if more pacific, opportunity for the practice and reinforcement of the same skill. They did not necessarily offer preparatory training in the skill; obviously, one had to be capable enough if presenting oneself in either sporting or martial capacity.

It was, too, always said that hawking and hunting were important for the upkeep of cavalry horsemanship and a sharpened eye for terrain. That is a concept neatly encapsulated in a stanza borrowed from Marriott Edgar's monologue, made famous by Stanley Holloway, *The Battle of Hastings*, with its 'aunting refrain:

> *There on the 'ill sat 'Arold;*
> *On 'is 'orse with 'is 'awk in 'is 'and.*

Again, the skills are analogous rather than supportive. At the very least, this portrays the natural whim of the horse rider to choose for diversion those activities that would exercise both steed and military man in pleasing fashion. The motif of amusement, without the end product, in this instant, of actually fighting and maybe killing someone for real, is the constant.

This martial excursion has to be included, because football is often branded a stylised battle, as if it were some kind of replacement or aversion therapy. George Orwell came close in 1945 - 'war minus the shooting' - to implying this in his accusation of sport being a sort of diluted 'warfare'. He was, it should be remembered, referring to a distorted form of international sport, with the distinct inference that the scowling political mask had been smeared across the smiling sporting countenance. It is, nonetheless, a much used analogy. In terms of the genuine reason why sport - why football - exists, it should be properly scotched. The focus must remain on its essential autonomy as a diversion.

It is relatively easy to describe how football emerged and developed. It is perhaps more difficult to analyse why. The rational explanation accepts football *qua* football, as a self-justifying amusement for its own sake and with its own values, without need of, rather imperilled by, being overlaid with extraneous validations. It is important to cling to that clean-cut perspective. Any journey through the story of football is beset by such pitfalls. Apart from tribal and nationalistic mystiques, we shall also encounter, *inter alia*, the dire educational myth that football, like cricket and rugby and other games, is character building. More of that anon; for the present let us, with Johan Huizinga, relax over the simple truth of football providing an 'interlude' for players and observers alike.

Football and Pre-Victorian Society

The words 'play' and 'interlude' convey a sense of tranquil gentleness, but many pre-Victorian pastimes, including the varied forms of football, were attended by a prodigious and bestial violence. The cruel baiting and slaughter of animals and the most vicious contests of fighting, cudgelling and the like were not uncommon. It was this degree of brutality, especially when it engaged a clamorous horde of aggressive folk, which alerted the authorities to the social hazards of sport.

This has been, from medieval times until the present day, a consistent element in the progress of football. Those in power were suspicious and fearful of games played and watched by undisciplined crowds. There were several aspects that caused concern. There were the possible political ramifications of crowds gathering for football matches and being used, spontaneously or consciously, as the cover for some subversive or anti-authoritarian act. In more humdrum manner, there was the collateral damage to crops and property that resulted from the mayhem of football in field or street. Additionally, on the economic front, there was the absenteeism from worthy labour and the perceived cost to employers of such high jinks.

The military mind was incessantly worried by games. In 1297, at the onset of yet another Anglo-Scottish war, the other ranks demonstrated a lack of purposefulness that shocked their commanders. The Lancashire and Cheshire levies apparently played football against Scotland's finest in what might be deemed the first ever football international. It was an event that foreshadowed the mingling and footballing of British and German troops on the Western front 600 years later at the Christmas of 1914. Once more it was the commandants who were not amused.

In 1314 a proclamation of Edward II berated 'certain tumults arising from great footballs in the fields of the public'; in 1365 an edict of Edward III banned a wide compass of ball games, plus 'the hurling of stones'...one could list a roster of laws, local as well as national, that forbade football in particular or as part of some general ban. In 1541, during the reign of Henry VIII, a statute expressly proscribed artificers, labourers, apprentices and servants from playing games except at Christmas and then solely under the beady eye and at the home of the master. Games, football included, were outlawed on account of 'country persons having invented new and crafty games whereof archery is decayed.' Enclosures and extended sheep farming in the 16th century had led to a similar protest: 'shepherds make but poor archers', moaned one gloomy Tudor commentator.

It is doubly interesting in that, as well as the powers-that-were being bothered about a shortage of archers, the would-be archers presumably preferred football and other games. In a moment Johan Huizinga would have recognised, they possibly found archery too much like real work and not sufficiently amusing and diversionary. The attempt to gear such activities to military ends is reminiscent of the Elizabethan demand for a meatless Friday. In spite of its superficial religious rationalisation, it was prompted by a Protestant government's wish to keep sufficient sailor-fishermen afloat, so that, come such a threat as the Roman Catholic Spanish Armada, there would be enough experienced seafarers to man the English fleet.

Indeed, such was this battery of legislation over several centuries that many ball games were notionally illegal until 1845, when that 1541 legislation was, eventually, repealed, although the statutes were honoured more in the breach by this time. Needless to say, the elite were normally free from such restrictions and the rich and aristocratic indulged in many sports, some of them of an expensive nature. There were, for instance, some sixteen real ('royal', as in Real Madrid) tennis courts, with their elaborate construction, in London alone in 1620. Much money was spent and wagered on games, particularly in the 18th century and Regency periods.

This penchant for such pastimes among the high and mighty was part of an ambivalence that typified the reaction of the upper classes to sport among the other classes. Briefly described, throughout this long later medieval and early modern epoch there was a swinging of the pendulum from outright abhorrence of sport among the lower orders to a benign recognition that time spent at leisure helped to keep the peasants and workers content. They could let off steam in bustling football matches and then, the thought ran, they would be less likely to mutter subversive sentiments and more likely to resettle quietly to their manly toil. The more the landlords, squires and employers were themselves involved and showing a fond interest in the appropriate sports, the more effective, many of them believed, would be the stratagem.

It is possible to trace an approximate trail of this exercise in social ambiguity. It changed from time to time and, of course, from individual to individual. For example, some Regency sporting aristocrats and plutocrats actively enjoyed joining or backing their tenants or workers in a string of games from hunting and horse racing to cricket, boxing and 'pedestrianism', the precursor of athletics. At one time and place the local big-wig would throw up the pig's bladder to signal the commencement of the football match. At another time and place he would be doing his best to have the game abandoned. Thomas Elyot's *The Governour*, his 1531 treatise on the education of the superior Tudor youngster, was quite elitist on the subject of fencing and tennis for the fledgling aristo, but scornfully dismissed 'the beastly fury' of football, along with the bad company to be found round a skittles alley, out of hand.

PRELUDE

This curious and contradictory situation was reflected in the attitude of the church, always with an instructive role to play in the story of sport, at least until about 1914. First the Puritan tendency, then the strict nonconformist sects, such as the Baptists, and later much of Methodism and the low and evangelical wing of the Anglican Church showed an unrelenting antipathy towards sport. It was licentious and brutal; it was frequently associated with the alehouse (skittle and bowling alleys again); and it led people astray, away from their prior requirement to worship, pray and perform good works. The broader and more latitudinarian groupings in the established church looked to find some compromise, hopeful that, by maintaining a social link through sport, they could the more efficiently recruit for and hold their parishioners to their religious responsibilities.

According, as with the political and economic aspects, to the degree of preponderance of a particular creed at any time or in any district, the clerical effect, over these scores of years, varied. The use or non-use of the churchyard for sporting encounters was one touchstone, while another and potentially more compelling one was Sunday observance. The purity or otherwise of the Sabbath is a significant thread running through the tapestry of nearly 500 years of sporting chronicles. Given that Sunday was the only generally free day from work, any crackdown on Sunday sport was disastrous for the would-be games player. It was a provision that was to affect British football until late in the 20th century.

The alliance of a more puritanical minister with a landlord or employer keen to enforce social discipline in the streets and passive attendance at the work-place was a powerful weapon. Equally, a sporting squire and tolerant vicar might have encouraged games to flourish. Sometimes it is difficult to spot the join between the religion and the politics. In 1555, during Mary I's Popish rule, action was taken to stop sporting activities because her advisers feared that 'unlawful assemblies, conventicles, seditions and conspiracies' might be being organised by treasonable Protestants behind the screen of games. On the other side of the theological divide, the oft-cited Puritan legislation against pastimes during Oliver Cromwell's Protectorate in the mid-17th century was motivated, in part, by the suspicion that renegade Cavaliers might be planning to overthrow the Roundhead regime behind the cover of merry recreations.

The Ambivalence of Old-time Football

Old-fashioned football itself had its own inner ambiguity. Unlike some sports, football was not of great appeal to the nobility. There were one or two examples of lordly support - the Earl of Sunderland and Lord Willoughby are reported to have arranged a match with equal sides on one occasion in Hanoverian times - but the hullabaloo of most festival football was not to the taste of the disdainful gentry. Their preference, certainly from the early 18th century onwards, was for horse racing, cricket and fisticuffs. The first two had the bonus of the 'gentle' and 'simple' folk being able to play together without too much loss of dignity, in that there was no actual physical contact of the major kind associated with the football then played.

Indeed, and partly because of the failure of the people in the top drawer to lend a hand, there was, by 1750, a dwindling of interest in football, with several of the annual games either banished or lessened in popularity. This was, according to most historians, typical of the time, with many ancient pursuits restrained by the impact of legal, labour, religious and social regulation, as a compound of urban, industrial and religious and other disciplines began to bite. It is intriguing to note that, just as the darkest hour appears before the brightest dawn, football fell away somewhat in its incidence just prior to the events that were to grant it lasting prosperity.

One of the reasons for this was the upside of non-aristocratic and squirearchial backing. A principle element in the upper crust affection for cricket, racing and boxing in the Hanoverian and Regency period was the opportunity they provided for gambling. It was this obsession with wagering that led to these pastimes being the first to be standardised and supplied with controls. Unless and until there was some agreement as to the format of the sport, arguments abounded over the heavy bets won and lost.

Although cricket's chroniclers, like non-striking batsmen trying to pinch a yard or so as they back up, are ever eager to push the beginnings of cricket further back into the mists of time, it was basically the 18th century before, from a complex skein of etymological and legal references to the sport, a recognisable form of cricket emerges in the south-east of England. Its earliest surviving rules are 'articles of agreement', dated 1727, for a match ('matches' were for betting; 'games' weren't) between the teams raised by the Duke of Richmond and Mr Alan Brodrick, especially for this purpose, and the 'London' code of 1744, the precursor of the present laws of cricket, was probably designed to ensure that the quite astonishingly weighty gambling associated with cricket was more peaceful a proposition than it might otherwise have been. At much the same time, when some form of London club, an antecedent of the distinguished Marylebone Cricket Club, was first active, the Jockey Club, with gentleman like Admiral Rous and George Bentinck to the fore, was established to bring stricter controls to horse racing for much the same reason. In boxing, there were the 1743 Broughton Rules, named after Jack of that ilk, whose Tottenham Court Road Amphitheatre was the chief venue for what, before the intercession of his code, was a comprehensively coarse and unruly sport. The Queensberry Rules, promulgated in the mid-1860s, were a sophistication of those earlier constraints.

Gambling, then, was the key to 18th century efforts to bring some semblance of order and sanity to pastimes often wrecked by the troubles to which heavy wagering is heir. The need to clean up and standardise these sports indicates how rife the corruption was. There was one infamous case in 1817 when the fixture between Nottinghamshire and England at Lord's was said to have been 'sold' on both sides, suggestive of a scene of batsmen endeavouring to get out and bowlers trying not to take wickets. Conversely, football, whatever its other horrors, was mainly free from the vice of gambling. Given the 18th century passion for betting this is perhaps surprising, but football's stalwart defence against the evil of wagering was its own primitive anarchy. It was too chaotic to call and, in consequence, too hectically muddled to fix. Even Hansie Cronje, for all his guile, would have had trouble fixing the Derby 'mellay' on a Shrove Tuesday.

That primeval innocence was to stand football in good stead. Particularly when the public schools were to search for appropriate games for their pupils, football was, whatever else, untainted as yet by the sinfulness of gambling. Moreover, the highly localised, even domesticated, incidence of football remained robust. As Britain became more urbanised, football had the advantage of being playable in streets as well as in fields. When the time came when football, like cricket, racing and boxing before it, was subjected by its middle and upper class aficionados to a more precise formula in the middle of the 19th century, the time was ripe for its large scale acceptance and utilisation.

Such are, in general terms, the reasons why football was sporadically and communally played across Britain, and possibly across much of Europe too, during the centuries stretching back to the generations not long after the

Norman Conquest. Again in generalised terms, and recalling that over such a wide terrain and extent of time the variables must have been numerous, some summary account of the social pros and cons has been added, indicative of what aspects of national life favoured and hindered its spasmodic existence.

So much for the knotty question of why. Next it is the turn of the slightly easier, because less theoretical and more factual, question of how. What were people actually doing when they participated in football? What were the aims and skills and conventions of this widespread sport that was so readily and speedily to become transformed into a modern, national game? So complete was the victory of football that A.E.Housman's *A Shropshire Lad*, was able, without exegesis, to include a couple of mentions of football in his despondently heart-rending verses:

The first, in stanza XVII, reads:

> *Twice a week the winter thorough*
> *Here stood I to keep the goal:*
> *Football then was fighting sorrow*
> *For the young man's soul.*

The second, in stanza XXXII, reads:

> *'Is football playing*
> *Along the river shore,*
> *With lads to chase the leather,*
> *Now I stand up no more?*

> *Ay, the ball is flying,*
> *The lads play heart and soul;*
> *The goal stands up, the keeper*
> *Stands up to keep the goal.*

This exercise in laconic melancholia was published in 1896. It was barely 30 years since the codification of football and yet, such was the sport's widespread recognition, that a nationally esteemed poet and his discerning readership were already at ease with football's citation in serious lyrical verse.

CHAPTER TWO

'GAMENESS'; THE PRE-HISTORY OF FOOTBALL

'Football Readiness'

THE PRE-VICTORIAN football we know about is unusual. It is the football about which we have little or no knowledge that is the more significant. That is to say that we are aware of the football that made a splash, that only happened once a year as part or whole of some annual festival and was addressed by contemporary diarists or chroniclers. Below that higher level of occasional celebratory action dwelt a lower, less considered but more imperative type of football. It scarcely registered on the radar of the literate scribes of the age because of its very ordinariness. This was the daily or weekly disportment of tiny groups of boys or young men who would randomly foregather for what later generations would call a kickabout.

All across the land, around scattered hamlets and in cramped city streets, man would be at regular 'play', with the instinctive urge to kick and throw uppermost. Important although the great festival football matches may have been, it is more surely this innate, commonplace delight in the primitive skills of kicking and throwing that mattered most when, in the last half of the 19th century, football became codified and formalised. The rapid spread of the game demonstrates the organic nature of its seedbed. This also applies to the quick-fire expansion of football to Europe and South America within decades of its British origins and to the rest of the world later in the 20th century. It has been to the great advantage of organised football that it has touched a tap-root in almost all societies. Educators speak, in regard of teaching children, of 'reading readiness'. Communities all over the world have, during the last 150 years, signalled 'football readiness'.

The pretty picture of a youngster kicking a stone about a medieval village, as prelude to the flair of a George Best, could be superficially dismissed as sentimental folklore. In fact, it is the reverse. It is a hard-headed notion. Organised football became ubiquitous because disorganised football had been ubiquitous.

Festive Football - Where and When

Nonetheless, the major festive football encounters had their impact and are certainly worthy of some methodological as well as social analysis. The various proclamations, already discussed, against football offer clues as to what actually happened. In 1576 'unknown malefactors of the number of a hundred' gathered illegally in Ruislip 'and played a certain unlawful game, called football.' The injunction makes it sound as if the sport was not too well known, although that may have been conscious judicial ignorance, just as the numbers involved may have been exaggerated a trifle for alarmist purposes.

Nevertheless, there is little doubt that large numbers were often engaged in football matches of this kind. That said, it would be wrong to assume that play was entirely incoherent and lacking in structure. As early as the 1420s there were football dinners in London, pointing to some decorous sense of ordered celebration. While gateways or the distance between two conveniently located trees or shrubs frequently served as goals, from Ireland comes early evidence of specially contrived hooped willow goals.

As the famous Iona and Peter Opie researches into child folklore revealed, arcane rules are commonly to be found being maintained with an iron discipline in the seemingly random play of children. Thus were there likewise, in similar folk games, oral conventions, some apparently quite complex, to bring an element of control to the fury of medieval and early modern football, especially in regard of restrictions on the basic violence of the activity. Haxey Hood, in Lincolnshire, had 'boggons', who had a supervisory role, not unlike today's referees.

Although the Reformation and the establishment of the Protestant church, no less the influence of a stringent Puritanism, reduced the number of saints' days available for recreational purposes, it is believed that, in the 18th century, between a half and two-thirds of parishes sustained the tradition of an annual feast or 'wake' or other form of revel, as well as keeping some other seasonal festivals. These were the times, of course, for the major fairs, whilst smaller parishes held what today might be described as a fete. Such holidays followed a pattern that comfortably compounded the theological and the economic. For example, Plough Monday - when the Haxey Hood game was played - was the first such day after Twelfth Night; Shrove Tuesday was a major holiday and the date for many football matches (and a school half-holiday in certain places until late in the 19th century), while it has been calculated that, around the Whitsun period, no fewer than 314 fairs were organised in England and Wales, many of them, inevitably, involving an agricultural or marketing function.

It must be stressed again that, unlike in the Roman Catholic areas of Europe where 'holy days' remained the norm and the church was intimately engaged, the Anglican clergy had become less involved. By the 18th century the joint factors were at work of a more tolerant, some would opine idler, established church plus nonconformist chapels with a distaste for gaudy and brazen recreation. Neither, then, wished to be engaged in popular merrymaking, but, in that the parish was the civil as well as the religious unit, there was an encouraging climate in which jolly social and cultural elements were to the fore.

In such jovial situations football would find itself but one of several ingredients in a cheery casserole of pastimes. Blindfold wheelbarrow racing, gurning through a horse collar, chasing a greased pig, hasty, that is hot pudding eating - here was all the fun of the fair. The pre-Victorian football match of this kind must be seen specifically as a part of this festive whole. Every place had its own format. Sometimes teams were ten or fifteen only; elsewhere there were swarms of a hundred and more. Sometimes the ball would be small and hard, like a cricket ball; elsewhere it would be an inflated animal bladder. Sometimes an enclosed meadow would be the venue; elsewhere an extensive terrain of maybe two or three miles would be chosen. Sometimes the goals would be small, if usually natural targets like a couple of bushes; elsewhere the goals would simply be, say, the well in one village and the church door in the next. Naturally, much of this depended on whether the game was internal to the township or parish, which was perhaps more common if less advertised, or had developed into a contest between two adjoining hamlets. The Bromfield Free School annual football match in Cumberland tested the youth of the east against those of the west end of the parish, with the goals accordingly located over two miles apart.

One of the most famous games, assisted by the fact that it persisted into the 19th century, was at Derby. Here representatives of the neighbouring parish churches of St Peter's and All Saints' met in yearly combat, although it seems there was sufficient flexibility to permit any resident of the borough to attach himself to either of the rival factions. The resultant congregations would be the envy of present-day vicars. Hosts of between 500 and 1000 men were embattled in the parochial cause and this was a long-drawn out affair. St Peter's goal was a gate to the south of the town, while All Saints' defended a watermill to the east of Derby. Strategies included waiting until after dark to attempt a sortie; plunging into the River Derwent and conveying the ball by a watery route; hiding the ball beneath a lady's petticoat, and, after the fashion of Harry Lime in *The Third Man* film, utilising the sewers. Like many of these great wide-games, the normal conclusion came with victory for the side that first managed to thrust the ball at or through the goal. There was a profusion of one-nil score lines in pre-modern football.

The adventures of the adherents of St Peter's and All Saints' live on in celebrated memory, for their years-old rivalry is commemorated in the coinage of the 'Derby' match for a contest between local teams.

That original 'Derby' match was scheduled for Shrove Tuesday. Other games that, according to the zealous research of Robert Malcolmson, took place on this last day of feasting before the constraints of Lent were Alnwick, Chester-le-Street, Sedgefield, Whitby, Ashbourne, Nuneaton, Corfe Castle, Teddington, Bushey Park in Middlesex, Dorking, Richmond, Kingston-upon-Thames, Hampton Wick, East Moulsley, Thames Ditton, Hampton and, aptly enough, Twickenham. Devonshire towns were more likely to favour Good Friday; the preferred date in Workington and in the Nottinghamshire township of Eakring was Easter Tuesday, while Kirkham kicked off on Christmas Day.

Festive Football - How and What

Vivid descriptions of the regional variation of 'camping', the football of East Anglia, particularly Norfolk, have survived, as did the game itself well into the 19th century. The goals were ten yards wide and they stood some 150 or 200 yards apart; the ball was 'the size of a common cricket ball'; an 'indifferent spectator' threw up the ball for which the teams, probably of a couple of dozen or so a side, struggled and fought; players could 'throw' but not 'give' the ball to colleagues; there was 'much time, many doublings, detours and exertions'; and a goal was called a 'notch' or 'snotch', similar to cricket's original notch, for a tiny gash in the scorer's stick to mark off a run; apparently it was conceivable that a team might forfeit a 'notch' if one were caught in possession of the ball; and the game, after the manner of a handball game like fives or tennis, was settled by the best of either seven or nine notches. In a foreshadowing of rugby, a goal was scored not by throwing the ball through the goal, but by carrying it thence, that is, the scorer retained possession as in the modern rugby touchdown. Such a tourney might have taken from two to three hours to reach completion.

It was sophisticated enough for the distinction to be made between 'rough-play', which included boxing, and 'civil-play', where only kicking and wrestling was licensed. The kicking was undoubtedly aimed more at the opponent than the ball and there was a further difference between 'kicking camp' and 'savage camp', for which particular shoes - one of the first mentions of special footwear, the forerunner of football boots - could be provided.

Cornish 'hurling' was very similar, except that in the extensive open spaces in the west of that county, the game was played over a very wide area with innumerable participants racing and fighting hither and thither. In the east of Cornwall teams of from fifteen to thirty engaged in a strategic battle of 'hurling at goales', a description of which survives from the early 17th century. The rules were, as in camping, quite stern. Players paired off and only one tackler or blocker was permitted per attacker; below the waist grappling was forbidden, as was butting, except the man in possession could butt the blocker's chest; the ball was hurled man to man, but, as in rugby and with a prescient hint of the offside law, hurling a 'fore-ball' to someone closer to the goal was not allowed.

Yet another variation was the Welsh 'cnappen' or 'knappen', a rumbustious struggle between large teams, and a game prevalent in both town and country. It was played as late as the 1880s in Neath, where windows were shuttered and the 'principal thoroughfares' yielded up to the contestants, such was the violence of the fray. Several other towns - Jedburgh, Chester-le-Street and Workington are instances - actually sustained their older version into the 20th century. By this time it was no more than what Richard Holt calls a 'folklore oddity', a somewhat artificial reminder of the past, not unlike the reconstruction of a medieval joust. Indeed, one might perceive in the lengthy history of many of these shire- and town-based football matches what was perhaps a rather forced desire to stay true to ancient tradition. The alignment of the football match with other aspects of the annual festival underpins this conjecture. It is, of course, likely that the players in all these many and varied diversions, and over myriads of years, enjoyed some dribs and drabs of footballing at other times of the calendar. It was just that the yearly encounter provided the one special opportunity for celebration and glory.

Two further comments, one general the other particular, may be added. Firstly, as one observes these versions of football throughout several centuries and in an array of locations, the unmistakeable perception is that much of pre-Victorian football was more like modern day rugby than soccer. The varieties of tackling and throwing or passing were legion, whereas kicking the ball appears to have been less popular. The delicate distinction is made between kicking the ball and the opponent, for hacking was a constant in most types of football and was - as chapter six will reveal - a significant factor in the schism that led to the formation of the Rugby Union. Modern observers, confronted with a version of the ancient sport, would be forgiven for wondering whether it more resembled the behaviour of present day supporters than that of, always allowing for notorious exceptions, present day players.

There may have been a number of reasons for this. One was strategic. Most games required the ball to be thrown or conveyed, not necessarily kicked, through the goal, the tactical essence being hand-held possession. In the Rugby codes today kicking is deployed either defensively or as an occasional attacking ploy. In Rugby League, in fact, it is utilised by law to place undue possession at some hazard, with the requirement to play the ball with the foot after a certain number of tackles against the penalty of turning the ball over to the opposing side. Kicking in much ancient football was simply too risky. Moreover, it may, in the swirl and ruck of those wrestling 'mellays', have not often been a feasible option.

Another reason was practical. Commentators speak airily of the use of the inflated bladder of a pig; it has become a cliché of romantic sporting storytelling. Until the advent of the industrially produced rubber bladders at a date as late as the 1860s, the animal bladder was the only air-filled sporting object. What is not entirely clear is the durability, especially before the use of leather casings, or the air retention and bounce qualities of the pig's bladder. Nor is it altogether apparent how easy or difficult it was to obtain a pig's bladder in an agrarian economy where multipurpose cattle or sheep tended to be more numerous than pigs. In some areas the bladder may have been ceremoniously used as part of the annual festivity. Certainly it could not have been a regular household item, as it is suggested the trustily hewn cricket bat was in many south eastern villages in the 18th century. It is patently apparent that the smaller ball, either flax- or hemp-stuffed, like a cricket ball, or carpentered and shaved wood, like a bowl, would have been much simpler and cheaper to make. This in itself may have helped to dictate the forms of football in given areas and the amount of tangible kicking that was likely.

Secondly, and on a more specific note, it seems that a captivating aspect of camping - and, of course, this may have applied to other types of football less well authenticated - was the ownership of the goals. Normally, and this obviously applies to the modern football codes and also to other field games like hockey, lacrosse and cricket, one protects one's goal or target from enemy offensive. The reverse was true of camping. This was a homing game, the objective being the conveyance of the ball through the goal to the security of one's own lair, rather as in those versions of hide and seek where players attempt not only to evade discovery, but also endeavour to return to the safety - 'kickstone' was the successful child's cry - of the starting point, the prescribed home or den.

The instrumentality was the same. Players defended and attacked goals, but the psychology was the converse of the norm, as they tried not to breach the bastion of the foe but to outwit the enemy who were preventing them from finding sanctuary in their own hideout. At a stroke, several of the cultural and allied theories about games playing, discussed in the preceding chapter, look decidedly topsy-turvy. It is further testimony to the imaginative extent of human inventiveness in terms of 'play'.

Casual Football - Isolation

However, for all the interest in the major examples of footballing prowess up and down the kingdom, it is 'the routine relaxations', usually arising out of 'the normal intervals of the working day' that, in their larger overall sum, are the more significant.

Robert Malcolmson, expert chronicler of the popular recreations of earlier times, concludes, 'it is likely that these routine leisure activities and family festivities were, in terms of the hours involved, more prominent than the large public celebrations and sporting events...everyday leisure was relatively subdued; it was usually rooted in informal, face to face encounters.'

To understand the motley variety of localised pastimes from the medieval period right through the early modern centuries until well into the 19th century, one must take earnest note of the isolated nature of much everyday life. At the celebrated date of 1066 the population of Britain was a meagre 1.5 million. With nine out of ten inhabitants in rural habitation, and with 10,000 manorial settlements during the reign of Edward I in the 13th century, this suggests average communities of just 200 or so souls. By 1700 the population had only advanced to 5.5 million and by the beginning of the 19th century it was up to 12 million. There were then 15,000 parishes in England and Wales, so that, discounting the few large towns and with agricultural labour accounting for two-thirds of the work-force, the average population of these rural societies was no more than 400 or 500 residents, suggestive of a young male contingent of approximately 80. Many, of course, would have been much smaller.

It was scarcely sufficient to support major sporting or other recreational endeavours, other than of a strictly limited and crude character. Yet there was an even more definitive restriction. Until the advent of the railways in the middle of the 19th century, this was a largely immobilised society. It is hard to overestimate how closely men and women were tied to their locality. This should not be confused with social mobility. Peter Laslett and other social historians have demonstrated that, even in the depths of the Middle Ages, there was a fair amount of movement for purposes of work and intermarriage. The portrait of the socially introverted and inbred village community is something of a myth. The problem was that when people did decide to migrate, seeking their fortune elsewhere than in their own locale, it took them a long time; Hannibal marched with his elephants from Southern Spain across the Alps and into northern Italy - but it took him seven months. Travel in Britain was not much more efficient in the hundreds of years before the railways. For everyday purposes, such as occasional recreation, it was barely feasible.

Thomas Hardy, writing in *The Mayor of Casterbridge* of his beloved Wessex as it was about 1830, commented, 'To the liege subjects of Labour, the England of those days was a continent, and a mile a geographical degree.' This was a pedestrianised society. It was this practical immobility that completed the circle of loneliness that began with the isolation of the normal village. There were minor improvements after 1750, but, in general terms, what has been called 'the unremedied badness of the roads' ensured that in winter or wet weather journeys by wheeled transport in many parts of the country were abandoned.

In 1821 the *Manchester Guardian* announced, in the tones that today might be deployed for interstellar travel, the momentous decision to use two horses, a 'light machine', a driver and guard, plus the mail, to race from London to Manchester. The trap was planned to leave London at 6 o'clock in the early evening, rushing overnight, with several changes of horses, at an average of eleven miles an hour, and reaching Manchester at 10.20 the following morning. It was thought that this would snip thirteen hours off the normal coach journey, for the very best a coach, carrying no more than fifteen passengers, could manage was a peak of nine miles an hour and the stoppages were perforce much longer.

Transport historian Jack Simmons calculated that, as late as 1837, 75 million trips were undertaken using public transport in the year, a matter of a niggardly four per head. This involved about 220,000 each weekday, of which 95,000 were negotiated in London and 85,000 by steam boat - a remarkable testimony to the wretched condition of the road system: it was still quicker by boat than road from London to Brighton, while a cross-Channel journey was usually a more comfortable prospect than a trip from the metropolis to York. This left 20,000 long coach excursions and just 20,000 journeys in the provinces and on minor roads.

Private transport, by horse or horse-drawn vehicle, was, of course, the privilege of the well-to-do minority. There were a million horses in Britain in 1800, but the majority were working horses, with only a fortunate few people having ready access to horseback. The vast bulk of the population walked. They carried their belongings or, should their trade depend on it, pushed a cart. Some were devoted pedestrians. Doughty hikers in the later 19th century, like William Gladstone or Charles Dickens, strode briskly over thirty miles. The classic novels of the 19th century, not least some of those by Dickens, that indefatigable walker, describe lengthy marches; *Jane Eyre*, *David Copperfield*, *The Old Curiosity Shop* and *Adam Bede* are examples. But walking could not conquer time. Brisk as they undoubtedly were, it took William Gladstone and Charles Dickens ten or twelve hours to complete their marathon treks.

Quite simply, it just took too long to make regular return journeys of any substantial mileage that incorporated a recreational diversion, such as a football match. This, plainly, is why the reported football matches often stand out as no more than annual affairs, with holidays allowing for some special effort to be made. For humdrum day-to-day purposes, inter-community activity was rarely viable.

Moreover, even when the horse was employed, it did not improve matters very much. For a day visit a journey of six miles on horseback was reasonably regarded as standard; fifteen miles was a dire extreme, with, say, the drawn farm cart making even slower progress. Much of this was affirmed by William Pitt the Younger, when, in 1803, he issued a prime ministerial edict about the formation of militias, a form of 'home guard' created because of the threat of Napoleonic invasion. Able-bodied men were required to muster for two parades a week, but he decreed that no-one should be asked to report at a point more than six miles from his home: 'no more than the sturdy English peasantry were in the habit of going when led to a cricket match or other rural diversion'. In the event, much of this moderate martial venturing proved none too practical. A twelve mile round trip, including military drill, may have taken six hours, too long for a reasonable evening out after work and too long for labourers to be spared from the fields.

There were attendant factors like time and money. The Victorians were wont, as smoky industrialism took hold, to reflect nostalgically on the delights of country life. It was not so delightful in practice. There was not the binding austerity of the factory system, but the agrarian routine was very demanding, even though its rhythms allowed for some seasonable highs and lows in terms of labour intensity. Working conditions were poor and, it is necessary to remember, child labour was not a function solely of the industrial age. It was far from being a healthy life and there was much poverty; hence the flight to the new industrial towns when these came into being. Some historians have raised the issue of whether, given the pitiable nutritional standards of those times, working men could have found, after their labours, the extra energy for regular strenuous physical recreation, such as the rough and tumble of football.

As for remuneration, the average weekly wage for an agricultural labourer in 1850 was 10s (50p), plus the equivalent of 2s (10p) in kind. This left little or nothing for leisure pursuits that might involve distant travel or the costs of attending sporting or other events. These facts are recorded briefly, but they contribute to a circumstance whereby, through lack of access, time and money, great swathes of the populace were locked into a fairly static existence.

The famed social historian G.M.Trevelyan, writing of the 18th and early 19th centuries, concluded that 'for most men the village was the largest unit of their intercourse. A village cricket match, a hurly-burly at football, or races on the village green were very different from the organised athletics of the modern arena...few villagers had seen anything of town-life. No city-made newspapers or magazines stamped a uniform mentality on the nation. In this isolation from the world at large, each shire, each hamlet, had its own traditions, interests and character.'

Casual Football - Variety

A contemporary observer, Charles Pearson, writing in 1846, claimed that almost all Britain's inhabitants were 'chained to the spot'. A consequence was that sport was among the 'traditions, interests and character' that were internalised. This honeycomb of parishes, an atomic mesh of mainly self-subsisting agricultural units, probably evolved some characteristic 'play' response. Arguably, this was true also of large tracts of Europe where similar conditions obtained. Throughout Europe we consistently find evidence of target and ball games, with or without clubs, as an ever-present. What appears to be a natural inclination to seek relief from mundane labour in the casual wielding of a stick or lobbing or kicking of a stone or other object seems to be a constant. Like the agricultural principle, there is a definite sameness about these diversions. Like the agricultural practice, there is as basic an individuality.

Local circumstances must have dictated that individuality. The number wishing to play; the size and condition of the available ground; the type of ball (stone, shaped wood, hemp stuffed or blown bladder) to hand; any other implements that might be obtainable; the forceful influence of personality, such as an innovative ring-leader or what sociometrists would term the 'star' in any such group; the requisite oral tradition: 'play' would have been both recognisable and peculiar in every instant.

What we might have found across Britain and much of the rest of Europe (the Italian 'calcio' is just one example of folk football overseas) would not have been several discrete games, but, more probably, thousands of games, each slightly different from the one in the next parish and also altering perceptibly from generation to generation. These have been called 'folk-games', but it is unlikely that their wide-ranging variance has yet been properly appreciated. It may be more accurate to speak of one amorphous game, multifarious in its infinite variety, yet, if one happened to move, permanently or temporarily, one would adapt easily. One might conceive of a primeval swamp of 'gameness'.

A clear parallel today would be the primary school playground. It plays host to its own particular brand of game with its own particular rules, obeyed with a scrupulous strictness, but with an incomer having sufficient of the common parlance to make adaptation easy. 'All is flux,' cried Bergson, and thus it was with sport. There was possibly a Quatermass-like morass of 'gameness', hundreds of examples of friendly romps. Gradually, these were thinned out into a much smaller number of regulated games, a process delayed for the most part until the last half of the 19th century. In games, as in life, many are called, but few are chosen.

Incidentally, this concept helps solve the confusions and controversies among sports antiquarians about the origins of their favourite pastime. In all those rows about locations and nomenclature they are equally right or, less charitably, equally wrong. All the references indicate that something of a disportive nature was occurring; the hazard lies in trying to trace an actual birth-place or time for any particular sport, such are the interlocking Heinz-like qualities of pre-modern diversions.

The modern sporting mind has difficulty contemplating a world without fixtures. Occasionally one sees in the press the facetious question, if Blackheath was the first rugby club or Sheffield the first football club, against whom did they play? The truth, of course, is that, in almost all sports, the establishment of clubs was to offer opportunities to members. Where team games were concerned, they were 'sides' clubs, a proclivity we shall further observe in the following chapters when the evolution of football clubs is analysed. Although there were occasional forays to nearby parishes and although, in the organic order of things, ideas and methods were transferred along the route-ways of society, by far the major part of pre-Victorian sport was of this inward-looking character. Localised groups of boys and youths just played among themselves at their variants on one or more sports on their own patch.

From both the higher-order games of shire and township and what little evidence may be discerned from the lowly diversions of localised folk-games, one may dimly glimpse some hints of the footballing format and its necessary skills. Ball and target are high on the list of priorities, with individuals or groups utilising the former to attack and, sometimes, defend the other. The targets range from holes as in golf and wooden bases, like skittles or wickets, to a wider goal, as in the hockey or football alternatives, the objective being the placement in, dislodgement of or thrusting between. Patently, the addition of sticks or clubs to assist in these purposes provided a further profusion of possibilities. The bewildering array of such embryonic sporting deeds may be exemplified by comparing the cricket wickets, reported by the cricket historian Rowland Bowen, which were six feet wide and a few inches high, with football goals just a couple of feet wide and not much higher. The curio of cricket being, like football and hockey, a chiefly double target game offers further witness to the intricate interbreeding of these primary folk games. Especially is this so when one recalls the lengthy cricketing phase in which there were but two stumps with a cross-bail, there was the convention of underarm 'bowling' as in bowls or skittles, and the charging of fielders was permitted.

The utilisation of two targets obviously appealed where the terrain was sizeable and the numbers engaged were sufficient to warrant the deployment of two opposing groups, while the skills required to throw and/or kick the ball away from and toward the other goal - a gateway, the distance between two trees or bushes or two improvised markers - were instinctive and general. Factor in the verve of running and the vigour of wrestling and struggling for possession of the ball, with their latent fascination for the youthful male, and the formula is almost complete.

It is well rehearsed that, for some centuries, 'the casual playing of football' had been, from the apprentices of London and other towns to the farm labourers of scores of hamlets, endemic. Often this was on a Sunday, when, as one contemporary observed in mid-17th century Maldon in Essex, 'the people did usually go out of church to play at football and to the ale house'. In the Wye valley in the 19th century it was noted that, following the harvest festival, 'after dinner all the men played or rather kicked football at each other and then it grew dark, when the whole game ended in a general royal scuffle or scrummage'. As Richard Holt comments, this was probably in furtherance of old-style football, although the 'kicking' element reminds that, when fewer people were involved in a more confined milieu, the rudiments of modern association football were the more likely to be developed.

It was exactly this set of skills and branches of interest that, however unconsciously, awaited the coming of those industrial and urbanised environs that would provide the appropriate context for the modernisation of sports, among which football would be the major winner.

CHAPTER THREE

SCHOOLS; FOOTBALL AND VICTORIAN EDUCATION

Barbarism - 'the Nurseries of Vice'

FAMILIAR TO many, an early set piece in Thomas Hughes' classic *Tom Brown's Schooldays* is the football match. Published in 1857, the book was 'the first great school story', the progenitor of thousands on much the same pattern. Crucially for our analysis, the story is set somewhat earlier. Thomas Hughes (1822-1896) enjoyed and celebrated his own schooldays in this lightly fictionalised account, placing the action around the late 1830s and early 1840s.

We know from other secure evidence that Rugby schoolboys played a form of football prior even to that date, but the novel provides two helpful corollaries. Although the game was organised by the older pupils, it obviously had the sanction of the school authorities - previously schoolmasters had frowned upon athletic activities, chiefly for the same reasons why churchmen, landlords, employers and keepers of the peace had often, in days of yore, suspected that sport and sin galloped hand in hand. Furthermore, it is evident, not least from the speedy popularity of Thomas Hughes's semi-autobiographical memoir, that the football references were intelligible to his widespread readership, both of lads of about Tom Brown's age and, one suspects, their nostalgically inclined fathers and older brothers. There is already the semblance of recognition that 'football' is a part of the life-style of young, literate, middle to upper class youth.

The Rugby format of football was internal to the school. Indeed, it is said Rugby never played an outside team at its eponymous game until 1867 and never played another school at rugby football until 1897. This autonomous game had settled into something remotely like what we know today as rugby by 1841 and the first rules were written down in 1845. The situation was rather different from that of cricket. In 1841 Rugby School (captained by Tom Brown in the near-realistic fictional account) for the first time played MCC, led by the corpulent but amiable MCC Secretary, Benjamin Aisalbie, according to laws already deemed acceptable in many districts of the country.

The exploits of Tom Brown serve to exemplify a curio central to the origins of formalised football. The game, which, for hundreds of years, had been associated with mischievous apprentices, coarse townies and uncouth farm-hands, was adopted by the young gentry, not in any disruptive or anti-authoritarian fashion, but in the corralled precincts of their scholastic institutions and, increasingly, under the beneficent eyes of their masters.

To grasp the significance of this transmutation requires some understanding of the underlying character of the emergent public school system. Ironically enough, the appropriation, to deploy Marxist terminology, of proletarian football by the bourgeoisie acts as a grim metaphor of what occurred in educational affairs. One of the flowers of the northern Renaissance in 16th century England was the growth of the 'free grammar school', with William Shakespeare, the brightest bloom of that extraordinary culture, himself a pupil of Stratford Grammar School. It has been claimed, possibly with some extravagance, that no boy - they were not intended for girls - lived more than twelve miles from such a school, and there was, amazingly, such a school for every 6,000 of the Tudor population. Their purpose was the production of personnel to man the administrative and commercial agencies of the Elizabethan state and to sustain conformity of religious practice; they were weapons in 'winning the west for Protestantism'. Each was to be a 'governour' after the fashion of Thomas Elyot, the Elizabethan pundit we met in the opening chapter.

They were normally founded by the charitable endowment, in land and monies, of some wealthy benefactor, but, during the 18th century, they fell into desuetude. The Hanoverian period suffered from a general decline in administrative efficiency and religious observance and the grammar schools were also buffeted by changes in urban life. By the early 19th century there were barely a hundred left and, in total, they boasted but 3,000 pupils; the once famous Leicester Grammar School, for instance, had sunk from 300 scholars to three day-boys and one boarder. Apart from a brief revival, from about 1920 to 1960, they never again prospered and today they number about 120, as opposed to 1,180 in 1965.

However, there was a countervailing tendency. During the immediate pre-Victorian era, a number struggled to establish themselves as what came to be called 'great schools'. Often utilising convenient legal loopholes, they did so by offering provision, at a price, to the rich and nobly born. The boarding element, which had played a negligible part - usually two or three staying in the schoolmaster's household - in the older dispensation, became central, with day-boys either despised or excluded. Gradually, the age-level rose, from a starting-age of seven or eight to thirteen, although preparatory schools took up some of the leeway.

In many cases, this meant some distortion or finessing of the founding charter. Put bluntly, several schools, in contradiction of the Robin Hood philosophy, were robbed from the poor and given to the rich. Rugby, for example, had been founded for the free schooling of local boys in 1567 by a rich grocer, Lawrence Sheriff, while John Lyon, a local benefactor, had established Harrow for poor neighbourhood boys in 1571. Others, such as Charterhouse and Christ's Hospital, had been intended for, in general terms, the needy gentry. Westminster School, with its geographic proximity to church and government, flourished eminently, although by 1800 Eton, with interest stimulated by royalty's preference for Windsor, became the greatest of the 'great schools'. Shrewsbury, too, rose from the crumbling dust of a fading grammar school to enjoy a new opulence, while Winchester focused more and more on rich fee-payers and built accommodation for them accordingly. When demand grew in the 19th century, there were purpose-built additions, like Marlborough, Cheltenham and Wellington, which made no bones about their target being the sons of wealthy gentlemen.

It is of interest that vestiges of the origins of the traditional 'great' schools remain in the paradoxical and arrogated usage of 'public' schools, that is, 'endowed' schools, as opposed to the later development of 'private' or 'proprietary' schools, few of which managed to vie successfully with the older brand. Nonetheless, the alternative private schools rapidly followed suit when the public schools adopted organised games.

For all the superiority of the early public schools, they were, in character, reflective of the worst features of the 18th and early 19th centuries, a period whose politics have been defined as 'oligarchy moderated by riot'. Indeed, that appellation serves equally accurately for both these types of school. It is difficult to determine which were the more brutal; the staff or the boys. 'Teaching and beating were interchangeable terms'; the flogging was indiscriminate and constant. In 1860 Mr Hopley, who kept a private school at Eastbourne 'for the sons of persons in a high rank of life', was sentenced to four years penal servitude for the manslaughter of the fifteen year -old Reginald Cancellor. The boy suffered from 'water on the brain', but his teacher interpreted dullness as a challenge to authority and, apparently with the approval of the father, subjected him to a fatal beating. In 1825 the thirteen year -old son of the evangelical social reformer Lord Shaftesbury died after an arranged fight with an equal, both having seconds to assist them, that lasted two and a half hours.

Those who quail with horror at the outrageous behaviour in 'the blackboard jungle' of some of today's secondary schools would recoil with even greater distress from scenes of the old-style public schools. Apart from the inveterate Flashman-type bullying, there was anti-authoritarian strife. Eton had an infamous rebellion in 1788 and this was followed by five such insurrections at Westminster between 1770 and 1818. Pistols, as well as stones, were used; property was destroyed; buildings were barricaded and defended. There were six riots at Westminster, one of which necessitated the presence of troops, with fixed bayonets, before it was quelled. The Harrow rebellion of 1771 lasted three weeks, while, apart from several serious uprisings before his time, even the sainted Thomas Arnold barely thwarted an insurgence as late as 1833.

One imagines prison riots of the modern age. Chiefly in respect of Westminster, the education historians John Lawson and Harold Silver have written, 'boys were herded together, largely unsupervised; the young were exploited and bullied by the older boys, and when they sallied out to roam the streets after lock-up, drunk or sober, they struck terror into the neighbourhood. Rich, arrogant and unafraid, the young gentlemen were hard to control in these unprecedented concentrations.' The unreformed public schools have been described as 'essentially self-governing republics, run by a prefectorial elite, in which the teachers rarely intervened'. Thomas Bowdler, whose 1818 edition of an expurgated Shakespeare gave rise to the censorious verb, called these schools 'nurseries of vice'.

Oddly enough, this 'barbarism', as Thomas Arnold's son, Matthew, the poet and schools inspector, branded it at large, was to prove an advantage for football. The schools certainly mirrored the boisterous and unseemly character of the ruling elites whence their scholars derived, and, in the social vacuum created by boredom and neglect, the pupils, rather resourcefully in some cases, constructed their own diversions. There were plenty of pupils and few staff - Eton about 1766 had nearly 500 of the former and just ten of the latter - and the teaching regime, while brutish in style, was sometimes short in time, leaving the youngsters to their own devices for hours and hours.

Crowded and locked together, they adeptly devised collective pastimes. These included, it must be admitted, not only poaching, bird-nesting, killing an astonishingly broad range of small creatures and fighting, but also, if there was an adjacent river, as at Eton, swimming and boating, as well as cross-country runs. Importantly, they incorporated into this Butlinesque scheme of more wholesome exercise some rudimentary borrowing of the games of their villages, estates and townships. Although 'still largely disorganised', the main contenders were forms of cricket and football. These were the folk-games of the ordinary populace. The older children of the estate or hamlet and the young servants and employees of the pupils' fathers would have played them. Needless to say, their sons would have scrambled along happily with them and with their energetic amusements, prior to going to boarding school. The pupils of Winchester College apparently played some form of folk football, upon which the headmaster, William Hornman, smiled kindly, from at least the beginning of the 16th century.

When Tom Brown/Thomas Hughes played football at Rugby in the mid-19th century, the absence of masters in any supervisory capacity was meaningful. The lesson to be learned is that the football introduced into the public schools, the football that eventually would be systemised and then rule the world, was begged, borrowed or stolen from the common folk. Moreover, the conduit for it and, critically, the conduct of it, was the pupil, not the master. The middle and upper class English boy was to become the major progenitor of the game that would attain comprehensive global status, following their graduation from educational establishments to the wider world.

Reforms - and Reformers

The next step in football's epic trek was its domestication by the school authorities. Having watched over it with increasing benignity, they gradually brought it, along with other games, into the construct of their establishments. It became a feature, one that might proudly be mentioned in advertisements, prospectuses and brochures. This incorporation of a slightly tamed version of football within the official school structure was itself an illustration of the reformed character of the public schools. This, in turn, was an example of a British society that was, by the onset of the reign of Queen Victoria, becoming more rational, disciplined and polite.

A major element in the reform of the 'great' schools was a dimensional change in their clientele. As industrialism flourished and fortunes were made by hard-working businessmen, there arose a wish to send the sons of such families to prestigious schools. This was in line with the social mobility of the 19th century bourgeoisie, who had pretensions to become landed and even ennobled gentry - not unlike, one might ruefully add, their counterparts in the 20th and 21st centuries. Matthew Arnold, like his father, one who felt sport overdid its reliance on 'fire, strength, earnestness and action', believed that games helped this admixture of 'philistine' middle class with 'barbarian' upper class boys.

In so doing, they were castigated by their erstwhile champions, Richard Cobden and John Bright, leaders of the free trade movement, and that set of radical political values sometimes described as Manchesterism. They were aghast at this betrayal of their clear-sighted, progressive principles. They were infuriated that mill-owners and cotton merchants should choose as their model a feeble-minded landed aristocracy. Richard Cobden, who had been shocked by Manchester council's adoption of the sort of fuddy-duddy regalia used by the antiquated London corporation, thundered at his fellow commercial men for 'glorying in being the toadies of a clodpole aristocracy', content with 'the very crumbs from their table'.

Britain was fast on the way to becoming a plutocracy, with landed and trading wealth intermingled. As the perceptive cultural historian Jeffrey Richards, has concluded, 'elite schooling gradually replaced noble birth as the identifying badge of the ruling class, and the public school system expanded to accommodate them.' To glance ahead a little, a third of the peers created between 1885 and 1914 were from the industrial and commercial classes. Previously there had been a mere handful lacking landed and noble pedigree. One example of a countrified trader was W.H. Smith, of the famous news agencies and a competent cabinet minister in his own right, who paid out £30,000 for a rural estate to become a landed gentleman. Robert Peel and William Gladstone are two Victorian premiers who came to the fore from commercial backgrounds, via public school (Harrow and Eton, respectively) and

Oxford. Robert Peel was born among the cotton mills of Bury, but his father, John Peel, while not he of hunting song renown, bought a large estate at Drayton near Tamworth, while Gladstone, whose father, the merchant prince John Gladstone, left £600,000 on his death, married into the Glynne family - his mother-in-law was a cousin of William Pitt the Younger - and lived on their Hawarden estate near Chester.

There were others who became better known as sportsmen. Among them was the Harrovian A.N. Hornby, a son of the cotton mills of Blackburn, who set himself up amidst the lush grassland of Cheshire at Parkfield, near Nantwich, with his country house cricket pitch, his gunroom and his string of sprightly hunters. Astutely dubbed by Neville Cardus as 'the Squire of Lancashire', he captained the red rose county and England at cricket, as well as being a Captain in the East Cheshire Militia. He certainly played football at Harrow; he played some soccer for Blackburn Rovers; he boxed; and he became one of the first double internationals by dint of winning nine English rugby union caps.

Another rather more random example is Reginald Hargreaves, a child of Accrington calico printers, educated at Eton and Christ Church, Oxford, and destined to lord it over a 160 acre New Forest estate, Cuffnells in Hampshire, for which county he played twelve matches and acted as president, as well as being doyen of the local Conservative Association, between times huntin', shootin' and fishin'. For good measure he married, none too happily, Alice Liddell, the original Alice in Wonderland. Her irate parents, the Dean of Christ Church and his snobbish wife, had astringently rebuffed Lewis Carroll's offer of betrothal; Queen Victoria kiboshed Alice's fervent romance with her fourth son, Prince Leopold, who instead was wedded off to the Princess Helen Frederica of Waldeck-Pyrmont, so she settled, rather unconvincingly, for 'Regi'.

That brief excursion into something like a sub-plot for an operetta like *The Student Prince* does indicate how quickly and how profoundly the social classes were altering in shape and personnel. A public school and varsity education offered a key to the door of social aggrandisement, and, especially as the railways some of them had built or financed came into regular use and travel was improved, off went the sons of the 'shopocrats' to Eton and Harrow. They may have been, as Cobden rightly accused, besotted by the allure of the landed nobility, but their business acumen remained intact. They still wanted value for money. They would not have handed over hard-earned brass for the rowdy, uncontrolled barbarity of former years. In a cyclic motion of adjusting to demand and insisting on supply, new money played a major role in reforming the public schools.

New money is, accurately, associated with the growth of professional football in Britain and elsewhere, as later chapters will delineate. It is not always recalled that new money, through its determination that the public schools should be reformed, also helped create a comfortable manger for the birth of global football.

The medium for public school reform was a batch of bold and assertive headmasters. In effect, they rescued the schools from the grasp of the pupils. The keepers regained control of the zoos. They saw their schools rather as younger Oxbridge foundations, with the pupils secluded and corralled away from the world in monastic style, so that their educative influence could be total and uncompromising. Thomas Arnold (1795-1842) of Rugby is correctly viewed as the archetype, although some of his influence had a mythic quality, albeit no less potent for that. He took over the headship of Rugby in 1828, his mission to create a mini-state of Christian duty. He was no sentimentalist about children, believing that 'a society formed exclusively of boys' resembled 'evil in the mass'. His task was to convert the pig's ear of the sinful child into the silk purse of the Christian gentleman. 'My object will be,' he announced, 'if possible, to form Christian men, for Christian boys I can scarcely hope to make.' He was not averse to vigorous flogging, but, with Thomas Arnold, you were more likely to be beaten for lying than for an inability to construe Latin verse.

He was, then, an avowedly energetic man - the shy testimony of his wife, Mary, alludes to how shaken she was by the avidity, and the consequent eleven pregnancies, of his sexual appetite - and he threw himself whole-heartedly into the scholastic fray, eager to cleanse the Augean Stable of the unreformed school. It is, however, simplistic to reduce his cure to more prefects and fewer bullies. Thomas Arnold was a Christian radical and a believer in continuing reform - 'my love for any place, or person, or institution, is exactly the measure of my desire to reform them'. He 'stood foursquare on the life and example of Jesus Christ' as the basis for political judgement, for, he urged, 'religious society is only civil society fully enlightened'. That zealous regard for holy and social life to be in concert, along with its corollary that intellectual attainment without devout impulse and rightful behaviour was purposeless, was a sophisticated doctrine. It was one that was to flavour much of political and academic life in Victorian England, even as the new scientific forces of geology, biology and textual criticism were attacking those sacred barriers.

The great historian, Sir Robert Ensor, has written, 'No one will ever understand Victorian England who does not appreciate that among highly civilised, in contradistinction to more primitive, countries it was one of the most religious the world has known'. He goes on to add, importantly, that 'its particular type of Christianity laid a peculiarly direct emphasis upon conduct'. Here was the reformed public school in a doctrinal nutshell and the Arnoldian dogma in a phrase. Christian, yes, but the outward signs of that inner grace happened to coincide with what were considered the correct attitudes of the Victorian English gentleman.

This behavioural, as opposed to just canonical, pattern was to find its surest footing in the rehabilitated schools. It was, plainly enough, the template for the good sport, with all that came to mean in terms of bravery, modesty, forbearance and affectionate fellowship. Football would soon be the vehicle on which these virtues were learned, practised and vindicated. When it comes to an assessment, not only of the durability of football in the renewed public schools, but also of its wider national dissemination in later years, the impact of this mongrel tenet of Christianised sportsmanship can barely be overrated. Without that component, it is inconceivable that football could have been successfully launched with the approval of the establishment as a countrywide pastime.

Thomas Arnold himself was not unduly interested in games. This element of the Arnoldian myth is partially the result of Thomas Hughes's exuberant delight in sport, as expressed through Tom Brown. Readers of the novel will recollect that Tom has not one but two alter egos; the dashing but reckless Harry East and the scholarly but timidly gentle George Arthur. The latter perhaps adheres to the master's teaching more strictly, after the manner of Arnold's favourite pupil and biographer, A.P. Stanley, Dean of Westminster. Thomas Hughes never quite lives up, in fiction or in reality, to the dream of academic devotion, and there were headmasters who, while genuine admirers of Thomas Arnold, inclined, like Hughes, to East rather than to Arthur as their guide.

These sporting mentors included George Cotton, a Rugby master and the original of Tom Brown's young master, a teacher who would have married Jane,

Thomas Arnold's favourite child, had not his mother been revealed as a boozy imbiber. He became a reforming headmaster of Marlborough, where frog-beating - gruesomely, the title is a literal reference to the slaughter of frogs with sticks - had been one of the unofficial diversions. There were also Edward Thring of Uppingham, E.W. Benson of Wellington, H.H. Almond of Loretto, John Perceval of Clifton and Charles James Vaughan of Harrow. Although they admired Arnold's slogan of 'Godliness and good learning', they were more concerned with the social community. Distinctive compulsory uniforms, as well as compulsory chapel going, were introduced; school magazines, school songs ('God give us bases to guard and beleaguer...Fights for the fearless and goals for the eager', warbled Edward Bowen's Harrow anthem) and other appurtenances of loyalty soon became the norm. The connoisseur might observe that, at Harrow, 'bases' were goals, a further illustration of that mesh of nomenclature and practice evident across a host of games.

Edward Thring, who transformed Uppingham, after 1853, into an esteemed 'great school' complete with the first public school gymnasium, pleasingly rejoiced, one of his pupils recorded, over 'a fool in form' who was competent at games. H.H. Almond, a proponent of the opened window and the chilly dip, listed his priorities in telling sequence as 'character... physique... intelligence... manners... information'. Richard Holt has pointed out that the Loretto uniform Almond introduced of open-neck shirt and long shorts looked uncommonly like a modern football strip. The watchwords of the public school became 'fortitude, self-rule and public spirit'.

Games - the Reasons

Moreover, games were central to this reformed culture. They became, it has been commented, 'compulsory, organised and eulogised'. Eton made games 'the infallible prescription'. Cricket was, of course, the summer game, and it outdid football in pseudo-religious symbolism - the Godhead as 'the Great Scorer' of Grantland Rice's verse - and mock-sacred lore - Henry Newbolt's subaltern rallying the ranks with his imperishable cry of 'play up, play up and play the game'. However, football had the advantage of being played in the two longer terms, while, given its still rudimentary stratagems compared with the more specialised skills necessary for the summer game, it allowed more boys to make some sort of a decent mark. As with cricket, the costumes and caps and colours were in profusion, with inter-house and other matches staged to foster the competitive spirit of fidelity to one's fellows and one's institution. Football also played its part in building the mystiques, the codes, the hierarchical gradations and the rest of the Byzantine-cum-Masonic devices that glued the social edifice of the school in place. The prefects were invariably selected from the 'bloods', the games' champions.

Although the advent of railways encouraged the beginnings of some very notable inter-school cricket fixtures, the travails of wintry journeys discouraged inter-school football matches. The house match remained the salient fixture and, significantly for the future development of football, the games remained largely internalised.

The cult of what was called Athleticism - so exceptionally well analysed in the work of the sports historian, J.A. Mangan - grew apace. The rationalisations were several. As well as instilling or reinforcing the essential quality of allegiance to school, form and house, it channelled the energies of sturdy youths away from the debauched activities of the Hanoverian and Regency schoolboys and into safer and more respectable outlets. It was hoped, too, that their dangerous libidinous animation might be virtuously dispersed through the wholesome booting of the football. Edward Thring made no bones about energetic hours of football being the antidote to what, in his thunderous sermons assailing the depravity of self-abuse, he called 'the worm-life of foul earthly desires'. A further advantage of football was that, unlike some of the field sports, such as hunting and shooting, of the old dispensation, it took place within the confines of the school in a restricted area and subject to immediate supervision.

It also reflected a theme to which we shall return when the nation at large is considered; that is, the anxiety about public and personal health. The cold baths, the open windows, the cross country runs and the non-luxurious fare of the typical public school, as well as the physical jerks and the compulsory football, certainly had a sternly moral bent, but they also reflected a concern about wholesome living. Cleanliness was next to Godliness. The microbiologist, Bo Drasar, argues that the school matron's constant check on bowel movements in such establishments did much to secure the British obsession with constipation, a complaint from which no-one, he mildly adds, has ever actually died.

At the extreme, the cult of 'manliness' was the opposite of Thomas Arnold's ideal, for it was resolutely anti-intellectual. It was directed at avoiding what, in

1872, one disapproving Victorian termed 'a nation of effeminate, enfeebled book-worms'. We know, from the engaging studies of the historian, Gerald Howat, that Tom Brown was also based on Augustus Orlebar, vicar for fifty years of Willington parish church in Bedfordshire. Tom's opponent in his fictional fight, Slogger Williams, was, in fact, Rev. Bulkeley Owen Jones. Both these ebullient clergymen were models for Thomas Hughes of what came to be called 'Muscular Christianity.' Thomas Hughes defined it succinctly as the training of the body 'for the protection of the weak, the advancement of all righteous causes and the subduing of the earth that God has given to the children of men'. Football was a boyish exercise, moral as well as physical, in this regard, as was even 'fighting, rightly understood'.

Along with two clergymen, the attractive author of *The Water Babies*, Charles Kingsley, and Frederick Denison Maurice, Professor of Divinity at King's College, London (until he was sacked for uttering the alarmist opinion that hellfire did not exist), Thomas Hughes's 'Muscular Christianity' overlapped into Christian Socialism. This argued that the earthly application of Christian love involved the organisation of society on co-operative lines. While many of Hughes' supporters would not have followed him to that extreme, this positive view that Christians should be proactive in this world as well as pre-occupied with the next found favour with lots of clergymen. A curio of the era, one helpful to football's spread, was that, as religion was firmly challenged by scientific and philosophic opinion, the otherworldly eggheads shied away from the church and the clerical vacuum was filled by the footballing 'musclemen'.

It would be the likes of hearty clerics such as Augustus Orlebar and Bulkeley Owen Jones who would be in the van when the time came for football to be carried forth to the urban and rural parishes of England and Wales.

Other factors were at work. As the 19th century wore on, the first Darwinian generation emerged. In spite of the entreaties of Charles Darwin's 'bulldog', T.H. Huxley, there was a crude distortion of evolutionary theory known as Social Darwinism. Herbert Spencer, the social scientist, coined the phrase 'the Survival of the Fittest' and Francis Galton, Darwin's cousin and the scientist who coined the word 'eugenics', were among those who promoted dangerous thoughts of planned breeding and racial superiority. Vague acceptance of these tenets became common and infiltrated the schools and colleges, underpinning the games ethos that offered youth the chance, through football, to exhibit its fitness to survive. It was the heyday of the healthy mind in the healthy body.

This chimed in with the assertive individualism of the Victorian climate. Charles Darwin published *On the Origin of the Species* in 1859, the same year that Samuel Smiles produced *Self-help*, his collection of hagiographical biographies lauding the principle of self-improvement. Without doubting the basic truth of the Darwinian thesis, it is intriguing that it was a Victorian mind that figured out the secret of the genetic selection process. Examinations - a means of 'maximising aptitude' opined Jeremy Bentham, the arch-advocate of individualism - were becoming all the rage. Their enthusiastic proponent, James Booth, claimed with some force that they led to promotion, as in the civil service, 'by competition rather than conspiracy'. Adam Smith, the free trade economist, had said that 'rivalship and emulation render excellency' - and the school football field was, in this respect, seen as the equivalent of the school examination hall. Curiously, therefore, football was recommended as excellent both by co-operative socialists like Thomas Hughes and rampant individualists like Herbert Spencer.

School football thus enjoyed the best of all philosophic worlds at the time when imperialism touched its apex towards the end of the 19th century. 'The scramble for colonies' augmented the British Empire, so that, by the death of Queen Victoria in 1901, it covered a quarter of the world's land surface and ruled over a quarter - a seventh of them of British descent - of the human race. The message of imperial responsibility was taken very seriously in the public schools. Its products, as missionaries, colonial administrators and army officers, would be at the forefront of the maintenance of the Empire. Again, the rough and tumble of football and the lessons learned herefrom were seen as integral to the instruction of potential empire builders and keepers. The army, in particular, as we shall have later occasion to note, was to the fore in the encouragement of football and the spread of its global tentacles.

Games - the Practice

All this encouragement of football and allied games had its opponents. In 1858 F.W. Farrar, headmaster of Marlborough and then Dean of Westminster, published his best-selling if gruesomely maudlin tale of fatal slippage down the primrose path, *Eric*, or *Little by Little*, a title which, incidentally, restored that splendid forename to much usage in the fifty or sixty years before World War

II, as the present writer might diffidently affirm. In that story Dean Farrar railed against the vanities and superficial partisanship of games, believing that they distracted boys from the greater glory of revealed religion. The book sold in its dozens of editions and thousands of copies, but no-one took a blind bit of notice of the message.

Rudyard Kipling, although the poet of imperialism and 'the white man's burden', came to view the school fixation on sport as perilous, and he blamed military shortcomings in the Boer War on the ineptitude of the public schools and their wasteful games bias. It was thus that in 1902 he wrote his accusatory lines in his poem, *The Islanders*:

> *Then ye returned to your trinkets; then ye contented your souls*
> *With the flannelled fools at the wickets or the muddied oafs at the goals.*

The muddied oafs of the establishment were none too pleased. Some rather blamed an incipient English 'sloppiness' about games, with the rhymester Norman Gale chunnering on about 'Female men are thick as thieves, with croquet, ping pong and the rest'. No one noticed the genuine fly in the educational ointment. Much of the promotion of football and competitive sport was based on a generalised belief that prowess in games was character building and informed a student's later adult capacities. Such fallacies about 'the transfer of training' are now largely invalidated; it is now believed that the highly pragmatic Duke of Wellington would never have uttered such nonsense as the daft remark that the Battle of Waterloo was won on the playing fields of Eton. It is rather that the same basic attributes permit of parallel achievement, such as being both a successful school football captain and a successful army officer. The ability to kick a football straight indicates little more than the ability to kick a football straight.

No matter. What is compelling is that school football and cricket could be and certainly was a controversial issue in the earnest discussion of martial failure. It had become that important.

Because school football remained mostly self-contained during most of the 19th century, 'football' continued as a generic term describing several different formulae. There is some evidence that Richard Mulcaster, head of Merchant Taylors' and then St. Paul's schools during the 17th century, had tried to organise school football years before, but it had not caught on. Samuel Butler, the headmaster of Shrewsbury, in the early 19th century, had dismissed football as 'more fit for farm boys and labourers than young 'gentlement' while an Etonian, speaking loftily in 1831, said conclusively, 'after all, the Yorkshire common people play it'.

When football became acceptable, the brand which was taken up in each scholastic establishment was determined by three interlacing factors. One was the sort of game already played by the boys on an unofficial basis, some of it perhaps with local 'townies' or with village boys at home in the holidays. Another - as was the case with games in the country at large - was the terrain. The third was the taste of the master in charge. As this latter stalwart was often an old boy of the school, the first and last factors linked nicely, whilst the terrain had possibly dictated the tactics of the pre-official version in the first place.

Charterhouse, cabined in the cloisters of an old Carthusian monastery, found dribbling to be the satisfactory mode, and Westminster, too, until the boys began to use the Tothill Fields for games, suffered something of the same restriction. Charterhouse moved out to Godalming in the 1870s, in part to find space to develop sporting facilities. Harrow had a large enough eight acre field, but it tended to be something of a quagmire in the winter months, making for a heavy, flattish, squiggling ball. To avoid the static scrimmaging caused by this and because it was difficult to find much length kicking such a leaden object, dribbling over the muddy surface was to the Harrovian fancy. By 1900, incidentally, the eight had become 146 acres. When Benjamin Kennedy replaced Samuel Butler as Shrewsbury's headmaster, he smiled kindly on football there. Dribbling - 'douling', as it was named in the sort of argot typical of the public school freemasonry - plus off-sides was the key, and Shrewsbury was one of the first schools to welcome back old boys as football players. Winchester's footballers had a very precise area of 80yards by 25yards and this placed a sharp premium on accurate and not indiscriminate kicking, together with more compact scrimmaging. It did not reduce the mayhem, for there were many cases there of broken limbs.

Between 1845 and 1862 seven of the major schools had written down the rules of their particular brand of football, with, for instance, Westminster's 'football ledger' dating from 1854. The lately reformed Tonbridge School also emerged as a strong footballing establishment. The Eton 'Field Game' was an eleven a side affair in which handling was forbidden. The melée or scrimmage

- the 'rouge' at Eton; the 'squash' at Harrow; the 'hot' at Winchester - was prominent in most codes, and it was not unknown for an enthusiastic master to plunge into the fray from the touchline.

In the wider open spaces of Rugby, handling was more commonly accepted. It is now widely acknowledged that the story of William Webb Ellis, who, in 1823, 'first took up the ball and ran with it', is a myth invented in 1895, as James Malvin has reported, by Rugby old boys, irritated that 'rugby' had not really started at their alma mater. Certainly, if he ran with the ball in 1823, not many ran after him. The famous description of football at Rugby near the beginning of *Tom Brown's Schooldays* makes no mention of such a solecism. There is running and scrimmaging and catching and kicking, but no catching and running with the ball as yet. The fags, Tom Brown among them, guard the line, attempting to prevent the grounding of the ball and subsequent attempt at a kicked goal. They come under violent attack from the older and strong-booted attackers, with some brave, quick lads, like Harry East, acting as 'quarters'. The game - between School House and the rest of the school - still engages huge numbers, again something more feasible on the usually more spacious fields of the provincial school in the countryside.

The intricacies of the varied sets of laws, all the more elaborate to meet the complex demands of the in-group jealously to sustain its own patois and mystique, were to prove a nuisance when, in mid-century, old boys of the several schools were anxious to find some common ground. There were, however, two or three salient, as opposed to peripheral, divisions of opinion. Perhaps the most telling was the problem that arose from the narrow urban and wide rural space available to the schoolboys. Very approximately, the former encouraged dribbling and the latter handling, accompanied by punting. That was to be very inconvenient.

Given the cloistered nature of the private boarding school, its charges effectively walled in and inward-looking, the metaphor of the womb is particularly apt. Football underwent a womb-like gestation in the early Victorian public school. It did so, one should remember, precisely at a time when, under the strain of urban, industrial and religious change, the folk versions of football were imperilled and dying. It was the task of interested public school old boys, many of them readers of *Tom Brown's Schooldays* and disciples of Thomas Hughes, to act as midwives and to deliver the babe of football to a wondering world.

CHAPTER FOUR

1863: THE FOOTBALL ASSOCIATION;
FOCUS AND CODIFICATION

'...FOOTBALL - a good game for boys, but in my opinion too savage for grown up men'; thus spake, in 1887, Christopher Wordsworth, nephew of the poet, William, not very successful head of Harrow, rather more successful Bishop of St. Andrew's, and a fine sportsman, who contrived to help organise and participate in both the first varsity cricket match and first boat race in the 1820s.

He was not alone in this trenchant opinion, and it is important to note that his jealousy about what he termed the 'ascendancy' of football was that of a fully-fledged sportsman and not - and there were quite a few of these about - a shrinking aesthete. It is significant, too, that he was still mourning the expansion of football as late as 1887, long after football's more general entry into the life of the nation. By the time cricket had become an essential part of schooldays, it had been widely accepted as a game for gentlemen and the nobility, even those of mature years. Although there could be injuries, it was more civilised than football, lacking the core element of violent contact, and, during the middle of the 19th century, it was rapidly acquiring its repute of being a saintly game. Furthermore, it was fast becoming an international game. The first tour of North America by an English team was in 1859 and of Australia in 1861/62, both before the formation of the Football Association.

Football still had the opposite image. Outside the schools, it was localised, working class and rugged. In a word, it was not yet respectable. What the public schools had accomplished was some taming of the game as a physical outlet for boys. Thus the next question in the trail of riddles that composes the historical journey of football is - why and how did football become a game for the gentleman amateur?

'Perpetual Adolescence'

Part of the answer lies in the factors already considered, in particular, the influence of Muscular Christianity, the Victorian emphasis on physical exercise and sound health, the insidious effect of Social Darwinism and the conscious attempt to relate character building to the professional role of public school old boys at home and throughout the extensive imperial domains of Great Britain. In 1864 the Clarendon Commission report on public schools gave official support to this view, congratulating those agencies on 'their love of healthy sports and exercise'. All this leant some credence to the value of football as a manly pursuit for men of middle and upper class affiliation. At the very least, it was a useful way of keeping fit and socially active in the winter months when there was no cricket. As we shall later discover, many football teams were, initially, the offshoots of cricket clubs. Indeed, although the likes of W.G. Grace thought nothing of playing cricket from March to October, the cricketers' arrogation of the warmer months for 'the summer game' forced football into the wintry season. It was to be years before footballers realised, or were prepared to argue, that a pleasant June afternoon is preferable to a frozen or muddy January Saturday for their chosen recreation.

There was, however, a clinching feature. The propagandist indoctrination of the public schools was Jesuitical in its intensity. Of course, many boys hated it: Lord Salisbury, for high-profile example, the highly competent Conservative premier of the late Victorian decades, was bullied so wickedly at Eton in the mid-19th century that he beseeched his father to remove him. Despite that definite proviso, it is arguable that, rather like the acolytes of some esoteric priestly sect, the public schools stamped out its products according to a carefully limited template. Moreover, the 'hidden agenda', that is, the codes by which the pupils lived aside from the strictures of the official school routines, was in cogent accordance with the authorised construct. Had it not been, as many educational agencies could dolefully confirm, the overall effect would have been mightily diluted. Rarely in educational history has there been such correspondence between the formal and unofficial aspects of a typology of schooling.

The public school was deemed to be a preparation for a life of arduous service, very likely in foreign climes, as soldier, missionary or administrator.

There was, in fact, a creepy inversion of orthodox religious beliefs, wherein there are usually thoughts of delicious rewards in the afterlife, consequent upon the travail through 'the vale of tears' of mundane existence on this mortal coil. In the Spartan ethic of the public school, there was no suggestion, let alone guarantee, that the post-school existence would be hunky-dory. Rather was school vaguely conceptualised as a juvenile Paradise, the happiest days of one's life, the heaven before the hell of the real world of unremitting service.

A principal upshot of this pressurised view, cultivated in the claustrophobic hothouse of the secluded boarding school, was the concentrated friendships of the boys and the celebration of boyhood almost as some form of devout cult. There is, predictably, evidence that this spilled over into homoeroticism, but the more powerful truth reveals the profound affinity of school-friends. It is, of course, an aspect described a thousand times over in schoolboy literature. This stretched a hundred years from *The Boy's Own Paper* and tales such as Talbot Baines Reed's *The Fifth Form at St. Dominic's*, via the massive output of Charles Hamilton - Frank Richards was but one of his 25 pseudonyms as he penned 70 million words, the equivalent of a thousand full-length novels, created 105 fictitious schools, including the Greyfriars of Harry Wharton and Billy Bunter - to the *Red Circle School*, a long-running tale from 1933 to 1958 in the *Hotspur* comic. Even allowing for the natural hyperbole of fiction, these narrative accounts of boyhood adventures and loyalties have a degree of authenticity, affirmed by many memoirs of the actual experience. What is more, the literature, like scriptural texts, served to reinforce the faith.

In practice, the 'manliness' of the schoolboy's code was echoed in the agencies of his later employment. In the Army, in the Royal Navy, in what was known as the 'broad' echelons of the Church of England and in civil administration, especially overseas, the unflinching steadfastness, restrained emotions and unyielding fidelity of the school and its playing fields remained the core values. It is no accident that Henry Newbolt's poem, *Vitai Lampada*, its rather pretentious Latinate title trailing its message, became so popular, for it embodied the notion that the values of boy and man were similar, the one set informing the other. The young subaltern rallies the ranks, when 'the Gatling's jammed and the colonel's dead' with the same rousing cry of 'play up, play up and play the game' that had successfully encouraged him when, at school, on 'a bumpy pitch and a blinding light', ten runs were required 'and the last man in'. Nor is it an accident that this same inscription now faithfully graces the external

Lord's cricket ground wall.

Sport was the outward sign of the inward creed. So approximate was the boy and the man in ideology that the concept of the 'boy-man' emerged, with the young adult anxious to preserve not only the values, but also the activities of childhood into adulthood. Gone was any acceptance of St. Paul's strict injunction to put aside childish things - and playing football typified this attempt to convey the serene joys of boyhood into the sterner environs of manhood. Crucial to this was, for many public schoolboys, the midway stage of university. Its cloistered corridors and secluded chambers had, firstly, inspired the design of the public schools and then, secondly, offered their old boys much of the same cultural diet for three more years. The academic pressures were none too burdensome and collegiate and school 'house' life was very similar. The universities were to play a critical part in the promotion of games, including football nationally. In his veiled autobiographical novel, *The Way of All Flesh*, Samuel Butler, late of Shrewsbury and St. John's College, Cambridge, has his narrator comment: '...the only things worth doing which Oxford and Cambridge can do well are cooking, cricket, rowing and games...'

At its extreme, the idea of the boy-man has been extended to encompass the notion of 'the eternal boy', or, in the more impressive Latin, 'puer aeternus'. This view was most succinctly analysed by the Old Etonian, Cyril Connolly, in his *Enemies of Promise*, published in 1938. This theory suggests that, because of the fervent and romanticised concentration of that school experience, emotional, intellectual and even physical development was arrested, producing what has been called a state of 'permanent adolescence'. He wrote that the pupils' 'glories and disappointments are so intense as to dominate their lives and arrest their development', resulting in a self-conscious ruling class of staggering immaturity. In adult life, this frequently, then and since, became confused with homosexuality, even with paedophilia and sado-masochism, but, without ruling out such aspects entirely, it was more delicately nuanced than that. Asexuality might be a more precise connotation.

Of course, this is a cultural explanation, not a scientific thesis, its base anecdotal observation and speculation, not hard empirical evidence. Nonetheless, it is persuasive. Indeed, Jeffrey Richards, in the modern era, has suggested that the whole Victorian state, with the public school 'the power-house of the nation', suffered as a result of this widespread inability to cope or come to terms with adult life. Several writers of ripping yarns for schoolboys seem to fall, in part or whole, into this boy-man category, including Thomas Hughes, Talbot Baines Reed, Frank Richards and on to P.G. Wodehouse, described by J.B. Priestley as 'a brilliant super-de-luxe schoolboy.' Several apologists of the public school system quoted the biblical friendship of David and Jonathan as being 'wonderful, passing the love of women.' E.F. Benson, author of the school story *David Blaize*, son of an Archbishop of Canterbury, a pupil of Marlborough and whose brother A.C. Benson wrote the words of 'Land of Hope and Glory', went further. Bizarrely, he wrote that 'in many ways boys are a sex quite apart from male and female.'

Unsurprisingly, the two great texts of a refusal to grow up were published in the Edwardian era, the peak of this development. These were J.M. Barrie's *Peter Pan and Wendy* (1904) and Robert Baden-Powell's *Scouting for Boys*; both authors had singularly quaint if relatively innocuous social lives, the former seemingly obsessed with childhood, the latter tagged 'a perennial singing schoolboy' by his biographer. A number of revisionist biographers have found characteristics hinting at fixated adolescence in Gordon of Khartoum, Lord Kitchener, Cecil Rhodes, Lawrence of Arabia, Captain Scott and Field Marshal Montgomery, while, among sportsmen, W.G. Grace - 'just a great big schoolboy in everything he did', an old school-friend of the cricketer told Grace's biographer, Bernard Darwin, in but one of several such assessments - is another who apparently ossified at adolescence in respect of intellectual competence, moral evaluation and emotional response.

It could be urged that adolescence is no bad juncture at which to ossify. 'Perpetual adolescence', whilst limiting in a humane sense, does have its virtues, along the lines of the 'cheerful Puritanism' by which slogan Talbot Baines Reed was identified. And even if one does not completely agree with Cyril Connolly in his acidic castigation of two or three generations of public schoolboys as frozen at or about puberty, one is forced to acknowledge the strength and suddenness of the shift to gentlemen playing ruffian games such as football. Visiting continentals certainly found the sight extraordinary and were quick to blame the previous incarceration of the offenders into unnatural single-sex bastions, isolated from the realistically warming streams of family and neighbourhood life.

Be that as it may, it was this boisterous band of boy-men who brought domesticated football out of the closet of the public school and - had they but known, they would have scolded themselves for such carelessness - allowed the world eventually to embrace it.

'The Simplest Game'

The obvious post-school starting point was the gathering together of old boys, anxious to continue playing the specific football code of their alma mater. That was well enough; the problem occurred when opportunities arose to meet and socialise with those who had attended a different school. Football was a genre. As Joseph Strutt makes clear in his *The Sports and Pastimes of the People of England* (1831), there was a simple outline to 'foot-ball', with 'two parties' trying to 'drive' the ball between the goals. Beyond that, there were many differences. Even Joseph Strutt's suggestion that the goals were 80 or 100 yards apart and that the goal 'sticks' were 'about two or three feet apart' is applicable only to a number of the classes within the genre. In short, rather like the man who could not describe an elephant, but would recognise one if it entered the room, football was easily identified in general, but the devil was in the detail.

It appears that, when two 'parties' representing differing credos met, the decision had to be made as to which rules to use, with the toss of a coin or the nomination of the host club being common devices. The difficulty was multiplied at the Universities of Oxford and Cambridge. Here the old boys of many schools naturally foregathered, and, as part of the expansion of games as a broadening of the undergraduate society both at college and university level, football grew in popularity. The colleges, as well as the parent university, had started to take sport seriously; it is about the middle of the 19th century when, as in the public schools, excellent facilities were first developed. In the last forty years of the century there was an enormous expansion of inter-varsity sports of all kinds, including association and rugby football.

Prior to that, however, football suffered from the fact that the student bodies personified a dozen or more sets of school rules and chaos threatened. Such was the students' ferocity of passion for their old school that they regarded as anathema the distasteful regulations of any inferior establishment. When the sporting press debated the notion of unified laws in the late 1850s, these divisions of opinions were made ferociously clear. The temptation was for cliques of old boys to indulge privily in their own sacrosanct pursuit, but this, in practice, became very piecemeal, and, in spirit, imperilled the very need of their college and university to inspire the devotion to the cause that had typified the students' schooling.

In 1846 two ex-pupils of Shrewsbury, H. de Winton and J.C. Thring, aided by a cluster of Old Etonians, endeavoured to break the impasse by devising a compromise version of football. It tried to steer a steady and equitable line between the kicking and the handling types. Some approximation to a Cambridge Football Club resulted and four trial games were played under this regime. Although the experiment languished a trifle, the move was revitalised in 1848, when fourteen undergraduates met, with George Sault and H.C. Malden, to revise and consolidate these rules, which showed a definitive shift to the dribbling propensities of Shrewsbury. This proved helpful, and not only at Cambridge, for, over the next close on twenty years, the Cambridge settlement was probably the nearest to a bridging regulo, although one or two other attempts at compromise rulings were tried elsewhere.

Its immediate impact must not be exaggerated. In the main, there was a studious avoidance of codification. The parallel development was the formation of football clubs, but, in general terms, these were more often than not 'sides' clubs, where members met regularly to play football among themselves, using the laws of the football typology they espoused. These formalised clubs obviously grew from the phenomenon of clusters of footballers, of all classes, enjoying their game together in various parts of the country.

The 1850s were a wholesome decade for the establishment of Britain's first football clubs. There was an intriguing development in the Sheffield area where Hyde Park had been the venue for informal football since the early 1830s. The Sheffield Club was formed possibly as early as 1855 and certainly produced its own rules in 1857. 1857 is now the accepted date of origin, with two local sportsmen, William Prest and Nathaniel Creswick, responsible for that start and for the collation of the laws. Around 1858 the Hallam club was established. In 1860 the two played each other at Sandygate, Sheffield in what may be regarded as the first ever fixture between two properly established 'clubs'. Sheffield won 2-0 - and the club is still playing.

One element was the contribution of Sheffield Collegiate old boys, drawn from the families of steel manufacturers and their professional attendants, such as doctors and lawyers. Their public school teachers - Old Harrovians, in the main, it is thought - had taught them the kicking game. John Goulstone, a sports archivist who has challenged much of the received wisdom about the origins of both cricket anf football, has also pointed to the links of the Sheffield clubs with the original folk football commonly to be found in that south Pennine district around Holmfirth and Penistone. Sheffield thereby illustrates three major factors in the early spread of football, namely, the wish of old public schoolboys to keep up their football interest; the influence of public school and varsity teachers in substantial provincial day schools; and the capacity of organised football to liaise comfortably with the local 'disorganised' game.

The pretty, if perhaps apocryphal, tale is told of Old Harrovians in south Yorkshire giving their homespun rustic opponents each a pair of white kid gloves to wear and silver sixpences to hold during matches. This was a preventative against the handling with which the folk-game was associated, although this prior example of sponsorship may have become exaggerated in the re-telling. What is certain is that Sheffield built up one of the first 'associations', that is federations of clubs, at much the same time that this was being contemplated by the London based clubs.

Further instances of provincial enterprise were the first Nottingham clubs, Notts County in 1862 and Nottingham Forest in 1865, while, in 1871, Turton, formed by two Old Harrovians, John and Robert Kay and a stimulus for J.J. Bentley, later a chairman of Manchester United and a President of the Football League, is usually regarded as the first of a wholesome crop of Lancashire clubs. In Scotland, Queen's Park was started in 1867 under the gentlemanly auspices of the neighbouring YMCA. Glasgow Rangers followed in 1873 and, by the middle 1870s, there was a group of some ten clubs in the Glasgow area.

The first of the metropolitan 'kicking' clubs was Forest, as in Epping Forest, formed in 1859, again with Old Harrovians indulging their 'humble desire' to prolong their footballing activities. They operated in and around the Snarebrook and Leytonstone area of Essex, not far from Forest School, but in 1864 they were transformed into The Wanderers, destined to be the first of the famously successful amateur teams, becoming inaugural FA Cup winners in 1872. Groundless, as their nomadic name implies, they played military and school sides, usually under a cheery motley of rules borrowed from varied dispensations. They played some of their matches on the public areas of Battersea Park.

There is evidence that football was played at the Kennington Oval even earlier, perhaps from 1849, just four years after the launch of the county cricket club there. Here is another constant in the early years of the football saga: cricket clubs playing host to football, usually as a means of occupying the bodies and hearts of the cricketers during the dark winter months. Members of the Surrey County Club, the Surrey Paragon Club, the South London Club and the Union Club were permitted to participate in this activity.

On the hacking and handling front, the Blackheath Club, formed in 1858, upheld the sporting traditions of Rugby school, while there were also signs of football becoming well-known further afield. The key reason was the wish of outlying schools to copy the great English schools. In Wales the incursion of public school and Oxbridge trained masters into establishments like St. David's College, Lampeter and Llandovery College saw the beginnings of formal football in the principality. In Scotland, Loretto, Edinburgh Academy and Edinburgh Royal High School were in the vanguard of this movement, and, in 1857-58, Academy former pupils started the Edinburgh Academicals Club. Meanwhile, Oxford University graduates with professional posts in Glasgow pursued a largely rugby-orientated route, utilising laws written down in their so-called 'Green Book'.

A further arena for football was the armed forces, partly as public school officers wished to sustain their boyhood pastime, and partly as bonding exercise and sinless pastime for other ranks. There are plenty of examples of army football, with, as elsewhere, varying degrees of team membership. The dictates of the army throw into clearer light the problem of such differently-sized teams - there was an obvious need to include everyone or as many as possible from a troop or squad, for the formalities had to yield to the more urgent needs of discipline and platoon or regimental loyalty.

Edward Thring, the supportive brother of J.C. Thring, who had been instrumental in trying to find a legislative consensus at Cambridge, was the enthusiastic head of Uppingham from 1853. He was now ready to try again; in 1862 he laid down, almost as if they were the Ten Commandments, the ten rules of what he entitled 'the Simplest Game'. Broadly based on the old Cambridge formula, they were to be the foundation of an acceptable format for football. They read:

> **1. A goal is scored whenever the ball is forced through the goal and under the bar, except it be thrown by hand.**
> **2. Hands may be used only to stop the ball and place it on the**

ground before the feet.

3. Kicks must be aimed only at the ball.

4. A player may not kick at the ball whilst it is in the air.

5. No tripping or heel kicking is allowed.

6. Whenever the ball is kicked beyond the side-flags, it must be returned by the player who kicked it, from the spot where it passed the flag-line, in a straight line towards the middle of the ground.

7. When the ball is kicked behind the line of goal, it shall be kicked off from that line by one of the side whose goal it is.

8. No opposite player may stand within six paces of the kicker when he is kicking off.

9. A player is 'out of play' immediately he is in front of the ball, and he must return behind the ball as soon as possible. If the ball is kicked by his own side past a player, he must not touch it, kick it, nor advance until one of the other side has first kicked it or one of his own side, having followed it up, has been able, when in front of him to kick it.

10. No charging is allowed when a player is out of play - i.e. immediately the ball is behind him.

To the modern eye, and although some of the essentials are in place, there are some issues, such as any handling at all, that seem surprising. Those who have played amateur football on wind-swept plateaux will appreciate law 6, which obliges the player who has kicked the ball miles off the pitch to recover it, while many will pore over law 9 and recall how tricky the offside rule was and is. Thring's laws were used for a match in Cambridge in 1862 between Etonians and Harrovians., and in 1863 nine Cambridge students, representing Shrewsbury, Eton, Harrow, Rugby, Marlborough and Westminster, drafted the 'Cambridge Rules', a fresh-minted revision of the old Cambridge code and something very close to Edward Thring's propositions.

Whatever its flaws, it must have been heartening for England's young gentlemen footballers to have the opportunity to play a standardised game. However, it was not easy to organise this in a constitutional vacuum. Football's protagonists were well aware that other more firmly established sports, such as cricket and horse racing, had procured a degree of stability only by dint of some kind of national authority.

'Football Association'

It was to this end that the fateful meeting was called on 26 October 1863 at the Freemasons' Tavern in London's Great Queen Street. Some fifteen or sixteen people attended, that is, one or two from each of eleven clubs, plus the odd 'unattached' gentleman and an observer from Charterhouse School and the rugby-minded Blackheath. The originating clubs were: Barnes, No Names (Kilburn), the War Office, the Crusaders, Forest (Leytonstone), Perceval House (Blackheath). Crystal Palace, Blackheath School, Kennington School and Surbiton.

The restricted geographic spread of the teams is instructive. They are primarily London based teams from south and south-east of the River Thames. There is some reference in various texts to the 'London Football Association', but it could scarcely, at the onset, boast even a metropolitan representation. The captains of the public school teams were canvassed - and that fact in itself is of further instruction. It demonstrates how the tradition of pupil oversight remained prominent, but there was always the obstacle of these youthful officers serving for one year only, before passing on to adult life, so that some continuity could be lost. A generation later and such a correspondence would have been with the master in charge of football. There was no direct provincial - Sheffield, for example - or university - Cambridge, for example - delegation in attendance. All in all, this was just a group of young gentlemen, all of public school extraction, one or two of them with military or scholastic attachments, all of them playing locally together, a fact underpinned by the then practice - as in country house cricket - of playing for more than one team.

Some dozen or more of these enthusiasts had the courage - some would say, the arrogance - to sense that there was a call for more overall organisation. That is the way these things often happen. Whether in sport or politics or the arts or the sciences, one often finds that the origins of spectacularly successful projects and groups are similarly humdrum. A close-knit band of brothers has many informal talks and then holds a formal meeting. Arthur Pember of the No Names Club, took the chair. They simply resolved to form a body to be titled 'the Football Association' and E.C. 'Cobb' Morley of the Barnes Club agreed to become secretary. Such was his helpful pioneer work, Morley is sometimes known as 'the Father of the Football Association'.

They were modestly keen to lay down 'some set of rules which the metropolitan clubs should adopt among themselves', but their rules soon became widely known and accepted. Before the end of 1863, John Lillywhite's 'British Sport Warehouse' was selling 'the Pocket Laws' of 'the Football Association' for 6d [2.5p], with postage thrown in for an extra penny.

History is about winners. To the victors go the cultural spoils of popular credit. Take the case of Orville and Wilbur Wright, the first, in 1903, to fly in what the *Daily Mail* called a 'balloonless airship'. There had, of course, been many attempts before that and many contributions towards the science of aeronautics; there are also one or two yarns of previous successful, but unwitnessed and unphotographed essays in flight. No matter... however forcefully revisionist narrators might argue, the glory and thus the inspiration belongs solidly to the Wright Brothers.

In the sphere of radio communications, as the lyrics of Starship's *We Built This City On Rock And Roll* tell us, popular wisdom has it that Guglielmo Marconi invented the radio. Some would argue that the Italian was merely the marketeer who saw the wider implications of the invention of a North Staffordshire pioneer scientist, Sir Oliver Lodge, hell bent on communicating with the spirit of his son who had been killed in the fields of northern France.

Similarly with the Football Association: for all Cambridge University's footballing students had taken the lead in the moves toward consensus about the laws of football or the Sheffield Club had pioneered the way forward in the provinces, this infant organisation was to prove the power-maker. Unchanged in name, it remains today the salient football body in England and the global model for national footballing structure.

A short succession of meetings were held to debate the rules, which were eventually issued as 'the Rules of the London Football Association', in December 1863. They bore, as might have been anticipated, a marked similarity to the Thring/Cambridge varieties.

Almost unwittingly, the newly formed Football Association also supplied the distinguishing label of 'association' football, when the need arose for some specificity over against the 'rugby' football breakaway. The public school patois is evident in the diminutives of 'soccer' and 'rugger'. They are of a type with 'champers' for 'brekkers' and 'starkers' at 'Twickers' and examples are still to be heard, jarringly, among the nicknames of sportsmen, especially cricketers.

Charles Wreford-Brown, a public school footballer and England cap and a vice-president of the FA, is credited with the coinage, once exclaiming in a heated discussion, 'not rugger, soccer'.

Associationism was the key. Although a consensual rulebook was one of the leading motivations, an institutional collectivity was not essential to that development. Other sports had agreed laws without such constitutional procedure. The MCC, the Jockey Club, the Royal and Ancient Golf Club of St. Andrew's and the 1867 Queensberry Rules offered a legislative and judicial fount for followers of, respectively, cricket, racing, golf and boxing, in some degree on an overseas as well as a British basis. For instance, the county cricket clubs were not, at this stage or for years later, locked together constitutionally with one another or with Marylebone Cricket Club, nor were local cricket clubs linked regionally with the appropriate county clubs - but they all played by the same laws.

What characterised the Football Association was that not only clubs, but also city and county 'associations' of clubs enlisted as members. Given the unrepresentative and limited nature of its start, the Football Association extended its membership with relative celerity. Nothing could more ably emphasise how much this was a concept ripe for its time. By 1868 the FA had thirty member clubs, all from the south of England, and fifty by 1871, while the 'London' FA enjoyed friendly contacts with the Sheffield Football Association (26 members by 1877), including representative matches between the two groups in 1866 and 1871. A Birmingham FA, which quickly had fifteen members, was established in the 1875/76 season, followed by Surrey, Staffordshire, Lancashire, Cheshire, Buckinghamshire, Berkshire, plus Durham and Northumberland by the end of the decade. Another set of FAs quickly came into being in the early 1880s, including Lincolnshire, Norfolk, Shropshire, Sussex, the East Riding of Yorkshire, Northamptonshire, Nottinghamshire, Derbyshire, Middlesex, Kent, Essex, Dorset, Cambridgeshire, South Hampshire, Somerset and Suffolk.

The prominent usage of the county as the ambit for these alliances echoes the progress of cricket's ongoing organisation, as well as underlining how persistently enduring was the political strength of the shire in Victorian England. Other sports, such as rugby and hockey, would also utilise the county formula. At the same time, there were a much smaller group of city or district unions. As well as Sheffield and Birmingham, these included Walsall,

Cleveland, Liverpool, Scarborough and a separate FA for London itself. In the twenty years after the establishment of the FA, some thirty confederate FAs joined the institutional fray. The swift creation of this impressive array of unions of clubs suggests, yet again, how much football, however rudimentary, was being played and how many teams, however elementary, were active in the middle of the 19th century, most of them willing and able to subscribe to the novel national regime.

It was the beginning of a quarter century of formalisation throughout the world of sports. Responding to the settled social environment and changing mores of the age, there was an epidemic rash of national bodies and competitions. By way of illustration, the Grand National Archery Association was formed in 1861 and Horace A. Ford became first champion archer in 1864; the National Cyclists' Union was established in 1878, only a few years after the invention of that useful machine; sticking with apparatus, the National Rollerskating Association came a year later; the English Billiards Association was founded and the first rules for that pastime agreed in 1885. The English Lacrosse Union (1892) and the English Bowling Association (1893; a year after its Scottish equivalent) are two final instances.

Following the convention of the authoritative club, the multi-skilled Wimbledon Club seized control of croquet - its rules accepted by all or most in 1868; with W.J. Whitmore the first champion in 1867 - tennis - Spencer W. Gore was the first champion in 1877, from a field of 22 and before an audience of 200; but tennis court dimensions were not agreed until 1884 - and hockey - the Wimbledon rules were accepted nationally in 1883 and the Hockey Association formed in 1886.

This general yearning for standard rules, for competitive devices, for championships, above all, for unions and associations, locally, usually at a county level, as well as nationally, underlines how clearly football was but one, albeit a significant one, among many sports seeking a national identity. So swift and effective, indeed, was the extension of the collective 'association' habit that, by the 1880s, the FA proper was more a society of societies than of direct membership. Of about a thousand affiliated nationally, only 200 were individual club members. The majority were affiliated through the network of shire and town associations that already covered most of the nation. Those FAs with fifty or more club members were automatically granted a seat on the FA Council and this system of representative democracy appeared to suit the needs of the clubs efficiently enough. One advantage was that of administrative continuity locally. Of the 39 FA registered clubs in 1870, a mere four were still in existence in 1900. The existence of umbrella bodies was a more efficacious method of sustaining football than a reliance on the rise and fall of transient club enthusiasms among groups of youths.

There had already been some informal cross-regional matches. In the 1850s, for example, an old boy of Cheltenham School, William Mather, gathered together in Liverpool some of his old school chums and former pupils of other schools and played against a similar outfit from Manchester. The 1866 Sheffield versus London game is recognised as the first genuinely official representative match, but, thereafter, 'association' type fixtures became common. Probably the first county matches of the new regime were those between the Middlesex FA and the Kent FA at Beaufort House in 1867.

'Accelerated Development'

In all this brisk encouragement of football, and its spread countrywide, the headache of varying rules remained a constant complaint. The Football Association provided a sensible forum for that debate on something akin to a democratic, or, at least, oligarchic, foundation. It was obvious that, with the game already quite widespread, no single club had the prestige to carry the day and have its authority accepted by all. The ability of a few noblemen more or less to impose their supremacy over their inferiors, as had generally been the case with the sports associated with massive gambling, such as cricket, boxing and racing, was over in this strikingly new Victorian age of middle class influence. In any event, it had taken many years before the need had been acknowledged, and the problem resolved, in those other sports. It is plain from the swift expansion of FA membership that many hundreds of clubs were ready and willing to talk through and reach an agreement. Apart from the major argument with the rugby-inclined clubs, a happy feature of the discussions was the broad-ranging anxiety on all sides to listen carefully and to yield ground tactfully.

The draft rules of the infant FA, while placing a premium on dribbling, allowed holding the ball and hacking, but this was immediately challenged by the Cambridge and Sheffield protagonists. They wished to minimise both the risk of injuries - and subsequent chance of absence from their professional or business duties and loss of earnings - and to encourage the use of the foot at all times. Even Thring's permit to control the ball with the hand prior to kicking (a ruling maintained, in yet another linkage between games, for balls hit above ground level in hockey) was frowned upon by the newer breed of footballer. In 1871, importantly, all handling was outlawed. by the Football Association. The break with 'rugby' was now enshrined in the laws of the game.

The inner arguments among the public schools also continued, for a distaste to bow to the dictates of any one of their rivals remained. Some schools decided to stick to their own rules. The London-based Football Association, however, did not stand upon its dignity, but acceded to these progressive overtures Its first secretary, Cobb Morley, was unyielding in his view that the continuation of hacking would mean a game abandoned to schoolboys, as 'no one who has arrived at the age of discretion' would participate.

Most clubs accepted the FA's enjoiners that the 'ground' should have a maximum length of 200 yards and breadth of 100 yards, be marked out with flags and have - unchanged today - goals eight yards apart and eight feet high, with a tape strewn across the 'sticks'. There was no centre circle or half way line, just a 'centre' of the ground from which the game 'was commenced by a place-kick' (the rugby parlance should here be remarked), with opponents keeping, as is still the case in both football codes, a distance of ten yards. Just as cricketers changed round after every over, footballers changed ends after a goal or, if none had 'fallen to either party', at half-time. Some years had to elapse before half-time became the sole occasion for a change.

The two intractable problems for the dribbling game were the ball out of play and offside. The Thring creed yielded up the ball going behind the goal to the defending team for what later would be called a goal kick. This substantially eased the task of the defenders, who retained possession should they happen to play the ball over the goal line. It was the avant garde Sheffielders who produced the capital answer of the corner kick and this was included in the national rule-book from 1872.

The ball crossing the sidelines created another conundrum. Unlike in the Thring dispensation, the throw- in - at right angles from its point of exit, but one-handed and often heaved mighty distances - was taken by the player who first reached it. This led to manic races and struggles to 'touch down' and claim the ball, as behind the try line in present day rugby. The Sheffield clubs are credited with the idea of the throw-in going, with the same logic as the goal or corner kick, to the team who had not kicked it across the boundary. It would be 1883 before agreement was obtained about how the ball should be thrown in with a two-handed overhead throw.

The vestiges of these ancient rites linger in football's joint language. The words and phrases 'in touch', 'touchline', 'finding touch', 'kicking for touch' and 'touch judge' are deployed constantly in all football codes, often without much thought as to what or who is being 'touched'.

One question that often evokes interest is the decision to have eleven members in a football team. There are two answers, the one elementary, the other complicated. Rowland Bowen, in his magisterial if spicily controversial *Cricket; a History of its Growth and Development throughout the World* (1970) asserts concisely that 'the number has been borrowed by soccer and hockey'. In brief, it is a straight pinch from cricket. In many of the schools where football teams were to be formed one's being a member of 'the eleven' meant cricket pure and simple. The borrowing was an obvious one.

That leaves the more complex question as to why cricket teams had ordinarily opted for eleven members, although, of course, there had been constant variants from an ancient version of four a side and single or double wicket matches to games against odds, such as eleven against twenty-two. Cricket archivists have been keen to trace the game back to a single birthplace, although the probability is that, like football, its rudiments have several origins prior to much later codification. Rowland Bowen opts for Northern France, in an area extending from the Seine and on into Flanders. Here there was a numbering system based on eleven, with eleven inches to the foot and the inch sub-divided into eleven 'lines' or 'lignes'. He also indicates that there may have been pre-Norman links between what he calls the 'eleven-based area' and south-east England.

The more traditional view of H.S.Altham (A *History of Cricket*; 1926) insists patriotically for an English nativity. He touches on the Anglo-Saxon usage of eleven in land measurement, with the 'goad' or 'gad' of 5.5yards, being a quarter of a chain, the width of an acre strip and, of course, at 22yards the length of a cricket pitch. John Eddowes, in his erudite *The Language of Cricket* (1997) suggests that the attraction of eleven could have been its reference to the eleven good apostles, after the apostasy of Judas Iscariot or, more pragmatically, as a team-building exercise, to 'the fingers of the hand plus one, a captain'.

In these regards it is worth noting that numbers had been one of the issues that had required a compromise decision when teams of differing vintage met. Edward Thring's ten rules do not mention numbers. Although eleven may have been assumed, it is possible that he hoped to meet the needs of those who employed more or less than the magic number. It is significant that, when the Rugby Union was established in 1871, twenty aside was the norm, typical of a game that relied more than soccer on the scrimmage and the foot-rush. In 1875 this was reduced to the present-day fifteen, although, of course, the rugby league code subtracted another two players in the interests of a more open and spectator-friendly game.

The offside rule caused some discussion, but not in principle. Once the rugby edict of everyone being behind the ball had been conceded, it was merely a matter of how many defenders were needed to keep an opponent onside. The Sheffield rules, obviously finding much favour in the north where the game was fast flourishing, were often the ones accepted, but there was give and take, with the offside rule proving an exception. Sheffield favoured no more than one player, but on a big field and with lots of rushes en masse, this could be difficult to assess. Three, the goalkeeper and two defenders, was the London fancy and this was agreed in 1866.

It did take some years to iron out all these legalistic creases, but, by the early 1870s, there was a surprisingly high degree of consensus. By 1877 there was almost complete agreement, although one or two northeastern strongholds held out until the 1880s. The actual style of play had not altered much and that may have helped in the resolution of the outstanding questions. There was an adamant desire to find sufficient accord for any club to manage to play against any other club. Dribbling was the key. It remained collective in strategy, something akin to what in rugby used to be called a 'foot-rush', and, despite the anxiety to escape injury, the charging was still very robust, with the poor goalkeeper especially unprotected. In the eleven a side game, eight were attackers, or forwards, the basis, of course, for the eight who compose the rugby union pack of forwards. The hope was that, if one's long, sinuous dribble was thwarted, the ball would roll to a 'backing up' colleague, and the dribbling attack sustained. The very much-outnumbered defenders were relied upon to seize the moment and hoof the loose ball up field towards their own prowling forwards. Falling back to help the defence was a futuristic notion. Indeed, the fundamental thread of football's strategic evolution is of a continuous reduction of attackers, from eight to, in some of the present day's formations, one striker.

It would be amusing to mount a case for this emphasis on outright assault reflecting the positive boldness of the self-confident Victorian as against the negative caution of nervy 20th century man, but that would probably be a cultural bridge of conceit too far. As we shall see, it more reflected a gradual tactical switch to a passing game, so that the positional placings became more individualistic and discrete. By the early 1870s, there were, as well as a goalkeeper and a full-back, first one and then another intermediary half-back seconded from the forwards, whilst, in 1877, Cambridge University introduced the phenomenon of the centre-half and played with only five forwards. He had been the second centre-forward, for the forward formation tended to be two on either flank, with three, then two, then just one in the middle. Through this construct, we draw close to the five forwards design and 2-3-5 format that would endure for eighty years.

The upshot was that, by 1877, tacit agreement had been reached on the laws by the 'association' fraternity. All around the nation plenty of clubs were playing something recognisable as soccer, even if the charging and rushing might have taken away the breath of the modern spectator. At least they were playing between set bounds, with a common shape of goal and, importantly, a leather encased rubber bladder, supplied by John Lillywhite or one of his colleagues in the retail field of sports equipment. Moreover, they were adhering to rules discussed and agreed under the aegis of a national body to which most of them were affiliated.

It is this social change in kind that makes the day 26 October and the year 1863 so 'memorable', to use the epithet for the odd outstanding dates in British history coined by W.C. Sellar and R.J. Yeatman in their text-book spoof, *1066 and All That*. The BC - 'Before Codification' - chronological branding was rendered redundant. Henceforward all, for football, would be AD: 'Accelerated Development'.

PART TWO

NATIONAL

CHAPTER FIVE

AMATEURISM;
THE SUCCESS OF THE FA CUP

Amateurs - and Gentlemen

ENTER CHARLES W. Alcock. His is a name to conjure with in the saga of sport, yet it is practically unknown. He enters the stage as the football scene is transformed from parochial to national. He is the father or inventor of modern football, in fact, one might go further - of modern sport.

One thinks of Charlie Chaplin or Walt Disney as the icons of cinema, or Elvis Presley as the icon of pop music, but substantial as has been the impact of these cultural phenomena, they have not, in singular from, conquered the planet as football has so decisively done. Yet football's chief progenitor is not well-known. Luckily, Keith Booth's recent solid and detailed achievement, *The Father of Modern Sport; the Life and Times of Charles W. Alcock* (2002) has done something to rescue this largely anonymous figure from the historical shadows.

Charles Alcock is another example of the child of commerce being trained in elitist seclusion. Born in Sunderland in 1842, the son of shipbuilding and marine insurance interests, his family soon moved to Chingford and he went to Harrow School. He did not attend university, but, after a brief flirtation with the family business, he devoted his life to sport. As player, annalist, journalist, but most spectacularly as administrator, he became one of the first men to carve out such a career. The critical elements were his becoming secretary of the FA in 1870, a post he held, salaried from 1886, until 1895, and secretary of Surrey County Cricket Club, from 1872 to 1907, the year of his death, aged 64, in Brighton.

PARISH TO PLANET

An effective amalgam of bustling energy and amiable tact, Charles Alcock had replaced his brother John, who represented the Forest Club at the inaugural Football Association meeting, on the FA Committee in 1865. He soon won the confidence of his colleagues and worked arduously to advance the game. His double role in football and cricket was advantageous to him, for he brought his experience of organising the one to benefit the other, as, in both sports, he administered seminal developments in respect of their competitive, international and professional aspects. Many of the practices and ideas he helped to introduce over this lengthy period of joint control were copied not only in football and cricket, but also, gradually, in other sports and other countries. Charles Alcock's career was one that both made its mark in the immediate present and also made prescient statements about the distant future.

Alcock's initial honorary status as the FA's chief executive and his life-long part dependence on his earnings from journalism and editorship reminds one how strictly amateur the game of football remained. The term had a peculiar resonance in Victorian times, for it tended to indicate not only an unpaid lover of the appropriate activity, but, by default, a person of exalted rank, to wit, a gentleman. The age-old distinction between 'gentle' and 'simple' (Simon, the worthy who met the pieman, was plebeian, not stupid) was gradually being converted into the more forthright sociology of middle and working class, but the concept of 'the gentleman', with all its gradations and labelling, exerted considerable force in social life.

A glance at the novels of Anthony Trollope will provide a discerning flavour of what this meant. In *The Last Chronicle of Barset* (1867) the richly endowed Archdeacon Theophilus Grantly meets the impoverished Josiah Crawley, Vicar of St. Ewold's, to discuss the forthcoming marriage of their children, and the latter is embarrassed by his daughter's lack of money. His superior, in rank and wealth, comforts him: 'We stand', said he, 'on the only level ground on which such men can meet each other. We are both gentlemen.'

The recognition was instant. By dress, schooling, accent, tastes and a score of other references, one gentleman could spot another. Cricket's 'gentleman', as opposed to 'player' is thus more precise than the vaguer 'amateur', in that it indicated the correct designation as being social rather than economic. W.G. Grace is but the most celebrated of the many cricketers who could not afford to play regular cricket economically as amateurs nor socially as professionals... hence the coinage of 'shamateur'. The Amateur Athletic Club, established in

1866 by Oxbridge men, was severely clear on this point. Its members had to be unpaid participants, to be sure, but there was also a clause excluding 'artisans and mechanics', plus all other manual workers. When the London Athletic Club moved to admit tradesmen (that is, the upper tier of manual workers) in 1872, sixty members resigned, consoled by the support of *The Times*, fulminating against the inclusion among gentlemen of 'outsiders, artisans, mechanics and suchlike troublesome persons'.

Amateurs - and the Rugby Schism

The schism between the soccer and rugger enthusiasts was a row between two sets of former public schoolboys. It is worth laying emphasis on that point, because, in the fullness of time, the games were to be associated with bourgeois and proletarian imagery. In essence, the split occurred quickly. By the Christmas of 1863, not many weeks after the formation of the FA, the Blackheath representatives had withdrawn from the deliberations about the rules. Handling was one issue and the infant FA, while under pressure from many quarters to outlaw such acts, essayed at some compromise. Minor handling had been permitted and, of course, it endures today for throw-ins and goalkeeping. The basic argument revolved around hacking.

The deliberate kicking of shins, as a debating point, stimulated much friction. Mr F.W. Campbell of Blackheath gave vent to a legendary and xenophobic outburst that reveals much about the mind-set of the hour. The abolition of hacking, he exasperatedly averred, 'savours more of the feeling of those that liked their pipes or grog or schnapps more than the manly game of football' and he offered 'to bring over a lot of Frenchmen who would beat you with a week's practice'.

It was an argument about the degree of violence that was consistent with proper masculinity. In a neat phrase, the always perceptive Richard Holt, in his *Sport and the British; a Modern History* (1989), suggests that these Victorian gentlemen were in search of 'courage short of cruelty'. The soccer adherents wanted to allow other skills to emerge that tripping and hacking spoiled, but they were not averse to heavy charging. It was not a contest between softies and hearties.

After an uneasy lull, the Rugby Football Union was founded in 1871 and three of its alumni, A. Rutter, C. Holmes and L.J. Maton, drafted rugby's rules. Interestingly, probably to Mr Campbell's sorrow, they banished any semblance of kicking or tripping an opponent. These were gentlemen, but they were no leisured aristocrats with unearned incomes. Football, of either code, provided a Saturday escape for business and professional men who could not afford to be maimed. Rugby undoubtedly involved, with its tackling and scrimmaging, a more aggressive outlook, and the two games now also grew significantly apart in strategy.

Rugby became more and more a handling game, with passing by hand paralleling the passing by feet that soon became popular in soccer, which, for its part, forswore almost all handling. Kicking from the hand remains a rugby tactic and, for some eighty years, dribbling continued to play a part in rugby forward play. Since about the time of World War II that specific skill - which was still being taught in rugger schools in the 1940s - has sadly fallen into decay. Another widening difference was in individual and collective play. As rugby became more enamoured of the close-knit game, with forwards bound together in scrum, ruck and maul and working together at line-outs, soccer turned more to the personal holding and release of the ball to a colleague at some little distance away.

Faced, as we shall later observe, with the haunting wraith of professionalism, the two codes found differing solutions: tenuous compromise in football, as in cricket, not least through Charles Alcock's influence in both sports; harsh separation in rugby, with the advent of the Northern Union, later the Rugby League. To glance a little ahead, as Association Football encompassed working class youth, as well as a minority of paid players in the top flight, many, if not all of the public schools forsook it and concentrated on rugby union. Having made soccer possible, the elite schools opted for rugger. The continuum of this class opprobrium against soccer may be observed even at the present time, when the labels of several top-ranking clubs - Wasps, Harlequins, Saracens, for instance - reflect that gentlemanly ethos and are reminiscent of the nomadic and country house cricket elevens of the era, such as I Zingari ('The Gypsies'); Quidnuncs, Incogniti ('no names'), Free Foresters, to say nothing of Harlequins, who first played cricket in 1852.

The fall-out from the rugby defection was especially bothersome in the influential sphere of the public schools, not least because of the knock-on effect for varsity and old boys' football. Oxford University and Richmond were two early recruits to the union colours, but, in general terms, the fast spread of the FA's brand of football soon compensated for this. There was some concern that both the Manchester and Liverpool clubs, and some of their neighbours, chose the Blackheath by-pass, but, as history demonstrates, that was not an irrevocable blow to soccer in those cities. Another north-western example is Sale, formed in 1861, like many football teams, as a winter adjunct for the cricket club, which began in 1854. Sale is now the sole yet sprightly, banner-carrier for top-flight Rugby Union in the region, and, like many rugby clubs of pre-1871 vintage, continued to describe itself simply as a 'football club'. It would be some time before common parlance accepted the not terribly accurate terminology of 'football' and 'rugby' to differentiate between the codes.

Of course, time would tell that there was plenty of space for both these games and many others. It was perhaps an advantage that the matter was settled quickly. It was at only the fifth meeting of the Football Association, held in December of 1863, that the hacking dispute caused the rupture. Although there was some of that acrimony that is drearily characteristic of the committee system, the organisational boil was lanced and there was no lingering suppuration. Charles Alcock was one who acted diplomatically and encouragingly towards the nascent Rugby Union, and, all in all, it was, among the disastrous splits that litter institutional history, a comparatively friendly one. Amazingly, and unlike practically all religious, political and cultural creeds, football has suffered no major schism since.

Amateurs - and the FA Cup

It was in the same spirit of the amateur tradition that Charles Alcock moved to bolster the FA's competency and prestige in being primarily responsible for the inauguration of the FA Challenge Cup. This was a device that, like Helen, was to launch a thousand ships - and several thousand more, as, in sports of all kinds as well as football, the knock-out tournament became a standard competitive mode. Charles Alcock certainly believed and claimed that the FA knock-out contest was the first of its kind. It is true that the fourteen clubs in the Sheffield FA, which covered an area wider than the precincts of the city, played for a cup for the 'champion club', but, while it is not precisely clear how that was arranged, the likelihood is that it may have been on more of a league basis.

The patent disadvantage of the knock-out approach is that half the clubs fall by the wayside at each stage, making it less attractive, at least as the primary format, in any one district. As the years drew by, it became the norm in most districts to add the cup competition as a tasty extra to a programme of league or friendly fixtures that kept everyone involved. The Sheffield FA do not seem to have made any formal complaint of institutional plagiarism and the Sheffield Club was included in the draw for the third of the cup series in 1874, one of the first northern clubs so to be engaged.

The conventional tale of the Harrow Cock House trophy holds some credibility as being the inspiration for the FA Challenge Cup. The boarding school 'house', sometimes named after its current house master, was, quite simply and accurately, the accommodation base for a portion of the pupils. It naturally served as a device for inter-sports rivalry, with house representation later a stepping-stone to the school teams. One or two public schools had inter-dormitory competitions on the same lines. The prominent day schools for older boys, like the main grammar schools, soon began to mimic this notion, thereby producing the curio of pupils belonging to, in respect of building, a non-existent 'house'. Four 'houses' was a typical number, lending itself to a cheap and cheerful competition of some kind, within the plethora of school and other fixtures. The avian symbol of the cock was borrowed from the notion of the 'midden', on top of which one male bird would lord it over the others. At Harrow School the metaphor was slavishly followed. The non-champion houses fought out for the right to challenge the champion house to see if the challenger could assume pre-eminence.

It is for this reason that the FA Cup was originally - and still remains in title - a 'Challenge' cup, although this convention was only operative in the second year of the competition, when the first winners had a bye to and were allowed choice of ground for the final. They did not have to play in what the rules called 'the trial matches'. This rite of struggling to be the one to try his luck at toppling the champion was not uncommon in the sporting field, and remains, to some extent, an aspect of boxing; film-goers will remember how, in On the Waterfront, the mumbling Marlon Brando mournfully confided that he 'coulda been a contender'.

The gentlemen who joined Charles Alcock in the offices of The Sportsman, one of the journals on which he worked, in 1871 to discuss his proposal were all familiar, in some form, with the concept. They gave the suggestion their immediate and happy backing. There were six of them, composing, with the hard-working Alcock of the Wanderers Club, the FA Committee. Public schoolmen all, they were A. Stair of the Upton Park Club and also the FA treasurer; C.W. Stephenson of Westminster School; J.H. Giffard of the Civil Service Club; D. Allport of the Crystal Palace Club and Francis Marindin of the Royal Engineers, a young captain destined to play a major part in the FA's history. Charles Alcock's motion read: 'that it is desirable that a Challenge Cup should be established in connection with the Association, for which all clubs belonging to the Association should be invited to compete.'

This was July. In October 1871 they reconvened, this time with representatives of eleven metropolitan clubs, the above mentioned sextet, plus Barnes, Harrow Chequers, Clapham Rovers, Hampstead Heathens (how the Victorians loved puns!), Windsor House Park and - how Blackheath's Mr Campbell must have scoffed - Lausanne. Not only was the idea accepted, the first rules were ratified and arrangements were set in train for the competition to take place in the current season just beginning.

The eighteen rules reflect the conditions of the times. A ninety minutes playing period is stipulated, as if it were not yet a common ruling in all football matches, while the knock-out approach was sufficiently novel for a convoluted rule six that waxed romantically about teams being 'divided into couples'. Immediate provision was made for 'provincial clubs' to be exempted from the early 'tie-drawings' and to be drawn against neighbouring teams. In the event, many clubs already had cluttered fixture lists and were unable to compete in the first cup competition, but fifteen aspirants became the historic few to play out that first tourney.

They were comprised chiefly of the London clubs which had been represented at the inaugural rules meeting. These were Wanderers, Harrow Chequers, Barnes, Civil Service, Crystal Palace, Upton Park, Clapham Rovers, Hampstead Heathens, plus Royal Engineers from Chatham. Hitchin, Reigate Priory, Maidenhead and Great Marlow, all within reasonable distance of the capital, joined them. The other two were Donnington Grammar School, Spalding and, from far away, Glasgow's Queen's Park Club. Charles Alcock and two committee colleagues were appointed to purchase a Challenge Cup, the £20 cost paid for out of subscriptions from the contestants, including a guinea (£1.05p) - a sixth of that year's income - sent by Queen's Park.

The competition's authors were sensitive to the financial posers set all-amateur clubs, as well as the questions asked of busy salary earners who had little time to travel long distances. Donnington School scratched, allowing

Queen's Park through after a first tie bye - and then they were granted another bye to the fourth ties, that is, semi-finals, both of which were played at the Oval cricket ground. Queen's Park contrived to travel to London with the help of a public collection in Glasgow. There they met the formidable Wanderers in what was described as 'the most remarkable event in modern football' and they held Wanderers to a tough and well-earned scoreless draw. Unluckily, they could not afford to hang on for a replay, so Wanderers, who, with a bye here and a scratching there, went magically through to play the Royal Engineers, victors over Crystal Palace in the other semi-final and 7-4 on favourites for the cup.

18 March 1872 was the date of the first FA Cup final. Just under 2,000 spectators paid what some believed was an off-putting one shilling each for the privilege of watching a strongly fought contest. Wanderers had the best of the play, but the only goal came after fifteen minutes when R.W.S. Vidal, 'the prince of dribblers' from Oxford University, outwitted several defenders, steered the ball to M.P. Betts (with his pseudonym of A.H. ('arrow) Chequer), who triumphantly smashed home the famed Cup Final's first goal. The Engineers team had been incommoded by Lieutenant Cresswell breaking his collar bone when only ten minutes had elapsed. It was the first recorded injury in a very lengthy list of such incidents in Cup finals. With typical Victorian phlegm, 'he maintained his post to the finish of the game'. The Wanderers triumphed 1-0 and Charles Alcock, Wanderers' captain and the perpetrator of a disallowed goal, cheerfully lifted the 18 inch silver trophy he had invented, selected and bought. It was formally presented at the Wanderers' annual dinner.

The two teams characterised the amateur tradition. The Wanderers Club, arising from the old Forest Club, was started by Alcock and, typically, he was their autocratic captain and secretary. Their ranks were made up of Old Harrovians and other former public schoolboys, and their homelessness is reflected in their title, one that, along with 'Rovers', remains in modern football nomenclature for the likes of Wolverhampton and Bolton. Equally typical of the public school motif was their garish costume of orange, violet and black, the sort of confusing, dazzling clash of hues that is still to be found in the rugby union. For their part, the Royal Engineers team were all officers, two captains and nine lieutenants, a further demonstration of amateur elitism.

So it was to continue. Wanderers were 'challenged' next year by Oxford University, whose semi-final opponents, Queen's Park, had not made the journey because of the work commitments of several of their team. Wanderers, as was their right, chose Lillie Bridge, West Brompton, as the venue, not far from the better known Stamford Bridge. The Lillie Bridge site is now covered in rail tracks. The choice may have had something to do with the proximity of the Boat Race course, for the final was played in the morning of 29th March 1873, so that the players could watch the varsity eights in action. Wanderers won 2-0, with goals from C.H.R. Wollaston and Kinnaird. This was the first of an amazing nine final appearances by the Hon. A.F., later Lord, Kinnaird, he of the red beard and red trousers. The newspapers describe him 'threading a way between a forest of Oxford legs'.

Wanderers were soon to have a hat-trick of wins, 1876, 1877 and 1878, and, although Charles Alcock did not play in another final, he refereed twice, in 1875, plus the replay, and 1879. Royal Engineers (who undertook the first-ever football tour, playing Sheffield, Nottingham and Derby in three gruelling but triumphant days in 1874), Oxford University, Kinnaird's Old Etonians, twice, Clapham Rovers and the stylish Old Carthusians were the others among the first eleven victors.

Whatever the rather trivial controversies about the origins of the FA Cup, it is correct to state that it was the first knock-out contest organised for a team sport on a national basis the world had ever known. By this stage the number of entrants had more than doubled to 37, and the spread was more geographically equitable, with nearly half the teams hailing from the north and midlands. What is also very important to observe is that, very soon, the local FAs began to promote their own cup competitions, adding a lively zest to neighbourhood and county struggles.

The FA Cup was a very purposeful competition. The intention was to raise and consolidate standards. It was an attempt to suit the practice to the preaching. While expense and time constraints meant that fixtures predictably remained localised, there was the hazard that the standardised code would be only half-heartedly accepted. The programming of a popular tournament was the ideal instrument for tuition in both the letter and the spirit of the law. The disadvantage of the knock-out approach - its abrupt curtailment of rivals by half at every stage - was now its initial advantage. Clubs were prepared to have a go in a competition that only engaged them in one or two matches, as opposed to a series that necessitated long and expensive journeys for several away matches.

Amateurs - and the Laws

Moreover, this was no static exercise. The dynamism of cup football led to or was accompanied by a surprising number of additions and sophistications, even during that initial bedding-in period. The 1872/73 season saw the introduction of the free kick for handling, a borrowing from some public schools, who already included this in their autonomous rules. The following year the free kick was applied to interference when in an offside position and for encroachment when a free kick was being taken. In 1875, when the Royal Engineers won the final after a replay, the changing of ends after a goal was replaced by the sole such exchange at the halfway mark; crossbars, first mounted for a Cup Final in 1882, were allowed instead of tape - and Lieutenant Sims, one of the gallant Sappers' backs, is reputed to be one of the first players to introduce heading. In 1878 Samuel Widdowson, of Nottingham Forest, invented and wore his own shin pads.

On the subject of crossbars, already in use in the Sheffield area and elsewhere, modern commentators have wondered aloud why their utility was not recognised earlier. Like the ancient use of the pig's bladder, there were pragmatic grounds to consider. If, like Wanderers, one was reliant on public parks or open fields for a temporary playing pitch, conveying two sticks and a tape may have been difficult enough; carriage of two stout posts strong enough to hold aloft a crossbar, together with that selfsame beam, may have proved arduous, if not impossible.

Such reforms arose to solve queries thrown up by the march of football, its pace quickened by the peremptory needs of the new cup competition. One very direct consequence of cup football was a recasting of disciplinary procedures. Recognising that, with a cup at stake and a requirement to maintain uniform standards, the old order would not suffice, the FA designed a new mechanism for cup-ties. Hitherto, law and order had been left to the respective captains. It was a system predicated on the amateur gentleman's credo that no-one would intentionally break the rules. This self-regulation involved an expectation that a player accidentally committing an infringement would release possession or back away, rather as, to their immense credit, snooker professionals today confess to a cuff touching a ball and step back from the table. The captains would speedily deal with other issues. Plainly, in its rudimentary form, football permitted such licence that official supervision was scarcely required; it was only as first one act and then another was prohibited, or as judgements as to offside or balls out of play grew more complicated, that a third party became necessary.

Borrowing from the world of cricket, the FA determined that two umpires, one for each half of the field, in the manner of modern day hockey officials, should be appointed. They were included in the rules from 1874. Later in the 1870s and first mentioned in the laws in 1881, the referee was added, to whom the case could be 'referred' if the umpires disagreed. As in club cricket, each side produced its own umpire, so this concept of third party tribune was probably sensible. Appeals, normally made by the captains, were, with perhaps a glance sideways at cricket, rapidly dealt with, usually by a decisive wave or raising of the arm. It was in 1878 that an umpire first used a whistle, in a match between Nottingham Forest and the oxymoronically titled Sheffield Norfolk. All this also explains why today's referee is not someone to whom matters are referred. Over the next thirty years, and with the rules growing ever more complex, the balance of judicial power shifted. In 1891 the referee was more or less empowered to assert full and decisive control, armed with the shrill instrument of the whistle, with club umpires relegated to neutral linesmen by 1898.

In 1872 the size of the ball was regulated at a circumference of between 27 and 29 inches, while in 1883 the two-handed throw was sanctioned. It was in the 1890s that additional refinements were added and affirmed, such as a ban on charging the goalkeeper (a personage not mentioned in the laws at all until 1871) unless he was playing the ball or obstructing an opponent. Goal nets were patented by a Mr Brodie of Liverpool and deployed for the first time by Old Etonians in 1890. They were an instant success, so much so that they were made compulsory the following year. They were first deployed at a Cup final in 1892.

The penalty kick, the bright suggestion of J. Reed, secretary of the Irish FA, was introduced late in 1891. There was an incident at the tail end of an FA Cup match between Stoke (City was not added to their name until the granting of city status to the 'six towns' of that bustling area in 1926) and Notts County in February 1891. The Potters were 1-0 down with the 90 minutes fast running out when the Magpies' full-back, Hendry, punched a goalbound shot off the line. Referee John Lewis awarded a free-kick for handball, the only decision within his powers at the time and, with the ball almost on the line and a defensive row of County players lined up, the kick was easily cleared. The injustice rankled with Lewis, who also happened to be a prime mover in the FA's legislative committee, and the penalty was enshrined in law in time for the 1891/92 season.

Having been involved in the creation of the penalty kick, Stoke swiftly became the victim of another heinous crime which led to the advent of a sub-section of the current law 7 which declares: 'If a penalty kick has to be taken or retaken, the duration of either half is extended until the penalty kick is completed.' Facing Aston Villa, and, late in the game, being a goal behind yet again, Stoke won a penalty. But the Villa keeper, conscious of the lateness of the hour, booted the ball over the stand and before it was recovered the referee was forced to blow for time. Logic soon held that time would be added on for a penalty to be taken.

There were several convulsions of thought and action over the relevant dimensions and markings. The earlier penalty area measured twelve yards outwards and stretched right across the pitch, while the kick itself was taken from the mid-point of that line. After one or two modifications, the current design and measurements of goal and penalty areas were settled upon in 1902. The penalty area arc was not added until 1937. It was, however, 1912 before goalkeepers were banned from handling outside the penalty area. Hitherto they had been able to handle up to the halfway line, insisted upon only from 1882, simply because there was no other marked line. Indeed, it was only in 1882 that white or otherwise distinct boundary lines became compulsory.

Most early clothing rather resembled cricket and school wear and it was 1909 before a distinctive costume was made compulsory, an old tale suggesting that an out-player handled in the penalty area and an acute goalkeeper nonchalantly took up his colleague's outfield position, while the handler remained in goal, leaving everyone none the wiser. The green goalkeeping jersey became standard a year or so later. As with early cricket, first the individual and then the team uniforms were usually flamboyant and several teams went through a variegated range of mauves and crimsons, until a more humdrum prescription prevailed. Again, it was partly a matter of meeting the needs of spectators, many of whom were removed a distance from the play. Single or double primary colours, contrasting sharply with those of the opposition, were what were required. Numbers on shirts followed, for the same reasons of improved spectator comprehension, in 1928, and were made compulsory for Football League games in the 1938/39 season, somewhat later than one might reasonably have been anticipated.

AMATEURISM

Curiously, it was 1913 and 1914 before yielding ten yards at a free kick or corner respectively became law. Presumably, the spirit of letting the game proceed had previously ruled against the negative and un-Corinthian tactic of forming a human barrier, standing on the toes of the takers of free kicks and corners. The centre circle was an 1887 innovation, introduced for the same reason of allowing some space for the game to proceed from a kick-off.

Initially, the referee was appointed 'by mutual consent of the competing clubs', and cup fervour continued to drive the legislative zeal of the FA. For the 1880/81season, the 'caution' for 'ungentlemanly conduct' and the dismissal for 'violent conduct' was introduced. The persistence of 'gentlemanliness' as the standard to be preserved is noteworthy. Gradually, the FA appointed match officials, not only for the final, but also for matches in the later rounds, eventually to the point where all such appointments were made centrally, as is today's practice.

Amateurs - and International Football

The amateur ethos - and Charles Alcock - had another contribution to make to football's narrative before the onset of professionalism. This was in the matter of international football. The term itself is utilised anachronistically, for, of course, there was no conception of sports of any kind between nations at that time. The speed of change in sporting history was to be bewildering and it is as well to recall that great 19th century statesmen, like Gladstone, Bismarck or Abraham Lincoln, would not have understood the meaning of the phrase.

The Canada and United States cricket matches of 1844 have some claim to be the first-ever team games between two sides labelled nations. They certainly preceded the first Australia and England Test match of 1877. This was advertised as a fixture between 'The All-England eleven and a combined eleven of New South Wales and Victoria' and described by W.G. Grace, a participant, as merely when 'an Australian eleven for the first time beat an eleven of England', the accent being on the even-handedness, for they often played against odds, and on the indefinite article, that is, it was not 'the' eleven. In short, the beginnings of international combat are often messy, with matches only later dignified by such terminology, perhaps to add to the prestige of the sport and to lengthen its historical heritage.

'England' certainly played football before this, but, again, the onset is a trifle haphazard. Furthermore, the geopolitics of international sport are a very tricky subject. 'England' illustrated this by playing its opening international matches against three other regions within the United Kingdom or, as Jane Austen more precisely entitled them, the United Kingdoms. For Scotland, Wales and the whole of Ireland then fell legally, along with England, under the sovereign aegis of the British crown in parliament. Football's international dimension was thus launched with what came ambivalently to be called 'home internationals'. The three outlying kingdoms all formed football associations. The Scottish FA quickly recruited 133 members, seventeen of them still playing in Scottish senior football at the present time. In 1882 there were moves to form an international board, which continued the good and rightful work of insisting on parity of playing conditions. It ruled, for instance, on the optional size of the ball and on the legitimacy of the modern throw-in, on line markings and on the use of crossbars.

In consequence of this impetus, Great Britain was allowed to have four 'national' teams, with Northern Ireland continuing after the main part of Ireland had won its independence in 1921. In the fullness of time, the sceptic might muse about whether other nations are content to see the United Kingdom thus disunited, and a solitary World Cup victory from this truncated quartet fuels the furiousness of that thought. Certainly, our European rivals have never sought to enter their distinctive regions - Bavaria, say, Catalonia or Normandy - in European or world tournaments. Rugby Union followed suit, although a cross-border Irish team was maintained after the advent of Eire, whilst the British Lions tours offer a periodic shadow of geopolitical sanity.

The development of a foursome of national bodies did, however, set the useful precedent that, for international contest to work efficiently, one had to have both an acknowledged nation and a prescribed focus of officialdom. Some cricketing countries, including both England and Australia, have suffered on occasion from this lack of an identifiable and creditable sovereign body. Football managed, in most cases, to avoid that error, as it extended its wings and flew across the globe's surface. Political scientific pedantry apart, the gentlemen administrators of the late 19th century might have rightly protested that there were no other countries to play football against at that stage, and they did, at least, have the gumption to raise the stakes and seek out ways of lifting standards by instigating a representative tourney.

AMATEURISM

The opening games were no more than appetisers before the coming feast. In 1870 a game was organised at the Oval between what was called 'the Scotch (sic) and English sections', meaning that all the players were London based, and further such games were planned for 1871. They roused a spark of interest, not least among the rugby union fraternity, who were quick to latch on to the international motif. In 1872 the FA took a team to Scotland, to play a team chosen by Queen's Park and, in fact, consisting entirely of that club's players. This duly constituted the first 'international' football match of all time. Perhaps ominously, no goals were scored. There was a return match in London in 1873, which England won 4-2, and those fixtures drew decent crowds of 2,000 and 3,000 respectively. Wales began international operations in 1879 and Ireland in 1882, leading to the establishment in the 1883/84 season of the Home International Championship. It was a sporting series that was to last exactly a hundred years.

Amateurs - and the 'Passing' Game

The inventive amateur tradition had one final contribution to offer. The medium consisted of two fine all-amateur clubs, one from each side of the Anglo-Scottish border, and the content was an advance in footballing technique. They were Queen's Park and Corinthians, and they pioneered the passing game.

The Queen's Park club was formed in 1867. The club motto, 'Ludere Causa Ludendi', in the style of a Victorian municipal epithet, translates as 'Play for Playing's Sake'. Although now languishing amid the lower orders of the Scottish leagues, they have honoured that injunction for close on a century and a half, and, as the owners of Hampden Park, the club has obviously been an important cog in the wheel of Scottish football. At the onset, and wearing their rugby-style hoops of black and white, they were simply dominant. One or two other teams - Vale of Leven and Dumbarton, for instance - contributed, but it was Queen's Park's pre-eminence that saw England beaten in eleven of the first nineteen international fixtures, with only three wins and five draws.

Fast and resolute, Charles Campbell, reputed to be the first effective header of the ball, was the leading light. He controlled the game from half back, in a 2-2-6 formation, but the key to dominance was short passing as an alternative to the long kick and the mazy dribble of the English. 'The Scottish game', with its alert tactical acumen, benefited from improvements in the manufacture of the ball and law changes that authorised, under careful conditions, the propulsion forward of the ball to a fellow player. The English game soon followed in the wake of this mini-revolution, especially through the migration of Scots to the northern clubs, as the spectre of professionalism reared its disconcerting head.

It was partly as a counter to this distasteful process that Corinthians were formed in 1882 to sustain the amateur ethic - and also to see what might be done to halt the supremacy of the Scots. The team was chosen from among the best amateurs of the day to play occasional games in the holiday periods, rather after the manner, and with the same motive, of rugby union's Barbarians today. Among their early luminaries were William Cobbold, the next to inherit the long-standing nickname of 'the Prince of Dribblers' and an experimenter with shin pads, and the brotherly full- back pairing of A.M. and P.M. Walters, known to their friends as Morning and Afternoon.

Corinthians, while never playing competitively, did much to raise standards and they often outclassed strong professional combines. They once trounced a certain Manchester United, then known as Newton Heath, 10-0, for example. It was about this juncture that the FA tried to bring together the amateur and professional associations more securely under one protective shelter. Several amateur clubs were opposed to such controls and the public schools, in particular, were irked. It accelerated the schools' adoption of rugby union. Corinthians later merged in 1939 with another club to become the Corinthian Casuals, and are still to be spotted in the Isthmian League, having finally found a home just off the A3 in Tolworth, Surrey.

The moment had passed, but, like Queen's Park, Corinthians had demonstrated the value of the skilful passing game. Artfully, they tried to perfect the technique of drawing defenders, creating space and then releasing a more telling pass.

It was to be the last breath of foremost amateurism. The mythic lore is related that Corinthians, in honour of the amateur ethos, kicked penalties wide and instructed their goalkeeper to stand aside should one be ordered against them, sniffily shocked by the abhorrent scandal of playing for or against men who would commit such offences. A sending off led apparently to expulsion from the team. In a convention also used in lacrosse, they withdrew one of their own players should an opponent have to vacate the field because of injury. That aspect of their value system had little wider appeal now or then in football circles, but, however disdainfully aristocratic their delicate consciences, they were, alongside Queen's Park, the Che Guevaras of methodology. They promoted the revolutionary transformation of football from a mainly dribbling to a chiefly passing sport.

CHAPTER SIX

URBANISM; FOOTBALL'S SOCIAL FRAMEWORK

IN 1863 A DOZEN or so clubs started the Football Association. Twenty years later there were already a hundred entries for the FA Cup and the country was awash with football clubs. Forty years later, into the Edwardian period, there were 35,000 clubs registered with the FA and 580,000 listed participant players, while a similar number of some 500,000 were in weekly attendance to observe professional league matches.

Organised football came of age with astonishing rapidity. It represents one of the largest spontaneous outbreaks of voluntary activity in the social history of a nation in which such voluntary action has played a conspicuous part. In addition, with the building of designated stadia, the charging for entry and, ineluctably, the paying of players, football was soon switching, at its highest level, to being a major element in the nation's developing entertainments industry.

Urbanism

To make sense of this sweeping success one needs to understand something of the very national social history of which is was a part. In negative terms, it would not have been possible, practically or psychologically, for the rise of spectator football to occur before 1850. Casting a bow at a venture, it may not have been possible after 1950, but that is a more abstruse conjecture.

The practical issues are the more straightforward of the two. They involve the growth of population and of towns, both at once the cause of and a response to the challenge of industrialism. These processes, in turn, implicated the mobilisation of people and of services, most dramatically through the railways, the peak achievement of the primary industrial revolution. As the years drew on, rail transport was assisted and rivalled by public road transport, first the tram and then the bus.

To all this must be added a wide range of social improvements, both personal - higher wages and increased leisure - and civic - the provision, for instance, of public parks. Quite simply, to play or watch football on a regular, weekly basis became a practical proposition.

The other dimension, the psychological one, is of a more complex order. And without one or the other condition, football would not have come to dominate society as it does today. There was some peculiar mind-set about Victorian society that encouraged and at the same time shaped football as a national pursuit. Some of the elements - Muscular Christianity; zeal for physical prowess and well-being - that had triggered the public school adoption of the sport also powered the middle class determination to make football's respectable benefits available to the lower orders. It was an example of 'rational recreation', a concept beloved of the Victorian social thinker. At bottom, football was an improvement on getting inebriated in the pub and brawling in the street.

The fact that it was so successful a venture suggests, however, that the reformers were pushing at an opening door. In other words, both the do-gooders and their potential clients must have shared something of the same values and aims. In *The Screwtape Letters*, the Christian apologist C.S. Lewis suggests that you can always tell who a do-gooder is doing good to from the hunted look on their faces, but, with football, the two parties seem to have been in cheerful accordance. Even with professional football, Victorian crowds were, contrary to some gloomy forebodings, pleasingly well behaved.

In summary terms, the first fruits of modern football were both a social and a cultural expression of the industrial and urban revolution. Without one or the other, the impact would have been much less potent. It was this interaction of the more material with the more mental factors of urbanism that ratcheted up the intensity of football's development. The result was that, by 1900, football had chalked up two telling records. First, the number of people regularly playing football - something like a sixth of all males between 15 and 44 years of age - was higher than in any other sport. Second, the numbers paying to watch football were higher than for any other sport, having, about this point, edged above the temptations of cricket. In terms of both participation and spectatorship, football already stood high in the lists of leisure pastimes in general.

Urbanism, as the social and cultural bailiwick for modern football, is a significant concept, worthy of dwelling on because of its wider ramification. The process of industrial urbanisation, pioneered in Britain, soon spread across the developing world. As it did so, football danced attendance. By the end of the 20th century, and with the exception of one or two regions of special character, the commercial or industrial city without a professional football team was the exception rather than the rule.

'Congregation'

The political scientist Herman Finer described the sort of society emergent from the industrial revolution by the laconic term of 'congregation'. The word admirably conveys the sense of an ever more concentrated press of people, quite different from the smaller communities that more characterised the agricultural and commercial economy prior to about 1750. 'Congregation' made itself manifest in three circles of human activity. More people crowded into the cabined conditions of more factory-type workplaces within the cramped environs of more towns.

There is considerable academic speculation about the chickens and the eggs in this process. Did prospering industry prompt population growth, for example, or did the demands of more people lead to advanced technical solutions? The relative weightings of cause and effect need not detain us unduly. Suffice it to emphasise that the swirling, intersecting action of a demographic explosion, a plethora of factories and the like, and the unprecedented growth of towns presented football with the ideal circumstances in which to expand.

800 years before that first representative football match between London and Sheffield, William the Conqueror landed in southern England and triumphed at the Battle of Hastings. In that memorable year of 1066 the population of Britain was a meagre 1.5 million. 100 years before Cambridge University issued its seminal football rules, Bonnie Prince Charlie was attempting vainly to emulate him. In 1745, the year of the second Jacobite rebellion, the total population had struggled on to a still sparse 5.5 million, less than four times as many in some 700 years. In the 1871 census, the first after the formation of the FA, it was a flourishing 31.5 million, a six-fold rise in a century.

URBANISM

It was truly a demographic revolution. The numerical key was the decline in the death rate, falling almost a half to 22 per 1,000 population, whereas the birth rate stayed constant at about 35 to 37 per 1000. That is a fact worth noting, for later global population growth - so important to the spread of the football cult - would follow the same arithmetical pattern of consistent births gradually outstripping falling deaths.

Another very significant pointer to the future of global football was the youthful nature of a rapidly escalating population. In the mid 19th century the mean age of the British people, the age above and below which one found half the population, was 26; it is currently approaching 40. 60% of the population was unmarried. This looming predominance of young people raised political eyebrows and gave rise to furious debate. Football was just one, if one of the most successful, of the answers that were rehearsed as to what to do with all this youthful energy and vim.

A similar model that was to have worldwide ramifications may be discerned in terms of urban growth. As population exploded, then, size-wise, what were thought of as villages became towns and towns became cities. But there was an overriding factor of many towns growing more quickly than the norm, just as, once more, the last fifty years has witnessed the same proclivity among developing nations. In the first fifty years of the 19th century, London doubled in size to 2 million inhabitants; Manchester and Salford jumped astronomically from fewer than 100,000 to 500,000; Leeds from 72,000 to 172,000 and Blackburn from 13,000 to 65,000. Bradford was yesterday's Jakarta - its inhabitants sprang eight times in number from 13,000 to 104,000.

These commercial and industrial foci were both reproducing at the new improved national rate and receiving additional recruits by way of inward migration. Britain lost about 1.5 million souls a decade as overseas emigrants, with that figure increasing as the century wore on, while, internally, about 500,000 people in each decade made their way from the country to the towns. Only 166,000 people inhabited Lancashire, destined to be the pioneer industrial county, in 1701; that had risen to 673,000 by 1801 - but by 1831 it was 1.4 million. Now a tenth of Britons lived in the County Palatine, where, in 1701, there had been but a five-hundredth. The great range of cotton and allied trading towns, from Liverpool to Manchester, were, of course, responsible for this. Moreover, the county, as a whole and not just those urban districts, was, after London, the most crowded area in Britain. By 1831 there were 1,000 people per square Lancastrian mile.

This dreadful overcrowding was connected with the impact of steam-powered industry. This necessitated the packed concentration of men, women and children in unprecedentedly large numbers in the work place. This might generically be called the factory system, although, needless to say, the designation altered from one industrial type to another, from mill and mine to iron foundry and pottery. With no short distance cheap transit schemes in early evidence, accommodation was built for the factory workers close to the workplace. By the mid 19th century, 2 million Londoners were crushed into an area of 4 by 6 miles; 250,000 Mancunians and Salfordians were cramped into just one square mile of territory, and there were 66,000 Liverpudlians, 38,000 of them in cellars, cabined into each square mile of the city.

The 'cottonopolis' of Manchester was 'the shock city of the 1840s' and the world's first industrial town. In the 1780s there had been two water-driven cotton mills in Manchester - then the first steam -driven loom was used in 1789, allegorically, the year of the French Revolution. The Industrial Revolution was equally compelling. By 1800 there were 500 power looms in the country and Manchester now boasted 52 steam-driven mills and 61 attendant iron foundries and machine shops. By 1833 there were 100,000 power looms in Lancashire alone, while Manchester hosted 213 mills, plus a vast array of supportive dye, bleaching, printing and calico works and engineering premises.

Until this time, work places had mostly been small affairs, with many outworkers, like George Eliot's weaver, *Silas Marner*, working at home in solitary state. Suddenly, the advent of steam led to large-scale enterprises. By 1850 the average number of workers per employment unit was 200, an average that, of course, embraced some vast gatherings of employees. From a situation where agricultural labour had long dominated the employment statistics, we discover that, by 1850, five out of ten British manual workers were in the industrial trades, with many others in back-up services like transport, and with another fifth in domestic service.

The upshot may be summarised by the statement that when Queen Victoria came to the throne in 1837, more of her subjects lived in the country than in the towns, and that when she died in 1901 the reverse was true. And by a substantial margin... in the ratio of 28 million in towns (deploying the standard urban measure of communities of more than 5,000 inhabitants) and 8 million in the country, an urban/rural split of 78% to 22%.

This was to be the setting for mainstream football, but urbanism of itself was not a sufficient factor. The numbers were recruited in urbanised close proximity to play and watch football, but they had to have the time and the money. The next chapters, then, in this socio-economic saga are the finding of some leisure time and some spare cash.

The first inroads into the gruesome labour conditions of the primary factory system came through regulations designed to limit the hours of work of women and children. As they normally assisted the adult males, the latter, too, found their hours limited, although 'relay' shifts of women and children were sometimes used to keep the men working for longer periods. In any event, the real reason for the reduction in hours was the gradual technological improvements that made, in mill or mine, the toil of ancillary workers less necessary. To use a dramatic martial illustration, the powder monkeys, of what today would be regarded as junior school age, who scuttled about the decks of the royal navy frigates at the battle of Trafalgar in 1805, had, by the battle for the Falklands in 1982, been replaced by electronic and computerised equipment. In more mundane style, much of the work done by women and children in the factory set-up was taken over by ever more ingenious machinery and they became redundant.

The consequence was that, by the middle of the 19th century, many tradesmen were working a ten hour day or perhaps a little over, heading towards the 60 hour week that was common among manual workers in the last quarter of the century. From about 1847, and with considerable variance from place to place and industry to industry, the Saturday half-day began to appear. This was critical for both the participants in and watchers of football. With Sunday frowned upon as an opportunity for such activities, the free Saturday afternoon was, perhaps literally, a godsend. In effect, this usually meant a finish at 2pm, for work began between 7am and 8am.

Workers were free to play or spectate and, obviously enough, the Football League kick off of 3pm was, in part, dictated by this system - or, just to underline the point, 3.15pm at Stoke, for the potteries had a slightly different working pattern with shifts ending at 3pm.

This was the prime move favouring the fortunes of football, but there were some other reforms that helped. Sir John Lubbock introduced the idea of what Lord Salisbury entitled 'bank' holidays in 1870. The several 'holy' days of the old rural tradition had largely vanished, while the grim disciplines of the Victorian factory regimes were much stricter, so that St. Monday was not as freely celebrated. Many workers, including clerical workers - sympathisers of Bob Cratchit, Ebenezer Scrooge's lowly clerk in Dickens's *A Christmas Carol*, will recall that he was one such - could count on only Good Friday and Christmas Day for rest days, apart from Sundays. The closure of the banks on three Mondays - at Easter, at Whitsuntide and in August ~ plus Boxing Day, had the knock-on effect of shutting down most other businesses and those holidays became general. The first bank holiday was Whit Monday, 19th May 1871. Well into the 20th century, the Football League would often cram three fixtures around Christmas and the Easter weekend. Incidentally, the term 'weekend' first became common in 1879. Prior to that time only Sunday was a rest day from work.

The next stage was the coming of holidays, just a few days at first, then the regular 'wakes' week, when industrial townships closed, lock, stock and barrel, for an urban crusade to the seaside, and then the beginnings of paid holidays. Commercial and professional workers were the first to obtain some days off with pay. The general post office gave a week's holiday with pay to its thousands of 'letter carriers' in 1867, and the paternalistic railway companies soon followed suit. Among private companies, the Wills Tobacco firm in Bristol offered their labour force a week's holiday with pay in 1891.

The notion of a summer holiday did not affect football directly, except in so far as it represented a liberalisation of industrial conditions and a sense of more time and money being available. The factory owners were becoming more aware that a healthier workforce was a more productive and thus more profitable one, deserving, by that token, some tolerant consideration. There was also the argument that a complete shutdown facilitated essential maintenance of structure and machinery. The 'wakes' or 'feast' type holiday also emphasised the communal character of Victorian town-life with its customary mono-economy of reliance on one trade, frequently one agency of that trade, such as a colliery, a mill or a shipyard. There was one town; one job; one holiday - and one football team. Not for nothing did some football teams gain nicknames based on those manufactures - potters, cobblers, saddlers, hatters, gunners, railwaymen and so forth.

Continental workers envied their British counterparts. The British labour force had some liberty to play and watch football regularly well before their European colleagues did so. The reasons why the British 'invented' modern sport are wrapped up in social detail of that kind, rather than - as is sometimes implied - some sort of English genetic flair for games.

As the economy prospered and the regimen relaxed a trifle, the wages also improved. It is a complex question to examine over many industries over many years, but, in the most approximate terms, there was some amelioration on that front, enough to allow for sixpences to change hands at sports ground turnstiles - first introduced in 1871, possibly not coincidentally the year of that initial bank holiday.

To provide some frame of reference, Mrs Isabella Beeton informs us in the first edition of her admirable *Book of Household Management*, published in 1861, that if one had an income of £1,000, then one would be likely to employ five servants, and, if it were £200, one might still have one servant living in and one out. Even the impecunious Micawbers in *David Copperfield* had a poor drab maid, self-defined as 'a Orfling'. Middle class incomes ranged from as low as £150 to £1,500, whilst £5,000 per annum was regarded as rich indeed. Put another way, small shopkeepers, teachers and senior clerks might have hoped to earn £3 a week.

Below this, some 10 million industrial workers were progressing nicely. Between about the time of the establishment of the FA in 1863 and the outbreak of World War I in 1914, the lowest paid unskilled workers saw their earnings rise from 12s a week (60p; £30 a year) to 18s (90p; £45 a year) and the highest paid skilled workers' wages likewise from 35s (£1.75; £88) to £2 5s (£2.25; £113). All in all, these fifty or so years witnessed a 60% or 70% increase in manual workers' wages, but, as there were drops in rent and prices, with food especially becoming cheaper, it amounted to a rise in real terms of 80%. It was calculated that £1 10s (£1.50) weekly income for an average 48 hour week could reasonably keep a normal family in decent comfort, with maybe a little over for those tanners at the turnstile.

If conditions for these artisan classes had progressed with some steadiness, it is salutary, having advertised the funds available to the middle class layer, to finish off the sandwich with a word about the bottom tier, many of whom may have wanted to play or watch football. The agricultural labourers, now but 1.2 million in numbers, earned on average 10s (50p; £25 a year) around 1860, rising to 15s (75p; £37) in the late 1900s, plus the equivalent in kind of 2s or 3s (10p or 15p). There were also 2 million domestic servants, with an impressive hierarchy of remuneration. In this same time-span, the lowliest of maids advanced in yearly earnings from £9 to £12 and the loftiest of cooks from £30 to £69 a year, inclusive, naturally, of the not to be sniffed at perquisite of full board.

By and large, the later 19th century wage economy liberated the respectable artisan and lower middle classes to indulge in a little leisure, without which neither the recreational game, which also could make some small financial demands on those engaged in it, nor the professional game would have flourished as wholesomely as it did.

Transportation

One of the most exhilarating aspects of this epoch of urban and industrial construction was the transport revolution that galvanised the whole of society into mobility. The static society of earlier times had been shaken up a little by the advent of the canals and the promotion of road works. Even building the first faltering steps of industry required reasonable transport. When Josiah Wedgwood launched his famous pottery in the mid 18th century, he lost a third of his wares through breakages, as the only effective carriage outwards from his Burslem depot in Staffordshire was by packhorse.

Canal engineers like James Brindley and road engineers like Thomas Telford and John Macadam had begun the transformation of the transportation map. By the first years of the 19th century, there were some 6,000 miles of canals and of England's 130,000 miles of primitive highway, a fifth had been made good by the turnpike trusts, supervisors of superior and dedicated toll roads. There were improvements to stagecoaches as well. Nonetheless, the canal journey from Manchester to the Mersey estuary (some 30 miles) took a wearisome twelve hours and the canals were chiefly, if valuably, used for freight. As for the 'flying coaches', the reforms meant that the previous three day journey from London to Manchester was reduced only to something less than 30 hours, still a tedious slice of time.

The major breakthrough came with the advent of the railways after 1830. The opening in that year of the Liverpool and Manchester railroad lit the fuse for an explosion of railway lines. Twenty years later, there were already 6,000 miles of railways in Britain and by 1880 there were 16,000 miles. It was to reach a maximum of 24,000 miles by the beginning of the 20th century, only to be sadly reduced to 11,000 miles in the last generations. In London, the underground system was commenced in 1863 with tunnelling from Farringdon to Baker Street and was patently destined to play a significant role in the leisure - including football - of Londoners and visitors to the capital.

In future years Herbert Chapman played a significant role in having the name of Gillespie Road tube station ceremoniously changed in November 1932 to the name of the club he managed, Arsenal. The Gunners were quite literally put on the map. Chapman had spent months lobbying for the change, which meant that thousands of tickets, maps and signs had to be replaced. Even machinery had to be re-configured. 'Whoever heard of Gillespie Road?' Chapman famously asked at one point in the talk,. 'it's Arsenal around here'. Football was beginning to dictate matters.

In 1842 there were 25 million railway passenger journeys. In 1912 there were 1,800 million such journeys. It is difficult to exaggerate the seismic change wrought in British life by the railways. What made it so earth shattering was its effect on everyday life. A man on the moon was a clever scientific stroke, but it has not been repeated, let alone become an experience that is daily taken for granted by thousands. There was also the pace of the change. By comparison, it was fifty years after the first manned flights that air travel really entered the consciousness of the ordinary Briton, and then only for a holiday trip once or twice a year. Most people were using the railways regularly within a few years of the building of the first one.

The public authority came to keep a careful eye on the railway system; there was a clear acknowledgement of its national value. The 1873 Railway and Canal Traffic Act, for example, set up the Railway Commission as comptroller of the then 28 private companies. The famous 'parliamentary' train, at a penny a mile, had, since 1844, ensured there was always some opportunity for the not so well off to travel, and the first, second and third class division, however much it clung to social caste determinants, ensured the poorer folk had that chance.

Trains were quicker and more reliable than their rival modes. Sea travel remained cheaper, but who would choose a boat, fare 7s on deck, 15s for a cabin, that took a day and only sailed once or twice a week from London to Plymouth, against a seven trains a day service, a journey of seven or eight hours, at a price of 18s 8d? One bought a ticket before departure, whereas, with a coach, unless you booked and joined it at its point of departure, you might have had to hang about at a crossroads or a tavern, hoping there might still be a place for you, when and if it showed up. The Liverpool to Manchester service almost immediately began to transport 1,200 passengers a day, compared with 500 by coach, but at half the price and in half the time. In 1830 the coach from London to Brighton cost £1 3s (£1.15), but it took so long that there was the further expense of refreshments en route and tips were all but obligatory. Eight miles an hour was par for a coach; twelve miles an hour was exceptionally good. Within a decade or so, trains were conveying ten times as many visitors to 'London by the sea' as the now vanishing coaches had done in a quarter of the time.

Convincing evidence of the force of the railways relates to the change of attitude towards the time. Until this stage, time varied from town to town, rather as lighting up times still do today. No one could ever move from one place to another quickly enough for it to matter. Fast and dependable, trains made a nonsense of this, and the railway companies were keen to publish timetables (the term comes from the 'tables' of tides used in association with sea journeys). The railway companies locally brought pressure on town and city corporations to adopt standard 'London' time and this eventually became nationally adopted. It was quite late on before, in 1880, the Statutes (Definition of Time) Act made Greenwich Mean Time the legal base for timekeeping in the United Kingdom.

R.S. Surtees, country gentleman, writer and creator of Jorrocks, the sporting grocer, was captivated by the way railways were 'whirling as many passengers along as would have filled the old coaches for a week, unlocking the country for miles, and bringing parties within a few hours of each other who formerly had been separated'. Others - for one, Charles Dickens, victim of a nasty train crash - were less enthused, and there were financial scandals and social despoliations to mar the progress of rail development.

For all that, it may be safely said that, without the railways, no national sporting competition, no FA Cup or Football League, could have been contemplated. It was not just that the charter trains would bring the crowds to London for the FA Cup final or, on shorter runs, ensure that local spectators a little distanced from the stadium could enjoy watching their favourites. The first duty and task for the railways was to convey the teams in good and fast time to the away grounds, so that fixtures could be safely scheduled.

Trams, what Richard Hoggart fluently called 'the people's gondolas', came in the next phase of transportation history. The buses, outside of London and some of the large cities, were really a between the wars phenomenon, but the horse trams completed the urban network of public transport. They radiated outward from town centres, often with the railway station as the hub, imposing a compact pattern on urban life. Although one could live further out and travel to work by tram, the tramlines were obviously limited in extent and flexibility, so that towns found themselves bound in by another form of economic frontier. They were a boon to the ordinary leisure seeker and, as such, a major player in the carriage of spectators and teams to football grounds.

(The author's father, crafty inside-left for Sale Holmfield and Sale United in one of the Manchester leagues just about the time of the 1914-1918 War, would reminisce of such tram journeys as an amateur player. His party piece and the club song, warbled on the top deck of the tram, was the maudlin music hall favourite, *While London Sleeps*, originally sung by Arthur Lennard. He related how fellow-passengers would weep at their recital, but his cynical offspring were wont to wonder aloud whether the lachrymose effect was caused by sympathy or anguish.)

After some desultory experiment, the first trams arrived in Liverpool in 1869, in Blackpool and London in 1870, in Glasgow in 1872 and in Birmingham and Sheffield in 1873, all of them already strong football centres. The usual method was for the local authority to lay the track and let out the tram franchise to private hands. Then - Huddersfield in 1882 and Manchester in 1901 are examples - the municipalities took over the whole show, and the next step was the electrification of the vehicles and the departure of the horses.

Trams were twice the size of buses, originally viewed - and priced - as a more middle class mode of travel. Trams, with their penny and twopenny fares, were the first genuinely working class means of transport, with no one worrying about a bit of dirt being left on the wooden slatted seats. In the years just before the First World War, London annually catered for 505 million tram rides and Manchester for 206 million such trips. Nationally, there were 3.3 million journeys a day in 1914, the majority of them in electrified trams.

Let us take stock of the transport situation generally at that juncture. In 1910 the British undertook 5,000 million jaunts annually by public transport, 1,300 million by rail, 3,000 million by tram and 700 million by horse bus. Less than a hundred years before the average number of public transport journeys taken a year by each British subject had been four. In 1910 it had catapulted to 124. Many were for work, shopping, visiting family and the like. Many of them were for going to play or watch football.

As a postscript to this travelogue, mention should be made of the honest bicycle. The first 'safety' bicycle, the Rover, was manufactured in Coventry by J.K. Starkey, nephew of James Starkey, 'the Father of the Bicycle', and pneumatic tyres, courtesy of J.B. Dunlop, were added in 1888. From then until after the Second World War, the bicycle, among its multiple uses, was often the vehicle of choice, not only for biking to football grounds, but also for youth teams making their way around the away grounds of junior leagues.

Municipalisation

In the 1980s there was superficial talk, mainly from Thatcherite politicians, about a return to 'Victorian values'. These they construed as strident individualism and private initiative, untrammelled by public control. They were no more than half right. The Victorian middle classes were fierce protagonists of public intervention. Sometimes with the central state and the local authorities in partnership, often with the municipalities taking a brash lead, there were vast civic undertakings across a range of subjects. The motives for this combining of public with private action were a mix of religious piety, social awareness, fiery civic pride and an eye for the trading interest.

The evangelical streak in Victorian religiosity called for good works as the sign of inward grace, while what is sometimes called the 'intolerability' theory forced people to respond to unutterably dire social conditions, especially in terms of poverty and sickness. Self-interest was never lacking. The virulent fever epidemics, such as typhoid and cholera, that swept through Victorian towns had a nasty habit of spreading from the poor to the well-to-do districts, while desperately pauperised men might easily turn to social disorder. Civil self-importance was also to the fore. Towns and cities vied for prestige. Mill owners wanted to have the tallest chimneys, and the new urbanised seaside resorts liked to have a long pier. The mock-Gothic town halls of the new industrial cities were but the crown on architectural efforts at municipal grandeur.

What the more far-sighted Victorian industrialist and capitalist sought to construct was an environment amenable to the pursuit of burgeoning trade. If ordure and other refuse clogged the streets, then the wheels of commerce were, quite literally, halted. In Manchester in the 1830s the dung-hills, some of which now had a weight of 30,000 tons, were re-named dung-mountains. If the alleys and streets were unlit, then petty theft - 'depredations' from shops, for instance

- might be masked. If workers were unnecessarily ill, they were absent from work and business suffered. It made economic sense to 'keep the ring clear', as the contemporary phrase ran. What the right-wing politicians of the 1980s neglected to consider was the huge effort the Victorian 'individualists', self-helpers and free traders put into the public business of guaranteeing that the ambit in which they strove to make money was cleared of the physical and other obstacles impeding that purpose.

The ambitious engineering schemes that brought fresh water to and removed sewage from the industrial towns were the most momentous illustrations of this confidence in public works. It was also by far the most effective answer to the public health question, but there were plenty of other examples of civic vitality. An urban landscape is still within living memory of a series of gaunt structures, each catering for some social need or ill. The school, the hospital, the workhouse, the asylum, the prison - they loomed darkly at some corner of the city, as if mimicking the nearby factory or barracks, for, in another instance of local pride, many towns hosted a neighbourhood regiment. The Victorians were acutely conscious of the factory formula as the model for their social agencies and, obviously, they served to illustrate Herman Finer's precept of 'congregation'. Children, patients, paupers, lunatics and criminals were herded together, sometimes in groups of 2,000 or more, insulated from the buffets of outside existence, and, in particular, offering no threat to the peaceful bustle of trade and business.

At the last, there was the ultimate in 'congregation': the resting place - after a torrid battle with the church, which had a vested financial and proselytising interest in keeping burials within its churchyards - of the municipal cemetery.

There were, of course, less gloomy examples, such as libraries, museums and art galleries, many of them built out of municipal largesse or through the benevolence of local civic-minded dignitaries. The comparison is sometimes made between the ebullient conceit of the new industrial cities and that of the late medieval Italian city-states, such as Venice or Florence. It was an easy step, both for employers and employees, to transfer some of this sense of local patriotism to the town's football team. The mayoral welcome of and reception for the FA Cup winners, usually following a parade through streets packed with enthusiastic supporters, was an early demonstration of this shared communal pleasure. Moreover, the 'congregation' of thousands on a football ground was in accord with the collective nature of urban activity, whether for business or pleasure.

Recreation

The municipal action that had the most direct relevance to football was the provision of parks. Again the public health movement joined up their thinking with that of the churches. The parks became, it now appears with not much scientific veracity, the 'lungs of the city', while the pious were pleased to see workers further distracted from the bottle. Mill and mine owners were satisfied on both counts; healthy and sober employees were much preferred, for the devil makes work for idle (factory) hands.

The parks were, in the words of Jacques Carré, an historian of parks, 'a spectacular manifestation of Victorian civic art'. There have been three options for park design. One is the Italian baroque convention, where the park was a theatrical focus of urban honour, not a relief from urban squalor. Florence's Boboli Gardens are an example. The second is the oriental convention, with the park an emblem of paradise, 'an oasis of beauty blooming in an earthly desert'; the Taj Mahal being a wonderful example. British parks bent the knee to both those traditions. The bandstand, the statuary (Crystal Palace had a sculpted jungle) and the children's playground stand surety for the former and the colourful floral displays, greenhouses and aviaries (Kew is the leading exponent of these themes) for the latter.

It was the third option, luckily for football, that won the day, for the Victorian park was slavishly based on the landscaping pattern associated with Capability Brown and Humphrey Repton of the preceding century. It aped the country house estate and was at one with the Victorian 'romantic' belief with its fondness for nature. Hiding the park from the meanness of the city streets was a high barrier of walling or foliage, broken by a grandiose gateway or two, enclosing a rolling tract of turf, with, just inside the frontier of shrubbery, a circular macadamised way, eponymously known as the 'Brownean' path. Across the nation these parks flourished. Not without a good deal of argument about the relative needs of the sportsmen manqués and the gardeners manqués, possibly interested, having no gardens of their own, in the rosarium or arboretum, the turfed enclave became used for games. At first informally - Wanderers in Battersea Park - then formally, they were deployed for thousands of games of football. Later, clearly designated playing fields would be supplied, but, all in all, it is right to praise the Victorian authorities for ensuring that generations of British urban youth could play football.

Here they kept fit, enjoyed their games, strutted their stuff before the scouts of important clubs and played out their dreams of emulating their heroes. A significant characteristic of British football crowds has been the high proportion of their numbers who have themselves played football. This gave them not only a heightened grasp of what they were observing but also a more intense identity with the local professional team. These were the champions you not only admired, but had tried to imitate on a park pitch perhaps within the sound of cheers from the professional arena.

As early as the 1830s, parliament had urged the necessity of wholesome 'public walks', specifically as an antidote to drunkenness. From 1840 some public funds became available, while there were philanthropic donations. The crown made available, for example, Victoria Park, Bethnal Green in 1845 and Battersea Park in 1857, and, at the end of the century, a quarter of London's parks were crown lands. Sir Robert Peel laid out £1,000 for Salford's Peel Park, while Manchester had three parks by 1846. Joseph Hume and Robert Slaney were the pioneering radical MPs at the heart of the early parks campaigns and, later in the century, Octavia Hill fronted the Open Space movement with the same ends in view.

Park designers emerged, among them Sir Joseph Paxton, constructor of the Crystal Palace, Edward Vamp, responsible for Southport's Hesketh Park and Liverpool's Stanley Park, John Gibson, who became Superintendent of London's parks, and Edward Miller, the architect of parks in Halifax, Preston and Buxton. As one tiny example, by 1930 Liverpool offered 172 municipal football pitches to its young citizens. It amounted to an immense contribution to urban life in general and football in particular. Jacques Carré has written with some truth that the parks were the 'testing ground of the new urban ethos'. A contemporary enthusiast for parks, Rev J.F. Clarke, caught the essential compound of godliness and public health when he exclaimed of parks, 'REcreation, the creation anew of fresh strength'. In 1841 the snooty *Times* caught the essential compound of good works and social distinctions when it spoke of 'the redemption of the working classes through recreation', suggesting the value to them of 'the liberty of taking a walk in the more plebeian portions of the park, provided they had a decent coat on.'

A complex of social and economic factors thus conspired to make Britain safe for football. The advocates of 'rational recreation', what one of their number, Robert Slaney, called 'regulated amusement', were drawn from a number of middle class sources. There were vigorous churchmen, so much so that, for example, 25% of Birmingham's football clubs in the 1870s and 1880s were closely linked with churches. There were keen schoolteachers, for whom area organisation was the key, such as the Liverpool and District competition, first played in 1886, or the Brighton Schools' Football Association, founded in 1892. There were paternalistic employers, such as the railway works in Crewe, transformed from a hamlet to a thriving township of approaching 50,000 inhabitants by the Edwardian period. The bosses provided athletic facilities for the young railwaymen 'to make them healthy and in that way tended to make them better workmen'.

If the industrial urban environment was propitious to the promotion of football, so was the mind-set of the influential citizens, those who had oversight of the vocational and the cultural lives of the youth of Victorian Britain. There are few blacks and whites in the printout of social history, so that, of course, it is easy enough to point to the many exceptions to this variable and flimsy rule. There were ministers of religion who regarded sport as frivolous or, if sportively inclined, utilised their gifts to ingratiate themselves with the high and mighty; there were teachers who did not give a fig for games, and, indeed, it was to be some time before such activities became a formal part of the elementary school syllabus; there were employers who believed that they should control, with an absolute rigour, the working hours of the working man and intercede not one jot with the few that remained for his leisure.

The evidence is also sometimes mixed as to whether the workers or churchgoers were more to the fore than the owners or clerics in starting football teams. The advantage of the workplace or the church as a setting for such an activity had an inherent appeal, so that the bottom-up was almost as likely as the top-down approach. This, of course, is a further indication of the eagerness among the lower orders to play at football. For all this, there was zest, at best, and, acquiescence, at worst, among their lords and masters for the formation of football teams. For instance, the Victorian gentry, and the policeman paid for out of the rates they paid, preferred the youth of the town to play an organised game of football, connected however loosely with the local church, than a disorderly one in the streets, however much exercise and noisy enjoyment might be gleaned.

Commentators have been right to emphasise the historical theme of football as a sport borrowed and customised by the middle class and handed back to the working class. What should not be lost is the quick enthusiasm shown by the recipients. If middle class reformers thought that football, among other pastimes, was the right and proper pastime for those they regarded as their inferiors, then there was brisk agreement among them.

The remaining and overall question of the urban football spectator per se and of professional football as an actual business in Victorian Britain will be addressed in chapter eight. In the meanwhile, this examination of the construct and ambience of the Victorian town demonstrates how significant it was as a bailiwick for both professional and recreational football. The history of football after 1863 tends, not without justification, to concentrate on the top-flight professional echelons of the game, suggesting that the popularisation of the game was led by the establishment of the national cup and then league competitions. However, the study of the primary urban environment is a useful reminder that the amateur game, relevant social factors and the genesis of mass transport were and remain basic ingredients in football's story.

CHAPTER SEVEN

PROFESSIONALISM; THE FOOTBALL LEAGUE

IT HAS BEEN argued that the pace at which football conquered the kingdom was breathtaking, further testimony to the thesis that the ad hoc footballing, which was some centuries old, was good and ready for national codification. There has been a tendency for commentators to be a trifle dismissive of pre-historic football as being little more than a series of jolly romps and violent escapades. Rather must a vague yet widespread consciousness of the footballing prototype have very much assisted the spread of a codified format. Equally, it should be recalled that early-modernised football, even when codified, was relatively unsophisticated, so that the continuities were possibly as pertinent as the changes for players in many areas.

Amateur Pleasure versus Professional Business

However, revolutions, sporting as well as political, may often be unstoppable, with their consequences not always to the taste of their begetters. The Gospel according to St. Matthew enjoins us not to pour new wine into old bottles, the political interpretation of that proverbial counsel indicating the awful disasters that might be consequent on inflicting novel procedures on to ancient systems. Historians of the French, the Russian and other traumatic revolutions endlessly debate the consequences, expected and unsought, of these seismic shifts in the political landscape. At the less momentous and less gory level of the English football revolution, there is certainly room and evidence for such a perplexing discussion. The changing speed and fundamental switch of events is sometimes bewildering, the germane factors not always immediately perceivable even at a retrospect of almost a century and a half's distance.

PROFESSIONALISM

Interestingly enough, a prominent feature in the onward spread of football was the social class element, commonly regarded as a relevant aspect of more potent revolutionary subversion. The creation of a national football formula was a middle class, even an upper middle class invention. As we have observed, for a variety of cogent reasons, the bourgeoisie, to employ a not inapt Marxist epithet, encouraged the proletariat to embrace the new football code - and this it did with some energetic assiduity.

The originators of football watched this process with an ambiguous mix of pleasure and anxiety. It would be wrong to assert that the working classes took over the game and made it their own, although there is, in the literature, both contemporary and modern, comment that flirts with this suggestion. The sons of toil certainly adopted and enjoyed the game, but they never really gained control of it in the same way in which, for instance, they initially kept oversight of those agencies - trades unions, friendly societies, co-operative stores - that rose directly from the ranks of labouring men and women. What basically occurred was that, in the upper reaches of the game, there was, according to historical predilection, either another shuddering tremor in the same revolution or a second revolutionary earthquake.

It amounted to a rather untidy contest between the older 'Corinthian' public school masters of the game and the industrial middle class businessmen, with their new money and new values, who spotted and responded to a business opportunity in this novel situation and sought to manage the heights of the game accordingly. In other words, this second phase revolution amounted to a schism between echelons of the middle classes, not some sort of stampede from the lower orders. The velocity of all this activity was tremendous and it is this rapidity of growth that permits of the judgement that this was a revolutionary process. Only 22 years divided the start of the FA in 1863 and the reluctant espousal of professionalism in 1885. In historical time, and following several centuries of purely local endeavour, this signifies basic change at a bewildering pace.

There were three principal building blocks. There was the incipient shift to making payments to players, primarily in the industrial areas of the north west of England. There was the decision to move to a league basis, with the formation of the Football League crucial, introducing a disciplined schedule of uniform competition, with home and away fixtures and the simple award of points for wins and draws. There was the sudden complication of large scale paying spectatordom; it was a far cry from a few thinly spread friends and relatives, gathering to watch teams of public school old boys in spirited contest, to thousands of working men paying to crowd together to cheer on their waged heroes.

As is the way with historical elements, this threesome interacted, each one affecting the other two, in an accumulative cycle. The ramifications of the spectator aspect are of such weight that they will be examined separately in the next chapter. As in other sports, the pressure of the spectator factor influenced not just the fabric of football in its upper tiers, in regard of the physical question of the construction of stadia and other financial investment, nor merely in respect of the psychology of spectating, but in respect of community identity. There was also the meaningful facet of its effect on the very rules and playing style of the game. It amounts to a major topic and must await particular analysis.

This leaves the two rather more internalised features of professionalism and the league system to form the main subjects for this chapter.

The Coming of the Professional

The evolution of the football professional is roughly analogous to that of the paid performer in cricket, its predecessor as a puller of crowds and a payer of players. There were three interlocking stages. Many of the earliest cricket professionals were employees of the rich noblemen who sponsored and often played the game, as, in the 18th century, it adopted something approaching a common design. Thomas Waymark, the so-called 'father of cricket professionals', was a groom in the service of the Duke of Richmond at Goodwood, whilst James Aylward was recruited by Sir Horace Mann, the patron of Kentish cricket, as a bailiff - 'a poor one', according to contemporary accounts, indicative that the job was a sinecure. This also applied to 'pedestrians', the runners, the athletes, of the age, men who were frequently the footmen of mighty estates, one of their duties being the conveyance of messages or the task of racing ahead of the typically slow-moving coach to warn those at the destination point of its impending arrival. With horse racing's appeal to people of all classes, it is scarcely surprising that the first tranche of lower class jockeys were also the grooms and stable boys of aristocrats interested in the turf.

PROFESSIONALISM

In the second phase, there was something of a mood of independence, with cricketers hiring themselves out to all comers on a match to match basis. These were often small-time tradesmen, such as tanners or lace-makers, who were able to combine two profitable skills. This phase culminated in the famous 'Exhibition' elevens of the mid 19th century, with the All England XI, organised by Nottingham's William Clarke, the most profitable of these mercenary teams. Other popular sports - boxing is an illustration - tended towards this degree of independence, although there were, as with the racing fraternity, 'stables', such as Jack Broughton's Tottenham Court Road Amphitheatre in the 18th century, to which boxers, like jockeys, were primarily committed. It was never a widespread practice. It was as late as the 1860s before the term 'professional' was used in sporting parlance as a noun to indicate a paid player.

Thirdly, a significant aspect of the dominion of the county cricket clubs from the middle of the 19th century onwards was the recapture of the paid performers. As county cricket became the main drawer of spectators and thus controller of cricket's chief stream of revenue, the county authorities were able to re-exert control of the professional cadres. The cricket 'pros' undertook extraneous jobs, like bowling to members at practice and work on and around the ground. In this they were comparable with all the oldest golf professionals and many of the contemporary breed. The cricket professionals were supervised with strict discipline, notably in regard of inflexible contracts that bound them to one county. Birth or a two year residential qualification came to be the necessary criteria for eligibility. Although this was defended on the somewhat specious grounds of building teams with a county identity, its main purpose was to tie the working cricketer to the employing authority.

Football professionals negotiated a similar pathway. In the first place, jobs were found for promising players either in local factories or - and here the number of work-based teams had a marked effect - on the shop floor of firms that sponsored football teams. The industrial employers performed the same role for football as the landed gentry had earlier done for cricket.

In the second place, there was a whiff of independence as some talented players acted as mercenaries, plying their trade and auctioning their skills for different teams. It never reached the cricketing level where groups of professionals had organised themselves collectively, but the practice had sufficient weight to cause dismay among both local and national Football Associations in the matter of cup competitions. Players would be invited, at a price, to play in a crucial cup tie and strengthen a side for that special occasion. It was not unknown for the gifted among them to play for more than one team in the same competition.

In the third place, just as the county cricket clubs, nationally organised under the banner and aura of MCC, insisted on something of a legalistic straitjacket for their employees, the Football Association agreed, after anxious debate, a similar set of arrangements for the professionalism that was already rife among the emergent leading clubs in the country. The 'retain and transfer' system that was inaugurated, and which endured with little or no alteration for the best part of a century, bound the professional footballer tightly to the employing club. As throughout the entire economic network of agriculture and commerce, the Victorian master held forceful dominion over the Victorian servant.

One variation between cricket and football was that, because of its earlier connection with the landed nobility, paying players had not been frowned on as a principle. Cricket for years enjoyed the advantage of being a sport where the social classes reached some accommodation in respect of its playing, in the sense that 'Gentlemen' and 'Players' were included in the same county and international teams. This only mirrored the composition of many a village team, where, traditionally, curate and blacksmith temporarily lowered the class barriers in the common cause. With the 'pros', in a typical division of labour, doing the bulk of the bowling, and with cricket lacking the possible physical indignities of a contact sport, this compromise was maintained for decades, well past the middle of the 20th century. The problematic questions had arisen in cricket only when, temporarily, the upper crust lost some control of the paid performers.

In football, as in athletics, the very principle of waged players was regarded, in many quarters, as an evil. Beforehand, the delicate balance of the football world was challenged by the intervention of wholly professional clubs. The argument among the footballing hierarchy was, in chief, between two groups of gentlemen amateurs who detested the influx of working class professionals. One cluster were the ostriches who buried their heads in the sand and refused to countenance such a betrayal of the amateur ethos; the other bunch were the pragmatists who, conscious that there was no defence against the spread of professionalism, sought to determine how most effectively to manage it.

One aspect of incipient professionalism touched on a genuine issue of social inequality. As standards improved and, especially in regard of cup competitions, some training became essential, most working men were placed at a bleak disadvantage. Unlike their more leisured middle class superiors, they could not afford to absent themselves from work either for training or, indeed, for extended travel, should fixtures be any distance from their homes. Thus arose the question of 'broken time' payments, where clubs sought to compensate players out of pocket on these grounds. As we noted briefly in chapter five, this was the issue that led to the schism in the Rugby Union later in the century.

Such payments were, of course, only a little removed from outright wages, particularly as the perceived need for extra training and coaching grew. The answer to the 'broken time' problem was easily settled for work-based teams or where a job could be found for a player with a compliant local employer. Newton Heath, later to be more famously entitled Manchester United, had grown out of the Newton Heath (Lancashire and Yorkshire) Cricket and Football Club. This depot and carriage and wagon works employed men, initially Welsh internationals such as Jack Powell who had played for Bolton Wanderers, to bolster the football side. In 1887 Pat O'Donell famously walked from Glasgow to Manchester to take up employment in the carriage works and sportive deployment nearby on the squelchy North Road football pitch. Whilst it perhaps lacked the kudos of working for the Duke of Richmond, these were the equivalent of cricket's 'retained men', employed on landed estates.

Elsewhere, and in parallel, neighbouring Lancashire clubs, funded by wealthy businessmen, were happily breaking the rules and making illegal payments to players. Suspicious rumour maintains that Peter Andrews and James Lang were paid for playing for Heeley, the Sheffield club, in 1876, while Hugh McIntyre, an upholsterer and Glasgow Rangers player, is presumed to have become a professional when he moved to Blackburn Rovers in 1878. The first out and out professionals are usually deemed to be James Lowe and Fergus Suter - 'the Scotch Professors' from Partick - who played for Darwen when they took the Old Etonians, the eventual winners, to a second replay in the quarter finals of the 1878/79 FA Cup. It was later alleged that Fergus Suter was paid the then weighty sum of £100 to defect to Blackburn Rovers. It was said, in the early 1880s, that the leading Lancashire clubs paid players a specified amount for a loss, double for a win, plus practice money.

This, for a very brief respite, was when some skilled professionals, like cricket 'pros' in mid-Victorian times, acted as mercenaries, marketing their skills, like any other independent craftsman, to the highest bidder. The activities of Messrs Lowe and Suter were anathema to the authorities as much for this disruption of the natural order as for their acceptance of cash. The various cup competitions were the focus of this practice, for, both regionally and nationally, they were the fulcrum of competitive success and attracted the habit of surreptitious strengthening of teams for such occasions. 'Importation', commonly underpinned by payments, was the crime. In 1883 Nottingham Forest had placards posted concerning the illegibility of three 'imported' Sheffield Wednesday players. In 1882 one or two county associations legislated separately to impose two year residential qualifications on players in their county cup competitions, together with a rule that a footballer could only play for one team throughout the duration of such competitions. In 1883 accusatory remarks were passed about the Bolton Wanderers accounts, in which a considerable sum of expenditure remained unexplained.

The Football Association, backed by the astringent Birmingham and Sheffield Associations, struggled to retain the amateur ideal - the very word 'amateur' specifically to designate an unpaid player only came into vogue in the 1880s. In 1882 a cure for the 'disease' was applied by way of prohibiting payment beyond match expenses and loss of earnings solely 'while taking part in a match' on pain of banishment from the cup competition. Accrington was the first club to be banned from the FA Cup for making illegal payments in 1884. Matters came to a head later in 1884 when London's Upton Park protested against Preston North End on those grounds, subsequent to a drawn cup-tie. Major William Sudell, ex-soldier, now mill manager, and the shrewd, not overscrupulous operator and key to Preston's rising success in opposition to the power of Blackburn Rovers, sought to banish the hypocrisy that befogged the issue. He made no bones about it. Not only Preston North End players, he plainly confessed, but also players with other wealthily backed Lancashire clubs were being remunerated. 'Preston are professionals', he exclaimed, 'but if you refuse to legalise them, then we will be amateurs, and you cannot prove otherwise'.

Preston North End were, of course, disqualified, but such candid admission forced the authorities to reconsider the issue with some gravity. Charles Alcock and a well-known southern player, N.C. Bailey of Westminster, the winner of 21 England caps, proposed to the FA General Meeting that 'professionalism be legalised'. Outrage was expressed, notably by J.C. Clegg and C. Crump, on behalf, respectively, of the Sheffield and Birmingham Associations, both a little riled by the constant and, to their minds, unfair success of the north-western clubs. That said, professionalism was by no means unknown in the midlands or in Yorkshire, but the representatives of those areas were also conscious, not without some truth, that their powers would dwindle still further should the Lancashire clubs gain even more momentum. The proposition was lost, and, later in 1884, fuel was added to the glowing fire of controversy. The FA ordered that payment of lost wages should be restricted to just one day a week, that no 'imported player' should play in the FA Cup and that, as far as English clubs went, only English personnel should be eligible.

The rather prissy response of the vocal anti-professional brigade has, in retrospect, earned some justification, for few would argue that there has been no collateral damage, on and off the field, in consequence of football becoming thus commercialised. There has been a darker side. Excited competitiveness and rank sharp practice have often disgraced the beautiful game. Nonetheless, there is little doubt that the purport of the defence of amateurism was largely class-based. W.H. Jupe of the Birmingham FA believed it was 'degrading for respectable men to play with professionals'. It was an attempt to preserve the game, especially in its higher levels, for the middle and upper classes. The success of northern professional teams at the expense of southern amateur teams in the FA Cup had shocked and scandalised followers of the latter group.

Later, when James Forrest, the outstanding Blackburn Rovers half-back, became the first professional to be capped, aged nineteen, for England against Scotland in 1885 there was turmoil in both camps. The Scottish FA protested - but there was nothing so outlandish in the tiny International Handbook as a hint at anything as sinful as money changing hands, so the young Blackburn Rover escaped on a technicality to win a footnote in football history. As if to underline the travesty, and as a sop to the Scots, Forrest was ludicrously obliged to wear a different coloured shirt to distinguish him from his amateur colleagues in pure white garb. Thus James Forrest played for England against Scotland wearing dark blue.

The northern clubs were incensed by the southern intransigence. Meetings were held in Blackburn and in Manchester at which plans were laid to form a British Football Association, a breakaway move from the Football Association. Of the 36 clubs represented, 26 were from Lancashire. The 'British' title was presumably meant to embrace the many Scottish, Welsh and Irish professionals in these teams, and possibly hinted at the inclusion of any major clubs from Scotland that might espouse the professional ideal. It is interesting to conjecture on what such a development might have implied for the formation of, for instance, a United Kingdom premier league or even national team, as against the insistence on the four 'kingdoms' having separate identities for footballing purposes.

Charles Alcock took the view that, in what was to become a famed phrase, 'veiled professionalism is the evil to be repressed', and his pragmatic belief was shared not only by such Lancashire stalwarts as R.P. Gregson and Dr E..S.. Morley, but also by some of the FA grandees, key figures such as Lord Kinnaird and Francis Marindin, now the FA's President. The debate continued fractiously. The Sheffield, Birmingham, Walsall and other provincial Associations continued to oppose the reform. Finally, at a special meeting in July 1885, and by a narrow but constitutionally necessary two-thirds majority of 35 to 15, waged players were recognised, subject to conditions. The cautious bid for control had defeated the more frantic bid to suppress.

Some of these riders were directed at preventing corruption in the cup competitions. Charles Alcock introduced something akin to the standards of eligibility used in county cricket, another example of the way in which he transferred some of his experience in cricket to football administration. Any payment other than 'expenses' (a source of handsome revenue for many cricket shamateurs) was the criterion for the professional designation. Only professionals born or resident for two years within six miles of the club's ground or headquarters were allowed to play in any of the cup tournaments. It is fascinating that, as in cricket, the same provisos did not apply so emphatically to amateurs. However, partly because the professionalised clubs were thicker on the ground than the elite cricketing shires, the residential and birth rulings were soon found to be over-restrictive. No professional was allowed to serve on any committee or in any like official capacity.

In parenthesis, there were to be other cricketing sidelights, such as arguments about differing accommodation and dining arrangements for those who were regarded as masters and 'paid servants', especially at international level. In the 1894/95 season the paid servants beat their bosses 9-0 in a trial at Nottingham, but, as in cricket, an amateur was selected to captain an otherwise all-professional eleven. In justice, it should be added that the first English professional football captain, Bob Crompton, accepted that responsibility in 1903, almost 50 years before Len Hutton emulated him in cricketing terms for a fully designated England eleven.

PROFESSIONALISM

In an important step, the FA insisted that no professional could play for more than one club per season without express permission and that all professionals had to be registered with the FA. This was the basis of the lob-sided contract of retain-and-transfer. Annually, players could have their employment renewed, discarded or, by gainful transfer, located elsewhere. The professionals were inexorably tied to the clubs. Those high and mighty performers who had demonstrated some independent spirit would be, exclaimed the *Athletic News*, 'impressed with the reality of the fact that they are only servants'. The Scottish FA followed suit in 1893 and registered 560 players from 50 clubs in Scotland. By 1908 the English FA registered as many as 5,000 professionals from over 150 clubs.

The energetic wind of professionalism had been tamed, even as it had been accepted.

The Advent of the Leagues

Close on the wheels of the one revolution came another. In 1888 William McGregor, of Aston Villa and a Scottish titan of the Birmingham Association and an enterprising draper in the brisk tradition of midlands business ingenuity, contacted the owners of the twelve leading English clubs, with a view to establishing an autonomous competition, and earned himself the sobriquet of 'the Father of the Football League'. Proud Preston, in their late Victorian pomp, won the first title in 1889.

In one sense it was a re-run of the British Football Association threat of a year or so earlier, with the significant rider that the Football League remained under the legal aegis of the FA. What, in administrative effect, the Football League soon accomplished was a takeover of the professional game, thereby becoming the management of the senior formation of English football, whereas the FA concentrated on what, self-evidently, remained the majority interest, the thousands of amateur clubs.

In another sense, it was the very success of the FA Cup notion that urged William McGregor to opt for a national league. The plethora of shire and city cup tourneys, which had been so effective in ensuring that the FA code was accepted nationwide, disrupted the economic flow of the major clubs. Instead of a healthy crowd paying good money for a big game, a well-known club might find itself drawn in a cup-tie against a little fish, with certain financial and potential, and equally embarrassing, sporting loss. Thrilling as might be the knock-out competition, it patently offers but 90 minutes of football to half the original participants.

Overall, a natural ambition to be successful both in business and sport motivated the founders of the Football League. Commentators suggest that the organisation of American professional baseball - there had been an all-professional league since 1871 - was an influence on the establishment of the Football League, in that it gave an inherent structure to the top teams of the country. It is also probably true that there was a glance across to the activities of county cricket, which, whilst still a little primeval in construct, lacking either a constant fixture list or an undisputed method of choosing the champions, had demonstrated the attraction for spectators of a regular round of high-class encounters. It must also be remembered that county cricket, in spite of its pastoral shadows, was primarily an urban, even a big city, enterprise, heavily reliant, as would be the Football League, on a catchment area full of likely spectators and one in which public transport was efficient and plentiful.

The league concept was immediately infectious. The Irish League was formed in 1890; the Scottish League in 1891 and the Southern League (for the Football League was initially manifestly non-southern in scope) in 1894. The league principle was taken up quickly and there was even some schoolboy league football as early as the mid 1890s. Rather like the knock-out concept, the simplicity of the league formula, with teams playing each other twice, home and away, with two points for a win and one for a draw, is indeed potent. A routine wondering occurs of why no -one had thought of it earlier. Nevertheless, it was eschewed by, for instance, the Rugby Union for the best part of another century, presumably on the grounds that the convention of the 'friendly' fixture list was more compatible with the amateur ethic. In football, at home and abroad, it quickly became the spinal column of the maturing game.

The first twelve Football league clubs were Accrington, Aston Villa, Blackburn Rovers, Bolton Wanderers, Burnley, Derby County, Everton, Notts County, Preston North End, Stoke, West Bromwich Albion and Wolverhampton Wanderers. All but Stoke, Derby County and Notts County were from the West Midlands or Lancashire - and they formed the bottom three in the first contest of 1888/89. A Second Division was established in 1892 and by 1914 there were 40 clubs in the Football League. Even then only six were from the south, including Arsenal (1893), Chelsea (1905) and Tottenham Hotspur (1908), while the only mild success for the southern branch was Bristol City's championship of Division II in 1905/06. By 1914 the Southern League had 36 teams in two divisions, of which 24, some of them on but a temporary basis, would become future members of the Football League. In 1920 many of these were absorbed into the new Third Division South, which was followed in 1921 by the formation of the Third Division North. The Lancashire monopoly reigned supreme in the years prior to the First World War; the Football League established its headquarters conspicuously at Blackpool in Lancashire.

In its foundation year the twelve Football League clubs mustered 448 registered professionals, suggesting sizable average squads of 37. By 1896 there were 675 professionals registered, an average of 42. Partly because of the need to sustain reserve teams and use them for trial purposes, a high proportion of those enlisted never actually played first team football. The majority, even in the upper echelons of the leagues, were, at this point, semi-professional, eking out their day job with a Saturday afternoon pittance, something impossible for the first-class cricket 'pro', often committed to non-stop three day matches.

For it should not be imagined that riches untold fell into the pockets of these men. Initially, trend-setters like Blackburn Rovers only paid their artistes 10s 6d (52 1/2p) a week, while Sheffield Wednesday offered 9s (45p) for a home and 11s (55p) for an away game and - in a distant cry from the era of the vast sale of replica shirts - the players had to provide their own togs. The advance of the Football League improved matters, so much so that, by the mid 1890s, the leading clubs were paying an average of £3 in the season and a £2 summer retainer to their recruits. Grudgingly, payment was made to artisan internationals; in 1886 it was 10s (50p), rising to a more reasonable £4 in 1907.

The variations were considerable, with the allure of tasty winning bonuses or appetising signing-on fees a commonly utilised temptation. The system was tweaked in an attempt to control such inducements. In 1892 the Football League determined to limit that fee to £10. Then, after much heated debate, the FA legislated for a maximum wage in the 1901/02 season of £4 a week or £208 a year, including bonuses. In 1905 the top level was increased to £5 a week or £260 a year. A little leeway was allowed for talent money and, after cricket's model, benefits were permissible after five and ten years service. On the whole, the smaller clubs, which could never afford the higher pay, welcomed the maximum wage, feeling that it evened up the competition for players. However, and although its advocates pleaded a somewhat spurious fairness about these arrangements, the overall effect was to impose further restraint on the footballing trade. Nor was there anything as progressive as a minimum wage, so clubs could afford, given the desperate ambition of many young men to seek a livelihood in the game, to sign on lots of hopefuls at rock-bottom cost. This was another reason why clubs were able to sustain such large lists of players. The Football League became and remained something close to a wage-fixing cartel. Given that this model became accepted across the world, it is perhaps not surprising that the European Court of Justice should find for Jean-Marc Bosman in his landmark case in 1995.

In 1904 the FA also ceded supervision to the Football League of its own finances, a further step in its powerful onward march. The FA was probably glad to be released from such burdensome duties, but it was unlikely the Football League chairmen were prepared to be too harsh on offenders from among their own breed. It would seem that abuses continued. Some were in kind, like cheap or free housing or what in the army would have been called 'cushy numbers' in bogus local employment - just before World War I the Liverpool captain was appointed a bill inspector, with a responsibility for scrutinising the posters advertising future matches. As with the railway companies and some other responsible businesses, there was some degree of paternalistic succour provided by the Football League. Several clubs helped injured players and, by 1908, the Football League launched an insurance scheme to protect against such distress.

There was no proactive scrutiny of the clubs' accounts. Action was only taken when corruption was signalled. Sunderland, for example, were fined £250 and three directors were suspended in 1904, while the Manchester City scandal of 1906 caused quite a furore. Breaches of the regulations were revealed when the great Billy Meredith, discovered to be on £6 to £10 a week, plus bonuses, had apparently tried to bribe Aston Villa players to throw a match in 1905, allegedly on the instigation of Manchester City's secretary. There was also an allegation that the City players had been promised a £100 bonus if they won the league title. The club were fined £250, two directors were suspended, the chairman and manager given lifetime bans from football, and no fewer than 17 players were suspended for at least two years, fined a total of £900 and forbidden ever to play for City again. The sports historian Richard Holt has pointed up the irony of some of these players, including Billy Meredith, and the current 'Prince of Dribblers', being signed by Manchester United, presumably at inflated signing-on fees, plus other monetary sops. After they had served their suspensions the likes of Meredith and goalscorer Sandy Turnbull proceeded to make the United club a national name by helping them win their first FA Cup and League titles.

Transfer fees were actually paid for these players who had been barred from playing for the club they were leaving, a reminder that transfer fees had now become an accepted practice. It was a reminder, too, that unretained players were also subject to transfer fees, and, if they were not forthcoming, the unfortunate professionals could find themselves ousted from football. Transfer fees were intended to stop the poaching and tempting of players and were seen as a curb on the richer and more predatory clubs, but their allied alternative effect was a further restriction on the players' freedom of labour mobility. As early as 1892, just three years after its foundation, the Football League began publishing lists of players available for transfer.

In 1905 Alf Common grabbed himself a mention in history when his transfer fee from Sunderland to Middlesbrough was the first to pass the £1,000 mark. Characteristically, the tubby, undersized Common was a lethal goal poacher, one of many such to figure in profligate transfer deals. His footnote in history is less negative than that of George Parsonage, who, about this time, was banned for life; on his transfer from Fulham to Chesterfield, he greedily asked for a £50 signing on fee, when the limit was £10. The FA had also vainly tried to cap transfer fees at £350, but had been compelled to leave matters to the clubs.

The next chapter on spectators will deal in more detail with the evolution of the major football clubs into businesses, most of them designated as limited companies, and on the labour relationship that involved the unsteady and spasmodic growth of trades unionism among the professional ranks. These developments obviously had high import for the future. Nonetheless, there were also two odd presentiments of present day habits. One was some primitive sponsorship, with famous players supplying endorsements for football boots and the like, while Manchester City further distinguished itself in 1905. The club added to the attempted subornment of Aston Villa an agreement for the team to advertise OXO. Moreover, by 1914, 80 players 'wrote' ghosted columns in local newspapers, another cue to the shape of things to come.

The other was the use of agents. Probably the best known were Lucas & McGregor of Preston and J.P. Campbell of Liverpool, their Lancastrian bases being non-coincidental. They advertised both for players and for clubs and, in

1891, the latter agent had almost 100 players on his books. Most clubs relied on accessible local talent or on hearsay and newspaper advertisements for 'importations', and thus such agencies could be very helpful to both employer and putative employee. It was a short-lived enterprise, as most senior clubs soon began to construct their own networks for scouting, but it was, in a slightly different guise, a phenomenon from the end of the 19th that would recur with heated impact towards the end of the 20th century. It seems to prove the old saying - there's nothing new, only something to be done differently

The evidence, based on the sporting press advertisements seeking men who doubled as craftsmen and footballers, suggests that most players were drawn from the respectable ranks of artisan tradesmen rather from the pool of uncouth unskilled labour - the adjectives are deliberately chosen to indicate Victorian prejudices. Much store was set on dependability and it was a Victorian dictum that the skilled worker was a steadier type than the unskilled labourer, a bias probably fuelled by the conflicting conditions of reliably regular and decently paid work as against casually sporadic and ill-paid toil. It was widely felt that the full-time 'pro', with a match a week and some desultory training, would find difficulty coping with untold free time. There were, of course, no Nintendos, Baby Bentleys or extravagant glamour models available at the time. The Victorian businessman fervently believed that settled and diligent 'hands' were to be preferred to idle ones. It might be remarked that the management of leisure time has not always shown an improvement among the plutocratic performers of today's dispensation.

This conformed to the cricketing prototype. The slightly romanticised characterisation of the Victorian and Edwardian 'Player' is of the solid, crusty Roundhead, coming from some industrial or agricultural trade, to ply his batting and bowling skills against the Cavalier 'Gentleman'. In so far as this was true, in either football or cricket, it stemmed from the unromantic fact that it was men from these circumstances who more often found themselves with a little health, a little leisure, a little money and a little opportunity to develop an additional money-making sporting skill. Most, by no means all, professional footballers and cricketers were, to use a military analogue, NCOs rather than other ranks.

Despite the fact that both cricket and football professionals laboured within a structure of extreme trade restraint and that both sports provided dismal tales of woeful penury, alcoholism and distress, the upside was that the rewards for the more effective players compared reasonably well with proletarian wages at large. In the last years before World War I, between 550 and 600 players in the Football and Southern Leagues were on the maximum wage and earning around £250 a year. At this point the first-class county cricket 'pros', of whom there were about 200, would, on average, have earned an annual sum of about £275. Factoring in the relative ease and pleasures of playing sport for a living, this was comfortable enough in working class terms. The average yearly income in 1914 for the agricultural labourer was £50, for the ordinary urban worker £90 and for the coal miner £140. The comparison thus drawn is between the top level of football and cricket and the average level of everyday employment. There were plenty of footballers and cricketers who were, plainly, on even lower incomes.

This relative degree of economic well-being was grounded in the burgeoning crowds of spectators, keen to proffer their coins at the turnstiles. It is to that feature that we shall turn attention in the next chapter, together with some analysis of the fashion in which the major football clubs organised themselves as businesses - and the players, less effectively, organised themselves as trade unionists.

CHAPTER EIGHT

SPECTATORDOM;
FOOTBALL AS SPECTACLE

WHEN IT WAS intrepidly decided to throw open the Great Exhibition to the general public, the ageing Duke of Wellington was aghast and proposed that 15,000 troops should be put on standby against the probability of insurrection. The horror of rebellion and the remembrance of the unruly mobs of the 18th and early 19th centuries died hard. In effect, the stolid behaviour of the huge crowds who flocked from all across the country to Crystal Palace in Hyde Park did much to convince the authorities, if not the Iron Duke, that all was well and that the British crowd had undergone a change of heart and spirit. The Exhibition welcomed 6 million visitors, some 5 million of whom travelled by train, many of them aided and abetted by the pioneering travel agent, Leicester's Thomas Cook. The Regent's Park zoo, with some new acquisitions, also cashed in; almost 700,000, a record, visited the zoological gardens in 1851. All was peace and calm.

The Crowd in History

Without this switch in collective demeanour it is unlikely, however successful football might have been as a purely recreational pursuit, that it would have prospered as effortlessly as a business capable of coping with the custom of thousands of working class clients. Earlier in this text there was a musing that, as well as being unfeasible before 1850, football might have also been unviable after 1950. The major ground for that speculation must be the change of character of the British crowd, or rather its return to its old barbarism. In the later decades of the 20th century, especially in the 1970s and 1980s, the misbehaviour of football supporters reduced the centres of many towns to 'no-go' areas for the ordinary citizenry on Saturday afternoons. Had those crowds remained as high in numbers as they had reached by and just after the Second World War, then the civil chaos and mayhem may have been even more disastrous. Had it been proposed in 1970 for the first time that more than a hundred British towns would suddenly host fortnightly events attracting twin hordes of antagonistic young people, it is possible that the police would have invoked public order legislation to prevent them happening.

Football crowds, for better or for worse, in sickness and in health, were destined to play so crucial a part in football's evolution that it is essential to comprehend something of the fundamental reasons why they were, for a hundred years, sufficiently (never perfectly - there were several nasty lapses) well behaved to be found acceptable to the official mind. Later, it will be necessary to answer the question: why did they revert to their savage ways? For now, we may content ourselves with looking on the bright side of crowded life.

'An imagined community': that was the evocative phrase used in 1985 by the scholar, Benedict Anderson, to describe a nation. With its flag, its anthem, its heroes, its coins, its stamps, its legends, as well as its sport, a nation-state seeks to preserve its identity and its citizens latch on to the cultural traits and embody them, coming to believe that this display of national character arises organically within the frontiers of that nationhood. Critically, for football support, this also applies to regions and cities as well, with people keen to exhibit what has come to be regarded as typical of the district. They play out its persona. They imagine they are actors, cast by nature to play out national, regional or parochial roles.

Given that humans share 30% of the genetic endowment of the banana, it is unlikely that genes have much to do with this tribalism, especially as there are basic alterations in regional and national character that occur much swifter than could be explained by a variable gene bank. The change in British society in the decades leading up to the successful spread of professional football is a case in point.

No-one has described the change more vividly and concisely than the eminent social historian Harold Perkin. Writing in 1969, he pronounced that 'between 1760 and 1850 the English ceased to be one of the most aggressive, brutal, rowdy, outspoken, riotous, cruel and bloodthirsty people in the world and became one of the most inhibited, orderly, tender-minded, prudish and hypocritical.' There could scarcely be a more unequivocal assessment. Without any transplant or transfusion of genes, the English gentleman suddenly became recognised by his hauteur, his understatement and his rather chilly courtesy. Baroness Orczy's Scarlet Pimpernel, brave but nonchalant in his rescue of French aristos from the Guillotine, and Jules Verne's Phileas Fogg, stoically resolute in his eighty days circumnavigation of the globe (particularly when played on screen by Leslie Howard and David Niven respectively) could be the prototypes.

The Corinthian sporting spirit, as well as the emphasis on 'respectability' that informed a less brutal approach to sports involving both humans and animals, was an illustration of this shift in the national humours. The great sociologist, Max Weber, has demonstrated how, with urban and industrial growth, a profounder rationality entered into the political discourse. At its simplest, it was about the rural tradition being more dependent on an oral system and the urban dispensation more reliant on a written code. Cities and nations came to need more bureaucratic and allied official structures for their maintenance. The extremely relevant example is the making and keeping of written rules for football. They automatically restricted and narrowed the compass of what might be done, in the interests of control and moderation.

This provision and acceptance of regimens of many kinds tempered the mood substantially. The rationalism of time, and its strict oversight of one's activities, was one such. The hollow moan of the factory hooter, the remorseless clang of the school bell, the shrill blast of the railway guard's - and the referee's - whistle provided the sound effects. Another example is the usage of uniforms to underpin uniformity. This applied not only to the armed forces, but also to the novel trades of control, in the newly formed police, the workhouse and asylum overseers, the Nightingale-styled nursing cadres, and the gowned teachers. In prison, workhouse, asylum and hospital, uniform dress garbed the inmates as well as their supervisors.

The notion spread, perhaps sadly, to the youth organisations that sprang up before and just after the turn of the century, while the concept of school uniform, a very British tradition, has never abated in its soulless intensity. Other services - domestic servants, postal workers, rail and tram transport staff, brass bandsmen, park keepers, even the personnel of large stores - adopted the craze for the often officious or martial uniform. For all of them there was a reasoned argument about identifying those responsible for certain duties or tasks, but there was an underlying urge to clothe and shape human existence according to given standards. Football teams began to wear distinctive shirts, admittedly so that they could identify their colleagues the more easily, but also, more importantly, so that the fans could identify the more readily with the team. They rejoiced in the uniformity.

Beyond that, there was a non-formal sartorial agenda by which men and women could indicate who they were and what they were doing. Of course, this social identification by distinctive clothing was by no means a new trend, but, at this time, it became markedly stronger. A colourful example occurred in 1880 when the winning boat crew of Exeter College, Oxford, took the ribbons from round their straw boaters and tied them around their necks. The old school tie was born. With it was born, with all its cultural attachments and rites, the lengthy dominance of the thin tie as a replacement for the sturdier cravat or ruff, which had had the rather more purposeful job of protecting one from a dagger strike at the vulnerable throat.

The ease with which these regulos were imposed is significant. There was contentious opposition, but it was never as potent as the willing support at most levels of society. This was not a regime inflicted upon a slave people. It amounted to a fundamental change in national character of the kind so forthrightly defined by Harold Perkin.

The perceptive cultural historian Jeffrey Richards has mooted the simple and persuasive theory that society has 'rough' and 'respectable' elements, both of which may achieve a temporary dominance, without ever becoming monopolistic. For example, even in an era of peaceable football crowds, there were some crowd troubles. Players were assaulted, and Preston's Nick Ross was knocked unconscious after his team had beaten Aston Villa in 1885; in 1895 the Woolwich Royal Arsenal ground was closed for six weeks in consequence of the referee being mobbed by angry supporters; a pitch invasion halted the fifth round cup-tie at Villa Park in 1888, when Preston North End were leading 3-1; and, in 1889, it took ninety minutes, such were the disruptions caused by spectators, to complete the first half of the Sheffield United/Liverpool semi-final replay, at which point the game was abandoned.

Such blemishes apart, Richards suggests that the 'rough' were in the ascendant before 1850 and then the 'respectable' component enjoyed the upper, if not exclusive, hand for the next hundred years, the exact period when football developed as a global spectator sport. After that point, there is something of a reversal to the Hanoverian and Regency character of 'roughness'.

Foreseeing the next question, he also offers a convincing explanation of why 'respectability' was all the rage in the Victorian period and the first half of the last century. Jeffrey Richards postulates the idea that, as an accompaniment and as an expression of urban and industrial settlement, the twin cults of 'Evangelicalism' and 'Chivalry' were at busy work. Both these strands have already been touched upon. The low Anglican and nonconformist creeds brought an earnestness of conscience and a prudence of attitude that distinguished both the ambitious middle classes and the aspiring working classes. Mr Pooter, in his Holloway retreat, observes, in *The Diary of a Nobody*, written in 1892 by George and Weedon Grossmith, the petty snobbishness, yet virtuous integrity, that were the mark of these severe codes of conduct.

'Chivalry' was the Victorian take on the Hanoverian liking for 'decency'. It was interpreted as pinched restraint, good if rather sterile manners and courteous instincts. It was, from a sporting viewpoint, Corinthian in style. It was flavoured with the Victorian affection for medievalism, something of a guilt trip back to rurality as an escape from the grimness, if economic solidity, of industry. Victorian culture is littered with samples of what has been called 'vibrant medievalism'.

A list of visions from the 'medieval dream' include the novels of Sir Walter Scott, such as *Ivanhoe*, Charles Kingsley and Charles Reade; the mock-Gothic architecture inspired by Augustus Pugin, such as St. Pancras Station, the Houses of Parliament and scores of town halls; a frightening obsession with gardening; the invention of folklore (the word is a Victorian coinage); the political use of medievalism in, to the right, the Young England movement and the Primrose League, both associated with Benjamin Disraeli, and, to the left, Robert Blatchford's *Merrie England*, which sold 350,000 penny copies when it first appeared in 1893...and so on.

Eric Hobsbawm, that notable historian of Marxian credentials, has reminded us that 'the heavy incrustation of British life with pseudo-medieval and other rituals' includes 'the cult of monarchy', its gaudy emblems largely the result of Victorian imaginings. Writing in 1947 about Victorian culture, the medievalist Ernest Barker marvelled at what he described as 'a mixture of stoicism with medieval lay chivalry'.

The primness of Evangelicalism and the civility of Chivalry combined to rare effect within the propitious context of flourishing urban life. Possibly the most astonishing consequence was that between 1857 and 1901 crime, considered proportionately to population, halved. Moreover, the then low level of crime remained constant, apart from a slight blip up and down, until the 1950s. There is no doubt that the organisation of a more efficient police service helped, with, after the 1856 Police Act, the nation fully covered by 239 police forces and 12,000 'bobbies' - the reverent 'respectable' sobriquet or 'blue-butchers' - the sullen 'rough' epithet. However, senior policemen, now as well as then, would ruefully advise that it is difficult to operate a civil as opposed to a military - gens d'armerie - police service without the ready consent of the majority of the population.

In a less combative society, and with a more humane judicial system, the number of executions dropped sharply from over 500 a year around the time of the Battle of Waterloo in 1815 to 50 or so in the middle of the century. Incidentally, the abolition of public executions in 1868 was not out of sympathy for the condemned person (being hanged secretly behind prison gates was, if anything, more frightful) but because it was debasing for the audience.

Football and the Respectable Crowd

Here was the secret. The later Victorian establishment and their successors in the first fifty years of the 20th century no longer feared the crowd. In Judith Flanders's feisty comment, 'the volatile mob had become the sedate consumer.'

The fulcrum of this essential 'respectability' was the prudish marriage of the hard-working artisan class and the diligent middle class. Dourly virtuous, smugly self-righteous, frigidly repressed, uncomfortably censorious, together they created a formidable bastion of devout gravity, for whom the anachronistic title of 'middle England' served more accurately than as a 20th century appellation. To complete the sociological geometry, beneath was a subclass of casual and vagrant folk, and, above, a thin slice of upper crust exuding meretricious gaiety. Nonetheless, by and large Britain was, in David Harrison's phrase, 'a peaceful kingdom (of) overall tranquillity'.

This coupling of, to deploy another anachronistic metaphor, the aspiring blue-collar and the complacent white-collar workers was clearly class based. It led to an 'integrated culture', in which the two allies in the respectable coalition took their pleasures, if not sadly, then wryly, dutifully and conscientiously. These were shared pleasures, enjoyed in division. The first, second and third class carriages of the railway trains offer the most straightforward example. Others include the paid and free pews in the same chapel for the same service; the select and cheap end of the promenade of the same seaside resort; the public and saloon bars of the same pubs; and the stalls and gallery for the same show in the same theatre. The family novel, associated with Charles Dickens, is another type of example, for, often with readings aloud in mechanics' institutes and like places, the Dickensian magic had that same joint and broad-based appeal.

A vivid illustration is the Savoyard genre of Gilbert and Sullivan comic operas. This was the first major exercise in developing a light music industry in and for an industrial society. It is their very consciousness of what the protagonists were doing that is so striking. This 'urban folk-ballad' style of entertainment, echoing as it gently guyed the stuffy politesse and chivalrous romanticism of the age, and shaped to suit a vast amateur interest as well as professional market, was to be an enduring success. W.S. Gilbert knew exactly what he was about. He constantly used culinary metaphors to describe his purpose. A menu of 'tripe and onions' might please the pit, but not the stalls; the reverse was true of 'sweetbreads and truffles'; 'a plain leg of mutton and boiled potatoes is the most stable fare of all'. This was, in his trenchant view, 'the gastronomic mean'. It has been said that by dint of the D'Oyly Carte Company's excellence both lower middle class and upper working class customers 'were weaned from the church to the playhouse'.

Predictably, the cricket grounds and racecourses of the day had their due accommodation for joint middle class and working class spectatorship, and the football stadiums followed in turn. 1875 is the year when the first racecourse - Sandown Park - was completely enclosed and everyone had to pay to watch. Most racecourses followed suit and limited companies, as in football, were to the fore in such successful investments, with the railways bringing excursion trainloads of people to form crowds as high as 80,000 for some meetings. Although the late 19th century and early 20th century football crowd is correctly described in the literature as largely working class, as well as the 'staging', later to be called the terracing, being packed with proletarians, there were always seats in the stands for the bourgeoisie. The former certainly outnumbered the latter, but probably only in the natural ratio of five to one that they did in the general population.

The scanty evidence we have about the class composition of those early football crowds does suggest that these respectable skilled workers out-spectated unskilled workers about three to one; what is certain is that this ratio genuinely reflects the ability of the craft worker to afford the usual sixpence - a slight rise from the 3d and 4d of the 1870s - for entry, or a shilling for FA Cup fixtures and internationals. Women and children under fourteen paid half-price. Such were the changelessness of conditions and the sheer weight of tradition that this pricing pattern endured until well after the First World War. For the casual or unskilled man the regular finding of that sixpence would have been more difficult. His life was not only less well financed, but also more disorderly in pattern. It was not only the earning of the sixpence, it was its being set aside for a specific purpose that counted.

Football and the Urban Crowd

Watching has always been an aspect of the 'play', as analysed in chapter one. Older men who had played games watched younger men and children take their place as players. Women and children would watch husbands, fathers and brothers at play. Friends and relatives formed a thin grey line around the Wanderers' pitch at Battersea Park. Perhaps a field would be hired and maybe a collection taken. The demographic and urban revolution magnified that tendency, just as dames' schools became huge three-storied elementary schools, local lock-ups and bridewells were transmuted into castellated penitentiaries and, as the root model, factories had replaced small scale and domestic manufacture on the working front.

The urban identity of the mainstream teams was very evident. Almost all the foundation clubs of the Football League had populations above, several of them well above, 80,000 and, by the end of the Edwardian decade, there were only eight towns with more than 50,000 inhabitants that had not succumbed to the allure of a professional football club. Between the launch of the league and the start of the Great War, approaching sixty new grounds were built by Football League clubs to cater for the swarms of urban dwellers wishing to follow, with enthusiastic pride tempered by caustic critique, the adventures of their local team.

The stadium evolved from the fenced-off field, sometimes shared with a racecourse, a cricket ground or other multipurpose arena, with advertisements added to the palings, partly for revenue and partly to impart some sense of identity. The next stage was the making of slopes to aid viewing. The slag of coal pits was especially valued, while other clubs asked locals to deposit their ashes, cinders and domestic rubbish on their grounds, while Simon Inglis, the dedicated scholar of football architecture, recounts how Fulham utilised the municipal sweepings of the streets as the base for its terracing.

Next the terraced field soon became furnished with a wooden grandstand and some primitive changing - sometimes no more than a tent ~ and office facilities. Often where there had been a shared sporting function, football cornered the market. Wrexham's Racecourse and Derby County's Baseball Grounds are explicit examples, while Leeds United's Elland Road had been a rugby ground and both Sheffield United's Bramall Lane and York City's Bootham Crescent had been cricket grounds. Industrial sites, what now would be called 'brown field' locations, were widely used. Grounds like Manchester City's Maine Road, Birmingham City's St. Andrew's and Charlton Athletic's The Valley were built on disused manufacturing spots or rubbish tips.

From about 1880 there was an exhilarating expansion of such venues, which were frequently opened with all the bravura and ceremony as the new town hall or other civic edifice. Blackburn Rovers, who had originally played at the East Lancashire cricket club, moved to their own premises in 1881; a stand for 800 customers was erected at the new Leamington Street headquarters. Those other front-runners of the hour, Preston North End, led the way with the construction of terracing. Everton's Goodison Park, opened in 1892, boasted one of the first major grandstands in the country, while Manchester United built brand-new premises at Old Trafford for £60,000 in 1911.

The engineering architect Archibald Leitch, another Scottish contributor to footballing history, was the main designer of many of these grounds. Building on his experience of factory and allied designs, he was at home with the functional, rather austere requirements of his clients. From Sunderland's Roker Park and Glasgow's three major venues of Hampden Park, Celtic Park and Rangers' Ibrox, via Burnden Park, Bolton and Villa Park to Stamford Bridge and White Hart Lane, he went about his seminal labour of adding a new prototypical edifice to the Victorian city.

From the midst of the packed terraced housing of those cramped cities, there arose these new temples, joining the gigantic music halls, the cavernous public houses and the new craze of spacious department stores as agencies of commercial entertainment...a bright antidote to the aforementioned range of less magnetic urban symbols, the barracks, the workhouse, the asylum, the school, the hospital and the prison and, of course, the factory-type work-place.

History moves in parallels as well as in linear mode. The great crowds in the cricket and football arenas and on the racecourses of Victorian England were assembled in a manner not really seen in Western civilisation since the cities of classical antiquity had built massive stadiums for a previous generation of concentrated urban dwellers. The Roman games in the majestic Colosseum, with space for 40,000 spectators, and there were seventy other such show-grounds in use during the long sway of the Roman Empire, first spring to mind. However, a more relevant comparison might be with the commercialised chariot races of Rome, Antioch and, in particular, Constantinople. In the age of Justinian, in sixth century Constantinople, the two major chariot-based factions were the Blues and the Greens. With showy shirts, the wearing of favours, segregated seating and even distinctive barbering, there was fierce and modern-sounding rivalry, with the hooliganism sometimes degenerating into organised gangsterdom and political skulduggery, such as the infamous Nika Riots that imperilled Justinian's hold on the Eastern Roman Empire. The ancient historian Procopius described how the competing bands of fans resided in separate districts, with the Greens occupying some of the poorer streets, and how the divisions gave rise to distinct administrative and military duties.

As the numbers grew, it was important to regulate the crowd. Fencing off the ground and charging for entry had been the obvious answer. Previously, many sporting events had been free of charge. A local tavern would arrange a cricket match on an abutting meadow and sell lots of ale and refreshments. Racecourses had remained open to the general public, and the general public was tempted by scores of itinerant salespersons and entertainers. That was where the commercial element crept in. Slowly, the commercial element became more direct. There was a necessity to control the now teeming crowds and, apart from any profit motive, the money raised by charging for entry paid for the apparatus for such oversight.

The size of British football throngs grew slowly. In 1875 there were two crowds reported of over 10,000. In 1885 there were eighteen such gates, including 27,000 to watch Preston North End play Aston Villa. The advent of the Football League was an important juncture. In the first season of the Football League in 1888/89 600,000 paid to watch the twelve clubs in tourney. In 1896/97 the total crowds numbered 2 million, when there were sixteen teams, and in 1913/14, with twenty hopefuls, it was 5 million. The average Football League attendances increased almost threefold from 5,000 a game in 1896/97 to 14,000 in 1913/14. By this point, the First Division crowd averaged 23,000. Another guide is the spectatorship at the popular FA Cup-ties. In 1888/89 the 31 ties attracted 200,000 spectators, while the same number of matches drew a sum of nearly 2 million in 1894/95. During the Edwardian period attendances at all British football matches touched on 7 million a year.

The Cup final itself records something of the same sort of graph. There were fewer than 2,000 at the Oval for the inaugural final in 1872. Charles Alcock, whose influence at the Oval as the county cricket club secretary was evident, may have smiled at the comparison with the much bigger attendances at many Surrey cricket matches. All but one (the second in the series, played at Lillie Bridge, London) of the first 21 finals was played at Kennington Oval and the hosts in attendance gradually increased, especially with the dominance and popularity of the professional Football League clubs. The 1889 final, when Preston North End beat Wolves 3-0 and the referee was Major Francis Marindin, was the first one where the gate passed 20,000. In 1892 25,000 crowded into the Oval on a sunny day to see West Bromwich Albion defeat Aston Villa in an all-midlands final, the first in which goal nets were employed.

The jostling crowds were obviously growing too large either for the anxious spirits on the Surrey committee, who feared for their sacred turf, or for the hundreds who were now making an often troublesome trip to find there were insufficient vantage points. There were no enclosures in London big enough for the Cup any more, so the 1893 final was the first - a replay at Derby in 1886 apart ~ to be organised outside the capital. It proved to be the sort of coupling of triumph and tragedy that leads to innovation. The Manchester Athletic Club at Fallowfield was hired for the occasion and, splendidly, over 45,000, almost double the previous best, turned up to cheer on Wolverhampton Wanderers and Everton, while thousands were locked outside. Unfortunately, the palisades were too feeble for such a huge and excitable horde and were broken through, with the touchlines and goal-lines threatened and the reserved accommodation overrun. A hard-working Wolves team of mainly local lads scuppered the vain hopes of the favourites, Everton, in dreadful conditions that must have affected the play. An enterprising builder erected housing on the site of Wolves' original ground, Dudley Road, and called it Fallowfield Terrace in memory of that stirring deed.

SPECTATORDOM

The next final in 1894 was played at Goodison Park in Liverpool, a self-contained ground with relatively sound safety features. The Fallowfield fiasco was an episode from which lessons were learned the hard way about the need for pens and crush bars. Gradually, these became the stark but reassuring impedimenta of late Victorian and Edwardian football grounds. 37,000 turned up to see Bolton Wanderers beaten with surprising ease by Notts County, the first Second Division team to win the Cup. It was a goodly crowd, but not an enormous one, a fact interpreted by some as a fearful reaction against the heaving congestion of the previous year. Another reason may have been the absence of a trip to London. Apart from London's advantage as a main locus for rail travel, there was, and this was to endure, the sense of enjoying a day trip to the metropolis for the Cup Final.

By now the Crystal Palace, re-erected at Sydenham in south-east London, had become a much-loved leisure centre. W.G. Grace, a friend and possibly a wiseacre adviser of Charles Alcock, was influential there; he assiduously managed and led the London County Cricket Club there from 1898 to 1908, being suitably horrified when the greensward was made over for the better paying proposition of tennis, and, as 'the Father of English Bowls', he captained England in the first bowls international against the experienced Scotland team in 1903, also at Crystal Palace.

There was a natural bowl-shaped area, ideal for the huge crowds that watched the FA Cup Final and wanted to have some peripheral amusement at that famous site. Crystal Palace became the second of the three major venues for the event. Over 42,000 watched the first final there in 1895, when an early Aston Villa goal accounted for West Bromwich Albion. The gates rose year by year, a tribute jointly to the advancing popularity of the Cup, now with well over 200 entries annually, to the growing support for the top-flight teams, and to the improved transport available both to and around London.

In 1901 Southern League Spurs and Sheffield United fought out a 1-1 draw, with the London team winning the replay at Bolton. It was a spectacular occasion in the original meaning of the word of some event being spectated. For the first time in football's history - probably in sport's modern history - a paying host of more than 100,000 - 110,820 to be precise, including those who clung from the overshadowing trees - was assembled. The stands and the surrounding banks were packed. One attraction was that, apart from the earlier days of solely amateur engagement, it was the first time a London team had

129

reached the final. Hitherto the Cup had been monopolised in the professional era by the great north and midland clubs.

Whatever the reason, that 1901 audience set a significant milestone on the busy road of football spectatorship. The Crystal Palace gates remained high and they included two more that each topped 100,000. 101,000 watched Aston Villa beat Newcastle United in 1905 and a record 120,000 saw Villa again triumphant, this time winning 1-0 against Sunderland. With those three attendances of 100,000 before the First World War, football spectatordom had become a major social and cultural phenomenon.

The presence of a large concourse of watchers had a marked effect on football's construct as a game. The most overt illustration is with regard to boundaries. That very word reminds one that cricket, and other sports, had all to look to their boundaries when spectators showed up in any number. Prior to this, most field games had been limited only by natural hazards, like brooks or hedges, or artificial barriers, like buildings. There were manly dashes, in both cricket and the football codes, to retrieve the ball, with spectators, were there any, scattered in the rush. Soon this became untenable and the interior dimensions of the football were regulated, with the ball 'dead' when out of play. In cricket, of course, the award of four or six was the compromise, against the chance of a bigger all-run score, although until well into the 20th century local rules often demanded that, for a six, the ball had to be out of the ground, not over the boundary line. It is intriguing today to watch the control of golfing crowds when a ball is wildly but not impossibly struck among the watchers. Large audiences are comparatively new to golf, and the surrender of most of the rough to the spectator sometimes creates the same sort of headache suffered by football and cricket a century and a half ago.

Football as Business

That said, the chief consequence of large-scale spectatorship was to transform football from a game into a business. Very rapidly the top British clubs adopted all the trappings of the Victorian capitalist concern, with many of them registered as limited companies. Where they differed in purpose from most other businesses is in that the profit motive was not always to the fore. Indeed, in the years before the First World War, only the merest handful of the sixty or so such limited companies were paying a dividend. Moreover, the FA also banned the payment of fees to directors. In a fashion that was to delight and plague the football industry in equal measure into the present day, the football club was frequently the businessman's glamorous accessory, rather than his solid foundation. The reasons for such indulgence varied from sheer philanthropy, via the purchase of local esteem, occasionally, but not often, for political ends, to an almost childlike gratification in the football club as a toy. Johan Huizinga's theme of 'play' underwent another twist of connotation.

The motives were mixed within as well as among the individual investors and directors too, but what is apparent is that men who would have looked askance at a business proposition as shaky as most football clubs proved only too willing to shell out good money to be involved with a football team. Presumably they experienced all the emotions of the ordinary spectator, but with a more acute intensity. Where the spectator could only shout grumpily for the player to be dropped or the manager sacked, the director could actually precipitate and execute such acts. The theatre again offers a parallel, not so much in the theatre circuits themselves, which were often quite profitable, but in the allure of being a backer for a show. Here again there were - there are - businessmen anxious to shelve the normative commercial criteria in return for a heady engagement with the gaudy lights of the stage. In other words, it was sometimes more a consumer luxury than an economic investment.

Between the coming of professionalism in the mid 1880s and the start of the First World War, about fifty clubs sought incorporation as limited liability companies or some like form of legal existence. Previously, many had been run by one or more individuals or by committees elected by a membership - Tony Mason reports that Aston Villa had 372 members and a committee of nine. However, the business of erecting and maintaining grounds and sustaining a wage bill often made - as it still does - for rocky finances. Average league club expenditure was about £2,000 annually at this time, and gate receipts alone were sometimes insufficient to meet these costs. Raffles and lotteries seldom raised enough to close the financial gap.

Club after club searched for extra financing, usually with an appeal to local businessmen to dig deep into their pockets. This often began with two or three well-to-do benefactors simply subscribing to the cause, but, not unnaturally, many of them felt the need for a more trustworthy legal and fiscal format. Shares and debentures became the norm. Share prices varied wildly from 5s (25p) to £20, but the usual price was £1. Although there is some evidence of a moderate take-up of shares from among working class supporters, it was, unsurprisingly, their richer superiors who funded most of these investments and, by so doing, took control of the major clubs.

The sterling researches of Tony Mason reveal that, in the quarter century before 1914, 46 of the leading professional clubs boasted a total of 740 directors, about fifteen to each board, quite a high ratio. They were almost entirely middle class in make up, and, apart from some members of the professions, they frequently came from the wholesale and retail trades, especially from catering and brewing. That last fact does throw some extra light on the motives of the businessmen concerned, for some of them did contrive to mix business with pleasure.

Three breweries had something of a financial hold on West Bromwich Albion and publicans and brewers were major shareholders at Blackburn Rovers, while Bolton Wanderers, Manchester City, Watford and Preston North End each had influential shareholders from the licensed trades. J.H. Davis, the benevolent saviour of Manchester United, had made his money from brewing and married wealthily into the Tate family of sugar fame and fortune. He was chairman of the Manchester Breweries, and five other United directors had direct or indirect links with that company. The case history of John Houlding, onetime president of Everton and owner of the nearby Sandown Hotel in Liverpool, is interesting. He provided refreshments at, and part-owned, their then Anfield ground, but, after an argument about the rent, the club moved to Goodison Park. Houlding stayed on the Anfield side of Stanley Park and more or less started the Liverpool club from scratch.

H.A. Mears bought the old London Athletic Club ground at Stamford Bridge. Having failed to sell it either to the Great Western Railway company or to St. George's Hospital, he created the football ground that he rented out to Chelsea for £2,000 a year and his catering firm supplied the refreshments as a flavoursome extra. Sunderland, Wolves (the Northampton Brewery Company had a major interest in the layout of the Molineux ground) and Tottenham Hotspur (The White Hart Inn) had publicans as landlords at some stage in their development, while the breweries were keen to open pubs close to football grounds. The explanation of all this eager interest is simple enough. The football ground offered three opportunities to sell beer and elementary foodstuffs - before, during and after. Franchises on the ground and licensed premises in close proximity made good business sense. In these several cases, the magnanimity of the investors had rather more than a desire for local respect and juvenile delight in being involved in football. What was lost on the swings of gate money might be won on the roundabouts of beer money.

In general, all these business-orientated regimes adhered closely to accepted capitalist practice. The Football League was basically what early economists would have called a 'combination'. With the connivance of the FA, the senior clubs struck an agreement on trading conditions, in particular, on prices and wages.

The response of the workforce, that is, the playing staff, was predictable. There were efforts to form an employees' 'combination', the more effectively to bargain with the bosses' alliance. Some of these endeavours were puny and this, too, might have been foreseen. Trades unionism tended to flourish where the workers operated together in relatively high numbers and usually with a sound level of skills, often sharing the same communal life. The 'craft' unions of miners, textile workers, railwaymen and shipyard artificers are examples. It was more difficult to organise labour where it was isolated and subject to direct strict personal control - merchant seamen, agricultural labourers, shop assistants. Footballers found themselves somewhere in the middle, possibly after the manner of postal workers, where the work depot was of middling size, but where individuals were still vulnerable to victimisation.

What evidence there is suggests that footballers tended to be from the ranks of the skilled, not the unskilled, manual classes, with the several works-based teams offering further confirmation of that point. In this they represented their watching brethren: respectable workmen diverting respectable workmen. Playing football at League level certainly demanded the same characteristics. The skills had to be patiently mastered; the discipline of often-tedious training programmes had to be stoically endured; the necessity to maintain a decent level of fitness required self-regulation and the commitment to a week-on-week concentration on football called for a degree of mental stamina.

In short, football was a craft and footballers were craftsmen. Naturally, there were mavericks and rascals, but, in the main, the football professional was a tradesman, like an engine driver or an iron welder.

There was an attempt to form a football trade union in Manchester in 1898 but, typically, the employers were dogged in their resistance. A timid creature struggled on, until, some ten years later, and with the Manchester United players Charlie Roberts and Billy Meredith in the van, it revived somewhat. To the horror of the bosses, there was a move in 1908 to join the Federation of Trades Unions. There were threats of strikes and counter-threats of employers' action. Thirty Manchester United players were suspended and forced to train at the Manchester Athletic Club, but the principled and fearless Roberts was undismayed. Eventually, a non-affiliated union was accepted, a compromise solution that saved the start of the 1909/10 season from wreckage through strike action. By 1914 there were 4,470 members of the Players' Union; the forerunner of today's Professional Footballers' Association.

It should not escape note that this immediate pre-war phase was a particularly fruitful and indeed vigorous time for British trade unionism. There was the Match Girls' strike of 1888 and the London Dock strike of 1889, while in 1911 there was a railwaymens' dispute, a long-running miners' agitation and a noisy strike of seamen and dockers. The nation's trade unionists grew in number from 1.5 million in 1892 to 4.1 million in 1914. Some historians suggest that, along with the Irish, Suffragette, land tax and other troubles, this fierce outbreak of unionism might have led to some form of social revolution in Britain, had it not been for the onset of the 1914-1918 war.

There can be little doubt that the footballers' craft union was of a piece with this pro-active mood among the organised work force. Unionised footballers, rather like the foundation in 1906 of the Variety Artists' Federation in the music hall, a genre managed on much the same lines as football, even to the influence of the brewers and publicans, completed the industrial analogy. Football's spectators were the customers of a service industry, managed by an alliance of not always efficient limited liability companies and staffed by a not always effective trades union.

The football club as a piece of industrial capitalism has led to some scholarly analysis of the psychology of the football crowd, itself mainly composed of urban working class consumers. For example, these skilled workers' affection for football has been attributed to its similarity to the industrial process, with specialist craftsmen - the tough defender, the wily, hard-working halfback, the speedy forward - contributing particular skills to the well-oiled machinery of the production line, all in the hope of manufacturing a goal. Three rather more straightforward points might be summarily made.

In the first place, as so often in this text, the case of football's simplicity must be urged. This was the pastime most of the spectators had played themselves, in the street or on the municipal recreation ground. It was easy to play and easy to follow. In the second place, it represented some escape from the tedium of the manufacturing and domestic routine; it was what Johan Huizinga would have termed an 'interlude'. Others, of course, did the physical playing, on their behalf. This was vicarious 'play'. In the third place, it was akin to some other leisure pursuits, such as the music hall, where there was a degree of identification with the artistes. Music hall audiences similarly had their favourites, their heroes and, in this case, heroines, several of them with local affiliations that, as with the footballers, added to their popularity. The competitive edge provided the extra spice in football. As well as the communal sharing of pleasure, as in the theatre or the pub, there were the highs and lows of rivalries with the other clubs, especially the immediate 'derby' ones.

It was this combination of emotions that energised the football spectator.

CHAPTER NINE

INTERVAL; BRITISH FOOTBALL BEFORE 1918

FOOTBALL SPREAD across Britain like a benign epidemic in the thirty years prior to the Great War of 1914. Henceforward the professional component would naturally command the most vivid attention, but it would be misleading to forget the recreational game, which, after all, fed the football entertainment industry.

The FA had 1,000 clubs on its books in 1888; it had 10,000 by 1905. By 1914 over 12,000 clubs and 300,000 players were registered with the FA. There were 158 professional clubs, also 12,000 boys' clubs, and, apart from complementary figures for Scotland, Wales and Ireland, soccer was often the game of choice for thousands more who played informally on the playgrounds, parks, factory yards and streets of the nation. By the 1880s the bigger district associations were very busy. The Lancashire FA had over a hundred clubs; the Sheffield FA and Nottingham FA had about 40 clubs each and the Sunderland FA had 200 clubs. On average, a club registered roughly 30 players, a reminder that most ran two teams, so that a district association, such as Sunderland, may have organised over a hundred fixtures every weekend.

In 1892, in response to the professional predominance in the FA Challenge Cup, the FA Amateur Cup was established and first played for in 1893/4; the north eastern clubs, Crook Town, Blyth Spartans and Bishop Auckland did especially well over the years in this new competition. There were even endeavours, albeit vain ones, to set up an amateur version of the FA, just as, years before, there had been threats of instituting a separate professional association. If anything, there was a tightening of the joint local amateur and professional associations.

It was around this time that the public schools, to be slavishly followed by many of the grammar schools that were founded after the 1902 Education Act with its emphasis on secondary education, turned away from the increasingly plebeian soccer to the increasingly bourgeois rugger. On the other hand, local authorities were inclined to favour plebeian soccer. The London County Council, for example, developed something like 350 football pitches, offering facilities to close on a thousand amateur clubs. Between the wars the National Playing Fields Association (1926) and the Central Council for Physical Education (1935) came into being, a helpmate to football and to other recreational games, as the yearning to 'keep fit' strengthened.

The FA's refusal to acknowledge any schism on amateur and professional lines was, of course, the opposite course to that taken by rugby. Arguments about the reimbursement of players for lost working time in the 1890s led to the formation of the professional Northern Union, renamed the Rugby League in the 1920s. There were marginal alterations in team numbers, plus the introduction of the 'play the ball' rule and other minor changes. There was an obsessively complete ostracism between the two codes for over a hundred years, a timely reminder that the soccer/rugger split was entirely sporting in character, while the union/league fracture was driven by class and monetary considerations.

The most colourful example of amateur football retrenchment remained N.C. Jackson's Corinthians. The elite of the public school brigade assembled to preserve the eponymous spirit of the Corinthians. In their dog days they were a splendid combination, their centre forward, G.O. Smith, a highly intelligent teacher, controlling their tactics of drawing defenders out of position before hitting the decisive pass. In 1889 they beat double winners Preston North End 5-0 and in 1903 they beat Cup winners Bury, who had not conceded a goal in that competition, 10-3. Their exploits had overseas effects, helping to inspire the foundation of Real Madrid in 1902 (the famous all-white strip being designed on the Corinthians model) and the Brazilian Corinthians club in 1910.

Footballing Origins - Examples

Just as Marks and Spencer began as a penny stall on Leeds market and Boots began with old Jesse and Florence Boot dispensing a few pharmaceutical wares from their corner shop in Nottingham, so did all the big football clubs start as little football clubs. The contrast between the rise of County Cricket Clubs and of Football League Clubs is rivetingly wide. The cricketing counties have a commonality of origin that is depressingly monotonous. Representative 'gentlemen' members of local clubs, usually with one pushy club taking a definite lead, meet at a hotel or other public building and form a county club, hopeful of raising standards in the district. They seek fixtures with other counties and employ professionals to assist them, chiefly with the bowling.

There are one or two slight exceptions - Yorkshire and Nottinghamshire, for example - but the foundation stones bear a remarkable resemblance one to the other. In the main they constituted themselves as subscriber clubs, after the Victorian pattern of voluntary organisation, with committees elected by that membership, and, give or take some changes in trading legislation, they conform to that format to this day. When short of money, they would turn to wealthy sponsors, such as the Duke of Devonshire who annually bailed out the Derbyshire club from his Chatsworth fastness, rather than succumb to the wickedness of the share-holding limited liability compass. Today sponsorship and television funding have replaced his ducal charity.

Despite some flirtation with the excitement of relegation and promotion, the grim decision was taken that there would simply be first-class counties and non-first-class counties. The system became set in stone by 1914 into a group of sixteen first-class counties, while the Minor Counties Cricket Association and related championship was formed in 1895. The first-class County Championship was to be a watertight and inclusive system. In almost a hundred years only two counties - Glamorgan and Durham - have joined the cream, while, more significantly, none has left.

Not for football such an exercise in stultifying petrifaction. Football engaged, willy-nilly and with hectic to-do, in the tadpole approach. Thousands of clubs were formed from a variegated range of beginnings - and a few frogs emerged from that demotic struggle of the survival of football's fittest to adorn the Football League. Even now, there is the space for the ambitious tadpole so to metamorphose. Alternatively, taking the gloomy view of the tadpole economy, of the 39 clubs registered with the FA in 1870, we are told by Tony Mason that only four survived into the 1970s. In reviewing the origins of some of the more noted clubs by way of illustration, it is, then, important to recall that they are frogs cited as representative of differing types of tadpole.

The educational provenance of the pioneering amateur clubs was not entirely lost. Old boys or teachers formed Sunderland, Darlington, Darwen and Northampton Town, in whole or part. Blackburn Rovers was founded in 1874 by Blackburn Grammar School old boys; Leicester Fosse was established in 1884 by former pupils of Wyggeston School, Leicester and became Leicester City in 1919,

INTERVAL

Chester, now Chester City, was born of old boys from King's School, Chester, in 1884, whilst Queen's Park Rangers started in 1885 from the rather lowlier educational level of Droop Street Elementary School, London, as St Jude's Institute FC. Bolton Wanderers began life in 1874 as Christ's Church Sunday School, Bolton, with support from both teaching staff and clergy.

Several clubs arose from the desire of cricketers to enjoy a winter sport together. Derby County was founded in 1884 by Derbyshire County Cricket Club; Hotspur CC formed Tottenham Hotspur in 1882 and Preston CC begat Preston North End in 1881. Spurs owe much to John Ripsher, a bible class teacher at All Hallows Church, Tottenham, who was president of the football club for many years, although he sadly came to a pauperised end. They joined the Second Division in 1908 and were promptly promoted at their first attempt to the First Division. Both the main Sheffield clubs fall into this category. Sheffield Wednesday established a football section in 1867, while Yorkshire County Cricket Club players, seeking a winter leisure pastime, were responsible for the launch of Sheffield United in 1889. Newcastle United arose from the amalgamation of Stanley FC and Rosewood FC, the former started in 1881 as the supplementary football section of a cricket club. Conversely, Burnley - started in the local YMCA in 1882 - Bradford City and Ipswich Town appear to have flirted with rugby before settling for soccer. Nottingham Forest was initially a 'shinney' or hockey club.

Even more influential, predictably so when the social arguments about the need for manly sports are recollected, was the church. Bury, Mansfield Town, Swindon Town (where the curate of Christ Church, William Pitt, was the instigator in 1881), Birmingham City (the doubtless cherubic choirboys of Holy Trinity Church, Small Heath, in 1875), and Fulham (St Andrew's Sunday School, West Kensington, in 1879, under the spirited leadership of the curate, J.H. Cardwell) all enjoyed clerical baptisms, while Everton formerly rejoiced in the less than laconic title of St Domingo's New Methodist Connection Sunday School, where the bible class supplied the first 'Toffeemen'.

Aston Villa was founded in 1874 by the bible class of the local Wesleyan chapel; in 1887 Barnsley was born, fathered by the assistant curate of St Peter's Church, the Trollopean sounding Rev Tiverton Preedy, and Manchester City first saw the light of footballing day in 1879 at St Mark's Church, West Gorton. Evidence from areas like Liverpool, Nottingham and Birmingham suggests that between a quarter and a half of football clubs had some religious connection, at least at their nativity.

An overt illustration of the clerical interest was the foundation of Glasgow Celtic in 1887 on a specifically Roman Catholic basis, partly as charitable fund-raising organ for the Catholic poor of the city. It also offered some sporting succour to the Irish immigrant community. Glasgow Rangers certainly found much of its support from among the Protestant working class Govan district, but, at this stage, the sectarian divide was not so keen-edged as it unfortunately became.

At the other extreme, as has been noted, were the pubs and the publicans, with Liverpool a pleasing example of that mode of birth. Many of Bristol's local clubs were pub-orientated, while numerous clubs took their name from their host pub, such as the Royal Oak in Sheffield. Sometimes - Walsall is an example - there were inter-pub competitions. Sadly, no present day Football League side celebrates a pub sign in its coat of arms. The Birmingham brewers, Mitchell St George, organised a football club in the late 19th century, but it never made the top grade.

Works teams were plentiful, and, with their built-in advantages of assets and offers of work, they figured prominently in the formation of what were to be successful professional clubs. Manchester United began life as the Newton Heath (Lancashire and Yorkshire Railway) Cricket & Football Club. The Dining Room Committee of this carriage and wagon works depot also ran 'classes of improvement' as well as these physical activities, a reminder that, as well as hoping to assure some loyalty from their workers, the paternalistically inclined employers were eager to promote a healthy labour force. 'Rational recreation' was very much required - and seems to have been effective. In the 1870s a quarter of working class wages were spent on liquor, with an average individual consumption of 35 gallons of beer a year, but, over the next hundred years this fell to less than nine gallons.

Companies and businesses often sponsored choirs, dramatic societies, horticultural groups and similar activities for exactly the same reasons. A helpful parallel is the growth of the brass band movement. By the end of the 19th century there were 50,000 brass bands blasting away, a thousand of them Salvation Army bands, plus lots of 'temperance' bands with nonconformist church affiliations. Many others, however, were work based - Grimethorpe Colliery; Foden's Motor Works, Hammond's Sauce, Black Dyke Mills and the Co-operative Wholesale Society among them. To press the analogue further, they readily adopted, as in football...and in choral, dramatic and horticultural interests...the Victorian keenness for competition. In 1908 at Belle Vue Gardens, Manchester 2.5 million people attended the national brass band championship, with 500 bands in contest. To complete the circle, Crystal Palace was home to brass band competitions as well as FA Cup Finals.

Other works teams included West Ham United, arising from the Thames Ironworks shipbuilding firm on Victoria Dock Road; Coventry City, originally the Singer Cycle Works in 1885; Crewe Alexandra, unsurprisingly, had links with London and North Western Railway Company. Crewe began as a cricket club in 1866 and added football in 1877 - Alexandra comes from the name of their friendly local hotel. Millwall was parented in 1885 by Morton & Co, the jam and marmalade makers. Most industrial districts had plenty of works teams - there were a score and more in both Birmingham and Sheffield as early as the 1870s. Many, of course, remained - or perished - as soccer's tadpoles. The Bristol tobacco firm of W.D. & H.O. Wills, creators of the Woodbine cigarette, ran a football team, as did the Midland Railway Company (Derby Midland FC) and Steiner's Dyeworks in Lancashire (Church FC).

Needless to say, there were many clubs that were the offspring of mixed marriages. Often it is hard to disentangle one thread from another in the sometimes obscure beginnings of some clubs. The Stoke club appears to have been formed in an alliance of Old Carthusians and the North Staffordshire Railway Company in 1863 and Southampton (Southampton St Mary's in 1885; Southampton in 1897) arose from some partnership of church and schoolmasters, having begun in the church YMCA. Wolves also contrived to have a joint cricketing and church heritage, courtesy of, in 1877, St Luke's Church and School, Blakenheath. Leyton Orient managed to illustrate three types of footballing motherhood by way of religion, education and cricket; in 1881 the Homerton Theological College's Glyn Cricket Club had a notion to add football to its list of activities.

Plenty of teams lacked any specific launching pad. Troupes of young men just started football teams. A team was informally assembled to play the Yorkshire Institute of the Deaf - and Doncaster Rovers was born in 1879. Although it had some cricketing links, Middlesbrough has one of the most jovial of footballing heritages; it resulted from a tripe supper held in 1876 at a hotel in Middlesbrough. That fine town also boasted, just for the 1893-94 season, the temporary might of Middlesbrough Ironopolis.

PARISH TO PLANET

Footballing Origins - Discussion

Two points must be emphasised. Firstly, the huge majority of these sporting nativities occurred in the thirty or forty years from about 1870 to 1910. Those decades might be described as a pressure cooker period for British sport. It is an era in which hundreds of sports clubs of all kinds were formed, with football always in the van - an obvious memorial from that age is the prevalence of jolly amateur usages - 'wanderers'; 'rovers'; 'rangers' - in club titles. Contextually, one might bear in mind the 500 angling clubs, the 1,200 golf clubs, the 500 rugby clubs and the 1,000 tennis clubs that had also sprung into existence by 1914, the great majority of them over that same relatively brief period.

Secondly, in all of these typologies there is a crack along an official and unofficial fissure. A group of workers would sometimes start a football team off - to adapt a cricketing metaphor - their own bat, before maybe seeking succour from the company, as opposed to the firm making a formal decision to run a football club. A band of young men might assemble themselves into a football team and then ask their local pub for assistance as a changing facility, rather than the hostelry or brewery being initially responsible. There were church teams who utilised the faith sportingly, not theologically. The premises were useful for meeting and changing purposes, but there were cases where the incumbent parson or minister was dismayed at a lack of ecclesiastical commitment and cast out the sinners - as over against the Thomas Hughes type clergy who were determined to form and lead football teams, the better to reinforce the faith. Nothing demonstrates the eclectic origins of British football clubs more vividly than these extremes of vicars, anxious to steer men clear of drink, and brewers, keen to ensure they kept a close proximity to alcoholic beverages.

As examples of these switches of allegiance, Christ Church School suffered a schism with its hosting church and became Bolton Wanderers in 1877, whereas Blackpool were originally Blackpool St John's, until a similar parting of the ways with St John's Church and a convivial linkage with the Stanley Park Hotel. Aston Villa also soon yielded up its clerical and cricketing - Villa Cross Wesleyan Chapel CC - connections. The truth is that schools and churches and works and pubs were buildings; it was frequently their shelter and material assets that were desired, not their message or products. It is fascinating to note that the theologically based Everton, the educationally derived Blackburn Rovers and the vocationally sponsored Manchester United all soon relied in their pre-histories on public houses; the Queen's Hotel, the Bay Horse Hotel and the Three Crowns, later the Shears Hotel, respectively.

Arsenal's story offers another instance of shifting fortunes. Whereas Arnold F. Hills, a Harrovian and Oxonian owner of the Thames Ironworks, had been characteristically prominent in the paternalistic formation of the team in 1895 that became West Ham United in 1900, it appears that Arsenal's birthright was a much more democratic one. Indeed, the workers had previously been denied permission to play soccer on the company's cricket pitch. It was a group of Woolwich Arsenal munitions workers who established the club as Dial Square in 1886, electing a committee to do so from among their number. They were encouraged by a couple of ex-Nottingham Forest players to contribute a few coppers to buy a ball. Even so, there was some recruitment of likely players with the aid of jobs in the munitions works. The club turned professional in 1891, but tried to avoid the capitalist solution of the limited liability company, preferring the voluntary membership model. However, pressure from the landowner of their ground forced the Royal Arsenal committee to seek, in 1893, the umbrella of limited liability, which also afforded them the chance of raising money to buy their own ground. £4,000 in one pound shares was the flotation, with 1,552 shares allocated to 860 workmen in the Woolwich area, most of them employees of the company.

Unfortunately, the weighty costs of professional competition and ground maintenance told against this experiment in proletarian management. Attendances were poor, partly the consequence of sparse transport services in the district. The Boer War did not help, for compulsory weekend overtime in response to the call for more armaments cut attendances still further. In 1900, facing a loss of over £3,000, one of the last major clubs to be run by workers succumbed to capitalist pressure and the businessmen moved in. They turned Royal Arsenal into one of the most powerful and wealthy clubs in Britain. The shift from Woolwich in southeast London to Highbury in north London, at a cost of £125,000, was a deliberate and successful ploy, principally engineered by the wealthy Henry Norris, to appeal to a bulkier customer base. In 1904 they became the first southern club to be promoted to the First Division of the Football League and from 1914 were simply and triumphantly known as Arsenal.

A final point about the 'tadpole' theory of footballing origins is in respect of a further comparison with cricket. The now eighteen counties that comprise the County Championship stand aloof from the rest of the counties and other districts of the British Isles. Unless one lives in or near one of them, or, more accurately, close to the chief headquarters of one, it is difficult to enjoy an active interest. The incidence of Football League and Scottish League clubs has been such that identification and subsequent emotional attachment has been intense. A town would as soon have a football club as a mayor and several towns are known almost entirely because of their football team. During the intense popularity of league cricket in the north and midlands, especially during the inter-wars years, something of the same level of emotional attachment was apparent in cricket. The neighbourhood football club became the focus of fierce loyalty - and there were enough of them to guarantee that a majority of citizens and their families could indulge themselves in the affecting pleasures and disappointments of supporting a leading football club.

Localised loyalty was not, of course, a novel aspect. 'Here's a stranger; throw a brick at him' was said to be the motto of many villages, while the virulent ardour provoked by pre-modern football has been alluded to already. The town football team was, however, destined to create a most intense passion. As well as possible works or church connections, especially in the early days, football spectatorship generated strong familial links. This tended to be masculine in style, although today that pattern is changing to involve more mothers and daughters. The traditional motif was father and son, perhaps uncle and nephew, and also elder and younger brother. Part of growing up was to be taken to the match by one's father and to be inducted into the close ties of the terraces. Later it would be more of a generational element, with young men - youthful neighbours, school-friends, fellow-apprentices - standing and cheering together.

Some commentators have not hesitated to speak of the pack mentality and male bonding in this regard. Eric Dunning, an academic expert on crowd behaviour, described the football hooliganism of the 1970s and 1980s as 'segmented bonding', with disaffected youth alienated from the common social fabric. That was - that is - the unhappy extreme. More positively, the rituals of mutual enjoyment and celebration of one's local football club have brought huge pleasure and psychological succour to many. The football team has the advantage of continuity. A locality might enthuse over, say, a boxer bred in the neighbourhood, but that is necessarily an ephemeral delight. The football team regenerates itself. Its history and its lore become part of the generational togetherness, as father brags of the heroes of his childhood and his son is suitably unimpressed, preferring the stars of the present dispensation. There is also the regularity of the experience. Of course, families used to visit the variety theatre or the cinema on a weekly basis, but that, for all its delights, was essentially a changing scene. The fortnightly home match involved the same cast, a group of players with which forcefully to identify, a band of gladiators to bring gladness or melancholy to the watching thousands.

It is right to pause for a moment to reflect on the sheer emotionalism of football spectatorship, for it is now paralleled in towns and cities on every continent.

Footballing Progress - Cups and Leagues

The watershed of the tidal wave of professionalism was the Cup Final of 1882/83. For the first time the provincial entries outnumbered the metropolitan candidates by 49 to 35, and, after the appearance of Blackburn Rovers in the final in the preceding year, there was a provincial team in the final tie for only the second time in twelve years. It was Blackburn Olympic, only five years old and destined to have a short-lived, if glorious, cup history. They were the first non-public schoolboy club to win the cup, and they did so symbolically by defeating the Old Etonians, with six internationals, 2-1 after extra time. By trades, the Blackburn Olympians were five textile workers, a plumber, an iron founder, a picture framer, a dental assistant (that was the goalkeeper), and, to the despair of the gentry, two 'professors', one of them Jack Hunter, coach and strategist. The short passing and regular training of the northerners told in a tough match, with Jimmy Costley, a cotton spinner, scoring the winner. An amateur side never again won the cup, although Queen's Park were the defeated finalists in the following two years, the last fling of the amateur dispensation. Indeed, it would be 1901 before the cup was returned to London, when Tottenham Hotspur beat Sheffield United 3-1, after a replay.

Blackburn Rovers then proceeded to win the cup five times in the next eight years, while West Bromwich Albion had two cup victories in 1888 and 1892 and Wolverhampton Wanderers did the same in 1893 and 1908. Aston Villa won twice in the 1890s, a feat emulated by Bury in the early 1900s. Sheffield Wednesday also won twice, in 1896 and 1907, whereas rivals Sheffield United won the cup three times in 1899, 1902 and 1915. The merry-go-round of the FA Cup brought satisfaction to a wide range of Lancashire, Yorkshire and midland teams in that era, but, the solitary Spurs victory apart, no other region had a glimpse of the trophy.

The industrial belts retained a robust hold on the Football League. The First Division was much more openly contested than is today the case. There were 27 titles to be won and ten clubs shared the spoils. Not one of them fell outside the industrial areas and Aston Villa, the sole midlands winner with no fewer than six titles, were the southernmost club. Beginning with the famous Preston North End, who enjoyed two wins and three runners-up spots in the first five years of League football, Lancashire had ten championships, the other eleven falling to the north east, where Sunderland were especially flourishing with five titles, and Yorkshire in the persons of the two Sheffield teams.

'The Old Invincibles', Preston North End, did the double in 1889, as did Aston Villa in 1897, feats not to be repeated until 1961. On the way to their double, Preston did not lose a league match and did not concede a goal in their cup run. Preston North End have the privilege of holding the English record for the highest goal count in a competitive fixture at the top level; in 1887 they beat Hyde 26-0 in an FA cup tie. The British record, however, is held by Arbroath in a Scottish cup tie, for such competitions, of course, sometimes threw unequal rivals against one another. They beat Bon Accord, with not a pair of football boots to their name, 36-0 in the same era.

The Scottish League started in 1890/91 and, after a brief phase of moderately varied fortunes, the Clydeside shipyard area of Glasgow exerted its duopoly. Rangers and Celtic between them won eight of the first twelve championships and then every one before 1939, except for one, when another Lanarkshire team, Motherwell, contrived to steal the Scottish thunder. The joint success of the two Glaswegian giants tended rather to devalue the Scottish League, and this was not helped by the rabid sectarian divide, with its Ulster overtones, of the Roman Catholic 'Nationalist' Celtic and the Protestant 'Unionist' Rangers. This close attachment of a politico-religious kind was never quite as rampant in the English experience, but it was to figure unhealthily in overseas club football, as that developed. The skilled amateurs, Queen's Park, won nine Scottish cup finals between 1874 and 1890. Although they struggled gamely on, they only won one more Scottish cup, for, as in England, professionalism conquered all.

Why was London left so completely out of the footballing picture? The usual answer is the somewhat shallow consideration that the country was divided into the dour north, invested with grim-visaged professional teams among the slag-heaps and dank canals of industrialism and the skittish south, charmed by dilettante amateur clubs among the verdant meadows of suburban London. It is an image akin to that conveyed by the English Civil War division between humourless Roundheads and laughing Cavaliers, satirised by W.C. Sellar and R.J. Yeatman (to borrow again from *1066 and All That*) as the 'right and repulsive' versus the 'wrong but wromantic'.

London is too readily left out of the industrial equation. The capital city played a major role in the Industrial Revolution and developed into a major industrial centre. Its burgeoning population - 7.25 million in the Greater London area by 1911 - demanded services that only industrial methodology could provide in the required bulk, particularly by way of building materials, foodstuffs, clothing and the like. London was the largest port in the kingdom, the focus, then, not only for finance, but the sheer carriage of imports and exports on a massive scale. The works teams already mentioned - Arsenal; West Ham United - should remind us of the industrial heritage of London.

Apart from the docks, where the labour force was only just coming to terms with trades unionism and the struggle against casual rather than regular work, London's industry was much more disparate than that in the northern and midland districts. London was a sprawling conglomeration, as befitted the cosmopolitan nature of the world's leading city. The basis of northern professional superiority lay in the peculiar conjunction of discrete urban settlements, each with a staple industry, staffed by a close-knit community, residing together in proximity to the workplace. The physical and emotional identity fostered underpinned the local football team in both body and spirit, with the money at the turnstile and the cheers from the terraces. Some commentators have gone so far as to describe this sentiment as tribalism. That may be a little extreme. The cheers were not unequivocal. Oftentimes they were moderated by mordant criticism and salty wit. But, for all that, the loyalty and pride was fierce - and the grounds of clubs in relatively small towns were surprisingly full.

Some of the London teams did not lack for support. Chelsea's Stamford Bridge was, from the mid 1900s, just about the best attended venue in the country. In an intriguing precedent for modern day Chelsea, it was the rich businessman, Gus Mears, who had the huge ground built and sought a place for the club in an expanded Second Division. Approaching 30,000 people often filed through Chelsea's gates, whether they were in the First or the Second Division. The supposition is that these were possibly drawn from various parts of London, utilising its efficient transport system and that some of them were going to a football match, rather than watching Chelsea per se. In fact, rather like Queen Park's home at Hampden Park, sometimes seen as Gus Mears's model for Stamford Bridge, it was rarely full, as it could hold 100,000 spectators, including 5,000 in seats. People knew they would have a comfortable view, as opposed to some of the provincial grounds where there was often overcrowding and difficulty in seeing. On the alternate Saturday some of these attenders may have visited another London ground, whereas, in those few cities that boasted two major clubs, it would have been a solecism on the part of a supporter to spend Saturday afternoon at the rival club.

Therein lay the ripe distinction between the metropolitan and the provincial culture. The forthcoming saga of British football was destined to narrate the wresting back of some of football's glory from provincial into metropolitan hands, those of London, plus a small set of regional metropolises. In 1800 London had housed about a million citizens in its 60 squares and 8,000 streets. It measured five miles from west to east and was 'a walkable city'. In 1900 London was seventeen miles across and there were 6.5 million crowded in the city, the equivalent of the combined populations of Denmark, Greece and Bosnia-Herzogovina. Annually, almost a million public transport journeys were negotiated in London. It was far and away the biggest metropolis in the world. The future of global urbanism, and thereby of world football, would lie with the 'conurbation', a term first coined, appositely, in 1915, by the visionary town planner, Patrick Geddes.

Global football would have the repercussion of extensive player migration. In these present days of this worldwide recruitment of players, it is interesting to read criticism in contemporary newspapers of the use of other than very locally based players at a time when parochial loyalties remained so intense. Welsh and Scottish 'professors' were in some demand among the major Football League clubs, but this was still frowned upon in some quarters. Francis Marindin, of Royal Engineers vintage and now President of the FA, refereed the semi-final in 1887 when West Bromwich beat Preston North End, with its full quota of Scottish stars. He visited the West Brom dressing room after the game and cried out, 'are you all Englishmen?' 'Yes, sir', was the lusty response. Francis Marindin, who would have received a dusty answer had he been able to pose that query in many Premiership dressing rooms today, wished them well, but, romance and football being unstable partners, Aston Villa took the cup by two goals to nil.

INTERVAL

Footballing Progress - Internationals

The transition from club to national representation was, as now, an uneasy one. Scotland sustained the amateur tradition rigidly and the clever play of its amateur combines, drawn from the likes of Queen's Park, Dumbarton and Vale of Leven, often proved too taxing for England. During the late 19th century about 70 Scots were being paid to play in the Football League, but they, and even other Anglo-Scots, like the classically amateur the Honourable Arthur, later Lord, Kinnaird, were rarely selected for their national side. Blackburn Rovers's Caledonian full-back pairing of Nick Ross and Fergie Suter are two such professional instances.

Peter Hartland argues persuasively that the more tightly knit clannishness of the talented Scots team gave them a psychological edge over the English sides, drawn from several rival clubs and perhaps thinking more of club than of national success. With only ten or so mainline clubs, the Scots probably turned more to international football to boost the game in that country, whereas there was possibly some disharmony in England teams made up of middle class amateurs and working class professionals. We have already seen how the first professional to represent England was singled out.

There were a record nine Corinthians in the English eleven for the fixture in 1886. Of the first nineteen international encounters, Scotland won eleven and lost just three, with five draws. Yet, apart from some sprightly runs by Queen's Park, no Scottish club ever won the FA Cup and English clubs tended to better Scottish clubs in direct combat. Moreover, Wales and Ireland won the Home Championship in the pre-1914 years, so that, despite the predominance of the two major countries, it was never too one- or two-sided a contest. Nonetheless, England's 13-0 defeat of Ireland in 1882 at Belfast remains their record victory to date.

That first goalless international in November 1872 was played at the West of Scotland cricket ground in Partick, before a crowd of 2,000 - much the same as for the first FA Cup final. They paid a total £100 for the privilege, yielding a profit of £38, with the aid of the English FA funding their trip from donations from members. The £38 was wisely invested in the expenses of sending the Scottish eleven, again with a majority of Queen's Park players, to the Oval in 1873. The Old Etonian, Alexander Bonsor, had the honour of striking the first-ever goal in international football to spark off the 4-2 England victory. There were gloomy moments, too. The Scotland-England game at the new Ibrox stadium in 1902 was the sorrowful scene of football's first of many major disasters. 25 were killed and 500 injured when a stand collapsed. The game continued in order to avoid further panic, as the dead and injured were removed on makeshift stretchers wrought from the debris of the collapsed structure. It certainly concentrated the minds of directors of clubs about the need for safety and, more cynically, the need for proper insurance cover.

With their conventional, as it was to become, formation of 2-3-5, and with skilled Queen's Park artists like Charles Campbell, Billy McKinnon, Harry McNeil and Walter Arnott to lead the dance, Scotland thus flourished. Not that England lacked for stars. Among those that shone brightly were the cerebral Preston and Derby County forward, John Goodall, Billy Bassett, the pacy West Brom winger, the prolific Steve Bloomer, top scorer in the First Division five times with 317 goals for Derby and Middlesbrough, Blackburn's Bob Crompton, a defender of legendary stature and a then fabulous record of 41 caps, the combative little Ernest 'Nudger' Needham of Sheffield United, prototype of the sturdy, tough-tackling wing half, Sam Hardy, of Liverpool and Aston Villa, an intelligent goalkeeper of studied nonchalance; and two physically strong but classically adept centre halves in Bristol City's Billy 'Fatty' Wedlock and Manchester United's Charlie Roberts.

From Chirk, in Wales, hailed Billy Meredith, who helped Charlie Roberts press for player unionism and chaired the inaugural meeting of the Association Football Players Union at Manchester's Imperial Hotel in 1907. Pale, wan and slightly wandering, he was a right winger who took on defenders with an abrupt directness and, rarely among contemporary wings, often turned infield in search of goal-scoring opportunities. From 1894 he enjoyed a thirty year career, toothpick ever clamped in his jaws, with Manchester City and then Manchester United, winning a record 52 Welsh caps along that brilliant journey. He has every right to be claimed as the first of the all-time greats. From Ireland came Bill McCracken, the Newcastle United full-back and a lynx-eyed reader of the game. His adroit shimmies upfield to exploit the old offside law are said to have single-handedly persuaded the authorities to change the law in 1925 to two rather than three defenders bringing immunity from the offside offence.

There is, among football chroniclers, a tendency to adopt a Whig Interpretation of History, whereby the sport heads upwards and onwards in a linear ascent of progressive improvement. Very perceptively, Peter Hartland has taught us, from his profound researches, to be wary of that Macauleyan fallacy, for the chess-like manoeuvres of those days brought great joy to thousands of watchers.

Football was different from, not necessarily worse than, the game in later times. He reminds us that, according to the knowledge of the day, professional footballers were requested to pay some attention to addressing the conundrums of unsatisfactory diet and excess drinking and smoking, as well as to a regime of fitness drill. A dull but exacting routine, focused on the important role of the trainer, of skipping, walking, jogging over distance runs, sprinting and exercising with dumb bells and Indian clubs was eventually the norm. Indeed, it was that level of dedication that the old-style amateurs found alarming, as when Blackburn Rovers, in preparation for both the semi-final and final in 1882, were funded by a local cotton merchant to stay together in a Blackpool hotel for a week. Judith Flanders has pointed out that their protein-laden daily menu of port wine, raw eggs, porridge, haddock, mutton and oysters must have made 'an astonishing difference', as compared with the normal millhand's heavily carbohydrated diet of potatoes, bread, with maybe a little cheese or bacon, plus sugared tea.

With a format of 2-3-5, sometimes varied to protect a lead by withdrawing a forward and making a 3-3-4 design, most professional clubs reached a good standard. Heading was still in its infancy as an art-form, but, then, kicking the ball above ground was regarded as clumsy, and a Corinthian player guilty of such crudity risked being dropped. The view has been thoughtfully expressed that, over against the increasing tempo of football after the First World War and, of course, more so after the Second World War, there was a much more deliberate and concise approach then. With a concentration on skilled footwork, choice of position and accurate passing, and even allowing for the toughness of tackling and the three-man offside obstacle, there was, in the higher reaches of football, a delightful array of talent to enjoy.

The 1914-1918 War, as in so many historical respects, is a grimly valuable point at which to pause. The 1914-15 League and FA Cup programme was completed, with the famous 'Khaki Cup Final' at Old Trafford won by Sheffield United in front of an audience chiefly of soldiers. Thereafter regional competition, based on Lancashire, the midlands and around London, was organised, each game of only 80 minutes' duration, with no interval, and with no mid-week matches permitted to avoid interrupting essential war work. Wages were slashed or even stopped altogether, for it was decreed that all professional footballers should be serving in the armed forces or otherwise engaged in war-orientated activity. This was in response to angry claims that footballers were 'dodging the column' and setting a bad example to young men. The 'Footballers' Battalion', the 17th Service Battalion of the Middlesex Regiment, was formed; and football matches were extensively used as arenas for recruiting.

Footballers and football fans were numbered among the 2.5 million who answered Kitchener's famed call to arms, and, after 1916, conscription completed the engagement of a generation of young men with that vile, bloodstained war. Of the millions of lives it claimed one was West Bromwich Albion's inside-forward Harold Bache. Having been recently recruited into Albion's ranks, the player had had an instant impact and was believed to be heading for an international call up after a mere fourteen appearances when war interrupted his meteoric rise. Bache, from a family of solicitors, and so an example of the gentleman player who still competed alongside professionals at this time, volunteered and joined the 10th Lancashire Fusiliers as a bombing officer; an elite group known, with the grim humour of the time, as 'The Suicide Squad'.

On 6 February 1916, Bache's company found themselves billeted on a piece of Flanders real estate, near Ypres, known as 'the Bluff'. A major attack saw the Germans take 600 yards of ground, including much of the Bluff. Bache's commanding officer, Major G.L. Torrens, chose to counter-attack before dawn, at around 4.15am on 15th February. The Lancashires' Regimental Diary shows Bache leading the central column of the three which formed the attack and describes the fighting as 'hard', presumably an understatement. The attackers reached the top of the Bluff and many dropped into the trench which they had occupied as of right some few hours before. Hand-to-hand fighting ensued and there were many casualties as the Lancashires were forced back, including Bache, whose body was never recovered.

Bache is but one example of talent cut down in its prime of unfulfilled promise, always asking the question what might have been. His name adorns the Menin Gate among the many thousands who died at Ypres. A gold plaque, unveiled in 1922, still adorns the West Bromwich Albion board room, paying homage to all of the players and staff who served in the 'war to end all wars'.

Although some football did continue in Britain, much of it of moderate quality, with the qualification that it was often played for war charity purposes, and while the armed forces tried to provide some chances for servicemen to play the game, there is no doubt that the First World War dealt a severe blow to the heart of British football. Perhaps the most famed match of these dreadful times was on Christmas morning, 1914, when, in one of the few sane episodes of that insane tragedy, scores of men from the Lancashire and Saxon regiments played football between the trenches.

It was perhaps not as disastrous an effect as that the war had on cricket, which mourned the loss of the spacious, golden days of its late Victorian and Edwardian glories and, it could be argued, rarely again rediscovered the momentum to look keenly forwards and not nostalgically backwards. Pragmatic and prosaic, football in Britain resumed its activities as soon as was at all practical after the 1918 Armistice. In the meanwhile, the nation had to recover from the shock of major and immediate continental strife, after a relatively peaceful period, stretching back to the Battle of Waterloo in 1815. This had been warfare that not only slew countless thousands of servicemen, but also caused emotional and material distress among the whole of the civilian population.

In its forbidding fashion, the Great War may have reminded many that there was a world out there to be considered. The British football authorities may have been blinkered to it, but it was a world that had already begun to assimilate the British version of football into its various national cultures. It is to the global destiny that we must now turn.

PART THREE

GLOBAL

CHAPTER TEN

DIASPORA; THE SPREAD OF FOOTBALL TO EUROPE

IF THE FA HAD anything to do with it, this chapter may not have been required to be written.

The Football Association deserves every possible credit for shaping and boosting the game in the British Isles, but, when it came to overseas expansion, it was only, at best, peripherally interested. Too much blame should not intolerantly be attached to the FA. Commentators are wont to find organisations culpable for the omission of tasks for which they were not established. The FA's job, after all, was to run football in England and keep a benevolent eye on soccer in the other parts of Great Britain. The rest of the world was, like the past, in L.P. Hartley's phrase, 'a foreign country'.

Moreover, the FA reflected the governmental policy and public mood of the hour. Apart from the intrusive, chaotic, agonising, but mercifully brief Crimean War in the 1850s, Britain had kept itself free from continental war for a hundred years since the downfall of Napoleon. Certainly the British coast had been immune from the hazard of invasion since the Battle of Trafalgar in 1805. The Royal Navy patrolled the oceans and kept matters cosily secure, so that, by and large, the European continent, while marginally useful for occasional aristocratic vacations and middle class trading exercises, was shunned.

Apart from this being the common cultural mood, it actually made political common sense. Especially in the last two decades of the 19th century, when Lord Salisbury was the principal political navigator with a firm hand on the tiller of foreign affairs, eschewal of formal alliance with foreign powers was advisable. Official connections by treaty, with written promises to act in this or that way in given circumstances, were anathema to Lord Salisbury and the Foreign Office. The preference was for picking one's national way warily through the complexities of foreign entanglements, aided by a mild admonition or threat, maybe backed by the sailing of a battleship or the marshalling of some battalion. Indeed, the onset of the First World War, with nation after nation tumbling into hostilities through the interconnections of treaty obligations, demonstrates the value of that less formally committed position.

Europe - Nationalism

As counterpoint to that non-continental stance, British eyes looked outwards to the wider horizon of Empire, a subject to be explored a little more fully, in sporting terms, in the next chapter. This, in turn, found the British faced by rival empire-builders, among them Germany, and, of course, it was to be the German plan to build up its colonial possessions and its naval armament that proved to be one of the several causes of eventual war. The 20th century Briton is sometimes amazed to find that, almost until the outbreak of war in 1914, France, not Germany, was regarded as the natural foe. German belligerence was an expression of its new-found national identity - and an understanding of Nationalism, perhaps the most influential of 19th century ideological dogmas, is a prerequisite for any sensible grasp of the development of world football.

After an age of kingdoms and empires, the concept of the nation-state took profound root. England and France, then Spain and Portugal, were the initial runners in the nationalistic race. Now the world is awash with omnicompetent sovereign states. Germany, beforehand a cluster of duchies and principalities, and Italy, hitherto, according to the Austrian statesman Klemens von Metternich, no more than a 'geographic expression', were latecomers to the nationalist feast. Around, respectively, the potency of Prussia and of Piedmont-Sardinia, they both attained ultimate national unity as late as the 1870s.

Nationality is now just about the only game in the global town. This division of the world into territorial slabs is not an exact science, as the vestiges of what, in political science jargon, are known as 'particularist' elements exemplify. Scotland, Wales and, especially, Ireland illustrate the discomforts of proclaiming nationhood as the sole key to modern politics. The determination to fashion African nations out of a Western pattern of colonisation, against the grain of more ancient tribal alignments, is another, and more disastrous, example.

Nonetheless, and for the most part, the worldwide nation couples an administrative entity with a strong draught of cultural identity. This patriotic, even xenophobic, fervour was in accord with political templates that either recognised some degree of democratic citizenship or, as in more totalitarian politics, encouraged some kind of popular vehemence. In either case, and increasingly, sport became a major outlet for this worship of nationhood, what the great historian of civilisations Arnold Toynbee, called 'the pagan deification' of the nation. Along with the language and the stamps and the coinage and the anthem and the flag and the nationalistic icons and heroes, sport was a leading mode for the nation at prayer with itself.

Individuals and towns began to mean less and less, in sporting terms, as nations began to mean more and more. Although, for example, club football has made a powerful comeback, especially in Europe, over the last fifty years, even club competition is normally ruled on a national basis, as in the first or second (and sometimes third and fourth) clubs from each of the national leagues joining in the major European-wide tournament. Because the nation is nakedly a political concept, the ingenuous plea for politics to be kept out of sport was rendered vain as soon as the nation-state was deployed as the sporting vehicle.

The worst example is the modern Olympic Games. The irascibility of the defeated Greeks, the internecine squabbles of Americans and the overbearing attitudes of Germans marred the inaugural 1896 Games - and that was with only a hundred competitors. In 1908 the Americans left London vowing never again to participate, given 'such cruel and unsportsmanlike treatment' by the prejudiced English judges. In 1912 the British, appalled by their impoverished showing, appointed the first ever national coach, the Canadian W.R. Knox, explicitly because such failure reflected on imperial standing. Away from the ideal of a city inviting the youth of the world to contest athletically, by 1932 in Los Angeles, there was separate accommodation for national teams, the national procession, the triple victory rostrum and the playing of national anthems.

Instances from earlier Olympiads have been cited to confirm the opinion that the nationalistic disease was injuring the Olympic movement from the start. The nationalism grew ever more open. The 1936 Berlin Olympics were used as a platform for the posturing of the Nazis and are regarded by some historians, among them Richard Mandell, author of *The Nazi Olympics*, as a signpost towards World War II - the attempt to stage a rival anti-Nazi Olympic Games in Barcelona was foiled by the outbreak of the Spanish Civil War. The post-war Olympiads have been cursed with problems, usually of a nationalistic flavour, from the mass boycotts - 32 nations from Montreal in 1976 and over forty nations from Moscow in 1980 - to the thirteen dead in the anti-Olympic protest rally in Mexico City in 1968 and the murderous attack by Arab terrorists on the Israeli team at Munich in 1972. President Ronald Reagan politically exploited the Los Angeles games in 1984 amidst a distasteful orgy of chauvinistic adulation. The security precautions were alarming for that demeaning occasion. Eighty helicopters, several hundred sub-machine gunners, 50,000 security officers and fifty marksmen adept in 'surgical shooting' all contributed to that far from frolicsome scene of gaiety and merriment.

Above all, it is essential, in turning to the overseas expansion of football, to apprehend how quickly the national referential frame was erected and how politicised, along with many other sports, such as athletics, football rapidly became.

In the beginning, all was organic and informal. There was little action by the FA. The England team toured Central Europe in 1908 and 1909, sweeping to victories against Austria and its territorial adjuncts, Hungary and Bohemia, scoring 48 goals against seven, and doubtless fuelling a smug sense of footballing superiority. Football was included in the Olympic Games for the first time at London in 1908, Great Britain, fielding its amateur team, won comfortably, as it did at Stockholm in 1912. Denmark was the runner-up on each occasion and, in 1908, France fielded elevens from two rival federations.

Some English clubs ventured abroad. For instance, in 1909, Manchester United, fresh from their first ever First Division championship in 1908 and having beaten Queen's Park, 4-0 after a replay, to become the first winners of the Charity Shield, visited the Austro-Hungarian Empire. They won all their matches and, in an atmosphere suffused with premonition, their 7-0 drubbing of Budapest League leaders Ferencvaros led to such hooliganism that the police had to draw their swords to cope with the rioting.

A whimsical footnote to this sparse overseas activity was in 1910, when Sir Thomas Lipton, the well-known grocer, was turned down, typically enough, by the FA, when he sponsored a club tournament in Turin and hoped for an English entrant. Northern amateur side West Auckland, County Durham, a team made up chiefly of miners, nobly responded to his invitation. In scenes later dramatised for television, with Dennis Waterman as player-coach, they beat Red Star Zurich and Stuttgart en route to a 2-0 victory over Juventus and the improbable, if unofficial, title of world champions.

Europe - Industry and Railways

The ease with which English teams, at club and national level, dealt with foreign opposition did little to encourage the FA to undertake missionary work. The FA authorities appeared to have had little consciousness of any global mission, preferring the Little Englander view that English standards were high and that there was no point in being involved in such footling essays. Thus the missionary task was left to random groups of businessmen, tradesmen and servicemen, operating overseas, who wished to continue playing their favoured game in exile and who soon recruited members of the indigenous population to join them. The very action of working for or with local citizens obviously supplied a pleasant opportunity for such cheerful cross-national escapades.

Very significantly, there was a confluence of organic forces. Forms of folk football were in evidence across much of Europe. Much the same testimony as to fierce and mob-like pursuit is to be found, for example, in France as in England, usually under the name of 'socile'. Germany had also experienced the vigorous joys of old-time football. In Italy, especially in the Florence area, there was the rather more refined 'calcio'; in Russia 'lapto' was the nearest to an equivalent - and even the Inuit enjoyed a kick (or throw) about at 'kalajuit'. Once more we find evidence of the ubiquitous incidence of 'play', often with natural and spontaneous parallels, such as the collective forcing, by hand and foot, of an object towards a target. In some of these instances, the format had become more sophisticated, but for the same reasons adverted to in respect of the English convention, there had been neither motive nor desire to codify the pastime on any other than strictly local lines.

Now, because of exactly the new set of parameters, among them the escalation of national feeling and administration, there was a willing urgency to accept the definitive regulation first that intra-national and, second, that international, contest might be possible. The phenomenon witnessed in Britain of an agreed formula being eagerly embraced by hundreds already playing and habituated to some more primitive or localised version of football or other physical pastimes, was now to be repeated, writ large, on the continental front. Beyond that, there were hundreds more, excited by the modernistic signals being hoisted by the United Kingdom, who believed, accurately enough, that football was an intrinsic aspect of the new and future life.

Furthermore, the necessary material conditions were falling into place in continental Europe, as the 19th century advanced. Britain, it has been argued, was the first footballing country because it was the first industrialised and urbanised state. As the European nations themselves created industrial and urban components, normally accompanied, as in Great Britain, by a major upsurge in population, so were they in a propitious position to develop a football culture.

What is truly amazing is the velocity of that evolution. MCC dates its origins - there are one or two sagacious voices that put it earlier - as 1787; the Imperial Cricket Conference first met in 1909, a matter of 122 years separating the first formal national agency and the first formal international affiliation. The footballing analogue is the establishment of the English FA in 1863 and the first assemblage of FIFA (Federation Internationale de Football Association) in Paris in 1904, a pause of only 41 years, roughly a third of the cricketing hiatus. The poignancy of the comparison is underlined by the absence of England, ditto Scotland, Ireland and Wales, from the latter meeting of eight countries, and England's presence at the former, hosting representatives from just Australia and South Africa at Lord's.

Grudgingly, the English and Scottish FAs were represented at FIFA's congress in 1905, with Wales following in 1910 and Ireland in 1911, although it is hard to dodge the feeling that they turned up to keep a beady eye on the foreign upstarts, rather than with any degree of cooperative sentiment, an opinion borne out by a reluctance to be over embroiled even after World War I. It is of incidental interest that, when the Austrian ruled area of Bohemia joined FIFA, the Austrian and German authorities threatened to make other regional or 'particularist' FAs members, although, of course, Scotland and Wales had already created that precedent. Although not at first too effective, FIFA's proclaimed role was to regulate international fixtures and transfers, so perhaps the FA's aversion, given its self-perceived mastery of such topics, is understandable, if not entirely excusable. By 1914 FIFA had 24 member nations, each of them with an FA of sorts and almost all of them with an established league or similar championship.

The heady economic cocktail of industry, population, transport and town-life, as in Britain, was gulped aplenty in 19th century Europe. The complicated relation of cause and effect in that intoxicating mixture is less relevant to this study than the exhilarating football result. As in Britain, it was as if some inexorable law was being obeyed. Toss those ingredients into the cocktail shaker - and out popped football. It is true that, in the United States, the brew was a little wanting in its footballing effect, although other forms of professional sport were soon in place in an industrialised and urbanised North America.

As the workshop of the world, Britain was, initially, the commercial sun around which other economies orbited in a series of reciprocal trading relationships. Local overseas products complemented British exports. There were, for instance, the dairy products of Denmark or the wine of Portugal, as well as the cotton of the southern states of the USA, the wool of Australia or the precious metals of South Africa. Beyond that, and as the Victorian era wore on, Britain was the primary source of machinery, capital and technical skill for nations seeking to become industrialised. Hence one would have found the business names of Thornton in Austria and Russia; Wilson in France; Mulvaney in Germany; Cockerill in Belgium and Evans in Czechoslovakia.

The historian, Eric Hobsbawm, has written that 'the universal spread of football...is largely due to the works teams started by British owners, managers or skilled operatives in all parts of the continent.' The other side of the footballing medallion was the incalculable band of young men who visited Britain, drawn by its trading opportunities or to study, frequently in industrially orientated subjects, like engineering. They travelled back home, full of enthusiasm for many things British and for football in particular. These Anglophiles turn up often in the early annals of soccer in the newly flourishing nation-states of Europe.

These developing nations first desired British input for what John Stuart Mill called their 'infant industries' - and then, as they matured, wished to defend against British competition by protectionist practices. In 1860 a half of British capital investment had gone to Europe and the USA, but by 1914 it had declined to a quarter, as these emerging industrial economies ripened. More spectacularly, the actual amount of all international trade had burgeoned from £400m in 1840 to £2,000m in 1870, an amazing burst of sharp commercial energy and a breezy signal of the ascent of industrial manufacture and trade.

Within this context of soaring growth, Britain's proportion obviously fell, simply by token of other nations entering the industrial field. During the 19th century, therefore, British industrial output declined not, it should be emphasised, in total but as a fraction of the world's entire manufacturing productivity, from almost 40% to 15%. Conversely, Germany's proportion was lifted from 10% to 15% and Russia's from almost nothing to a more respectable 8%. France, an early runner in the manufacturing stakes, also, like Britain, saw her fraction fall from 30% to 10%. By 1900 most European nation-states had some semblance of an industrial economy.

The most telling example of these changes was the development of the railway. Not only was it an industry per se, it naturally lubricated the wheels of commercial intercourse for all the other industries. Moreover, as throughout the United Kingdom, it enabled football teams to fulfil, and also spectators to watch, fixtures that would have otherwise been difficult, if not impossible, to arrange. This substantially assisted the spread and acceptance of the accepted code of laws and conventions. With British managers and workers in situ, there were both the means and the men to make football happen.

Almost within days of Britain's first railway forays the United States, with the Baltimore and Ohio Railway Company in 1830, had, in fact, sprung into the railway age, and continental Europe was not far behind. The invention of the railways was, of course, no sudden and enchanting spell. It was the consequence of much practical work, including horse traction on rails, some of it overseas and not exclusively in northern England. This helps to explain the rapid spread of the railways. There were lots of engineers across Europe and America waiting for the pieces to fall into place, principally the application of steam to locomotion. Nonetheless, the first railways and, in most countries, the bulk of the rail system, were built by British contractors using British staff as well as British materials. Needless to say, the termini of many of these lines were industrial in character, for, on balance, freight was the primary and passengers the secondary motivation.

One more baleful aspect must be considered. Not least because of its vital role in the American Civil War, the railway quickly caught the attention of the military leaders, who soon spotted the potential of the railway train as a conveyor of soldiers and munitions. This was a significant political booster and a partial explanation of the state encouragement and, in some countries, control or ownership, of the national railways. The famous English historian A.J.P. Taylor always argued that one major immediate cause of the 1914-1918 War was the tortuous set of plans staff officers had drafted from rail timetables for, in emergency, the rapid transit of troops. Once embarked on that unstoppable process, thousands of soldiers were mobilised and rapidly transported to, literally, their battle stations; the die was cast.

The French railway from St.-Etienne to Andrezieux had been a horse-drawn freight service from 1828 which changed to steam and added passengers as early as 1832. By that same year the St. Etienne/Lyons railway was also completed, and the first international railway, Strasbourg to Basle, was opened in 1841. By that date, France had 350 miles of railways. By 1902 the figure was 29,000 miles. Germany's rail industry was similarly productive. The first German steam line was Nurnburg/Furth, opened in 1835; by the outbreak of the First World War, a united Germany could boast almost 40,000 miles of track. Italy was not far behind. The Naples to Portici line was completed in 1839 and, as Italy also became a unified state after the 1860s, so did it gradually develop a major national rail network.

Spain, another country of footballing destiny, was a trifle slower, railway construction being delayed by the mountainous terrain of much of the Iberian Peninsula. The steam-driven track from Barcelona to Mataro was the first such railway, but, toward the end of the century, Spain had 8,000 miles of rail. Sweden, another pioneer football nation, had railway connections from 1856, with the 1862 Stockholm to Gothenburg link its first major railway. Russia had horse-drawn traction from 1836 and made a quick translation to steam locomotion in 1837. Its first major railways were Warsaw (then, as periodically it often was, in Russian hands) to the Austrian frontier, opened in 1848 and the 400 miles Moscow/St. Petersburg line, completed in 1851. There was great momentum from the 1860s. By 1900 Russia had 33,000 miles of railways and, by the time of the 1917 revolution, that figure had leapt to 44,000 miles. From Tolstoy's *Anna Karenina* to Boris Pasternak's *Dr Zhivago*, the train would play its distinctive part in Russian literature. Contrary to some Soviet propaganda, Russia had taken many steps towards industrialism before the 1917 Leninist Revolution, to the point where industrial unrest was a major contributory cause of the uprising.

The importation of railways and manufacturing into other European countries and, indeed, throughout other parts of the world, created a network that soon required apposite cross-national communications of other kinds, such as time-telling, postal and telegraphic - and, later, telephonic - co-operation. Just as Britain had established unities of trains, clocks, letters and telegrams, so now did the world at large need systematic schemes for the same purposes and reasons.

In short, in quick succession, much of Europe underwent the socio-economic transformation that Great Britain had experienced and, by dint of that showing, these European towns and cities were ripe for the fruition of professional sport. Three catalytic elements - the scattered vestiges of kicking pastimes in some situations; the strong presence of football-mad Britons; students and businessmen returning to their native lands with a delectable taste for soccer - guaranteed that, usually, the most popular recreational and then professional sport would be soccer.

Europe - North Western Nations

Sometimes the origins of football's continental Grand Tour followed the English pattern with a strange similarity. English schoolboys and English teachers were playing football and other Anglo-Saxon pastimes in and around Swiss private schools from the 1850s, while many young, sports-crazed Englishmen were to be found working in the growing Swiss trading centres. This led to the formation in 1860 of the Lausanne Football and Cricket Club, represented, oddly enough, at the FA meeting in 1871 that set up the FA Cup. Switzerland was one of the first nations to adopt the standard English model of alliance and competition.

The Swiss FA was established in 1895, and was a founder member of FIFA, while there were regional leagues and then a national championship based thereon from 1898. Nursing its reputation for political disinterest and military neutrality, Switzerland provided FIFA - and later UEFA - with headquarters. By the end of the century there were dozens of football clubs in Switzerland. Their names have the genuine ring of hearty English fellowship: Basle Old Boys; Berne Young Boys; Zurich Young Fellows and Zurich Grasshoppers, still playing in the blue and white quarters of Blackburn Rovers, one of their inspirations.

The English proclivity of gentlemen kicking off and then passing the ball to the workers lived again in Sweden, where British Embassy staff in Stockholm appeared to have played football. The by now usual combination of expatriate British and Swedes educated in Britain was responsible for the game developing. Orgryte IS, founded in 1887, was the kind of multi-disciplinary sports club familiar in the Scandinavian countries. Its footballing initiative led to some success for the game by the 1890s in Gothenburg, where Scottish shipyard workers had earlier proffered a plebeian account of soccer amidst the gantries and cranes of the city's docklands. Soon Stockholm also boasted two or three clubs, including Hammerby.

DIASPORA · EUROPE

David Goldblatt, in his book *The Ball Is Round*, has fluently described how, as in Belgium, Holland and Denmark, the Swedes out-Heroded Herod apropos English Corinthian values and were quite rigid about the amateur code. Perhaps more than anywhere, the clash of class-orientated teams remained overlong in divisive manner. Orgryte IS, for example, were as defiantly middle class as IFK Gothenburg were audaciously working class, a Marxist cameo of the class war that produced ructions on and off the field when such duos met. Sweden is not considered now to be the land of footballing hotheads and hooligans, but such was the truth, and some of this roughness attended the efforts of the national team to promote a calmer unity. The traditional fixture with Denmark began in 1908, with Swedish supporters encouraged to vent their tantrums on the unfortunate Danes, an intriguing gloss on the old motto of governments seeking to distract from domestic troubles by foreign adventure.

As for Denmark itself, British residents in and Danish visitors returning to Copenhagen, where Copenhagen Boldklub was formed in 1876, gave an early lead. British sailors were also to be observed playing the game around the dockyard precincts of Copenhagen and Danish workers soon adopted the sport. BK Frem, another Copenhagen side, this one of more proletarian makeup, was formed in 1886. Frem was to Boldklub as Blackburn Rovers was to Old Etonians. The Danish FA dates from 1889 and Denmark, as we noted, fared well in the first Olympic competitions. In 1911 Sheffield Wednesday, in a characteristically British footballing visitation to the continent, played the inaugural game on Copenhagen's Idraetsparken arena, continental Europe's first-ever purpose built stadium. Like its British equivalents, it had three working class terraces and a middle class stand on the fourth side.

In Holland, sports clubs, many with a cricketing bias, were formed in the 1870s, further examples of English missionary zealotry, but also of Dutch Anglophilia. Team names like Go Ahead Eagles and Be Quick are memorials to this Anglicised heritage. Haarlemse FC, started in 1879, was one of many cricket and allied sports clubs that gradually turned to football as the century wore on and where Dutchmen who had found a taste for Anglo-Saxon culture discovered a comfortable setting. Then Dutch industrial workers developed an appetite for football. Enschede, where many Lancashire textile operatives had found employ, was another seminal centre for Dutch football. Leagues evolved and railways developed; football became widespread ~ and Holland was to be France's major adjutant when FIFA was formed.

167

Belgium was another up and coming polity that evinced veneration for British political values and approbation for British cultural models, football among them. Great Britain was remembered in the Low Countries as the high-spirited liberator of those areas from Napoleonic tyranny. Belgium owed the additional debt, for Britain had been its safeguard when, in turn, its inviolability had been recognised on its separation from the Netherlands by the 1839 Treaty of London. Now the United Kingdom was the ideal template, with its technical know-how and parliamentary democracy, for the aspiring, if moderately sized, modern state.

The toing and froing was hectic indeed. British businessmen and engineers were busy in Belgian commercial centres; Belgian scholars were busy in English colleges. Football was the pleasing accessory to both exercises. The main foci for Belgian trade were the capital, Brussels, and the ports of Bruges and Antwerp. The English managers and workers played football and invited their Belgian counterparts to join in; the schools and colleges of those cities, many of them with English teaching staff, included football among the activities on offer. It formed the perfect equation for football fervour.

The British were heavily engaged in the rudimentary introduction of football into Germany. Commercial connections were once more the key. Teams were playing in Bremen and Hanover from 1880, while members of the Anglo-American club in Hamburg were playing football in 1881 and a club was started there in 1887. Ports, then, with their organic links with British traders and sailors, were a key to the expansion of football - the North Sea and Baltic littoral was significant in the beginnings of German soccer. Next, three clubs were established in Berlin, now capital of the unified German state, and, as in Spain - and as in England, with George V's attendance at the Cup final in 1914 - the interest of the Hohenzollern royal house gave some regal kudos to the expanding sport. Organised football was being played in German high schools by the 1890s, although there is some evidence of informal essays in the game twenty years beforehand.

By 1914 there were close on 300 clubs in Germany, with most of the large cities, like Leipzig or Stuttgart, represented. It has been estimated that roughly 10,000 to 12,000 players were regularly active by this time. The British social echoes are pervasive. There were prudish religious and anxious political doubts about football, indeed, about Anglo-Saxon influence in some quarters. As in England, it was largely an alliance of progressive middle class and aspiring lower class men who tried to push the game onwards, arguing that the folk game played in pre-modern Germany was a true ancestor of the new football. In 1900 the Deutscher Fussball Bund or FA was formed, with its headquarters in Leipzig; attempts were made to set up a national championship in the following years, and, prophetically, there were stirrings - a club was formed in Essen in 1907 - in the Ruhr, currently evolving into Germany's leading industrial region.

France, where, in spite of its enduring agricultural image, industrialism, encouraged by the greedy demands of the Napoleonic Wars, was developed earlier than among its neighbours, should have proved fecund ground, the more so as there was a prehistory, perhaps consequent on France's proximity to Britain, of folk football in the country. The very presence of a manufacturing complex, with a sufficiently well-to-do consumer base, to process the close on 4 million bicycles wobbling around France by the outbreak of World War I, is a reminder of its industrial legacy. All those cycles promoted what is still a popular professional sport in French eyes. Rugby, too, quickly gained some standing in France, principally in the South-west around Toulouse.

Nonetheless, the anecdotes are related of British sailors and, alternatively, of British graduates playing football in 1872 in the port of Le Havre. Anecdote, too, tells of cricket being played in France at even earlier times. The realistic question is not when the game was first played, but whether it was sustained and extended. It was to be 1891 before there was an organisational coup, when three clubs were founded in Paris, two of them - White Rovers and Standard Athletic Club - by expatriate Britons and the other - the self-consciously labelled Le Club Francais - by students with some British collegiate experience. The existing and exclusive Parisian sports clubs, established in the 1880s to supply a dose of physical medicine, of the English public school and varsity prescription, to the allegedly effete sons of the French ruling and upper classes, felt obliged to add football to their list of corporeal medications. Racing Club and Stade Francais were two such agencies that ran football teams from the mid-1890s, so that Paris was the dominant force in early French football circles.

Just as in Britain, it was the provincial industrial areas, many of them with British links, which disputed the hegemony of the capital city. The Lille, Lens and Nimes districts and the hinterland of the ports like Marseilles and those on the Channel coast were the most fruitful. Just as in Britain, there were black spots where football was more or less ignored, and, indeed, France, like Spain and Italy, took some time to centralise the sport and establish a genuinely national structure. Nevertheless, by 1914 there were approaching 200 football clubs in France.

Europe - Central and Eastern Nations

British commerce, and particularly banking, boomed in Vienna, a lively and progressive location. The avant garde home of classical light music and of psychoanalysis, it was anxious to be at the cutting edge of modern taste and it was a prime target for British consumer goods and cultural influence. The Vienna Cricket Club played soccer against a team raised from among the mainly Scottish gardeners of the Baron Rothschild estate in 1894. That was the dramatic beginning of football in Central Europe. With Austrian infusions, those two teams, the one middle class, the other working class, prospered as Wiener Amateurs and First Vienna. The former, when still known as Vienna Cricket, sponsored Der Challenge Cup as early as 1897, drawing in teams from across the Austro-Hungarian Empire. In 1898, in another aping of British footballing births, operatives at a Viennese millinery founded the works team Wiener Arbeiter FK, later Rapid Wien, and, by 1910, Vienna had formed a football league for the city and its surrounds.

Central Europe was visited by several English professional teams in the pre-1914 years and it appears to have had a special attraction for British coaches, like the legendary Lancastrian Jimmy Hogan, who contributed, inter alia, to the development of Austrian football. Hungary fell willing victim to the football disease, the gymnasia of Budapest being especially vulnerable to the infection. By the turn of the century there were a dozen or so clubs in Budapest and in 1901 the first Hungarian championship took place. Ujpest Sport TE, in 1885, was probably the first of these clubs, but, in yet another example of class-crossed development, MTK, originally the Athletic Club of Budapest (1888), and the well-known Ferencvaros (1899), established an enduring rivalry on bourgeois/proletarian lines. At the same time, and prototypically, MTK was the sporting home of dissident liberals and academics, opposed to the conservatism and centralism of the Austro-Hungarian Empire. Nationalism, that pungent brew, was boiling up in many parts of Europe; football was the aperitif that heralded nationality, as well as the toast that hailed its success.

Such sentiments were enthusing the intellectuals and independent-minded middle class of Prague, the patent focus for Czech nationalism. Football was a little slower arriving here, but a youthful and ambitious intelligentsia spotted the fascinating linkage of English football and English liberalism. Slavia Prague, founded in 1892, acted as political, literary and sporting club, its colours those of Czech nationalism. Almost on sociological cue, Sparta Prague was formed as the bastion of the capital's working class support. The two rivals supplied the substance of Czech football, aided by the normal backing of trips from British teams and trainers (Scotland's Johnny Madden coached Slavia Prague from 1905 to 1938) and the customary individual vocational visitors. Interestingly, Hungary, less of a threat to imperial authority than the fiery Czechs, was allowed by the Austrian authorities to mount a national eleven - it played against Austria itself as well as in the first Olympic tournaments - whereas such Czech aspirations, including the notion of a Bohemian FA, were resolutely thwarted by the Austrian government.

That overt authoritarianism is a salutary reminder that nationalist and democratic privileges were looked upon with distaste by the imperial heads. Elsewhere in the Russian, Austro-Hungarian and Ottoman Empires, there was a reluctance to encourage spectator sports, for, in an echo of Hanoverian and Regency Britain (and, as we shall later remark, the British Empire) there was a dread of crowds of spectators gathering for sports events, as they might have turned into excuses for political and social misbehaviour.

Nonetheless, the pressure of urban and industrial change was powerful and the great cities of Central Europe had soon developed popular football clubs. If football came more slowly to Eastern and South-eastern Europe, it was because of the combined effect of reactionary politics, demonstrated by a clampdown on dissidence, and primitive economics, demonstrated by the continuation of rudimentary agrarian practices.

The point is underlined by the lack of football in the pre-1914 era in areas like Poland, partitioned among the three Russian, German and Austro-Hungarian Empires and starved both of political independence and undue industrial development. Where the British had penetrated - such as Lodz, the textile centre - there was football, but it must be remembered that, when there was no supporting cast of indigenous men in professional occupations or, indeed, permanent British residents, evolution was often blocked. In Krakow, heading towards some degree of industrial potential in the south of Poland, aspiring youth struggled to form a couple of teams - Cracovia and Wisla - just before the First World War. The picture was much the same in Bulgaria, fast under the Ottoman heel. It was late in the 1890s before football was sighted there. Swiss teachers, among them one George de Regibus, introduced the game to the youngsters of Sofia, where a club was started in 1912, but there was little or no other development before 1914.

Romania fared better. The national construct was more pronounced, with King Carol I a regal fan and industry better established. The Standard Oil Company in Ploesti meant there were British managers and technicians here present to give heart to the nascent sport, while the country's Colentina textile manufacturers also attracted British staff with soccer interests. There were some footballing ventures by Romanians returning from foreign studies, among them Iuliu Weiner, an enterprising dentist who had trained in Great Britain. He was instrumental in starting the first Romanian club in 1899 in Arad, and, with Bucharest fielding teams, an infant FA was established in 1909 and a basic competition inaugurated.

Romantically, it is nostalgic to recall the British sailors and builders who, in the 1870s, kicked a football around in, respectively, the port of Zadar and the commercial centre of Rijecka in the Balkan regions that would become Yugoslavia. A kickabout without some guarantee of continuity, either through a permanent British work-force or a bunch of admiring converts among the students and young people of the native population, could, of course, lead down a blind alley. Realistically, it was the mid 1890s before football was properly introduced into Belgrade, with a tailor's son, schooled in Vienna, Hugo Bale, the chief protagonist. Here again it was university students and other middle class men, fired by dreams of nationalist and liberal progressivism, who followed in those footsteps. Greater Serbia, the Hawks, HASK and Serbian Sword were amongst the clubs formed, the political message sometimes clear in the medium of their titles. Belgrade and Zagreb were, obviously enough, the key foci and, in 1912, Croatia felt strong or brave enough to form an FA and to embark in 1913 on a species of national tournament.

Athens, the home of British and other North-western European professionals and rich Greeks of Anglophile education and affection, was predictably the location for the first football to be played in Greece in the 1890s. By the 1900s there was the semblance of league soccer and national organisation. Panhellenic, very much the creature of well-to-do Greeks and their rich British counterparts was a leading team, and, as in the early years of English football, much of the activity centred on the university and the armed services.

Just as the Swiss were the secondary missionaries of football in Italy and elsewhere, so did the Greeks bring the game to the Ottoman Empire. Along with players from other Christian minorities, the usual parcel of Brits amongst them, they were shooting and dribbling in Constantinople (modern Istanbul) and Smyrna (Izmir) from the early 1890s. This was something of a concession, for the Ottoman Empire wielded weapons of the most intransigent conservatism, double-bladed swords of political authoritarianism and theological traditionalism. A pupil of the Naval Academy, Fuad Husnu Bey, is credited with being the first Turkish footballer, despite the fact that his team, the Black Stockings, were reported to the police, just as, all those years before, the self-righteous and self-interested clergy and squires of England had used the law to halt football.

The Young Turk movement, with its willingness to consign antiquated traditions to the scrap heap, was instrumental, from 1908, in aiding the future of football in the old Ottoman Empire. It strongly influenced the more reformist administration that desperately endeavoured to enable the region to catch up with Western technology and armaments. Moderation was lightly afoot. In 1905 a Constantinople league had been created and two or three Turkish teams joined the existing handful of expatriate teams. Among the Turkish clubs were Galatasaray (1905) and Fenerbahce (1907), both formed by the pupils of elitist schools in the city. A Constantinople association was formed in 1913, at which juncture there were 5,000 regular players, a heartening number, about half as many as for the whole of Germany at that point.

After 1918, the British army, active in these Eastern European regions as an occupying force, lent the ready help of footballing tommies to the cause. Beforehand, German troops, martially operational in various parts of Eastern Europe, had had the more benign and pacific effect of also spreading the football code there. That said, most of the mainstream development of soccer in these parts would have to await the dictates of modernism, in the joint guise of nationalism and industrialism.

Generally speaking, the aftermath of the First World War afforded some breathing space for the development of football in Central and Eastern Europe. There was an abrupt switch from empire to nation-hood, from two or three large entities to numerous independent polities, and, as we have noted, football was soon recognised as a superb nationalistic standard bearer. The Russian

Revolution, for all its grim faults, did have the like effect of encouraging the growth of football across the wide tracts of the old Romanov Empire. The Soviet Union quickly understood the literal potency of the political football at home and abroad.

There had been some pre-1917 action in what would become the USSR. One hears tell of the usual rumours of British sailors in Odessa or British residents in St. Petersburg at footballing play, but these observations were, historically speaking, freakish, in that they had negligible impact locally. The cosmopolitan port of St. Petersburg fostered half a dozen teams of varied expatriates, but it was 1896 before Georges Duperont, an enthusiast of Franco-Russian roots, contrived to form 'Sport', formally the St. Petersburg Circle of Amateur Sportsmen, with players of indigenous stock. The foreign teams, chiefly based on the city's textile industry, began to admit Russian players, and all the teams competed for the Aspeden Cup, itself donated by an English businessman.

Russia, judged by the benchmarks by which Western Europeans assessed their civilisation, was backward. The tension between the longing for modernisation, associated with English technology and culture, and the yearning for traditional, if outmoded, fashions, were probably more pronounced than in other parts of Europe. To some extent, this contradictory stricture applied to football. One suspects, and there is some testimony to this effect, that the expatriate community, in the worst traditions of such bodies, was inclined toward condescension, and, before the onset of war in 1914, almost all their involvement was ended.

Moscow was another staging post. Two intrepid Lancashire textile merchants, Clement and Harry Charnock, were involved with the Vicoul Orozov textile company at Orekhovo, Moscow's incipient industrial environ. Their advertisement in *The Times* for British employees might be adopted as a descriptor for the whole of the global spread of football. They called for 'engineers, mechanics and clerks, capable of playing football well'. It was a recycling of the earlier English habit of appointing competent workers who could also energise the foundry football team or play the cornet in the colliery brass band. The firm grew and diversified and was renamed, thankfully, OKS, and then, less obligingly, Morozovsky. Its football team, Morozovtsi Orekhovo Suevo Moskva, something of a tongue-twister for the exuberant fan to shout, welcomed Russian workers to its ranks. With another echo of British social history, it was now encouraged by the authorities as an antidote to vodka and political unrest, two elements of pre-Leninist life that were an inseparable and fatal mix. As OKS Moscow, they won the Moscow Championship five times in the Czarist era, but then were taken over by the Soviet Electrical Trades Union after 1917. This time they were more famously re-titled Moscow Dynamo.

Despite this adventure, and the growth of a rail passenger network radiating out of Moscow that made possible other footballing enterprise, the Czarist regime was suspicious - shades of 18th century Britain - of the lower orders being involved overmuch in sport. It was, thought the Romanov autocracy in line with the Hanoverian administration, a mask for insurrection and a deterrent to hard work. Rather too late in the fateful day, the Czarist government realised that the thought had been father to the wish and that its oppressive actions were actually fermenting insurgency. Football was grudgingly recognised as a relatively peaceful emblem of modernity. Under the statesmanlike guidance of Georges Duperont, an All-Russia Football Union, chiefly comprised of Moscow and St Petersburg clubs, was established. International contest followed, at the Stockholm Olympics in that same year. There they met and were defeated by Finland, still technically, and until after the 1917 Revolution, a Grand Duchy of the Russian Empire, and by another country - Norway. Norway itself had only achieved freedom from its union with Sweden in 1905, and was yet another new nation-state that had learned its football from animated students returning from a year or so of studies in Great Britain. By the same token, the first president of the Latvian FA, for Latvia was a Russian possession until 1918, was an Englishman.

Europe - the Latin Nations

The Latin countries of Spain, Portugal and Italy were destined to surge to the forefront of European and world football. Turning first to the Iberian peninsula, British engineers, soldiers and supporting personnel mined and defended the copper deposits of Andalusia, under the shingle of the Rio Tinto company, and played football in their leisure hours. At the Rio Tinto base of Huelva, Spain's first football club, Recreativo de Huelva, was formed and played, initially, other teams of British workers. Later and stronger challenges emerged. Colliers and shipyard operatives carried football with them from England to what was to be the important Basque industrial district around

Bilbao. The local youth, some of whom had visited England as students, took up the gauntlet. In 1898 they formed Bilbao FC, while Athletico Bilbao was started in 1901, both teams being of mixed British and Spanish composition in those seminal days, although the latter was to prove the durable survivor. The British presence and influence naturally faded and soon a convention only to utilise players of Basque family was accepted.

About the same time, over in Castile, Madrid was injected with a mild dose of soccer fever. The players in the innovatory Sky club in Madrid were chiefly teachers and students with experience of studying and footballing in England. As elsewhere, the progressive element among the Spanish elites lived in admiration of the English liberal and cultural model. It split after some years into New Madrid FC and Madrid FC, later to be Real Madrid, its 'royal' designation some reflection of the keen interest of King Alfonso XIII. The Coronation Cup of 1902 was played with his blessing and won by Athletico Bilbao. This was the first of the King's Cups that served initially as the major Spanish national competition.

In 1899, as legend has it, a Swiss founder member of FC Zurich, Hans Kamper, raised a team of fellow foreign workers to play against a team of British matelots - and the Barcelona club was born. In 1900 Angel Rodriguez, a trainee engineer, immediately raised the Espanyol team - the 'Real' prefix was granted later - of Catalonian players. In 1901 there was a small Catalan League and, by 1904, even a Catalan FA. It was fast progess for the somewhat introspective Catalonia. However, that level of 'particularism', so peculiar to Spain, with its large, semi-autonomous and often inaccessible territories, made national advancement very slow. It was not unlike the fourfold division of the United Kingdom. Other clubs were founded before the Great War of 1914-1918, such as Deportivo La Coruña, usually with that same kind of regional tie. It would be 1913 before a Spanish FA finally struggled into existence and 1920 before a national eleven strode onto the field, although, to be just, the war halted almost all European international soccer in between those two occasions.

In Portugal it was, once more, that compound of British residents and indigenous students with UK college experience which was to be in the van of development. Two early Portuguese leaders in this regard were Guilherne Terreira Pinto Basto and Cosme Damaio. The former pioneer returned in 1884 from England, having completed his studies there, and endeavoured to introduce the game he had come to love into his native land. By the 1890s football was dominantly the national game. The famed Benfica club was opened, with English connections, in 1904. Unlike the other colonial and imperial powers, including Britain, which were frightened by the political threat of mass gatherings in their possessions, Portugal did not altogether discourage the spread of the sport to their African colonies. Portugal - as the fluently vibrant Eusebio would exemplify in post-war European football - was the first country to benefit from an influx of black African players.

In Italy, predestined to enjoy a glittering football future, that same combine of visitors to and from the United Kingdom, acted as the lever. Ineluctably, it was the industrial and heavily urbanised areas that attracted purposeful attention. Northern Italy, home of Italian industrialism, was the focus.

In 1887 a commercial representative involved in optical equipment, Eduardo do Bosio, returned from a business trip to England and recruited the clerks of his Turin firm for football duties. Soon there would be three Turin teams, although two were soon to merge. The founder of Torino, Vittorio Pozzo, had studied in Bradford and Manchester, where he had befriended and learned much from Charlie Roberts, the Manchester United skipper. In 1897 students of wealthy Turin families founded Juventus, its title a deliberate plea for youthful involvement..

In 1898, British and Swiss merchants, headed by Alfred Edwards, gathered together to form Milan Cricket and Football Club, later AC Milan. AC Milan won its first championship pennant in 1901. The rival Internazionale Milan was established in 1908, the 'Internazionale' logo perhaps redolent of the communist politics and Italian working class image of the club, although, at first, it had a large Swiss intake. Milan was to emulate Turin as a major Italian football centre.

There was to be another example of the close ties between Italy and Switzerland. In neighbouring Genoa, British residents, under the auspices of the British Consul, had founded a cricket and football club in 1892. In 1897 the club captain, an English medical practitioner and goalkeeper, Dr James Spensley, invited Italians and other non-British gentlemen to join, and a flourishing and truly cosmopolitan football eleven emerged. They played the three Turin based Italian clubs - and won the first Italian Championship in 1898. Indeed, they won six of the first seven such tournaments. Swiss players continued to dominate several Italian teams, although, as in Spain and other parts of Europe, there was a nationalist backlash. The all-Italian teams

Sampierdarense and Andre Doria (much later to portmanteau themselves as Sampdoria) were formed in Genoa.

There were developments elsewhere in Italy. In 1892 a fencing and gymnastic club in Pro Vercelli in Piedmont started a football team, fortified by Swiss players. In Rome Lazio was formed by sportive army officers in 1900. Palermo (1899) and Naples (1904) were other sides to be derived from English-style cricket and football cliques, whilst Bologna was founded by Italian students and British residents in 1909. Other teams in the south of Italy were of a post-war vintage, such as Cagliari and Salerno. Officially, Fiorentina came a little later, in 1926, but its origins have been traced to a meeting in Florence in 1907 of three Englishmen with a zest for soccer.

Rather like the second phase of English football history, when the industrial north out-gunned the south, including London, the opening chapter of the Italian story saw its industrial north in the ascendant, with its middle and southern sections, as distance travel was still a cumbrous exercise and often antiquated agricultural practice was still the main economic activity, lagging behind. The Italian soccer tale reflects that of Europe in general, with its industrial base, its English roots and its middle class protagonists, but, as a slightly later comer to the football feast, it also exemplifies another element. Religious proselytisation often advances in waves, with fanatical converts, sometimes from alien cultures, taking up the challenge. So it was with the football crusade. By the last decade of the 19th and the first decade of the 20th centuries, citizens of nations other than the United Kingdom were picking up the cudgels, the Swiss, as the origins of Italian football demonstrate, foremost among them.

By the commencement of the First World War in 1914, it might be claimed that the great majority of European capital cities, industrial centres and major ports had a football club. Much of the football was still unsophisticated, and one should not be dazzled by the primeval mention of clubs that, much later, would startle the world, but which were then but ragged bunches of schoolboys, toffs or workmen. For all that, it was the staggering result of a relatively short exercise in sporting enterprise.

The common denominator is what David Goldblatt cleverly terms 'the informal empire' in *The Ball Is Round*. In South America, the port of call of our next chapter, as well as in Europe, the British enjoyed a steady presence. It was not just the official British Empire. A host of traders, engineers, adventurers, plus a phalanx of attendant teachers, administrators, diplomats and other professional men, brought football to this unofficial empire. They did so as part of the conveyance of many aspects of 'English' life, for the top political and economic dog, as witness the Americanisation, the 'Cocacolaisation', of today's world, tends to spread cultural as well as material wares. Very thoughtfully, David Goldblatt has also clarified the mass of complications for us and he has factored in all the many nuances of regionalism, class-consciousness, political ideology and religiosity that here hindered and there accelerated the ongoing evolution of football and gave it some idiosyncratic colourings.

He has explained how, at bottom, English values, as well as some new respect for the English language, were much admired by continental elites, especially in respect of civil rights. Great Britain was not only the workshop of the world; it was the haven of democratic freedom and the rule of law. Furthermore, it was the salon of popular cultural fashions. These included the physical pastimes that were welcomed by communities concerned about bodily ill health and effete mentality. Football, alluringly simple and temptingly irresistible, was in the van, as, socially, England occupied large tracts of the European mainland.

CHAPTER ELEVEN

DIASPORA; THE SPREAD OF FOOTBALL TO SOUTH AMERICA AND ELSEWHERE

BOCA JUNIORS; Newell's Old Boys; Racing Club - the names have an English ring, but the teams are South American. If anything, South America took more avidly to football than the European continent, although the mode of conveyance of the sport - through businessmen and tradesmen working in the region or students returning thereto - was, in that respect, very similar.

South America - the Background

The British economic influence in South America in the latter part of the 19th century was immensely potent. The flourishing triumphs of the industrial revolution released vast amounts of capital and South America was a prime target for investment. Britain had shifted from being a conventional imperial power, swapping manufactures for raw materials. Until well into the 19th century, two thirds of her foreign trade had been of this character, but, by the last decades of the Victorian period, a quarter involved the exchange of manufactured goods, while, significantly, another quarter was bound up with invisible earnings. By the end of the Edwardian era, the annual average visible trade deficit was £140m, but the combined profits of shipping, insurance and brokerage and especially interest and dividends from investments zoomed to £346m, yielding a net balance of £206m. The United Kingdom was suddenly less the workshop and more the high street bank of the world.

Indeed, Britain invested more in the American continent than in Britain itself. Readers of Anthony Trollope's *The Way We Live Now* (1875), and watchers of the brilliant television adaptation of that splendidly pessimistic novel, may recall that the crooked financier, Melmotte, persuaded unwary punters to invest their all in the South Central Pacific and Mexican Railway. Trollope perhaps had in mind some recent dirty work at the stockbroking crossroads involving the Santo Domingo Loan, the Costa Rica Loan, the Paraguay Loan and the Honduras Inter-oceanic Railway Loan, all of which came under parliamentary scrutiny in the early 1870s. They indicate something of the fever that attended the lure of manifold investment in that faraway continent. At this time no less than a third of British cotton exports were shipped to South America, while the guano of Peru, the nitrates and copper of Chile and the beef of the Argentine pampas made the return trip.

British money was represented by a strong British presence in South America. Argentina was a major example. By the 1860s one in five - over 30,000 - of the inhabitants of Buenos Aires was British. It makes for an intriguing example of colonialism - that 'informal empire' again - without recourse to armed occupation or politico-administrative responsibility. Countries like Argentina, Chile and Uruguay were sometimes known as 'honorary dominions'. The introduction of football, then, was not just down to the caprice of odd eccentrics who had happened on South American shores. Although, inevitably, particular individuals contributed saliently, the base was a solid phalanx of British traders, engineers and the like.

It attached itself, of course, to populations largely European in ethnic type. As with the north European colonisation of North America and Australasia, the indigenous peoples had either been wiped out or reduced to abject penury, although, as in the West Indies and the Southern states of the USA, enslaved African labour had often been rife. For example, slavery was not abolished in Brazil until 1888, when 700,000 slaves were freed, over 50 years after slave emancipation in British territories and some quarter century after freedom had been granted slaves in the USA. Thus there was, in most parts of South America, a racial mix, with the European stock very dominant, a factor that would forcefully affect the format of football in the region.

In the wake of the successful attempt to cast off the metropolitan yolk in the American War of Independence, ending in 1783, and the subsequent creation of the USA, the European settlers to the south began similarly to dream of autonomy. Economic changes and political decline in the homelands of once mighty Portugal and Spain contributed thereto. In the outcome, and drastically cutting short a long and intricate political story, the Portuguese colonial empire of some score and more territories emerged in 1822, rather as had the USA, as a consolidated independent Brazil, while the main Spanish colonies retained something of their previous shape, contriving to become independent states. This occurred between 1811 (Paraguay) and 1830 (Venezuela), with the principal nation-states achieving self-determination just before and around the early 1820s. Argentina in 1816, Chile in 1818, Peru in 1821, Ecuador in 1822 and Bolivia in 1825 are illustrations. Further north, Mexico attained a somewhat precarious degree of self-government in 1825.

It was all done and dusted in a remarkably brief time, with British diplomatic and other help, and not merely for altruistic reasons, to the fore. The British government was not unhappy to see Spain and Portugal, old maritime rivals, reduced in status, not least in the aftermath of the loss, Canada apart, of their own North American possessions. These were exciting times for the nascent states, most of them opting immediately or some time later for republican forms of governance, following the American model of eschewing monarchy. This was a mark of their wish, once their political autonomy had been guaranteed, to be seen as and to act like modern powers, building cities and expanding commercially. The friendly and welcome British were on hand to provide the funds, at a price, and the expertise, at a cost. Part of this yearning for modernity included, no doubt, a measure of interest in new European cultural norms, amongst which football was a prime instance.

South America - the Football

Members of the English cricket club in Buenos Aires, where Thomas Hogg was a pioneer soccer organiser, were playing a little football as early as 1865, but the genuine national development came a trifle later. British workers and English schools, in particular A.W. Hutton's English High School, established in 1884 as a kind of Argentinean Eton or Harrow, ensured the game had a deep foothold. An Argentine league was established in 1891, only three years after the Football League had been set up, and just after the Scottish League had been instituted. It was chiefly composed of teams from Buenos Aires, but was extended more nationally in 1893 as the Argentine championship. By the early 1900s it boasted no fewer than four divisions.

Here were the teams with the English names, like Boca Juniors, Lomas Athletic and River Plate, most of them based in Buenos Aires. Even Independiente, formed by Italian incomers and locals, had its English connection, for its founders were employed by and had played for the City of London Store club in the Argentinean capital. It was an Irishman, Patrick McCarthy, who actually started Boca Juniors, but Italian immigrants soon became engaged in its fortunes. Similarly, by the turn of the century Italians and Frenchmen had joined with Britons in the establishment of the famed Racing Club of Buenos Aires. The railway centre of Rosario was one of the first provincial towns to give birth to football clubs, both of them under British auspices, with Newell's Old Boys also keeping the Union Jack flying in that city.

The entrepot cities on the River Plate were patently crucial bases for British trade, and thus across the river estuary to the north there was first commerce and soon football to be discovered in Uruguay. A British scholar at the University of Montevideo is credited with the first tentative forays into football in the country, but the capital city also housed the Central Uruguayan Railway Cricket Club, formed in 1891 for British engineers and the like. As elsewhere, and with the influence of other expatriate Europeans telling, it shortly turned more prominently, in 1893, to football. W.L. Leslie, a Scottish sports teacher, did in Montevideo what A.W.Hutton did in Buenos Aires, both men emulating the previous efforts of public school teachers with a yen for games back in the old country.

The names of Arthur Davenport, Frank Henderson, Frank Hudson and Roland Moor are also honourably recalled for their endeavours in this regard, and there is still a 'Liverpool' in Montevideo, although, once more, other immigrant nationalities, especially those of Italian origin, began to play a leading part. In 1898, Uruguayan-born men of home-grown Spanish stock proudly established the Nacional club, while the old Central Railways club was transformed, under indigenous management, into Peñarol in 1913. The two clubs rapidly became and remain the leading lights of the Uruguayan footballing firmament and, inevitably, stern rivals. The British helped set up the Uruguayan Football Association and a league was started in 1901 whilst, in 1909, it was a Scot, John Hurley, who coached at Peñarol and introduced the players to the passing game that had been perfected in his native land.

Evolution was swift and telling. There were games between Montevideo and Buenos Aires select teams in 1888, and in 1901 Uruguay played Argentina in

Montevideo, the first international match not to involve a British side. In 1902, in a compelling illustration of Anglicisation, the tea merchant and master grocer Thomas Lipton, ever something of a football buff, presented a cup for Uruguay/Argentina matches. Argentina's first match with Brazil was in 1907 and the Argentines organised a South American championship from 1910. There would later be a Robert Newton trophy in the region and from 1905 there were occasional and highly prized visits from top English sides, including Southampton, Everton, Tottenham Hotspur and Nottingham Forest.

Elsewhere in Spanish South America the same story was constantly retold of British influence yielding first to elitist leisure and then to populist fervour and finally the advent of professionalism. In spite of geographic restraints and cultural limitations, almost every nation fell before football's spell.

The British had cricket and tennis clubs in Lima, where Peruvian football took root in the 1890s among the local middle classes, while the working class Alianza Lima was underway by the 1900s. In Bolivia, the late 1890s saw the beginnings of teams formed in La Paz both by well-to-do English and Spanish residents and by railway workers. It was European and English-educated local students who introduced the game into Ecuador, where, perhaps predictably, it was the port of Guayaquil that proved to be the initial centre. It was also a port, Barranquilla, which initiated soccer in Columbia, where the city of Bogota was later fated to play a part in the story of British professionals' intrepid adventures overseas.

William Paats, a Dutch games teacher, brought football to the students and other enthusiasts of Asuncion in Paraguay, where clubs such as Olimpia, Guarani and Libertad were soon in business, and where league football and the embryo of an FA were in place by 1906. Chilean football began among the sports clubs, some of them inevitably British, of the port of Valparaiso. The game spread rapidly enough for Chile to have an organised federation active in 1895.

Apart from the Spanish-speaking states, the former Portuguese protectorate of Brazil was, of course, to evolve into possibly the most important of the world's football nations. Further north along the eastern coastlands of South America, Brazil was another locus for British investment. Football followed the trading flag. A São Paulo league of five teams began in 1901. Here Charles Miller, the son of a Brazilian mother and the scion of a rich Sao Paulo family, was an instrumental motivator. An experienced footballer, he returned to Brazil in 1894 after his studies and persuaded friends in the city's cricket club to try their luck at football. He was connected with the São Paulo Railway Company and, as well as building a team including railwaymen, he persuaded other businesses, such as the Brazil Bank and the English Gas Company to do likewise. Non-British residents started the aptly titled SC Internacional; German immigrants then formed SC Germania, whilst American and wealthy Brazilians also joined the fray. A São Paulo league came into being in 1901.

The Royal Navy, frequent visitors to South American ports, was a factor in bringing football to Rio de Janeiro and possibly stimulated the conception of the Santos club. Nonetheless, as in several European capitals, it was the playboys of the wealthy elite who were mainly responsible for launching the game. Oscar Fox, who had Swiss as well as rich Rio family connections, played football in Lausanne during his studies there. Having tried to inspire the Rio Cricket Club to aim for footballing glory, he did inspire the birth of the extremely exclusive Fluminese club. In a rarefied and Anglicised atmosphere, reminiscent of the Henley Regatta, other teams, such as America, Botafogo and Flamengo, followed suit. Rio de Janeiro started a league in 1905, but national consolidation was lethargic, a consequence of the inaccessible nature of the vast forested hinterland. Indeed, it would, unbelievably, be 1971 before Brazil contrived to form a fully national league.

The major Portuguese element naturally were pertinently engaged in Brazilian football, as were a number of German immigrants, but the white middle and upper classes were dumbfounded at and offended by the popularity of football among the majority black and mulatto races. Brazil, the last of the American nations to abolish slavery, witnessed a schismatic sporting rift on ethnic grounds, despite the efforts of some Portuguese to organise football in the poorer city environs. This racist problem, something of a forerunner of the troubles to afflict South Africa, continued well into the 20th century. Looking a little ahead, the Brazilian government banned the use of non-white players in the 1921 South American championship, known as the Copa Americana and played from 1916 on a league basis. Peter Hartland has described how the brilliant striker, Artur Friedenreich, progeny of a German father and a native black mother, was therefore omitted. Only six players are credited in football history with having scored a thousand goals - he was the first. A meagre eight were for the country of his birth.

These were the days when black or mixed race players were forced to iron their hair or whiten their faces with rice powder. Nine players quit the Brazilian team FC America when they signed a black footballer, while teams simply refused to play the Vasco da Gama club when they fielded black players. There was even a spurious attempt to hide racism behind a literacy test - this in a culture where black and many rural children had for generations been denied educational chances and where three quarters of the population, almost all black, were illiterate.

To complete the story with its happier conclusion, President Vargas, who took office in 1930, initiated a slightly more enlightened regime aimed at social inclusion and a more comprehensive national identity. After what seemed to be the style of many South American governments, Getulio Vargas mixed populist social legislation with rather more totalitarian traits, shifting the balance of power from country to city and from a local to a central focus. Astutely, his government encouraged football as one of the means to these ends of securing the 'Estado Novo', the 'new state', with its Mussolini-like trappings. By the late 1930s and early 1940s there were even some all-black combines in the upper echelons of Brazilian football. Something like the 'integrated culture' of late Victorian and early 20th century Britain, with a differential sharing of the same leisure and other forms, analysed in chapter eight, emerged. The richer white and the poorer black and mulatto populations approached football from their differing perspectives and both Brazilian society and Brazilian football were to be the joint beneficiaries.

The Brazilian story is a further example of how modern football has plainly been the creature of populous urbanism related to manufacturing and commercial economics. Between 1930 and 1964 Brazil's population increased and doubled from 33.5 million to 80 million, with the proportion of urban dwellers rising from a third to a half. The population has now doubled again to 160 million and there are seven cities with populations of over 1.5 million. Although agriculture remains a vital ingredient of the economy, industry is increasingly prominent. That pattern of the linkage of professional football to demographic and allied economic change was and remains a constant throughout the world.

That is to peer slightly into the future. In essence, football had made a major impact in the leading South American countries by 1914 - and the 1914-1918 war was to have two distinctive effects in the region. On the economic front, full-scale war was costly to Britain and there was much haemorrhaging of her investment in and a subsequent loss of her direct control of commercial activity on the South American continent. With this was lost substantial cultural influence. Alongside that, there was a natural feeling, emergent in several parts of the world, that nations should be their own masters. The South American economies and political systems were, in any event, maturing somewhat and there was less practical need for metropolitan intervention. From the 1900s onward, South American nations began to adopt the Spanish and Portuguese languages for official footballing purposes.

Mechanisation and urbanised populations had swiftly extended across the cities and towns of this vast region. Industrialism evoked more examples of that old European stand-by, the works team, such as the Companhia Progresso textiles firm in Bangu, Rio, formed in 1904. Such teams supplied a valuable opportunity for lower class players. In turn, the huge rises in population provided the paying support, when that should be required - by 1914, cities like Rio, Buenos Aires and São Paulo each soared to over a million inhabitants, more than a tenfold rise in half a century.

On the sporting front, World War I was not, for all its global title, as world-wide as World War II was to be. The South American states were fortunate to avoid the debilitating effects of those ghastly hostilities. South America largely evaded that lethal wound of a war, which is so central to the historical discourse of almost every European nation, especially at a juncture when their football was blossoming handsomely. From this one viewpoint at least, the South American polities, despite their own internal troubles, travelled serenely onwards. Peace was a bonus. There was no hiatus, as in Europe, in the continuum of South American football, the dividends of which were soon to become apparent.

The British Empire - the Background

What of the rest of the world? Given the extent of British trading and allied activity, there were, undoubtedly, sightings of football in all four corners of the world. There was reported, as early as 1913 and under the auspices of the navy, a match branded as China versus the Philippines. Outside of Europe and South America, however, the development of football remained fairly sporadic before 1914. The breakthrough in Central America, its hub the prevalence of the game in Mexico, was during the inter-wars years. The breakthrough in Africa and in parts of Asia, notably the Korean Peninsula, Singapore, Japan and eventually China, came chiefly in the post-imperial decades after 1945. It was then that the appropriate circumstances, created by the interplay of demographic, urban and industrial factors, took a hold in those regions.

The steady and occasionally spectacular progress of football toward world supremacy among sports thus leaves an intriguing lacuna. It is the curious case of the British bulldog that did not bark. With football in the gift of British trades and business people, one would have surely expected that a prime source for its fruition would have been the British Empire, that vast conglomeration of races and territories, with, about 1900, some 700 million souls covering 25% of the planet's land surface. It was here, self-evidently, that many Britons settled and made their homes, whereas in Europe and South America, their presence was more transitory, dependent on the demands of engineering, commerce and the like. It is true that there were resident British communities in some parts of both regions, but they were proportionately small compared with the extensive British settlements in, say, Canada or New Zealand.

But it was not to be. Nor has football always found a genuinely comfortable billet in the independent states that, in the aftermath of World War II, replaced the British colonial network in a rapid and wholesale exercise of political liberation. Apart from England itself in 1966, no former British possession, including the so-called 'home countries', has ever won the football World Cup. Chiefly because of sympathetic if synthetic attempts to ensure all global regions are represented in the competition, one or two, such as Australia or Trinidad and Tobago, have had walk-on parts in the drama, but rarely has one looked like taking the lead.

The explanation of this apparent anomaly is rather convoluted, partly because the regions themselves varied so much as to economic, climatic, ethnic and other conditions. However, the story begins, in general terms, back in the elitist culture associated with the English public school movement, described earlier in chapter three. In that this was the fulcrum for organised sport, within a context of social and political ascendancy, its influence on sport, as on everything else, throughout the British Empire, was immense per se. Moreover, it was also largely unopposed by any contradictory credo from among the indigenous populations. The soldiers, civil servants, lawyers and missionaries who formed the elites in many of the British possessions were of this kind. Their word, socially as well as politically, was law.

From the sporting standpoint, cricket was the main beneficiary of this narrowly imperial dispensation. Such has been its dominance in former British colonial areas that, in strict contrast to football, no non-former British territory has ever won the Cricket World Cup. One might add that, of course, England has never won it either...

Cricket - 'the holy game' - had the virtuous advantage of sanctity. Imperialism and Christianity were well nigh synonymous in the Victorian upper crust mentality: 'who dies for England sleeps with God', intoned the poet laureate, the egregious Alfred Austin, with an eerie presentiment of the beliefs of Islamic suicide bombers in the 21st century. Cricket, in turn, was, in the phrase of Lord Harris, cricket dignitary and Indian politico, 'the classroom of God', and the game served as the physical arm of this religio-colonial plan. Cricket was the essence of 'Englishry' and this identification was kept preciously. The cricket antiquarian Rev James Pycroft, wrote in 1851 that 'the game of cricket, philosophically considered, is a standing 'panegyric' on the English character; none but an orderly and sensible race of people would so amuse themselves', while *The Cricketer's Song*, first warbled in 1859, asserted that:

'Tis the King of Anglo-Saxon games - the type of our strength confessed;
Where the charm of perils bravely dared inspires each manly breast.'

Not content with urging the natural English affection for cricket, there was the additional argument that non-English people could not aspire to the sport. John Mitford, writing in *The Gentleman's Magazine*, in 1833, suggested that 'cricket is the pride and privilege of the Englishman alone. Into his noble and favourite amusement no other people ever pretend to penetrate'. The doggerel ran:

No German, Frenchman, or Fiji, will ever master cricket, sir,
Because they haven't got the pluck to stand before the wicket, sir.

The glorious adoption of cricket by native Indians and West Indians was something of an embarrassment to this brainless school of racial superiority. Extraneous characteristics - the wiliness and suppleness of the Indian; the energy and panache of the West Indian - had to be crudely invented to square the ethnic circle. Appallingly, such unscientific thoughts are still extant today. It never occurs to the inheritors of the Anglo-Saxon fallacy that if Pakistanis and Bajans have a genetic aptitude for cricket, then why not Egyptians and Cubans?

Thus cricket was pressed home hard in the dominions and colonies. James Walvin has written that 'the games that thrived in colonial society were those of the colonial elites'. Of course, rugby union, golf, tennis and yachting were established in addition to cricket, while hunting and polo were the leading equestrian pastimes in several parts of the Empire, underlining the military factor in the imperial equation. It is difficult to exaggerate the impact of the combine of Athleticism and colonialism. Although the Indian Civil Service had a mainly academic bias, recruitment for service in the other colonies included a major sporting requirement, justified on the grounds of it indicating a decisive personality and one vigorous enough to withstand unwholesome climates. Not for nothing did the Sudan become known as 'the land of blacks ruled by blues'.

Initially, games were the province of the rulers, offering them nostalgic leisure pursuits as a remembrance of home, and a morale-boosting exercise for the participants in what would now be called bonding. This frequently led to the English settlers being more English than the English. It was the kind of exaggerated chauvinism that made the Caledonian and Hibernian societies of the United States more extravagant than their homeland originals. Gradually, the indigenous populations came to adopt the games, especially cricket. The reasons for this were ambivalent. On the one side, there was a willingness to accept 'Englishry' and, so to say, collaborate with the occupation. On the other hand, there was also a sense of competing with and emulating the conquerors, utilising sport as the medium. Cricket, rarely football, offered this opportunity.

More pragmatically, cricket enjoyed what geographers call the impetus of a start. Codified and institutionalised earlier than football, it travelled more easily in the high noon of imperialism. Cricket was being played in most British colonies before the English FA had been formed. To take one instance, cricket was so advanced in the region that the South African Cricket Association was formed in 1890 and the first South African Coloured Cricket Association in 1897, both as the cricket governing bodies for their respective communities. At the hazard of undue simplicity, the nearest to a guideline might be to propose that cricket was carried to British colonies by civil servants and soldiers earlier than football was conveyed to non-British areas by businessmen and craftsmen.

Additionally, football enjoyed the significant bonus of many European and a few South American students and merchants visiting Britain and returning home to help spread the gospel of football.

Then time's winged chariot also took a sudden swerve. The public schools, having gifted football to a grateful nation, were scandalised, as we previously noted, by the rapid popularisation of soccer amongst the lower classes and came to regard it as anathema. One must appreciate the abruptness, in historical time, with which British football sprang from select top drawer pastime to populist industry. By way of aide memoire, in 1872 2,000 middle class folk languidly watched the first Cup Final, which had been competed for by fifteen clubs, all, directly or indirectly, connected with public schools. In 1913 120,000, the majority of them working class, watched the first final with a gate of over 100,000, for which had no fewer than 64 clubs, all of them professional, competed just in the first round proper. By 1914 there were 476 entries all told, involving qualifying rounds based on 24 districts.

Those forty short, busy years had transformed the sporting landscape. Many private schools snootily dropped soccer to concentrate on rugger. To some extent, the exclusive schools across the British Empire, such as Australia's so-called 'little Rugbys', parroted the fashion, just as, in early 20th century England, the rising tide of new grammar schools, consequent on the very hidebound and backward-looking 1902 Education Act, also aped their betters and turned to the handling code. Furthermore, one of the most startling elements in the sudden success of football as a spectator sport was, predictably enough, the marked expertise of the professional performers. Relatively small groups of white settlers could not hope to compete at the upper levels of the sport, while the colonies and dominions had neither the populace, nor the populace the wherewithal, to support expensive spectator sports. In New Zealand, Australia and South Africa, for example, such a compound of features ensured that the main option for a winter sport would be rugby. The British settlers brought strength and enthusiasm to what was for another century or more to be an amateur ethos, and did so with very favourable results.

PARISH TO PLANET

The British Empire - the Football

These comments are offered in the broadest of terms. Such were the differences from one part of the Empire to another that it might be helpful to add a word or two about a couple of specific areas.

Australia embraced imperialism most fervently. The heroic account of Australian sacrifice involved the 400,000 Australians, a substantial proportion of the male population, who fought in the First World War. 80,000 were killed and 200,000 wounded, sufficiently grim testimony to such resolve. By Occidental lights the small native population was of impoverished quality. As throughout the entire American continent, there was near genocide of the indigenous races, including the wholesale slaughter of the Tasman native. Although the Aborigines played some cricket, as, later, the Maoris played some rugby in New Zealand, Australasian sport was fundamentally the sport of white settlers. Cricket and horse racing were well established as spectator sports before football had had time to make much headway, while, importantly, Australian Rules football, first played in Victoria and with solid rugby links, was in solid place as early as 1865.

Australian Rules Football, like ice hockey in Canada or baseball in the USA, was embraced as a definitive national sport, especially after Australia was federated as a united state in 1901. All the British footballing originators, from pubs to churches, from schools and cricket clubs to the army and the work places, were recruited to form teams. The obsession, political as well as social, with Australian Rules left little room for soccer, although football did make a belated and rather tame arrival with British migrants in the latter part of the 19th century. What is astounding is that Australian Rules cup competitions and professional leagues were established in Australia prior to England's founding of such fashions in football. It was 1923 before the Australian FA was rightfully constituted.

Thus an unsurprising national loyalty offered resistance to attempts to introduce the alien Anglicised version, although, because of Australia's desire to create a broad-ranging sporting culture embracing all world games, rugby league and, especially after 1945, association football, fortified by emigrants from European countries other than the UK, ensured that Australians today enjoy four football codes at decent levels of excellence.

New Zealand, with the European residents outnumbering the indigenous population by four to one, remained defiantly Anglo-Saxon in tone and, not least with the nurseries of its schools, gave serious attention to engagement with rugby and cricket. Some pioneer efforts of immigrant Scots to foster soccer were none too successful and rugby was the favoured code as early as the 1880s. Soccer kept going, the chosen relaxation of some industrial districts, giving rise, for example, to the Tramways and Waterside FC in Wellington and the Harbour Board FC in Auckland. However, New Zealand is a good illustration of the point that some overseas white settlements were too remote and not populous enough to vie with the European and South American societies in terms of professional football.

There was football in the posts and settlements of South Africa as early as the 1860s and a rudimentary football association was founded as long ago as 1884, while, later in the century, the famous Corinthians toured the region. However, that mid-century football was probably of mixed sporting pedigree and the introduction into white schools of rugby - in leading cases by old boys of Rugby school - in the 1870s settled any contest. Soccer became the game played by the indigenous black and coloured races - among whom there was later to be a revival in the post-Apartheid era. Some of the football was of a good standard and several players moved on to professional careers in Britain. As if to underpin the division, Afrikaans youth took avidly to rugby union and have sustained an influence on South African rugby endeavours ever since.

The Indian subcontinent demonstrated the reverse of the Australian or Canadian situation, for here, of course, the British were very much in the minority and the native population was immense. Football was certainly played by well-to-do Indian pupils in the schools of the Raj, but, as is well-known, it was cricket that became the major Anglicising instrument in terms of the sporting culture. As the cricketing pendulum swings ever more definitely towards the Indian continent, one might remark the irony that, of all the British importations into India, including Christianity, cricket has proved the most enduring and triumphant. Hockey, too, introduced by army officers in Calcutta in the 1880s, caught the Indian imagination. It built - in yet another example of the manifestations of 'play' - on the widespread yet localised and differing brands of stick and ball diversions long extant in many districts of India.

There was some football. In the first place, the long roster of British regiments serving in India ensured that the great garrison depots across India would run teams, playing for the Durand Cup from 1888. There were British civilian clubs in administrative centres like Calcutta and Bombay, and, for years, the Indian FA was totally white in organisation. The Bengali community would seem to have been the first main Indian protagonists and, by the 1890s, there was a degree of Anglo-Indian soccer, with Calcutta's Mohun Bagan club in the van. After 1918 collaboration between occupied and occupier was better cemented, but, perhaps surprisingly, Indian football, while never vanishing completely, did not, as in so many other countries, seize avidly on soccer as a nationalist emblem. For a mix of internal - caste and other antagonisms - and external reasons - other Asian nations were not at that time very active in football circles - cricket continued to take precedence.

The West Indies, chiefly through the vehicle of its schools, was also mesmerised by the temptations of cricket, and, as on the Indian subcontinent, it became the national game, firstly, through an uneasy alliance of rich white settler and poorer ex-plantation workers. This resembled, the ethnic aspect apart, the social class divisions of the traditional 'gentlemen' and 'players' convention in England. Indeed, the first England/West Indian Test match in 1928 was probably the first played by England against a team composed of players of both European and non-European stock. By the middle of the 20th century, and with the progress towards political independence across the islands and territories, cricket became much more an Afro-American game. Football had its moments, but these were delayed until later in the 20th century with the modest success of Jamaica, while it is instructive to note how, under the heady pressure of American sway, basketball is waxing somewhat as a professional sport for West Indians, with even cricket on the wane.

Canada, too, has been and is subject to the cultural levers manipulated by the United States. Cricket, after an encouraging start, spluttered, as did football, introduced by incoming Scots, as both those games did in the United States. Rugby appeared in the 1880s, but neither code showed many signs of glittering on the world stage until the late 20th century. It was rugby union, however, played in the Canadian universities that led to contacts with the American colleges. Matches between McGill and Harvard in 1874 have been judged seminal in the development of American football. Typically, a football code only slightly at technical variance with American football then took root. The Ivy League colleges of the USA and the Canadian universities, such as Toronto and McGill, Montreal, encouraged each other to undertake a footballing interest; the Canadian Football Union was established in 1891 and there has always been some exchange of players and joint commercial concerns with the United States. Sports like athletics, curling, lacrosse and especially the very Canadian game of ice hockey also proved to be popular, whilst it must be recalled that there was an energetic French influence in Canada, perhaps a little unaccepting of the norms of Perfidious Albion. Soccer battled on obscurely, the pastime of incomers from Britain, in particular around Ontario.

This may be the relevant spot to discuss football in the former colonies that became the United States. Sport in the United States presents all the ambiguities one might expect from a former set of British colonies that became the global superpower of today. Cricket had its day. The first ever overseas sporting tour was by English cricketers to the USA and Canada in 1859, while Philadelphia remained a strong focus for cricket, even unto defeating the touring Australians in the 1890s. Nonetheless, baseball, especially around and after the American Civil War, grew to be the pre-eminent American game, despite some controversy as to its Anglo-Saxon or purely American origins. With a teeming polyglot population, the USA was faced in the late 19th century with the urgent need to fabricate some cohesive national culture; as elsewhere, sport was to be a decisive ingredient. From tennis and golf to athletics and the consciously invented game of basketball, the Americans came to crave and acclaim success in a wide range of sports.

From early years soccer was played intermittently by European migrants in several industrial districts, with St. Louis being possibly the most vibrant area. There were attempts to launch and re-launch the game in the USA. One such was in 1894 by baseball clubs, looking, like British cricket clubs, for an off-season option, if one with a commercial angle, but that dream soon evaporated. Across the wide-ranging stretches of the American continent, it appeared to be difficult to keep national leagues going or to avoid unhelpful contention between different organisations. There was and seems to remain some tension between the allure of a commercially tempting worldwide market and a determination to retain a national introspection about sporting activity. It is, perhaps, surprising to learn that only 16% of United States citizens have passports; the continental size of their nation offers them a plenitude of internal geographical and other splendours, and is a comfort to isolationism.

Nevertheless, the Americans enjoyed a purple patch in the 1920s, when its national league flourished and its national side reached the semi-finals of the 1930 World Cup in Uruguay. Unluckily, the Great Depression killed off much of this growth, as it did so much of other cultural plants. Despite that setback, the Americans embarrassed the English with a one-nil victory in the World Cup in Brazil in 1950 and, like Australia and South Africa, have latterly supplied players to the English leagues.

All that said, the genuine story of football in the USA concerns the rise of American football. The parallels with the English tale are uncanny. The American colleges on the Atlantic seaboard played informal campus versions of football, like their counterparts in the English public schools, from early in the 19th century, and, as in England, there was the same mix of horror and tolerance on the part of the authorities. Similarly, there were strictly no inter-collegiate contests. Princeton, for example, played a sort of soccer known, perhaps in self-explanatory mode, as Ballown. Then came the first college fixture, when, in 1869, Princeton, having drawn up and regularised its rules two years earlier, played Rutgers College at New Brunswick, New Jersey.

As in England, there were disputatious arguments, as college football developed, between adherents to the Princeton kicking code and the Harvard or 'Boston' carrying convention. Something akin to soccer rules were agreed in 1873, a year in which Yale beat a visiting English team, the Eton Players. However, not least because of the interest engendered by the Harvard/McGill fixtures of 1874, there were changes of heart and something close to rugby union was adopted and an Intercollegiate Football Association was organised in 1876. The machinations that led to the gradual makeover of the game into the highly formalised sport of the present time need not detain us unduly. In 1891 the game's supreme mentor, William Camp, published his authentic text on the sport, endorsing the sacred nature of the scrimmage line, legalised in 1880, and thus the characteristic gridiron markings of the American football field, while in 1895 professionalism and, subsequently, league competition was introduced. In 1906, under the celebrated aegis of President Teddy Roosevelt, a conference was assembled to reform and regulate the game; the modern American sport, with its beguiling heresy, apropos orthodox rugby, of the forward pass, dates from this point.

There are several minor and one or two major reasons why association football did not burgeon luxuriantly in the United States. A major one must be that, as with Australian Rules in Australia, the compelling existence of American Rules left too little space, especially in the influential field of collegiate life, for soccer.

DIASPORA - SOUTH AMERICA

In some senses this latter section has shown up the negative side of football's medallion. It has demonstrated why association football was largely avoided in some critical regions of the world, at least in its formative years. At the same time, it has provided an opportunity to observe the major growth of other football codes. Apart from describing such significant analogues as the crucial role of educational and occupational establishments or the place of acute political awareness in the history of all football, it has also drawn, in outline, something close to football's evolutionary tree. With one or two solitary exceptions, previously noted, the world's major football codes may all trace their history back to that meeting at the Freemasons' Tavern, Great Queen Street, London, when the rules of the London Football Association were published. The tree soon bifurcates into its two large branches of soccer, the heavier one, and rugger, but the primary origin, with its impulsion to agree and sustain regulation, is that common one.

The steamship did for football abroad what the railways had achieved for football at home. The United Kingdom built two-thirds of all ships launched; the British mercantile marine, weighing in at 12 million tons, was four times as big as the German fleet, which was the next biggest. Whereas the tonnage carried by sailing ships outnumbered that carried by steamship by five to one in 1860, by 1910 steam outweighed sail by eight to one; in the same period UK shipping earnings doubled from £38 million to £76 million. During this relatively brief span of forty years, steam displaced sail on many routes, including the Atlantic trade to the Americas. Jules Verne's *Round the World in Eighty Days* was published in 1873. It was a classy advert rather than sci-fi. By 1880 a ninety days round the world tour was on offer to tourists at £200.

In the 21st century, with all its marvels of transportation and intercommunication, practically all sports are played everywhere and by anybody who is so attracted, even if only in penny packets. There is cricket in Finland and Los Angeles and rugby in Romania, as well as an established American Football European league and association football in Hong Kong. Looking back to the globe before 1914, before, that is, any mainline civic use of aircraft, it is remarkable to observe that association football had, in a generation, migrated from Britain to so many parts of an ever contracting world - and that, in several other parts, its coadjutant pastime of rugby and rugby's offshoots had equally taken root.

CHAPTER TWELVE

INTROVERSION; BRITISH FOOTBALL, 1914 TO 1953

IN SO FAR AS the thesis that British football was healthy and stable before 1914 is arguable, then that wholesome consistency was sustained for near another half century. British football - its clubs; its players; its bosses; its grounds; its fan base; its finances; its coverage; its place in the national picture - barely changed. It continued serenely enough, albeit in something of a geopolitical cocoon. British football tended to ignore the world scene, apart from a few overseas international ventures, while it positively frowned upon English clubs anxious to make a mark in Europe.

The Social Continuum

In both directions - the smug continuity at home; the suspicious watchfulness abroad - football reflected the national construct and the national mood. Domestically, there was little fundamental shift in the shape of a society founded in the industrial convulsions of a century before. Globally, the gruesome callousness of the 1914-1918 War offered little evidence that forays in foreign parts were of advantage and the Pax Britannica of the post-1815 period, with, in fruitful addition, a large empire, was regarded with some affection. While sometimes amended and even improved by the process of technical innovation, the cultural superstructure created by this largely Victorian socio-economic structure was scarcely touched. This included the leisure industries, among them professional spectator sports like football.

What may be called the Age of Collective Leisure, an age that reigned from about the 1860s to the 1950s, was a direct consequence of life lived in collectivist fashion. The majority of workers still found themselves congregated in large consortia of their fellows, in shipyards, factories, collieries, mills, iron foundries and so on. Increasingly, huge commercial and financial firms were adopting similar lines of mass production, with soulless typing pools or telephone exchanges the norm and with women, as well as men, drawn into this joint economic strategy of larger scale units.

Leisure followed suit. The indispensable element of transport remained, for the majority, a shared activity. In the inter-wars years the motor bus and, to some degree, the trolley bus, enjoyed its heyday. Practically unknown outside London and the bigger cities before 1914, buses overtook railways as the chief passenger carriers by 1932. It was their flexibility that was so advantageous. The railway station, with its radii of relatively short tramlines, had sustained the compactness of the urban form. The bus helped to alter that design. It was one of the keys to what became known as ribbon development, those filaments of suburban housing that, between 1918 and 1939, edged outwards in narrow strips and columns from the urban foci. The construction of out of town council estates, like Manchester's massive Wythenshawe, or the 'new towns', like Welwyn Garden City in Hertfordshire, founded in 1920, were four-square dependent on bus transport. Rural life, too, was re-energised by country bus routes, while light industry was also able to follow the paths of ribbon development, its employees conveyed to and fro by buses. Mainly under local governmental control, the buses liberated both people and settlements.

As towns sprawled in pattern and grew in numerical size, the buses and trolley buses sustained the volume of football crowds, where once walking, cycling and tram travel had been the norm. Both trams and cycling continued as a means of access - many a backyard of a terraced house close to a football ground earned the householder a few coppers in exchange for a cloakroom ticket and a cluttered place for the cyclist to leave his precious bike. However, the familiar post-match scenario was of nearby roadways lined with 'football' buses, waiting to convey supporters to a variety of destinations.

The Saturday half day, normally now offering freedom from noon, was comprehensively allowed. 7 million workers also had a paid annual holiday, and, although this did not impinge as directly on football as much as on cricket attendances, the very trait of a vacation at a crowded seaside location - some 20 million had British seaside holidays in these summers - underpinned the notion of leisure as having a collective and outgoing character. No fewer than 145 places were officially recognised as seaside resorts by 1914. 'Going out', in fact 'going out' en masse, was the secret of the nation at leisure. The pubs and clubs, and a welter of societies, for high and low, from leeks to bridge, plus the allure of the palais de danse - this was the golden era of ballroom dancing for all - were other illustrations.

Music hall metamorphosed into variety, but the popularity of light theatre was unabated. Nonetheless, the salient example, other than spectator sports, was the rise of the cinema as an exercise in popular relaxation. The cinema was basically the application of industrial and technical precepts to the collective leisure of the industrial period. As early as 1916, still in the silent era, British ticket sales had reached 20 million weekly, that is 1 billion annually; by the 1940s this figure peaked at 30 million a week and 1.5 billion a year. Two-thirds of the population went to the 'flicks', as they were casually called, once a week and a third twice a week; four-fifths of adolescents visited the cinema once a week. There were 5,000 cinemas in Great Britain and a borough like Bolton had 47 cinemas within five miles, a few minutes' bus ride, of the town centre. In 1938 the cinemas' revenue was £4.5 million, compared with £1 million from the theatres and music halls.

The public, then, remained devoted to public leisure. As for the money required for such entertainments, the economy continued to have a low-cost construct, with prices and wages not significantly shifting before 1940. The consequences of the Great Depression, at their most rampant around 1929-33, were harrowing. At its nadir, unemployment touched 4 million, leaving, with family dependants, 7 million existing piteously on a dole that began at 15s (75p) a week There were still 1 million out of work in 1940, before the strident demands of war soaked up all available labour.

Nonetheless, the gap between one being in and out of work was not as desperate as in the grim recession of the 1980s. In the 1930s 60% had weekly incomes of £2 to £5; another 15-20% had incomes of £5 to £10, with a minority on higher salaries than that - but 20% had less than £2. To put that in some realistic context, an average council rent was then 6s or 7s (30 or 35p), while a modest mortgage repayment was no more than 8s (40p) a week. A bedroom suite was £28 and blankets £1 4s (£1.20p) a pair, with 'never-never' hire purchase schemes replacing the old-time tally man as the selling medium.

Such illustrations introduce the social curiosity of a countervailing stream amidst the storms of the depression. Between 1924 and the beginning of World War II, industrial output increased by a third, one of the highest rises in history.

INTROVERSION

Much of this was due to the growth of light industries, many of them located on the suburban edges of towns, geared to domestic products like processed foods, bicycles, artificial textiles and so forth. Electrical supply and electrical goods doubled in volume in this period. As for housing, there was a permanent switch from privately rented properties - 90% in 1914 - to owner occupation (3 million units between the wars) and municipal housing (1 million units). Less than 10% of British housing units are currently privately rented.

It betokened the upward drift of the integrated combine of prudent lower middle class and artisan class householders, settling into respectable accommodation, usually with a garden and converting to what was then satirically called 'the religion of home improvement', now transcribed into the acronym of DIY. Regular in income and habit, these were, in many towns, the ones who kept the ticket offices of the cinemas, the variety theatres and the turnstiles of the football grounds busy. They normally had a shilling or a half a crown to spare for such indulgences.

The Second World War reinforced some of these practices. Its course was different from the 1914-1918 war, when 900,000 British and British Empire servicemen were killed. 373,000 service personnel (including 76 professional footballers) died in the longer and wider-ranging second war, but, in addition, there were 93,000 civilian deaths, compared with less than a thousand in the first war. It was, then, total war with a vengeance, but, with it, there was a mature sense of commitment. A.J.P. Taylor chivalrously wrote that 'the British people came of age' and remained 'tolerant, patient and generous'. Despite the negative aspects of black market offences and other unhappy blemishes, this was broadly true. 'Wartime Socialism', with its regulations and planning, was intrinsic to this mood, and it is instructive to learn that rationing, which continued after the war, came more in response to public demand than to political will.

It was on the back of this wholesale and co-operative spirit that the Welfare State, its fulcrum the creation in 1948 of the National Health Service, was constructed during Clement Attlee's 'silent revolution' of 1945-51. It built this great edifice on the foundations of a long series of attempts to ameliorate the social ills endemic in industrial and urban life. One should always remember that the Welfare State was thus labelled as an alternative to the 'Warfare' state of the totalitarian polities of Fascist and Soviet persuasion, which had scoffed at the effeteness of parliamentary democracies, unable to cope with the social wounds wrought by capitalism's failures. It was a patriotic exercise, for, as its leading protagonist William Beveridge, no red he but a classical liberal, made clear, an underlying purpose of Welfarism was its universalist principle. All contributed and all benefited, in the belief that social well-being was the collective responsibility of everyone and that such universalism was reinforced by this common sharing of social provision.

This was the acme of the process, begun in Victorian times, of trying to discover a decently moral balance of civic responsibility and individual enterprise. In her pioneering work, *The Idea of Poverty*, the American scholar Gertrude Himmelfarb demonstrated how this social environment had been gradually created in Britain. It was conducive to lifting the poorer sector out of pauperdom and into employment, with a complementary emphasis on self-discipline, hard work, thrift, self-reliance and - convictions for drunkenness were down from 189,000 in 1913 to 53,000 in 1930 - temperance. Tea drinking was the norm, up from 1.6 lbs per person annually in the 1840s to 7 lbs in the 1930s. The always important yardstick of criminality continued to be favourable. In particular, crimes of violence, by the standards of the 18th or late 20th centuries, were low. They were fewer than 5,000 a year in the 1940s and early 1950s, compared with 21,000 in 1968 and over 100,000 by the end of the century.

Emphatically, this life-style permitted the prolongation of collective leisure, for huge crowds, except on isolated occasions, posed no real threat to civil order. The football crowd was the supreme example of this. In fact, the social symbol of the age was the queue. One queued for the cinema, for the bus, to clock on at the factory, at the shops, in the playground before school...for the football match...for the little boats to evacuate you from Dunkirk. It was the characteristic social institution. It displayed both sides of the social medallion. It was tedious and humdrum; it was fair and disciplined. It almost defined the British.

But along with this even national temper at home went a profound introspection. Certainly the 1920s and 1930s were a period of static and inward-looking torpidity, what that fine historian of the age David Thompson described as one of 'incorrigible immobilisme'. The prototypical mid-wars politician was the avuncular Stanley Baldwin, letting sleeping dogs lie and leaving dovecotes unfluttered. Then, of course, came the example of Neville Chamberlain and his infamous piece of fluttering paper and discourse on 'people of whom we know nothing'. Trying to forget the First World War, trying to pretend that a Second World War was not on the cards, battered by the Great Depression, there was a nervy and frenetic edge to these times apropos matters alien. Later, and valiantly as Britain behaved in World War II, the sense of fighting alone was pervasive and, with problems enough at home to solve, few could work up much interest in foreign affairs in the immediate post-war period.

Little wonder that Britain's footballers and football authorities found nothing magnetic about the game overseas. After all, if one subtracted the ten or a dozen war years and factored in other foreign horrors, like the Russian Revolution and the Spanish Civil War, there were not so many years between 1914 and, say, 1954 when travelling abroad to play football was either feasible or attractive. For all that, the disposition was negative; little interest was evinced in football abroad.

The Football Continuum - the Cult

In 1929 J.B. Priestley published his jolly picaresque novel *The Good Companions*, a jovial yarn of three individuals breaking the bonds of social propriety, striking out intrepidly, meeting up and helping to re-establish the fortunes of a rundown concert party. One of them was Jess Oakroyd, a mill-hand of Bruddersford, with its portmanteau tone of Bradford and Huddersfield. One of his last ritualistic acts before freeing himself of a harsh working and an embittered marital existence was to 'go to the match'.

> "Something very queer is happening to that narrow thoroughfare to the west of the town. It is called Manchester Road because it actually leads you to that city, though in order to get there you will have to climb the windy roof of England and spend an hour or so with the curlews. What is so queer about it now is that the road itself cannot be seen at all. A grey-green tide flows sluggishly along its length. It is a tide of cloth caps.
>
> These caps have just left the ground of Bruddersford United Association Football Club. 35,000 men and boys have just seen what most of them call 't'United' play Bolton Wanderers. Many of them should not have been there at all. It would not be difficult to prove by statistics and those mournful little budgets (How a

Man May Live - or rather avoid death - on 35 shillings a week) that seem to attract some minds, that those fellows could not afford the entrance fee. When some mills are only working half the week and others not at all, a shilling is a respectable sum of money. It would puzzle an accountant to discover where all those shillings came from. But if he lived in Bruddersford, though he might still wonder where they came from, he would certainly understand why they were produced. To say that these men paid their shillings to watch twenty-two hirelings kick a ball is merely to say that a violin is wood and catgut, that Hamlet is so much paper and ink. For a shilling the Bruddersford United AFC offered you Conflict and Art; it turned you into a critic, happy in your judgements of fine points, ready in a second to estimate the worth of a well-judged pass, a run down the touch line, a lightning shot, a clearance kick by back or goalkeeper; it turned you into a partisan, holding your breath when the ball came sailing into your goal; elated, downcast, bitter, triumphant by turns at the fortunes of your side, watching a ball shape Iliads and Odysseys for you, and, what is more, it turned you into a member of a new community, all brothers together for an hour and a half, for not only had you escaped from the clanking machinery of this lesser life, from work, wages, rent, doles, sick pay, insurance cards, nagging wives, ailing children, bad houses, idle workmen, but you had escaped with most of your mates, your neighbours, with half the town, and there you were, cheering together, thumping one another on the shoulders, swopping judgements like the lords of the earth, having pushed your way through a turnstile into another and altogether more splendid kind of life, hurtling with Conflict and yet passionate and beautiful in its Art. Moreover, it offered you more than a shilling's worth of material for talk during the rest of the week. A man who had missed the last home match of 't'United' had to enter social life on tip-toe in Bruddersford."

Priestley adeptly conveys the image of that 'grey-green tide' with his rolling swell of subordinating clauses. It was male and artisan and these working men remained as stoically loyal to their football team, as they did to their town, their firm, their family, their neighbours, their holiday resort, even their boarding house, and their regiment in time of war. Ambition was not high. There was less movement of jobs or breakdown of marriages. They did not expect too much from the workplace, the home or the football team. If events proved disastrous, it was accepted as the norm; if they proved triumphant, there was a backward glance over the shoulder to spot what Nemesis had in baleful store. J.B. Priestley also insists on the emotional charge that injected this social experience. Ignore the emotional factor in British club football in these years and understanding its potency is impossible.

Every Saturday between the wars, the Football League, with its forty or so match programme, clocked up well over half a million in attendances. The average gates at a Football League match over those score or more seasons were 20,000. The record attendances at 35 grounds occured in this period. Travelling away with one's team was, unless the fixture was with a close neighbour, prohibited by time, money and accessibility. A predominantly home crowd helped preserve the peace and, apart from isolated incidents - Millwall earned itself some ill-repute in the 1930s - there were comparatively few crowd problems.

Many watched the reserves, 'the Stiffs', as they were sometimes affectionately labelled, on alternate Saturdays. There was the advantage of being privy to half-time scores; one's programme (this applied also for first eleven home matches) had the fixtures listed and coded as A, B, C and so on. Tin numbers would then be pinned at half-time to a lettered scoreboard. If you were prepared to wait at full-time, you might be lucky enough to obtain the final score as well. In those sometimes blessed hours without a squeaky public address system, the changes were advertised by a youth, like the one in Longfellow's still popular recitation, *Excelsior* carrying 'a banner with a strange device', that is, a blackboard with chalked names and numbers upon it. Numbered shirts arrived comparatively late; becoming common in the mid 1930s - the first major competitive match to feature numbered shirts was the 1933 FA Cup final, which saw Everton's players numbered from 1-11 and Manchester City's players numbered from 12 to 22 - and eventually compulsory, although the New Zealand rugby union All-Blacks had added white numerals to their sable jerseys as early as 1905. Pre-match and half-time entertainment was often in the capable hands and mouths of the local brass band, the bandmaster's tossing aloft of his mace greeted with a mixture of derision and delight.

The emblematic event in this crowd-building story was the construction of Wembley Stadium, for, let it be whispered as one writes in the lengthening shadow of a steadfastly unbuilt replacement arena, a scheduled price of £750,000 in a scheduled time of 300 working days. 250,000 tons of concrete, 1,500 tons of steel and half a million rivets went into the making of the famous stadium, with a battalion of infantry marking time on the terraces for fifteen minutes to test its durability. It was erected to hold 127,000, somewhat less than, at a pinch, the 140,000 of Hampden Park.

The Empire Stadium was further tested four days after its completion by the FA Cup final of April 1923 between Bolton Wanderers, the 2-0 winners, and West Ham United. 126,047 spectators, 35,527 of them in the seated areas, officially passed through the turnstiles, but, such were the multitudes, that some put the figure as high as 250,000 and there is no doubt that well over 200,000 invaded the new arena. It was chaotic. The ground was difficult to reach because of unprecedented traffic congestion and difficult to enter because the novelty of a barely finished venue proved impossible to steward adequately. Having arrived, there is no doubt that many felt it was their God-given right to force an entry, but, once inside, the mood was cheerful enough.

Football lore relates the efforts of George Scorey - 'the policeman on the white horse', the name of which was the satisfyingly ordinary Billy - and his colleagues to push the masses back, as the band played on, apparently very harmoniously, in the centre of the field and George V was welcomed with a respectful rendition of the national anthem by his teeming but generally well-behaved subjects. Eventually, forty minutes late, the final was played out with 'human touchlines'.

Astonishingly, there were neither fatalities nor serious injuries. Just fifty casualties, with chiefly minor 'crush' damage, were listed as hospital patients, although several hundreds also received first aid treatment. 28 April 1923 should shine forth in social history as a day symbolic of the mature and mellow humour and patience of the British working class of that age. A perplexed Irishman said that night to W. Pickford, a veteran commentator and FA Committeeman of the time, 'not a pistol went off.'

After Crystal Palace, with its Epsom Downs on Derby Day fairground quality, the Wembley final, with its regal presence, its national anthem, its polite introductions of the team, its majestic Guards' military band and its community singing, with Arthur Caiger the best remembered of conductors and including the reverent singing of *Abide with Me*, quickly became a national occasion of some ceremony and renown.

In 1919 the first two Football League divisions added two clubs each, while over the next two years the Southern League and teams from the senior northern competitions created the Third Divisions, South (1920/21) and North (1921/22). It was in these post-war years that the southern teams, led by Arsenal and Chelsea in Division One and five clubs in Division Two, began to make a showing.

As well as these the 92 clubs in the four divisions of the Football League, there were, by the 1930s, 10,000 clubs affiliated to the Football Association, chiefly through the county associations, and 750,000 young men and youths played the recreational game every weekend. Although the switch to rugby continued in the upper echelons of secondary education, the elementary schools had grown more conscious of the need to provide attractive physical exercise, and schools football burgeoned. During the 1920s the County FAs took over supervision of schools football and its structure was further strengthened in the immediate post-war years. By 1968 there would be 14,000 schools formally engaged in football.

In 1922 the maximum wage for professional footballers was revised downwards from £9 to £8, in common with the tightening screw on wages typical of the time. With the possibility of £6 a week for the fifteen week break, this gave the best players an annual income of £386, but, of course, the best players were in a small minority. 1928 witnessed the first £10,000 transfer, when David Jack moved from Bolton Wanderers to Arsenal.

Trades unionism generally, after its fiery combativeness before 1914, took something of a battering, especially given the timidity of the General Strike of 1926 and the miseries of the depression. The Players' Union was no exception. Against the grain of the growth of the Football League, its membership declined steeply after the Great War to 434 in 1929. In 1913 the legal position of professional players had been further weakened by the judgment in the test case of Kingsby v Aston Villa. Loss of employment had been, it was alleged, the result of an excessive transfer fee having been hung round the player's neck. No club had taken up the offer and his livelihood was lost. The judge ruled in favour of the club, asserting that this was justified by the contractual terms of employment and that no malice had been involved. The Players' Union membership did, however, rise to 1,900 in 1939.

For all that the work force, both inside and outside football, was not pampered in these years, there was the penetrative spread of football as a cult as well as a pastime, particularly in ways that involved the laying out of even more money.

The press had always had a sporting instinct. Journals like *Bell's Life* (first published in 1820) and *The Field* (1852) had supplied the middle class sports lover with such fare, but, increasingly, the cheaper newspapers were promoting popular games like football. In 1859 the bi-weekly *Sporting Life* had begun operations and reached a 100,000 circulation by the 1880s, while, in the provinces, newspapers like *Manchester's Athletic News* started in 1875, price 2d, and had a similar circulation by the 1890s. Soon it supplied the remarkable coverage of 500 words for each match in the two top divisions of the Football League and also the Scottish League. From 1885 the *Sunday Chronicle*, at the cost of a penny, majored on the previous afternoon's football, and many papers carried the alluring attachment of action photographs from about 1911. According to that diligent researcher Tony Mason, almost every town had its own football paper by the 1890s.

Certainly by the 1920s, all the British daily and Sunday newspapers carried copious reports of and articles about football. The provincial press provided a colourful range of 'pink 'uns' and 'green 'uns', special Saturday evening editions totally devoted to sport, mainly football, and hot on the streets with some celerity. Without such sources, the wait to discover how your favourites, if playing away, had fared was lengthy and nerve-racking.

There were match-day programmes, informative but scanty, and there were all manner of football annuals, just as there were *Wisdens* and other publications in cricket, replete with records and statistics. *The Football Handbook*, edited by John Leng, and *Charlie Buchan's Football Monthly* may be mentioned as examples of a considerable genre. Another outlet for the young football buff was the cigarette card, with albums available in which to stick the player's pasteboard picture, comforted by the reprise of the data on the back of the card pre-printed in the album itself. The vast consumption of cheap cigarettes, like Wills' Woodbines, in those years - the cigarette, hitherto thought of as exotic, substantively replaced the pipe as the smoke of the proletariat during the trench warfare of 1914 to 1918 - was such that most youngsters contrived to fill most albums.

For those eager to view larger pictures, the cinema newsreels, like British Gaumont or Movietone, started to show clips of important matches, most notably the FA Cup final, while the 'wireless' slowly began what was to be an invaluable service. Along with the gramophone, often used to pump, for instance, Charlie Kunz records over the tannoy sytem before matches, the radio was the first of the non-collective technical devices of any enduring impact. Unlike most organised leisure, it was privately consumed in the home, a clue to the shape of things to come. At the same time, the instantaneous reception of broadcasts gave it an essentially congregate flavour. Everyone heard the same programme at the same time, so that, for instance, the morning after a wartime airing of Tommy Handley's *ITMA* extravaganza, the playgrounds, shops and workplaces of the nation were full of people repeating and imitating the familiar catchphrases and gags.

After some bickering about who could or could not do what, a consortium of British wireless set manufacturers was granted an exclusive license to broadcast in and to the United Kingdom. This was in 1922 and it was called the British Broadcasting Company. The dominant feature was the sale of receivers, from which resulted what now seems the odd device of funding this public service through the post office sale of wireless licenses. The company had a licence to broadcast and the householder had a license to receive.

In 1927 this agency was transformed by Royal Charter into the prestigious British Broadcasting Corporation, under the austere directorship of John Reith. In January of that same year the first broadcast of a football match, Arsenal versus Sheffield United, was aired. 2 million people had a wireless license and, with a curtsey to the righteous side of honesty, they represented those who had a wireless set. In the spring of 1927 George Allison, later to be Arsenal's manager, commentated on the Cup final for the first time, describing for thousands how his future charges were belittled by a humiliating goalkeeping mistake to allow Cardiff City to win their first FA Cup, take the trophy out of England for the first and so far only time, and set a question which would become familiar to pub quiz participants for years to come. There were soon to be rumblings about costs and the losses clubs felt accrued from the broadcasting of games, a tiny premonition of later high finance squabbles over media rights towards the end of the century. Fortunately, the breaches were eventually healed and football was soon widely broadcast.

By 1939 there were over 10 million radios, and nine out of ten British households had a wireless. The golden age of radio began in the 1930s and lasted until the late 1950s, embracing the splendid contribution of the BBC in the Second World War, which was to prove to be the only major war in which radio was the most important medium. During this time, the BBC built an impressive reputation for sports broadcasting, with Raymond Glendenning the household voice of football commentating and with a trusty results service to boot. This all gave a comfortably glossy image to the game.

Not to the taste of the puritanical John Reith, but a big hit nonetheless, was the introduction of the football pools. Gambling was beginning to substitute for drink as the curse and vice of the working classes. As well as horse racing, greyhound racing became suddenly popular. By 1928 there were 60 tracks in Britain, some of them circling football pitches. The electric hare first sped past the traps in 1927 at Belle Vue dog-track, Manchester, where crowds of 27,000 watched, shouted and betted. From the onset of professionalism in the late 19th century, bookmakers had touted for custom around the bigger football grounds, while, from the mid 1880s, some newspapers introduced the practice of betting 'coupons', a habit vigorously attacked by the anti-gambling campaigners, still gloating over the success of their crusade to outlaw off-course betting on horse races. There was also some on-field football betting, the most infamous instance being the Liverpool and Manchester United match of 1915, when players, anxious to make a few pounds as the encroachment of hostilities threatened their livelihood, fixed the match.

The FA, still hobbled by its complacent sense of virtue, backed the Ready Money Football Betting Act of 1920, an attempt to prohibit all gambling in football. The nascent pools industry negotiated a careful path through the legal tangle, initially by collecting the bets, after, not - as 'ready money' - before the games. Its supremo was the shrewd Merseyside entrepreneur, John Moores, then an employee of the Cable and Wireless Company. Buying his share of the idea for a few paltry shillings from his more anxious partner, the eponymous Mr Littlewood, he sought the assistance, like The Rt. Hon. Joseph Porter in *HMS Pinafore*, of his 'sisters and his cousins and his aunts'. In 1923 they distributed 4,000 pools coupons outside Old Trafford and the first foundation stone was laid in the construction of a lucrative industry.

With a brilliant display of marketing acumen, Littlewood's and their rivals, such as Vernon's, brought respectability to the otherwise seedy reaches of gambling, its innocent pools coupons ingenuously welcomed as a mild but not sinful flutter in almost every home. The football authorities tried to counter the horrors of betting by refusing to divulge the fixture lists until a day or so before

In 1541, during the reign of Henry VIII, a statute expressly proscribed artificers, labourers, apprentices and servants from playing games except at Christmas and then solely under the beady eye and at the home of the master, although the statutes were honoured more in the breach.

Pictured left, the Harrow Footer team of 1871. Public schools were the breeding ground of organised football.

Queen's Park, right, the oldest Scottish football club, took part in the first FA Cup competition but were forced to scratch at the semi final stage due to the cost of travelling.

Newton Heath, left, were formed by the workers of the depot and carriage wagon works and in 1902 became Manchester United, arguably the most famous football club in the world.

Above: Charles W. Alcock, who deserves the soubriquct 'The Father of Modern Sport', pictured in his office at Kennington Oval. He was the key figure in the formation of the Football Association and founded the FA Cup.

William 'Fatty' Foulke, right, was one of the first great crowd-pullers in the UK. He was bought from Sheffield United by Gus Mears, the founder of new club Chelsea to bring the crowds into Stamford Bridge.

Not far behind was Billy Meredith, left, who starred for Manchester City, Manchester United and Wales until he was nearly 50. He was also instrumental in the founding of the Players' Union.

Jimmy Hogan, above, was the most celebrated of British coaches who travelled Europe, both West and East, preaching the footballing gospel. He is widely credited with being behind the emergence of Hungary as a force in world football after the Second World War and coached the Austrian 'Wunderteam' of the 1930s, of which Matthias Sindelar, below left, was the star player. Another influential Briton was Sir Stanley Rous, bottom right, who followed his secretaryship of the FA with the presidency of FIFA from 1961 to 1974.

Old Trafford showing the damage inflicted on it by Nazi bombing during World War Two. It would be re-built and added to in the next 60 years to become an urban temple of a stadium hosting more than 75,000 spectators.

The most iconic stadium of all; Wembley and its original Twin Towers. Here Wolves' Norman Deeley (fourth player from left) scores one of his two goals in the 3-0 defeat of Blackburn Rovers in the 1960 FA Cup final. Wembley came to mean something more than just a football ground to generations of supporters. It stood for hope, glory and aspiration.

Above: The official attendance at the 1901 FA Cup Final at Crystal Palace of 110,820 was, at the time, the largest ever for a football match. Note the composition of the crowd, exclusively male and largely working class. The profile of the spectator changed much during the 20th Century. Below, a scene from a match during the 1970s shows a mixture of ages and classes, including a number of women and youths, who would make up a much larger proportion of crowds by the early years of the 21st Century.

Brand Beckham: The biggest global marketing phenomenon of all; David Beckham, talismanic England captain and the face of everything from soft drinks, to sunglasses to aftershave.

Stanley Matthews was Beckham's predecessor as the first truly global football star, albeit rather more prosaic a hero. Matthews too endorsed products such as Craven A cigarettes, despite the fact he did not smoke, and Brylcreem.

Above: World Cup Final 2006 - Italy captain Fabio Cannavaro clutches the World Cup in front of a global television audience of over 3 billion. Proof, if ever it was needed, that football truly is the all-encompassing passion of the entire planet.

Right: Tibet v Gibraltar - Football has even permeated the most remote parts of the globe. Here two 'outcasts' from the modern political world, Gibraltar and Tibet, express their nationality by doing battle in the 2006 FIFI Wild Cup, held in Germany prior to the official tournament, but for 'countries' which do not officially exist.

the matches, a device that backfired thunderously, as irate fans were also inconvenienced and irked at this information blackout. A compromise was reached, with the pools firms paying for prior knowledge of the fixtures. From its Liverpool base, the main bailiwick, interestingly enough, for the more primitive press coupons campaign, it soared to dizzy heights of affluence. By the 1930s £800,000 a week was being invested and prizes as high as £22,000 were being won. The industry offered jobs in an era - and area - of dire unemployment to 30,000 people, many of them women. The annual turnover was £30m, rising to £50m in 1939; it was still five times smaller than the £150-200 million expended on betting on the 'gee- gees', but it was generally deemed to be less addictive, in part because of its single weekly occurrence and moderate wagers, whereas horse racing was a daily event, tempting punters into pitfalls of debt.

Littlewoods flourished so profitably that it diversified into the mail order and stores businesses, with such success that the football pools became something of a side show for the company. After the Second World War (during which the pools firms allied, with the help of the press, into a single patriotic Unity Pools mode) the jackpot of £75,000, for the 'Treble Chance' triumph of picking eight draws, was launched in 1946. It was the tempting equivalent of today's million pounds' bonanza on the National Lottery - Littlewoods' first millionaire had to wait until 1986. In 1946, 25 million postal orders were delivered to the pools companies, now the employers of 100,000 men and women. It was the nation's seventh largest industry.

Socially, the pools industry enjoyed a high degree of penetration and its function as a football educator is significant. At its height, the business attracted 8 million punters a week, a fifth of the adult population and representative of nearly two-thirds of the nation's households. This was approaching fifteen times as many customers as paid to watch Football League matches on most wintry Saturdays in the late 1920s and early 1930s. That 8 million also represented another strata of accomplices, such as family members or work-mates, choosing a line or a fixture on the coupon. This amounted to a quantum leap in the spread of an elementary knowledge of football, not least among the female portion of the population, who had largely been denied access to this arcane masculine realm.

That point about the encompassing of women into the footballing culture prompts some reference to women's football per se. There is some flimsy evidence about women occasionally appearing in the midst of one or two games of mob football in the olden days, although it is not always clear whether this was by accident or design. Such incidental mentions should not divert attention from the primarily male dominion in football, as in most sports. Mary, Queen of Scots may have played golf and the notorious Mrs Stokes may have earned some repute as a prize fighter in Hanoverian times, but these were hardly precedents. By the 19th century, some gentle sports were encouraged among gentlewomen, especially those, such as croquet, lawn tennis and battledore and shuttlecock, which might serve as an excuse for flirtation and courtship. Until the feisty young Charlotte Dod arrived in 1886 to terrorise her opponents with vigorous smashes and 'man-like' athleticism, lawn tennis was a static game for ladies. Even with hockey - East Molesey (1887) claims to be the first women's hockey club - it was not too over-strenuous, while, in 1909, Eleonora Sears was dispatched from the polo ground by her captain for wearing trousers. Cricket, too, had had its female adherents for some time, and was even beginning to be played in girls' schools, but it, too, was regarded with typical masculine condescension.

Baron Pierre de Coubertin, founder of the modern Olympic Games, gravely pronounced that 'women have just one task; that of the role of crowning the victor with garlands'. The Victorian conception of the 'private' role of woman, over against the 'public' part played by man (an argument often used to deny women the franchise) upheld the ideal of the chivalrous male as protector of the meek female. This attitude was assailed, in practice, by the stock of unmarried middle class women who were obliged, as well as ready, to find employment in careers like nursing, secretarial and clerical work and teaching. The 1914-1918 War tragically added to the volume of unmarried women, whilst, as is the way of wars, it had something of a liberating effect politically and socially. The 1918 and 1928 Parliamentary Acts finally brought suffrage to women and, slowly, especially in individual sports like swimming and gymnastics, there was a little more encouragement of sportswomen.

There is testimony to some women's football from the 1880s, while in 1895 there was a home counties encounter in London between women's sides drawn from the south and north of the capital, but, true to its innate and abiding conservatism, the FA was in disheartening mood, preaching the unhealthy effects of soccer for the distaff side and instructing its members in 1902 not to be involved in such unseemly antics. Truth to tell, although women's football occasionally drew good crowds, the motivation was suspect, as many men appeared to be even more derisory of their efforts than when the male teams were in contest.

The first saviours of women's football were Dick, Kerr's Preston Ladies. It is fascinating that the work-place, begetter of so many male-orientated sides, should again be the source of origin. The Preston electrical works could, of course, offer some sponsorship, but it was a sign of the times that sufficient women were employed in the new light industry of electrical components to supply a core squad. Formed, if rather sporadically, pre-war, they made quite a splash, raising money for charities during the ensuing war and often attracted big and increasingly affectionate crowds. Later they made overseas tours to play exhibition matches, including some in the United States, and, as the one major and purposeful women's team, they were rarely beaten. France was another country where there was a similar blossoming of women's football. Dick, Kerr's continued through to and after the Second World War, and there were occasional glimpses of stars peeping, such as Joan Whalley, known as 'the Ladies' Stanley Matthews'. Their enduring influence was to keep the flag waving and to encourage women to start teams and play football in what was still an unpropitious atmosphere.

Although the employment of women expanded during the Great War, both in substituting for men who had been recruited and in trades, such as munitions, where more workers were suddenly required, the working woman was not everywhere a novel factor. This was true of many industrial districts, like the textile towns of the north and midlands or the potteries of Stoke and its environs, precisely those places where football had taken a strong hold. One has thus to look at the liberating effect of the 1914-1918 War as a stepping stone in the rather difficult journey of women's football. Unluckily, it was a short-lived phenomenon. Particularly in Lancashire, several teams were established and, by the end of the war, it is thought over a hundred were in existence. The peak of this small revolution was in 1920 when Dick, Kerr's Preston Ladies met St Helens Ladies in front of over 50,000 spectators at Goodison Park.

As often happens with social progress, there are backward as well as forward steps, with, as an example, some resentment among troops returning from the frontline after both world wars about women holding down jobs they had assumed in wartime. There was such a setback for women's football after the First World War in 1921, when the FA determined that such games must not be essayed on the grounds of clubs affiliated to the FA. In regarding the FA as dinosaur-like in this as in other regards, it should not be forgotten that its diktat was accepted without much demur among the assembled masculine ranks of English football.

The Football Continuum - the Club Game

The foregoing sections attempt to paint a rough canvas of British life and society in the first half of the 20th century and the fashion in which it was so deeply penetrated by football. The football itself continued to be of a satisfactory standard. The regulo of the maximum wage and the diffusion of sizeable crowds across the nation maintained a steadily common level of skill and endeavour throughout the Football League and some of the same applied to the Scottish League.

A sign of such relative parity was that as many as ten clubs shared the twenty First Division titles contested between the wars. Furthermore, no fewer than sixteen teams achieved Cup Final victories in that same phase, with only Bolton Wanderers, with three trophies, Newcastle United and the new all-conquering Arsenal, with two wins, breaking that sequence of single victories. In 1920/21 there were a record 674 entries for the FA Cup. The system of geographical divisions, introduced way back in 1881, was now quite complex. There were 26 such regions by 1927 and it would be 36 by 1951. A sophisticated grading of exemptions prevailed throughout the qualifying competition and into the 'Competition Proper', so that, in effect, the quest for Cup glory began almost as soon as the football season itself.

Huddersfield Town, having only been formed in 1912, soared to the peak and won three First Division titles on the trot, 1924, 1925 and 1926, becoming the first club to do so, as well as being runners up in 1927 and 1928; they never won the title again. The names of their players, among them Roy Goodall, Alec Jackson and Clem Stephenson, were oft recited by Harold Wilson, that famous child of Huddersfield and one gifted with legendary memory, when in conversation with Russian and other European politicos during his premierships. Huddersfield's luckiest call was en route to their first success. Cardiff City came close to being the only Welsh team to win the First Division title as well as the FA Cup. It went to the wire of the last round of fixtures, and had goal difference, not goal average, ruled, they would have done.

The Merseyside influence was growing. Liverpool, with the sleek Elisha Scott in goal, won two championships, while, and neighbours Everton won three championships. Everton's centre forward was that mighty header of the ball, the much acclaimed and highly popular William Ralph 'Dixie' Dean, scorer of 310 First Division goals at a record ratio of 0.86 an outing. His 82 (60 in league matches) goals in1927/28 remain a record for a season's haul. Only the quick-witted, if sometimes argumentative, Scot, Hughie Gallacher, playing with Newcastle United, Chelsea and Derby County, comes close to him in this era, with a ratio of 0.72.

The Huddersfield manager, Herbert Chapman, moved to Arsenal after Huddersfield's second title season and enhanced his glowing reputation. The equally successful George Allison followed him. In 1930/31 Arsenal, with a record tally of 66 points, won their first ever title, and then added four more and a couple of Cup Final triumphs for good measure, all in the 1930s. It was a magnificent achievement. It was the type of single long term domination never before seen in British football, for even in Scotland there were two clubs, Glasgow Celtic and Rangers, jostling for hegemony. It had about it the futuristic look of the much later dominance of Liverpool, then Manchester United, in the upper flight of English football. Moreover, in almost half a century of trial and tribulation, Arsenal's initial triumph was the first time a southern side had won the First Division title. In addition, they were twice second and once third in the league, beaten Cup finalists twice and in the last eight on another six occasions, all in the spell from 1925/26 to the outbreak of war.

Northern commentators spoke glumly of the effects of the depression on football in the industrial wastelands of the north and midlands, and it is true that London weathered the economic tempest of the inter-wars years with more equanimity than the manufacturing provinces. Its largeness of population and variety of economic activity told, where the single staple systems, the textiles, the shipbuilding, the coalmining, of the purely industrial districts, slumped. In this sense, there was another futuristic glance ahead, to a time when, across the globe, it would be the great conurbations, signally identified with national and regional capitals, where football would burgeon.

Satisfying although such sociological explanations are - and they should never be discounted - one has then to clarify why Arsenal, and not, say, Chelsea, with its formidable supporter base, did not bring the championship to the metropolis. At that specific point, a more purely sporting elucidation is required. Basically, Arsenal was a very talented and efficaciously organised team.

Herbert Chapman was, by a long chalk, the leading manager of his generation, bringing success to both Huddersfield Town and Arsenal. Both George Allison and he were bright and capable men who brought a novel style to management. They directed their teams in a way largely unknown in an era when players were expected, with a little help from the trainer, to resolve on-pitch issues among themselves. The directors and secretary, it was hoped, had knowledge enough to recruit players and pick sides, but it was not anticipated that they would be involved in the actual tactics, anymore than the works manager in the iron foundry would have grasped the finer points of welding.

The two Arsenal managers introduced, or, at least, enjoyed the earliest consistent success in introducing, a definitive organisational and strategic flair. To this was added the comfort of sufficient money to pay transfer fees and keep a sufficiency of top-rate players on a maximum wage. Modern football history suggests that the science of football administration combines two branches: the physics of material wealth and the chemistry of man-management. Arsenal was one of the first clubs to experiment profitably in this joint laboratory.

The strategic element involved a sensible riposte to the havoc wrought by the new offside law, introduced in 1925. The three man bar had gradually produced an over-defensive outlook. With wing halves marking wingers, defences had pressed opponents backwards, so that play was often stuck in a narrow passage either side of the half- way line. The 1925 ruling reduced the trio to a duo, normally the goalkeeper and one other. The consequences were probably more disruptive than the FA planners had believed likely. In the first season played under the revised legislation, over a third more goals were scored in the Football League. In 1927 players were allowed to score direct from a free kick, with further additions to the goals columns. It is no coincidence that many major goal scoring records date from that era. 'Dixie' Dean is a fitting case in point, whilst the top-flight club record, held by Aston Villa with 128 goals in 42 matches in 1930/31, also hails from this period. With defences stumbling in retreat to retain some authority, space opened up and speedy wingers glided away. Quick, darting passes and lofted centres produced many goals, and 'Dixie' Dean, that virtuoso header, would score two-thirds of his goals in this manner in some of his most gainful seasons.

What Arsenal did was make full use of these new advantages, while, at the same time, seeking to stymie their opponents from emulating them. This they did apparently on the advice of Charlie Buchan, as near to a footballing scholar among players as the game has produced. A blunt speaking but highly intelligent inside forward, he was transferred from Sunderland to Arsenal and there made his presence felt corporeally - he scored 258 First Division goals for his two clubs - and philosophically. Herbie Roberts was instructed to concentrate on being, not a centre-half, but a centre full-back, whereas previously the three half-backs had been deemed to be all-rounders, attacking and defending. In the past, there had been some third back play, but usually to protect an early lead. The full-backs now marked the opposing wingers, and the three backs pivoted to cover each other. It helped that the full-backs in question were the England pairing of George Male and the England skipper, the exceptionally talented Eddie Hapgood. The wing halves, as the label suggests, had hitherto kept an eye on their opponents' wingmen; now they shifted inwards and marked the inside men - and with Wilf Copping, reputedly the hardest tackler known to the English game, this was marking of the most painfully efficient order.

The complement to this stern bolstering of the rearguard was the withdrawal of an inside forward for playmaking duties - and Arsenal's signing of the mercurially creative Alex James from Preston North End procured this maestro for that scheming role. The other inside forward, of necessity, also shared some of these duties, leaving space for the other three forwards to wheel and deal, the centre forward - that tough raider Ted Drake - foraging purposefully, the wingers - such as the quick-footed Cliff Bastin - being expected to cut inside and score goals. The overall effect was that Arsenal scored lots of goals, sometimes a hundred in a campaign, and conceded very few.

Everyone copied them - and the so-called W or W-M formation ruled over a long reign of thirty or forty years, not just in Britain, but the world over. The clincher for Arsenal was that they had been able to gather together brilliant players in almost every position. Over this time, they provided the bulk of the England team - famously seven of the England team which defeated World Champions Italy at Highbury 3-2 in November 1934 - and the leading light -

Alex James - of the highly successful Scotland team. Other teams were, self-evidently, not as good individually and the 'third back' system did often lapse into a defensive fog. For all that, it more or less concluded the evolution of the soccer formation from a rugby-type forward pack of eight or even nine to the 'sistema', as the continentals came to term it, of a more balanced ordering of attacking potential and protective capability.

It happened at a point approximately half way between the modern codification of football and the present time. The format has endured and, indeed, its seeming revisions in and since the 1960s have been no more than an increased elasticity of positioning of players, itself a result of heightened stamina levels as well as avant garde strategic thought.

The Football Continuum - the National Game

The home international tournament enjoyed some of its best moments during these years. A fascinating trait was the capacity of Scotland to perform so competently throughout the 1920s. Its narrower club base might actually have helped. Rangers, a chief provider, won no fewer than fifteen league titles between the two wars. International teams usually gathered just in time to kick off, with barely a thought about national coaching and systems. Not until Arsenal supplied the core of the English eleven in the 1930s did the consistent togetherness one saw in the better club sides emerge. Games were played at the same time as Football League fixtures, the commencement of that smouldering feud between club and country. Players retained some obligatory loyalty to the wage-paying club, as opposed to the occasional tit-bit thrown to them by the nation. In an interview not long before his death, the great Eddie Hapgood said that £5 was the most he ever earned playing for England, although, in justice to him, he valorously proclaimed he would do the same again, if chance offered.

1928 marked the 5-1 drubbing of England at home by the 'Wembley Wizards', as the press dubbed Scotland's best ever eleven. Apart from the inimitable Alex James and the lethal Hughie Gallacher, there were the wingers Alec Jackson, a member of the successful Huddersfield team, and, from Glasgow Rangers, Alan Morton. They harried a flustered English team into humiliated submission. Yet even tiny Wales, helped by the likes of Bolton's Ted Vizard, a fleet-footed outside-left, won three Home International championships in the 1920s, against England's none.

INTROVERSION

In Ireland, torn by partition and the creation of the Irish Free State in December 1921, football, too, was divided. The FA of Ireland, formed that same year, was affiliated to FIFA in 1923, while the Irish FA, based in Protestant Belfast, stuck to its rather stifled guns. Along with England, Wales and Scotland, they initially refused to play the autonomous Irish national team, another sad reminder of the depressing interplay of football and politics. Ireland, small and divided, rarely shone thereafter as a footballing concern.

By 1939 the England team had restored some of its former dignity. Then came war. Football had a goodish war in Britain, where it avoided the disdain that had confronted its efforts to complete the 1914/15 season. The 1939/40 fixtures had scarcely begun and, with government edicts, fearful of mass bombing, forbidding the gathering of large crowds, football was suspended. Then, with government encouragement, it soon recommenced, with a series of regional leagues, interspersed with cup competitions. Some crowd and other restrictions remained for some time, travel and equipment caused problems, while guest players, from the ranks of mobilised footballers now based in army and RAF camps in the vicinity of clubs they now appeared for, were widely deployed.

The official view was much less blinkered than in the blood and glory days of the First World War. It was recognised that the morale of weary servicemen and war-workers could be boosted by football and that sport was a useful fund-raiser. Sporting events raised £3 million for war charities, football's contribution approaching a third of that total. The football authorities did much to help services football, not forgetting the needs of the 100,000 prisoners of war in German and Italian camps. Dominion troops joined in football's hurly-burly; there were, for instance, some 84 Canadian service teams in Britain prior to D-Day in 1944. In a show of Anglo-American friendship, Field-Marshal Eisenhower, commandant of the allied forces in Europe, attended one of the wartime cup finals in 1944.

Another major difference was the totality of the citizens' war. It was both more global and less concentrated in specific areas than World War I. It was also a war of fits and starts. There were long periods of waiting, first for an invasion that did not transpire; second, preparing for one, in the other direction, that did. Most of the bombing was by night - Old Trafford, Highbury, West Ham's Upton Park, Millwall's the Den, and the grounds of Plymouth Argyle, Stoke City and Swindon Town were among those damaged - but, by and large, considerable football was played and considerable numbers assembled to cheer the players on. Soccer was played with amiable heart; Peter Hartland does right to remind us that handshakes all round stem from the friendly spirit in which football was played as an antidote to what were called wartime blues.

Another curio was that during the 1939-45 War, expenditure on leisure rose 120%. There were two reasons for this. On the one hand, from 1940 there was full employment and, with the help of Ernest Bevin, the shrewd trade unionist and Minister of Labour, wages rose to reasonable levels. It is an oddity of the age that butter and bacon sales increased after they had been rationed, simply because most people could now afford such tasty comestibles. On the other hand, with food, clothing and petrol rationed, with other goods in short supply, with holiday making at the seaside discouraged and, with the prices of essential foodstuffs kept low by government subsidy, there was actually quite a lot of money over for pleasure. Football was one of the beneficiaries. For instance, there were 85,000 spectators at Wembley for the League Cup South final of 1944, when Charlton Athletic beat Chelsea 3-1. These were good omens for post-war football.

Two clubs that were particularly advantaged by the guesting mode were Aldershot and Blackpool, respectively the main depots for the army and the RAF, where many footballers were retained as physical training instructors. Tommy Lawton, the worthy inheritor of the 'Dixie' Dean tradition for Everton and England, Stan Cullis of Wolves and England, and Sheffield United's inventive inside forward Jimmy Hagan, all graced the army Aldershot colours. At Blackpool there were, among other airmen, Jock Dodds, a high-scoring Scot, the hard-shooting Stan Mortensen and the first real notable celebrity of British football, Stanley Matthews.

Matthews had made his glorious name with Stoke City and England, demonstrating an uncanny dexterity as a dribbler, coupled with an abrupt acceleration from a standing start and a delicately precise knack of centring. Later knighted, it was, as sometimes happens with great sportsmen, the combine of heavenly gifts and earthly ordinariness that caused such adulation everywhere he played. Keeping himself consistently fit, he played at the top level of English football until the age of 50 years and 5 days, and became the first British footballer to occupy, and meritoriously so, the plinth of national hero.

He played a major part in a wartime international match at Maine Road, Manchester in 1945. England beat Scotland 8-0, Tommy Lawton scoring four of them, before a gate of 60,000. The concentration of English footballers in national army and RAF sides, plus the number of international fixtures, for England played 36 such games, winning 22, during the War, created a telling lesson in the advantage of continuous contact in national team-building. With Stanley Rous, the perceptive FA Secretary at the helm, it proved the value of blending international teams more smoothly through more constant collaboration. By one of those unlucky curiosities, and in spite of the fact the Scottish team was not at full strength, the outcome was that many commentators judge that this was the best performance by the best England team there has ever been, but, of course, as a wartime game, it had no official sanction.

'Familiar in his mouth as household words' were the titanic and secure Manchester City goalkeeper Frank Swift; the assured full back duo of Laurie Scott (Arsenal) and the new captain George Hardwick (Middlesbrough); the rhythmically creative half back trio of Cliff Britton of Everton, the majestic Stan Cullis and Joe Mercer, also then of Everton; and the scintillating quintet of Stan Matthews, Raich Carter (Sunderland and Derby County), Tommy Lawton, Jimmy Hagan and, replacing Cliff Bastin, his Arsenal compadre Denis Compton, cavalier prince of cricketers.

Such were the fortunes of war that Frank Swift, certainly one of the top three or four England keepers ever, was followed, with decided equanimity, in the Manchester City goal by the former German prisoner of war Bert Trautmann.

Militarily speaking, peace was, naturally, a huge relief and solace. Otherwise things were much the same as and sometimes worse than before. Materially, bombing and the unavoidable neglect of infrastructure, such as house building, had shattered the nation. Financially, domestic capital and overseas investment were down £3 billion each; the national debt was £3 billion and exports had dropped by two thirds. Socially, the mood and structure of society, was, for better or for worse, much the same. Rationing and shortages; the continuation of national service and the stationing in the UK of American troops in the wake of the Cold War, plus flashpoints like the 1950-53 Korean War and the 1956 Suez crisis; the regular impact of radio and cinema (one in ten of the world cinema audience was British in 1950); the transfer of wartime planning and control into the formation of the Welfare State, together with an essential slate of nationalised industries, likes the mines and the railways; the mellow civic disposition, with crime, already low, dropping a further 5% in the first five post-war years - day to day life was not so different.

Certainly football picked up the pieces and flourished in a post-war economy of full employment and reasonable wage levels. Relieved to be free of the drudgery and the perils of war, people flocked to the match. Football League annual attendances in the five post-war seasons never fell below 39 million and twice they burst over the 41 million mark. In the first full season, 1946/47, 86 of the 92 clubs made a profit, and the overall revenue was £4 million. Football made a splendid peacetime comeback; in 1950 there were 32,000 clubs registered with the FA, of which 500 had full or part professional staffs, with 7,000 professional players in all, half of them full-time.

The only setback was the ageing and decrepit condition of the grounds, the result of years of neglect, because of the war and because of the greed or cynicism of football directors. In March 1946 the Bolton disaster occurred, when, during a match against Stoke City before an audience of over 50,000, the Burnden Park barriers yielded to the crush. 33 died and 4,000 were injured, a substantial proportion of those there present. It must be said that the major cause was pressure from locked out fans forcing an entry from the railway line adjoining the ground. The government, faced with many construction challenges, was rightfully reluctant to give football grounds too much priority, and, despite the money pouring into the game, progress on ground redevelopment was lethargic.

On the brighter side, there were few disciplinary problems off or on the field. During the record-breaking season of 1948/49, with 41.25 million people crowding on to rarely very attractive or well-appointed terraces, incidents of crowd misbehaviour were pleasingly uncommon. Indeed, the yearly average of incidents reported by the police for the first thirteen seasons after World War II is ten or eleven.

Other leisure outlets were also prospering. In 1946 15 million went to the speedways and 45 million to the dog tracks, while the nation's main 450 dance halls were frequently packed with quickstepping couples, and, as the 1938 Holidays with Pay Act came into effect, up to 27 million holiday-makers scurried to the seaside resorts and the Butlin's holiday camps. It was the last grand flourish of the Age of Collective Leisure.

World War II ended too late and - with the unexpected use of the atom bomb reducing its length by an estimated fifteen months - too precipitately in

1945 to organise a full league programme. The FA Cup was contested in that first post-war season, the Derby County of Raich Carter and Ireland's Peter Doherty beating Charlton Athletic 4-1, and then, with demobilisation well under way and post-war resettlement underway, the full league programme was re-launched in the 1946/47 season.

The first club to spring to major prominence was Manchester United, which, having slumbered uneasily in the inter-wars years in the shadow of Manchester City, found a saviour in Matt Busby. A thoughtful and dedicated man of football, his wartime experience as an army warrant officer gave him valuable experience in man management. Where previous management, even when capably undertaken, as by Herbert Chapman or George Allison, had been slightly aloof, in the manner of the works manager, Matt Busby found a vade mecum between board and shop floor, after the fashion of the respected foreman or, in his own model, the regimental sergeant major, bridging the gap between officers and other ranks. Busby was as much at home on the training ground as in the boardroom.

The first of his three great teams flowed effortlessly to success, with a championship and three runners-up spots in the first six campaigns after the Second World War. Led by Johnny Carey, perhaps the first of the really cultivated full backs, they also beat Blackpool 4-2 in the 1948 FA Cup Final, since assessed as the classic footballing banquet of all those appetising Wembley feasts. The forward line - Jimmy Delaney, Johnny Morris, Jack Rowley, Stan Pearson and Charlie Mitten - was greeted as the brightest such quintet ever fielded in club football.

It is worthwhile concentrating for a moment on that cameo of footballing flair. The immediate post-war Manchester United team comprised servicemen returning from sometimes arduous military duties, tricked out with one or two who had spent the war in civil defence or war-work. Apart from the signing of the balding helter-skelter outside-right Jimmy Delaney, from Glasgow Celtic, they were all pre-war United players or products of local football, much of it under the auspices of the Old Trafford club.

They were not paid much money. After a threat of strike action, the maximum wage was lifted in 1945 from £8 to £10 in the winter, with the summer retainer up from £6 to £7.10, an annual income of £465, with maybe some bonuses for (the rider must always be added) only a minority of experienced and skilled players. After the wage rises of wartime, there was some slippage between these earnings and those of the average manual worker. In 1947 there was a further winter rise of £2 per week and a summer adjustment. This raised the annual wage to £510. It was determined by one of the Labour Government's new labour tribunals, one of its packages of improved rights for working men and women, while it also insisted on a minimum wage for junior signings, always - and often still - an area of gross maltreatment. Matt Busby's own first annual salary of £750 was indeed twice as much as he had earned as a sergeant major, but it looks meagre compared with the later ages. The happy-go-lucky Charlie Mitten's tale of the 1948 Cup final says it all. He related how that magnificent eleven shared £220; the band that played at the interval shared £330. Jack Billington, Burnley's twelfth man at the 1947 Cup Final, was paid 10s (50p) for his role.

And yet there was a sense of looking forward about these men - a sense of youthful elasticity of creativeness, of elusive speed and genuine panache. Their football looked ahead to glittering years of flood-lit celebrity footballers and, in particular, to years of sophisticated European tourney.

As the refrain of Leo Dryden's 1891 ballad *The Miner's Dream of Home* has it, 'the bells were ringing the old year out and the new year in'. That Manchester United team contrived to represent the last of the old and the first of the new.

CHAPTER THIRTEEN

EXTRAVERSION; WORLD FOOTBALL, 1914 TO 1953

IN 1945 MOSCOW Dynamo, on a goodwill trip from our then Soviet allies, visited Britain and played four games against British sides. Football fans were appreciatively attentive to the slick talents of the Muscovites. One tiny detail intrigued a public habituated to austerity. The Dynamos always lavishly took the field with three balls for the kick-about, then an unheard of extravagance. It was the nearest most people approached, in the flesh or through the press and newsreels, to European exotica. The British football authorities were inward-looking. After all, there was a certain whimsy about the arrogance of the four home nations forming the International Association Football Board in 1882 to make the rules, beginning with a statutory fixed crossbar, and run the Home International tournament, from 1884. While Britain fiddled ingloriously at home, the world burned furiously away, its football developing in all parts and at all levels.

Internationals - the World Cup

British national sides did have some limited contact with the continent. Having grudgingly joined FIFA a year late in 1905, England, accompanied by the other British associations, left the nascent international body in 1920. The British authorities were not keen to see any external tinkering with the rules, feeling, rather like the MCC and cricket's laws, that their ancient and originating role granted them some pseudo-theological right to protect the ark of football's covenant. Then they re-enlisted in the FIFA ranks in 1925, this time in part to exert authority on the same grounds - they wished to convert other nations to the delights of the two-man offside law, and this they effectively did.

As for the Olympics, Britain fielded an under-strength team in 1920 at Antwerp and no team at all in 1924 at Paris, where a skilled Uruguay, with the prolific goal-scorer, Hector Scarone, starring, won and, in so doing, created the first shock wave of South American football in Europe. Olympic football was suffering from the canker of professionalism that would later infect the entirety of the Olympic physique. FIFA echoed the British FAs in its rigid declaration on the topic. A player was 'either amateur or professional'; it was like pregnancy, one could not be a little bit one or the other. As with the old disputes both in football and rugby union, the issue of 'broken time' compensation for wages lost because of football commitments was the bugbear. Many European associations had licensed senior clubs to make such payments, but it was open to wide abuse - the Uruguayans who won the 1924 Olympics had been given make-believe governmental jobs to ensure they had an income, resembling the English cricket practice whereby needy amateurs had been given almost fictitious posts to support them financially.

Then FIFA and the Olympic Council, prior to the 1928 Amsterdam Games, came to an agreement that lost working time might be compensated. The UK FAs, marshalled by the somewhat dogmatic Frederick Wall, the English FA secretary, were intransigent on the subject, with most of their fellow FIFA delegates annoyed by so obdurate a position. It was the age-old dilemma that had bedevilled several English sports: it was the clash between the ideal of the amateur in societies, where many simply could not afford so to compete sports-wise at the top levels, and the shame of shamateurism, which tainted the purity of both true amateurs and genuine professionals. Once more, the British associations took their leave, departing through the revolving doors of FIFA membership.

The British teams also refused to play former enemy states, further grounds for evading international regulation, but England did play continental sides on 46 occasions during the inter-wars period. They won 33 of these, enough to preserve the proper sense of superiority, especially as - again like the England cricket team when touring other than Australia - they often fielded unrep-resentative elevens. Of the remaining 13 games, five were drawn and eight lost. The first team outside the British Isles to hold England to a draw was Belgium, 2-2, in 1923, while the first loss was against Spain, 4-3, in 1929. During the same period Scotland played just 15 such games, Wales only two and Northern Ireland none - whilst the Republic of Ireland, rising from the smouldering ashes of civil commotion, indulged its new FIFA membership to the tune of 33 fixtures. To offer some scale of comparison, Italy played 133, Austria 138, Germany 139, Switzerland 144 and Hungary 155 international games in that same inter-wars phase.

As music hall customers sang in those far off days, 'let the great big world keep turning'. Football grew in wisdom and stature all over the planet. FIFA had twenty members at the outbreak of the 1914-1918 War; this more than doubled in the post-war years to 52; there was a further surge after the second war, so that, by mid century, the figure was a very satisfying 68. As the figures cited above for Italy and other countries suggest, the appetite for international tourney was ravenous. Between 1919 and 1939 the leading eighteen continental nations played no less than 870 fixtures, an average of twenty each season.

The creation of more nation-states after the First World War and the nationalistic empowerment of others fuelled this excitement. As well as international fixtures, there were lots of trans-national club fixtures, with, it must be mentioned, a continuation of the tradition of British clubs touring abroad. The penchant for competition began to change the flavour of such sporting combat. Contests were both national - from the Baltic Cup, for example, for the three tiny states of Estonia, Latvia and Lithuania, to the Dr Giro Cup for central European countries and the massive edifice of CONMEROL, the South American tournament - and club - the Mitropa Cup, a two-legged knockout trophy for the best clubs in the central European region.

It was on the back of such activity, and in recognition that the Olympic Games was not answering the overall question of how to assess world football standards, that the World Cup was mooted. The Olympic champions, Uruguay, offered to host the first competition in 1930. A trophy, later named after the then FIFA president, Jules Rimet of France, a keen protagonist of world football, was specially made. Uruguay, then enjoying a relatively fruitful patch of economic prosperity and social orderliness, was anxious to utilise the event to celebrate the centenary of its independence, hence the ostentatious title of the brand-new Centenario stadium in Montevideo, the largest football arena outside the British Isles and, globally, possibly then the most impressive; hence, too, governmental investment in the whole operation.

In footballing terms England's notoriously churlish refusal - Frederick Walls' 'I am instructed to express regret at our inability to accept the invitation' - has the same resonance in football history as Chamberlain's 'piece of paper' appeasement speech, a few years later at the time of the 1938 Munich crisis, does in political history. Many have sought to beat the English FA with the rough-hewn cudgel of insularity. They may have been right so to do, the more so that the footballing world often looked to the British pioneers for a lead, but there is a kind of insularity in ignoring the accompanying widespread absenteeism from the inaugural World Cup tournament - there was no Germany, Italy or Spain involved either. It was a new and untried venture, while many national associations did not have the funds to sustain such an enterprise.

Eventually, France, Belgium, Romania and the newly formed Yugoslavia sailed to join nine South American teams in a contest of four groups from which the semi-finalists emerged. Amid memorable scenes of frenzy and turbulence, and with, as David Goldblatt wryly describes, the Belgian referee, Jean Langenus, promised all manner of protections and escape routes, the hosts methodically defeated their Argentine rivals, 4-2 in the final.

The 1934 World Cup was awarded to Italy. There was a reverse geographical distinction, with Uruguay, its players rent by dissension, absent and Argentina, frustrated by the poaching of players into the Italian league, underrepresented. The same grounds of distance and money were part of the problem. Nonetheless, there had to be a qualifying contest to winnow the nations down to a manageable sixteen, of which Egypt, the USA, Brazil and Argentina perished at the first hurdle, leaving the field a completely European one. The Austrian 'Wunderteam', focussing on the adroit Matthias Sindelar, was favoured, but it was Italy, well marshalled in smothering defence and coached by the disciplinarian, Vittorio Pozzo, who finally managed to beat the skilled Czechs, including the high scoring Oldrich Nejedly, 2-1 in extra time.

That 1934 World Championship in Italy had some of the connotations of the Berlin Olympics of 1936, although, as Peter Hartland tells us, Adolf Hitler is only known to have attended one football match in an official capacity, when Norway beat Germany in those Games - General Franco's obsession with football pools suggests he was the keener addict. We have observed the rise of popular nationalism and its search for heroic emblems. Although few nation-states were free, almost by definition, from this predilection, in the corporatist Fascist states it took on an overtly governmental and highly conscious awareness, to the point where, by 1941, Joseph Goebbels, the head of German propaganda, attempted to restrict Germany's national sporting ventures to those where the result could be favourably predicted.

EXTRAVERSION

In the 1934 World Cup Benito Mussolini, *Il Duce*, the Italian dictator, took an avowedly eager interest in that festival of football. The extent of his direct intercession is disputed, but there is little doubt that an expectant atmosphere was created, by the press and among the public, that Italian football was superior. It was the second, and not the last, World Cup to be won by the hosts. The psychologies and physicalities that usually made home teams the favourites in domestic football were being played out on the larger geographic scale. And, if not the hosts, then a regional neighbour was likely to be the victor.

The 1938 World Cup was staged in France. The UK, despite an appeal to send a combined British side, was again unrepresented; Uruguay and Argentina were absent, although Brazil appeared and in sprightly shape; Austria had been annexed by Nazi Germany - and some of her footballers were annexed in consequence, including two who played in the German World Cup XI; Czechoslovakia was under threat of similar appropriation; the Spanish Civil War had been raging cruelly; Japan was already at war with China - all in all, it was a depleted roster of nations that assembled in a distinctly uneasy diplomatic atmosphere. Italy again showed toughness and method in defeating the relative newcomers, Hungary, 4-2 in the final. Germany offered to stage the World Cup in 1942...

During the 1930s, England had been drawn willy-nilly into the diplomatic imbroglio of European football, occasionally helped or hindered by discreet Foreign Office advice. The two games that are usually recalled from the 1930s are the so-called Battle of Highbury in 1934, when England beat the pumped-up Italian world champions 3-2 in an unsavoury contest for which the cliché 'bruising encounter' does scant justice, and the notorious game in Berlin in 1938, when the English team were obliged to raise their arms in the Nazi salute, but ran out satisfyingly as 6-3 victors over Germany.

Professionals - the Spread of Commercialism

On the whole, however, the British authorities were taken by surprise by, where they were not dismissive of, this sudden welter of international football. The range and intensity of this international embrace indicated how quickly soccer was developing. Structurally, the chief enhancement of the game, where globally it was firmly established, was in its financial and sociological character. Once more, the evolutionary trail followed the British spore. Over and again, top level football in country after country forsook its largely middle class and amateur origins and adopted a populist mould. The players became professional. With that payment of full and part-time professionals came the inevitable reliance on the working class sections of the population for recruitment, with a complementary culling of amateurs, either too well salaried in their chosen careers or too socially superior to consort with the plebeian ranks.

As the crowds grew that funded these paid performers, and as these artists carried out their tasks more lavishly and attracted larger audiences, the social component of these hordes became overwhelmingly working class. This was not the sport of kings. The warning must be added - as in Britain - that this is scarcely so astounding, given the relative bourgeois and proletarian ratios of population. In some nations this was as high as nine out of ten in favour of the latter echelon. Almost everywhere there was seating provided, as well as widespread terracing. This accommodated a minority of the reasonably well-off, presumably middle class, customers, of the type who had supported the old-style amateur sides, often based on more generalised upper crust social clubs. Their continued presence may give rise to the argument urged for British crowds, that, in many districts, the gates possibly represented the corresponding proportions of social divisions in their catchment areas.

The post-war epoch of the 1920s and 1930s witnessed a wholesale increase in crowds both in Europe and also in South America, probably a five-fold augmentation, with 50,000 gates where there had been but 10,000 in the 1900s. There was an element, certainly in Europe, of escape from the miseries of war, although that should not be overplayed as a reason. The static nature of the First World War, whilst horrendous for the combatants and those immediately involved, had, unlike the roaming devastation of Napoleonic warfare or the 'total' character of the Second World War, left many societies bloody but unbowed and able to support a degree of normality. The commercialisation of football was perhaps more to do with the acceleration of those socio-economic prerequisites already addressed, of an industrial and urban character.

That said, it is true that the war and its aftermath produced political conditions that encouraged the spread of industry and urbanism. A prior example is Vienna, which, contrary to its popular repute as the haven of the Strauss waltz and of sweet-centred Franz Lehar operettas, like *The Merry Widow*, was the often grim and dirty centre of heavy industry. The reforms of the post-war Austrian republican government, including the reduction of working hours, encouraged even more playing and watching of football than in the previous generation. Austria, now a single state of just over 6m people following the disintegration of the Austro-Hungarian Empire, had some 40,000 registered footballers, many of them drawn from the street football culture of the Viennese industrial districts. In 1924 the first official national professional league outside Britain was formed, its author the secretary of the Austrian FA, Hugo Meisl. As he was also responsible for the launch of the Dr Gero national and Mitropa club tournaments and acted as coach for both FK Austria and the Austrian national side, he might be described, without undue Anglo-centricity, as a Viennese Charles Alcock. As often happens - 'ecce homo' - the man and the moment are dependent one upon the other.

What was Alcockian about Hugo Meisl's resolve to legalise professionalism was his determination to make transparent that which was already occurring and could not be halted. It is the legitimacy of the income that is important. As had happened in England, at Preston North End and among several leading north-western clubs, payments across the world were illicit or surreptitious, covered ~ 'veiled', it may be remembered, was Alcock's adjective - by ridiculous claims for expenses, by make-believe jobs and by simple deceit. The leading Austrian teams were Viennese, among them FK Austria, with something of a business and professional base socially; the Jewish club, Hakoah Wien, and Rapid Wien, the pride of the workers.

Once the Austrian league was under way, two other fragments of the old Empire, the new Czechoslovakia and Hungary also established professional championships. There was the diffusion of the notion to neighbours, that kind of social 'contagion' familiar to cultural historians, especially where, as in both Prague and Budapest, similar economic conditions prevailed. There was also the pragmatic point - vide Scotland in relation to England - that Czech and Hungarian stars would otherwise have been siphoned off by the Austrians.

The sense of new or refurbished nationhood was prominent in the tale of the professionals' progress. In Italy the Fascist authorities were actively involved in the creation of a tidy and unified system out of what had been a fairly chaotic mix, with a national league, soon to be placed on a professional base, promulgated in 1929. That insistence on La Liga being nationally compre-hensive featured recognition of football in the ailing south, itself a fillip for the well-being of the region. In La Liga, Juventus, backed by the Agnelli family, of Fiat fame, and Bogota, like other main Italian clubs favoured by Fascist support, came to the fore in the 1930s.

In Spain, relatively unscarred by the Great War, football was alive and well, but still riven by the particularist antagonisms of its semi-autonomous regions. Barcelona, for instance, while founded by Englishmen, was and remains something of a symbol of Catalan independence. However, several Spanish clubs, Real Madrid chief amongst them, were outward-looking, ambitious and businesslike, and an over layer of unity was found. It was expressed in the formation of the Spanish national league in 1928, while, in this instance, the acceptance of professionalism came two years later. Spanish football, like everything else Spanish, caught the blast of internecine war from 1936 to 1939, although its neutrality in World War II allowed Spain, and its football, a chance of internal recuperation in the early 1940s. The building of Real Madrid's Bernabeu Stadium, named after the club president and highly effective organiser, Santiago Bernabeu, was the architectural peak of this process. It must be added that the Franco regime marked that recovery with an extremely politicised approach to footballing affairs, with Barcelona, a focus for both republican and regional dissension, especially severely treated.

France was now a major footballing nation, in so far as there was an abundance of teams, competitions and spectators. One side effect of war is to spread ideas through the disruption of populations. The mass mobilisation of men, and then their mass demobilisation, has the result of ideas being picked up and then carried back to places from which they might otherwise remain hidden. Football became ubiquitous in France; much the same effect was achieved for baseball in similar military movements of personnel during and just after the American Civil War. By 1919 the FFF, or French FA, had finally been formed from the disparate elements that passed for football administrations and a national cup competition was launched. The legalisation of paid players was, nonetheless, slow in arriving, the argument being - another hint of British déjà vu - that the tritons would soon swallow up the minnows in the bidding for players.

David Goldblatt has described how the impasse was broken by the pressure of a new brand of clubs backed by industry, such as the car magnate, Jean-Pierre Peugeot's backing of FC Sochaux or the sponsorship of Lille by the wealthy brewer, Henri de Jouris. Brewers were a familiar reminder of British football funding, whereas motor car manufacture was a novel sign of the times. In 1933 the FFF permitted a form of contractual registration for players on fixed wages, but professionalism, while now a characteristic of the top flight of soccer, was not widespread, a fact accountable for by the enduring rural nature of much of French society, with industrial urbanism - the fount of commercial football - potent but limited to a few loci.

The comparative feet-dragging of the French serves as a midway example between the powerful professional elites of England, Scotland, Spain, Italy and Austria and the clutch of European nations where amateurism remained the constant. That statement requires the major qualification that licit professionalism is the theme of this discourse. In France, for example, plenty of francs changed hands before 1933, and the same was true of these purportedly amateur football nations. They included Denmark, Sweden, Holland, Belgium and Germany, all countries where industrial and urban progress had advanced hand in hand and where, by and large, social conditions, with reasonable hours of work and decent levels of pay, were at hand or shortly to be promoted. Most had national leagues - the Swedes formed theirs in 1924 - but professionalism was not officially accepted. Apart from Germany, these nations were small, and even unto today, whereas they have often assembled strong national elevens, their individual clubs have not overly flourished in European tournaments. They suffered from having a comparatively tiny industrial base.

There were attendant and idiosyncratic factors. The Danish espousal of the English Corinthian spirit was one such, while the DFB, that is, the German FA, also adopted an early English approach to the canker of professionalism. Most of these nations had a strong religious force, typically Lutheran, that was po-faced about the antics of football and football crowds, especially where, as in Sweden, they were frequently drunk and disorderly. There were played out in Sweden scenes reminiscent of pre-industrial England, with churchmen and the forces of law and order puritanically condemning the behavioural excesses consequent on spectator sport. A crucial element was the sober-sided attitude (previously observed in Europe in pre-1914 days) of trade unionists and socialists who saw football as demeaning for the workers and, not without some truth, a distraction from their fighting for improved rights and conditions. In Sweden, the coming to long-term power of the Social Democratic alliance, with all its profound and beneficial effects on Swedish economic and social existence, led to a cleansing of the footballing stable and a reduction, if not an obliteration, of Sweden's extensive culture of shamateurism.

In Germany, as in Sweden, it was the rise of working class clubs, eager to pay their players, in growing industrial areas that tested the old conservatism of the middle class authorities, just as the Lancashire cotton town teams had threatened the propriety of the English FA. Malmo in Sweden and Schalke 04, from the Gelsenkirchen mining area of the German Ruhr, were among the leading culprits, both subjected to stern disciplining by their respective FAs. In Germany, where football, among the German army during and the industrial civilian population after the war, was advancing by leaps and bounds, there was pressure to legalise the patently professional game.

The Hitlerite regime inevitably took command of the DFB, with young men's football the creature of the Hitler Youth movement and football clubs with racially or politically suspect backgrounds overridden. It would be distasteful to claim that Nazi treatment of Jewish football was, in the context of the Holocaust, especially scandalous. However, the detail, like the careful closure of all Jewish football clubs in Holland, is indicative of the mind-set that was to formulate the Final Solution. The Viennese Jewish side, Hakoah, was abolished and all the teams it had already played against were credited with 3-0 victories. That gruesome daftness hints at the official lunacy of a bureaucratic administration later bent on genocide.

The emerging totalitarian states, including a bunch of lesser nations, like Portugal, Greece, Hungary and Rumania, with right-wing dictatorships, embraced sport for its physical worth, in so far as they boasted of health and strength as a virtue, over against the fragility of the liberal parliamentary democracies, as well as an expression of fervent national pride. Football was, ideologically speaking, infinitely elastic. Thus the Soviet Union, preaching an anti-Fascist doctrine of Leninist principles, also found a seat for football at the table of Marxist dogma. What had been viewed as the equivalent of Rome's circuses, pap to divert the masses, football, and other sports, became part of the national armour. Although one or two clubs - Spartak is the prime example - retained some degree of independence, the majority were closely controlled and funded politically.

The Stalinist administration adapted its approach to suit the overwhelming desire for football among the Russian people. Moreover, the incredible and mighty endeavour of the USSR to industrialise under state management was, materially, a magnificent triumph, provided one did not factor in the ghastly cost in executions, imprisonments and all the other nastiness of a dictatorship intent on success. What, in effect, happened over relatively few years was a replication of what occurred - itself not free from associated miseries -- during the British industrial revolution; although, of course, Russia already had an embryonic manufacturing and communications system. The triple components of primary industry, intense urbanism, widespread mechanised transport links and a massive rise in population were suddenly present. It was a situation tailor-made for the lift-off of football. Crowds were plentiful and interest was wide.

In another reprise of the British convention, companies sponsored some of the teams, although, in this case, the industries were nationalised, like the Torpedo club, from the Moscow vehicle works or the Lokomotiv railway side. The state agencies, such as the army, with its CSKA Moscow team, funded sides. If one may be permitted an analogous conceit, Francis Marindin's Royal Engineers from soccer's early days in Victorian London, lived again. The use of the armed forces to oversee football would become a regular feature of sport in so-called Communist Eastern Europe after 1945. In effect, by one means and another, a professional football stratum was created in Soviet Russia. By 1936, a professional national league and attendant cup tournaments had been established.

Over in South America, untouched by the rigours of the 1914-1918 War, economies initially went on expanding, cities went on growing and populations went on increasing. Football, at both club and national levels, was acknowledged more and more widely as the new culture, celebrated by both the social elites and the huge masses of impoverished workers and migrants. South American nationalism was still comparatively young and immature; it was still seeking some novel definition of its identity. Football offered an answer. In the turbulence of South American politics and economics, which, at this stage, was rather like the restlessness and frenzy of a large-scale gold rush, football brought leisure but also a mixture of emotions for the people to enjoy. It also began to bring income to its stars, but, as in parts of Europe, the payments, some of them quite extravagant, were clandestine. There was player action, such as the 1931 strike by Argentine players, who contrived to demand freedom of contract from the stance of amateurism.

The transition to legal professionalism was imminent. Again, one sees the domino effect, witnessed in Britain and then in Europe, with neighbours forced to consider professionalism to protect their own human resources. In 1931 all the major Argentine clubs opted for professional staffs and the first professional league operated from that date. In 1944 the Argentinean professionals formed their first union, strong enough to strike in 1948 for improved contracts and wages, which were granted the following year. In 1932 the top leagues in Brazil were officially acclaimed as professional, in many cases the de jure merely replacing the de facto position. Uruguay and Chile also allowed professional contracts to be offered, although most of the smaller South American countries, rather like their counterparts in Europe, were too under-resourced, in urban, population and manufacturing terms, to support a formal cadre of professional teams and players. In Central America Mexico launched its first professional league in 1944.

In a dramatic illustration of the global context of football, that knock-on effect took on a world-wide dimension. If one team or one league turned lawfully professional, then there was a temptation for other players to sign on the dotted line and become a bona fide paid performer. Previously, that had happened in or close to the city or country involved. One reason why the South Americans resolved to license professionalism was the attempts made to poach their star artists for service with European clubs, recently professionalised, notably in Spain and Italy, where there was a Latinate affinity with the southern parts of the American continent. There were Argentineans of Italian descent in the Italian World Cup winning team of 1938. It was a meaningful omen.

The South American experience in the pre-1945 era is instructive because of its analogous nature to the European practice. For example, the 1929 Wall Street crash and subsequent depression was as debilitating for Latin America as for Europe. As the economies crumbled, there was, as in Europe, a grumbling restlessness among the unemployed and disadvantaged many, and, as in Europe, the heavy-handed response was all too frequently the emergence of one or another species of military and authoritarian rule. Juan Peron, courtesy of his musically commemorated wife, Evita, is but the best known of scores of dictators who tried, sometimes with material success, to forge populist support, even at the price of lost civil liberties.

It followed that, as in Europe but perhaps more belligerently, football was a major device in these exercises in national regeneration. Boca Juniors, for instance, was a Peronist club in a real political sense that has never been emulated in British football. Argentina, indeed, was the leading football nation of the region at this time, winning five out of ten Copa Americas, the annual Latin American national tourney, around this time. It displaced the feisty and dedicated footballers of Uruguay, now feeling, like some of the smaller European states, the pressure of sustaining world football status off a minute population of only 3 million.

As well as Buenos Aires, where the Peronist influenced Racing Club was beginning to shine, the other urban centres of the country, like Santa Fé and Cordoba, were developing proud footballing traditions. Independiente, San Lorenzo and the well-connected and well-supported River Plate teams were among those that arose - and Juan Muñoz, one of River Plate's exciting forwards also distinguished himself by prefiguring the lifestyle of George Best. Even more interesting was the opening in 1938 of El Monumental, the River Plate 70,000 capacity stadium, not only Argentina's first such modern industrialised construction, but perhaps the first in the world to welcome communal participation, in that it sensibly encompassed medical and educational facilities.

On the back of all these ventures into large scale football commercialism on both sides of the Atlantic came the cultural accompaniments that had adorned or otherwise the British game, as it flourished. In all these nations where football surfaced as an outstanding professional sporting spectacle, one also found the press and media dancing attendance. Everywhere there was extensive coverage in the popular press, the publication of dedicated football periodicals and annuals, often the inclusion of gambling, of a 'pools' or other variety, the use of footballers in advertising or, for instance, as the inspiration for music and dance, and the utilisation of radio broadcasting, with newspaper columnists and match commentators sometimes enjoying as much notoriety as the top players.

The totality of the football experience, and its express part in the daily lives, habits and emotions of millions of people, was built steadily across much of the world in the first half of the 20th century.

Football at War

Such were the sometimes uneasy preludes to full-scale war, in which a minor feature was the acknowledgement that football had a role. The British approach - 'We Can Take It' was the slogan - involved battling on in adversity, with football sustained, even if the competitive component was re-jigged to conform to wartime difficulties. This was copied across the continent, with some of that same emphasis on bringing some leisure to the weary lives of troops and war-workers. What marked this attitude was the insistent support and intervention of national governments. It amounted to a change of heart from World War I, where politicians had been largely indifferent to sport, and what it indicated was football's swift capture of the public imagination. The Orwellian adage about sport and warfare had that extra dimension, whereby sport was a propagandist armament.

The totalitarian administrations utilised football as a benign reminder that their martial supremacy was such that the daily round of ordinary existence need not fear disturbance. War, perhaps, was a necessary, even normal, circumstance, but people need not fear it would be unduly disruptive. A like tactic was attempted in some German occupied territories, with football a sign that the 'new order' restored normality.

The advent of Nazi rule in 1933 had led to an overhaul of the German game, with sixteen Gauliga or district leagues, whose leaders played out a contest for the national championship. As areas were annexed, new Gauliga were added, such as Alsace and Sudetenland, so that, at one stage, eighteen clubs from those two regions and also Austria, Poland and even Luxembourg were competing in the German leagues. Indeed, Rapid Vienna were 'German' champions in 1941. By using the British precept of sub-dividing districts to save on precious transport resources, Germany maintained competitive football right up until 1945. Particularly in the early wartime years, there were plenty of international fixtures, against countries such as Hungary, Yugoslavia, Finland, Spain and Italy. As Jack Rollin has pointed out in his excellent *Soccer At War*, a 70,000 gate watched Dresdner SC beat Hamburg 4-0 in Berlin to lift the German championship - twelve days after D-Day and the Normandy invasion.

Mussolini, and his Fascist placemen who organised sport, were also keen to keep football going, and, until 1943, sustained Italy's peacetime programme, whereafter there was some regional reorganisation, both before and following the allied invasion and the deposition of Mussolini. Ottorino Barassi, one of the Italian sport's administrators, did his bit by keeping the Jules Rimet trophy in a shoebox under his bed during the latter part of the war, fearful that the Nazis might lay greedy hands upon it. Spanish football actually resumed normal service in the 1939/40 season, subsequent on the formation of Franco's Falangist government, heralded by what was the short-term success of the air force team, Atletico Avoacion, a Franco-style merger of Atletico Madrid and Club Aviacion, managed by the gifted Spanish goalkeeper, Ricardo Zamora.

EXTRAVERSION

Other neutral countries, like Switzerland, Sweden, Portugal and, after its brief and inconclusive military bout with Russia until 1940, Finland, actively developed their domestic game, and, although international fixtures were restricted, one still finds that, for example, Switzerland played France right in the middle of the war. As German co-belligerents, Hungary and Rumania also played on, their league programmes more or less intact. Turkey, too, suffered from the minimum of dislocation in a footballing sense, whereas Greece, the locale of rancorous fighting, found it difficult to keep up any football activity. In Yugoslavia, with war waged bitterly within its frontiers, football came to much of a standstill, except in German-controlled Croatia, which fielded a quasi-national team. Poland, too, ravaged to west and east by Germany and the Soviet Union, saw an end to official football for the duration. Slovakia, rather like Croatia, enjoyed, for a time, some degree of neo-nationalism under Nazi oversight after the secession of large tracts of Czechoslovakia to the German state. With that neo-nationalism came a neo-national football team with fixtures against Germany and its co-partners. Slavia won five successive all-Czech club championships during this wartime phase.

Football was played in the other occupied nations. France had a zonal competition, in the occupied north and the unoccupied Vichy south, while forms of professionalism were preserved, including, for a spell, a national pool of paid players in fourteen regional squads. It has been estimated that about 300 professionals eked out a living, on a par with policemen and postmen, in front of goodish crowds and that some 300,000 young men participated in amateur football. Both Holland and Belgium, where the accent was still on part-time professionalism, contrived to conduct normal league programmes throughout the war, these being finally disrupted by allied invasion rather than Nazi occupation. Denmark, too, maintained an even football keel in spite of German control; having offered little or no resistance, it was not subject to the most spiteful rein. Norway, of all the northern European occupied countries, found it difficult to organise overmuch official football; here there had been bitter opposition to the occupation, and a defiant populace boycotted Quisling-style soccer.

The exploits of Moscow Dynamo in England in 1945 came as a surprise, in part because it was well rehearsed how traumatically the Russians had suffered in the war. The statistics, severally calculated, underlined this sentiment. The seven bloodiest battles of the war were Russo-German in contest. 1.6 million

239

men were killed in the conflict after the German invasion, compared with, say, the British losses of 4,650 at El Alamein. The western alliance was responsible for a fifth of Germany's 3.5 million dead. Soviet forces accounted for the other four-fifths, and lost 11 million combatants themselves, plus, grievously, another 11 million from amongst the civilian population. The British and American armed services death toll combined was about 300,000, while British civil losses were 0.01% of the population, compared with 25% of the Byelorussian civilian population. The Soviet military dead included about a million shot by their own political commissariat, for, as the great Marshal Zhukov remarked, 'in the Red Army it takes a very brave man to be a coward'.

And yet, and in spite of a dread of crowds that Stalin inherited from his Tsarist predecessors, football was played and watched by large crowds throughout these fierce hostilities. It is estimated that a million players were involved in formal competitions in the USSR during these tragic years.

The Post-war Settlement

It is important to recall the continuities of football during World War II. Rightly, we tend to remember the war for its horrors - the sickening acts of genocide; the appalling waste of human resources - and, inevitably, the nadirs of defeats and the zeniths of victory. It is not easy to factor in the mundane, the trivial, matter of football amidst such events, and yet, for reasons both social and political, a place was found for football in the interstices of existence throughout Europe, so much so that, in many regions, it emerged relatively and surprisingly strongly.

There was no area more astounding in this respect than West Germany. East Germany was in Russian hands, but the three western zones in American, French and British control rose swiftly from the wreckage of total war. The West German 'economic miracle', showing spectacular growth in industrial output of 10% and of exports of 20% in some years, was an unrivalled success, and, in that atmosphere, it was less amazing that football re-found its feet rapidly. By 1948 a form of national championship was resumed, with the process further eased by the 1949 establishment of the Federal German Republic, its 32 million inhabitants far outscoring the 13 million in East Germany. Saarland, which had remained French, also returned to the Germanic fold, having, in a small but telling example of football's interaction with politics, been a FIFA member for four years.

EXTRAVERSION

Although Germany was not allowed to compete in the 1950 World Cup or the Olympics of 1948 and 1952, the unionisation of the zones served as a signal for the re-launch of the Deutscher Fussball Bund (DFB) in 1949 and, in 1950, its first post-war international fixture, with Switzerland, before a large gate of over 100,000. The drawing tight of the Iron Curtain had caused a swift reshuffle of allies, with the Russians and their Warsaw Pact colleagues demonised and the Germans hailed - and soon rearmed - as chums. Nazi sympathies were soon overlooked among scientists, industrialists or administrators who might assist in the resurrection of a strong buffer state. Football benefited from this mood. It was a valued ingredient in the business of providing leisure and a taste of national pride to a hard-working people and former Nazi sympathisers, including Sepp Herberger, the old coach, were restored to post.

A stern if homely devotee of the game, Sepp Herberger, in alliance with the German skipper, Fritz Walter, set about restoring and extending Germany's football fortunes, rather more successfully than was managed by several of Germany's recent victors and victims among the western democracies. The Low Countries and the Scandinavian teams were relatively sluggish in riposte; Italy was wounded by the Superga air crash that wiped out the excellent and standard-bearing Torino team in 1949, including 10 internationals; and Spain, even allowing for the mature progress of Real Madrid, was at something of a standstill.

The divide between east and west was strict and complete. The Soviet Union's oversight of most of Eastern Europe was soon all-embracing. With state ownership as the referential frame, football clubs, as in the USSR, were primarily run by the state. The indubitable affection for football among the subjects of all these satellite states could not be ignored, while the chance could scarcely be wasted to demonstrate, through sporting accomplishment, that Stalinist Communism, like justice, was being seen to be done. It was art for Marx's sake.

The post-war accommodation of Soviet bloc club football is eerily similar. The state agencies either invented or absorbed clubs. There were army teams, like Poland's CWKS, Czechoslovakia's Dukla Prague or Rumania's Inter Steana. There were sides organised by the security forces or interior ministries, like East Germany's Dynamo Dresden, Bulgaria's Levski or Poland's Guardia. There were clubs based on state-managed industries like Chemie Leipzig in East Germany or Rapid Bucharest, the team of Rumania's railway combine. Even in

Yugoslavia, which had, under the tenacious governance of Marshal Tito, gained a precarious independence from Joseph Stalin's dictates, the same format occurred. Partizan Belgrade was the army team and Red Star Belgrade was the party team. As events later in the century would horribly bear witness, Tito needed all the devices he could muster to enable him to hold Serbia, Croatia and Slovenia in cohesive shape. He was anxious to ensure that football did its bit for the cause of Yugoslav unity.

But imagine a post-war English First Division in which Arsenal was managed by the War Office, Tottenham Hotspur by British Railways and Chelsea by Special Branch.

Hungarian football was also organised in this institutional fashion, with Kispest, later Honved, the army team, and MTK taken over by the security forces. Hungary, however, had built a decent pre-war base for its football, and, under the powerful influence of its coach, Gustav Sebes, would rise to challenge Germany, England and others for the hegemony of European and world football. The other aspect of these institutional clubs was that they allowed the easy creation of 'jobs' for the likes of Ferenc Puskas, Hungary's famous galloping major, allowing them to train full-time and also retain amateur status so they could enter the Olympic tournament - a competition Hungary won at a canter in 1952.

Hungary and Germany would also find the gauntlet thrown down by the enduring quality of the South American countries in the immediate post-war years. There were glowing signs of Brazilian promise, assisted by the coming to terms of the football and political authorities with the contribution offered by the Afro-Brazilian quarters of the populace and the diverse compound of what was called Brazil's 'mulattoism'. The great white, modernistic Maracana stadium was being erected in Rio in anticipation of the 1950 World Cup contest, and, with its titanic capacity of 160,000, it would overtake Hampden Park as the largest football arena in the world. Indeed, as with the huge bowls being dug out and concreted throughout Eastern Europe, as not very inspiriting architectural centrepieces for national adulation, the nationalistic dictators of South America were just as keen to see stadia rise in tribute to their reigns.

For all that activity, possibly the most portentous Latin American happening of that time was the extraordinary buccaneering league of Colombia. Colombia, then as addicted economically to caffeine as later it would be to cocaine, boasted, on the swell of its gainful coffee trade, a useful professional league, based around its capital, Bogota. Amid the kind of internal rows and tumultuous outrages that bedevilled the national, and thus the footballing, politics of the hour, FIFA had been persuaded to outlaw the DiMayor League, as it was known, in 1949. The human mind is resourceful and enterprising. It was realised that being cast off from the bureaucratic shackles was liberating. There were no regulations and no nonsense about transfer fees, wages, status and the like. The Colombians simply started a pirate league and travelled the world to invite foreign players to join the party.

The older British football fan will recall the furore and consequent bans that surrounded the emigration to Colombia in 1950 of Neil Franklin, a most stylish centre-half, then holder of the English record for consecutive appearances in the national team, and George Mountford of Stoke City, Charlie Mitten from Manchester United, doughty Roy Paul of Manchester City, Bobby Flavell of Heart of Midlothian and Billy Higgins of Everton. Insularity may have masked the fact that they were but a quintet among over a hundred alien visitors, fifty of them from Argentina. The programme that had inscribed on its colourful pages the names of Billy Higgins and the great Argentinean forward, Adolfo Pedernera, must have made for spellbinding perusal. A young Alfredo Di Stefano was another migrant, showcased and then recruited for his marvellous exploits with Real Madrid. The clubs, Millionaros, Independiente Santa Fé, and the rest, were packed out like exhibition elevens, and the crowds flocked to see them.

The rewards were immense. Charlie Mitten and his wife received a £2,500 signing on fee, £35 win bonuses and a £1,500 end-of-season bonus, as well a detached house, with maid and car. Although Neil Franklin found the ambience too tense and returned home after a brief, unhappy sojourn, the more extrovert Mitten stuck it out for a year and probably thought, relative to £12 a week in England, his six months ban and £250 fine was a small price to pay. Nonetheless, one wonders how often or how far he drove his shiny new vehicle through the Bogotan streets. It is estimated that 60,000 Colombians were killed annually in civil strife that served as a dreadful canvas to this episode over its four years duration. Finally, a bargain was struck at Lima in 1951, whereby the bootleg league was permitted two more years of profitable activity and Colombia was allowed to re-enter FIFA. Fifty years on, the equivalent of such rewards would become commonplace for leading footballers and the transmigrations of players around the globe would also become routine.

There is perhaps a lesson to be learned from this vital comparison of German teams battling out of the debris of a smashed totalitarian society, of Soviet bloc teams struggling amid the intense scrutiny of cruel left-wing tyranny, and of Latin American teams fighting for glory, often against a background torn by civil discord and ruled by preening despots. Both during the Second World War and its often contentious aftermath, people, unless conditions were completely barbaric, sought to play and watch football. This pertinent ability, this pressing necessity, to compartmentalise human acts and, for a while, to find the escape and refreshment, what Johan Huizinga would have called the 'interlude' of 'play' is encouragingly apparent.

At the same time, commentators became wont to relate sports such as football very specifically to political and cultural determinants, seeing direct and concentrated links between religious, ethnic, ideological and other characteristics and sporting styles. A cultural shorthand of doctrinal metaphors was made available to the press and media and they used them to reinforce the prejudicial emotions of spectators and the increasing volume of adherents who followed the game through newspaper and radio coverage.

We previously rehearsed, in chapter eight, how 'the imagined community' of a nation or a region may adopt a cloak of cultural identity and play out that 'persona' accordingly. That certainly happened with football, as it was incorporated into the visualised personality of each nation. The bravura of the Brazilian game or the workmanlike nature of German football are cases in point, and there is no doubt that, in the minds of players and onlookers, either friend or foe, something of this mythic belief had its telling effect. Cricket, with its more literary overtones, has a similar allusive quality, with West Indians indefatigably ebullient and Indians unfailingly, mystically sinuous. In football, these nationalistic interpretations were, after 1918, more overtly larded with ideological annotations, and, after 1945, there would be many games, such as the 1954 World Cup final between West Germany and Hungary, that were luridly branded as contests between Capitalism and Communism.

It might be timely, at this stage, as the politicisation of football became quite pronounced, to enter a caveat or two. One qualifying element is the similarity of the human condition, except under the direst of stress (and, admittedly, there were too many examples of that for global comfort during the 20th century) and thus the irrelevance of typologies of governance to many humdrum corners of ordinary existence. The amazing continuity of football during World War II, that constant insistence on 'play', is an illustration of this. As the saying has it, life goes on. At worst, one tyranny, left-wing or right-wing, is much like another, in terms of its effect on the ground where ordinary people eke out their lives. The poverty that results from a capitalist slump, such as the 1929 American led Great Depression, is much like the distress that arises from the crudity of statist mismanagement behind the Iron Curtain.

Moreover, political ideology, like the tenets of organised religion, is are open to an infinite range of interpretations. The great Hungarian team, just making felt its presence on the world scene, was applauded as a freewheeling representation of the Marxist ethic in beautiful action. Even its coach, the highly organised Gustav Sebes, firmly believed that, and probably that faith inspired him and his players. But had the Hungarians been Brazilian, then the spin would have been talk of exhilarating fiesta time. The very career of Pelé illustrates the point, for he ambitiously mustered his superb gifts with a carefully observed regimen of rigorous training and sensible life-style that could easily have passed for 'Germanic'. Some smoothly flowing batsmen have produced that same effect of facile, natural ease - the fluent Indian Prince Ranjitshinji is an example - through dint of tough and arduous practice.

Economics are the keys. The big rich industrial nation will normally beat the little poor agricultural nation, not because of any overtures of political science, but because the human and material resources are sufficiently large to create the circumstances in which a professional spectator sport might flourish. That is the formative structure. The rest is superstructural gloss, not, to be sure, of no account, but certainly subservient to the mainstay economic determinant.

At the close, there is the pragmatic point that international football is fundamentally the sport that was shaped by the Victorian gentry all those years before. It concerns twenty-two men and their concerted ability over the very constricted time-scale of 90 minutes. Moslem or Christian, Latin or Nordic, Marxist or Free-market, anything can happen in that short time-span. Usually, the compound of the fitter, better motivated, more talented performers, coached and organised by the more gifted managers, will win through, but not always. This is a reminder that to trail football as a yardstick for ethnic, theological or ideological superiority is a dangerous conceit. The most exact guide would be the underlying economic circumstance, free of all political construal...and even this will let you down, on occasion, over that brief passage of 90 minutes; that being the beauty of football.

CHAPTER FOURTEEN

EXPANSION: BRITISH FOOTBALL TO NEAR THE END OF THE 20TH CENTURY

DESPITE THE complaints of some critics, it is probably unfair to aver that British football declined in standard and quality in the first half of the 20th century. Both at club and national level, the home countries, especially England and Scotland, were rarely outwitted and outrun, while British coaches continued to be welcomed all around the world. It might be more reasonable to accept that, if Britain did not fall back, it did not rush forward; moreover that other countries caught up. There was complacency. The systems and structures worked well enough, both in sporting and financial terms, with plenty of exciting games and plenty of sizeable crowds. There was no genuine interior motivation to make alterations.

Britain, as the first industrial state, was to observe this phenomenon over and over again in railway construction and other branches of the engineering sciences. As pioneers, there was initially a rush of inventive genius, followed by a fallow period of reflection and inward-looking smugness; it has occurred too often and too regularly to be anything other than a national characteristic, although one has to observe that these are always issues associated with being the first. Other nations seized on the models, dodged the unavoidable errors of the template and embarked on the secondary phase of development with energy and clarity. So was it with football.

Furthermore, the football controllers of the continent and of South America were constantly looking outward, not least towards Britain, with a view to progress forwards and upwards. Britain was the recognised leader. As any account of the rise of world football reveals, it is the respectful copying of British methods, from the laws of the game and the modes of competition to the onset of professionalism and the use of the media, which catches the eye. Even allowing for the dictates of the same determining conditions of urban and industrial life falling into place, the degree of institutional cloning is very evident. If British football between the wars looked a little suspect and enfeebled, it was more because the rest of the world's football authorities had set their sights on catching up and, on occasion, surpassing the British game.

Home Rules

From about 1950 English football poked its head around the door of insularity and ventured fitfully abroad. It did so against the grain of the retreat from imperial grandeur, as, beginning with the granting of independence to India in 1947, the remarkably short-lived British Empire, assessing its longevity against that of the empires of antiquity, was dismantled in reasonably fair order. For all that, the fiasco of the dodgy Suez adventure in 1956, when the United Kingdom vainly tried to cling to some authority in the Middle East, is fairly judged as the moment when the nation realised, with a grave shock, that Britain was no longer a super-power. It did so as air travel began to be a more familiar and not solely military mode of transport, for a nation that, through the expediency of war, had learned at first or second hand of foreign lands. Soon this would be reinforced by the phenomenon of the overseas holiday, as the call of hot sun and blue ocean summoned, by the late 1950s, as many as 10 million Britons to the Spanish Mediterranean beaches. There was also inward migration to highlight the new cosmopolitanism. 150,000 Jamaicans arrived in Britain to boost a numerically dwindling workforce, the real beginnings of our multicultural society.

There were signs that the rational and co-operative methods and spirit that had served admirably both in war and reconstruction were wilting, and that people were now growing resistant to 'austerity', that then in vogue descriptor of a fair-minded but drab existence. There was an understandable demand for a colourful and diverse life-style. With full employment and relatively high wages - earnings rose by 130% between 1956 and 1969 - there were adequate funds to expend on novel goods and services. Between 1950 and 1965 the number of washing machines, for example, sprang from one to seven in every ten households and by 1971 a third of homes had central heating. Expenditure on furniture, electrical apparatus and other such domestic appliances doubled between 1951 and 1964 from £500 million to £1,000 million, with only a slight nod to inflation.

The turn to a consumer focus hit British football badly in the pocket. With a much more varied array of recreational options, football, a little passé and with an accurate image of rundown and primitive settings, suffered. Football League attendances fell sharply. The 40 million spectators of the 1949/50 season dropped to the 33 million of 1955/56 to the 28 million of 1964/65 to the 18 million of 1984/85, that is, worse than a halving in thirty years. In the meanwhile, the 1s 3d (6p) price of 1946 had doubled to the 2s 6d (12.5p) and rising of 1960. In the new dispensation, the leading clubs did not endure the same damage as the smaller fry. They maintained reasonable support, and that translated into healthy crowds for the Premiership towards the end of the century.

However, there was to be no renaissance for the lower division clubs. They were never to recover anything like their mid-century backing. In the 1961/62 season Accrington Stanley, under these pressures, withdrew from the Football League, one of the first, but not the last, of such casualties, for many, many years. 2005/06 happily marked the saving of the lost sheep of Accrington as the reborn Stanley returned to the Football League, but the financial omens were not too promising for the lesser footballing breeds in the 1960s.

Floodlighting was a bow towards the consumer. Football's archaeologists speak reverently of a floodlit match in Sheffield in 1878, but the first illuminated modern league match was Portsmouth versus Newcastle United in 1956, after which there was a steady acceptance of the attraction of evening football. It banished football's enslavement to daylight and often produced a theatrical atmosphere that became particularly related to cup football.

The golden age of collective leisure was dulled. Cricket was even more disastrously harmed, with a precipitous three quarters decline of County Championship attendances to under a million spectators by the early 1960s. That glittering symbol of collective recreation, the cinema, was another victim. By the 1960s over half of Britain's 4,700 cinemas had closed; in 1980 the nadir of only 101 million ticket purchasers was reached. Today it has risen slightly to 160 million a year, exactly a tenth of the 1946 figure. Trams disappeared, bus services were decimated and the railways, assailed by Dr Beeching, lost a sixth of the network after 1963.

EXPANSION - BRITISH FOOTBALL

The two chief engines of social change were the motor car and the television. Henry Ford's major contribution to socio-economic history was not so much mass production as the dream that the car could be the poor man's mode of transport and not - as its initial designs of the 'horseless carriage' intended - the internal combustion replacement for the rich man's conveyance. There had been 2 million vehicles on the roads in 1939 and about the same in 1948; by 1960 it was 6 million and by 1970 that had doubled to 12 million. In 1959 the motorway network was initiated.

A decisive moment was in 1953, on the day when Queen Elizabeth II was crowned, not so much for the regal glory, but for the fact that an estimated 20.5 million people, nearly half the population, clustered in groups of neighbours and relations around 5 million television sets, watching the muzzy, flickering pictures of that dignified event. This was the moment when, realistically, the post-war world began in Great Britain, heralding, as it did, the onset of a monopolising art-form, and one that would be supported by all manner of electronic gadgetry such as videos, computers and mobile phones. It was the onset of the 'miniaturisation' of society. Just as the ice storage units, to the temporary abandonment of ice-rinks, yielded to domestic fridges and then freezers and the public washhouses and laundries retreated in the face of the washing machine and the tumble drier, so was the cinema reduced to a niche in the corner of the living room, with the concert hall contracting, in turn, to the music centre on the sideboard. By 1960 the average power utilised in a kitchen equalled that of a cotton mill in 1860.

You no longer had to leave home and join others in the co-operative enjoyment of sport or the arts. And, if you did wish so to do, you no longer needed to climb on the bus or train with dozens of others, you could follow personal routes and private trails in your motor car. People were liberated at a stroke. They were freed in the value-changing context of an end to rationing and to controls, of a 'sexual revolution', energetically inspired by the deployment of the contraceptive pill from the 1960s, of a tripling of divorces from the pre-war average of 3%, from the 1950s, of the proclamation by Bill Haley and the Comets that the rock'n'roll cult was on its way, of the subversive messages contained in the *Lucky Jim* of Kingsley Amis and the *Look Back In Anger* of John Osborne, and of the popping of 'purple heart' pills as a mild prelude to the current entrenched drug culture.

A parallel and equally important televisual happening in 1953 was the screening of the FA Cup final, the one in which Stan Matthews gained his sole winner's medal. 10 million fans tuned in - that was four times as many as had paid and watched all the score or so Wembley finals thus far. Television was beginning its almost merciless capture of football, eventually reaching the juncture where the income from its deep penetration of the market made it master rather than servant of the game. The BBC's *Match of the Day* highlights programme was first broadcast in 1964 and soon commanded large audiences of 13 million - about half as many as were passing through the Football League turnstiles in a whole season. Especially when first colour and then satellite TV arrived and the coverage grew very sophisticated, there was a sense in which, apart from the sheer atmosphere of being present at the living event, one could watch the game more clearly on the screen. Spectatordom was amplified many times over.

The social character of the crowds began to alter in concert with the changing values of post-war society. The 'integrated culture' of aspirant workers and ambitious suburbanites slowly crumbled. The very proper feminist appeal for equity drew many men into a more family-focused life-style, very unlike the old masculine dominance of the football terraces, a process much aided by the liberty of car usage. There was an accent on youth. During the previous generations, the communal and family restrictions on adolescent misdemeanours had been underpinned by the organised youth agencies, such as the Scout and Boys' Brigade movements or an array of youth clubs, many of them church orientated. Now, and, in particular, where urban decay and anomie mouldered, the communal disciplines of street, work, church, national service, school and club foundered. An aspect of the shift of values after about 1950 was the flaring up of a more truculent and independent breed of adolescent behaviour, sometimes garbed in cult uniform, as with the Teddy Boys of that era. Paradoxically, given that discord often arises from economic despair, it was fuelled, in part, by the full employment that supplied almost everyone with a moderate income.

Football was a magnet for youth. Anecdotally, one observed the average age of football crowds drop steadily. A mix of vigorous loyalty to the team and the search for an outlet for preening macho bravado led to an increase in crowd troubles at and around the major football stadia. The new motorways conveniently contributed to this outbreak of misbehaviour, for the phenomenon arose of far larger contingents of 'away' fans. The days of watching one's club's reserves on alternate Saturdays was replaced by car and coach, as well as some train, travel to other outposts of the Football League. Conflict resulted. One sad outcome was the necessity to separate crowds, segregating the 'away' faction at one end or in one pen, a most unpleasant and unwelcome development.

Home Games

Matt Busby trailed the path of British clubs into Europe. His second great team - 'the Busby Babes' - caught the imagination of a nation where the accent was on youth. Youngsters, many of them locals, brought verve and panache to Old Trafford, as, contrary to FA advice, Manchester United resolved to engage in European contest. Champions Chelsea had been forbidden from entry into the first European Cup competition of 1955/56, the FA and the Football League believing such antics to be a distraction from the even tenor of domestic activities. The rather sporadic Inter Cities Fairs Cup was also introduced in 1955, a year after the formal launch of the UEFA, the alliance of European FAs, but did not really become properly established until it changed into the UEFA Cup in 1971.

Matt Busby understood that players, spectators and revenue would all benefit from the excitement of European club football, and so it proved. His team, at that first dramatic attempt, were defeated in the semi-finals by the majestic Real Madrid combine. Frank Keating, the long-serving and eloquent *Guardian* journalist, has recounted how the Football League was quietly smug that, without floodlights, United could not compete. Matt Busby persuaded his cautious chairman, Harold Hardman, that if they borrowed Maine Road, where Manchester City had installed lights in 1953, the Busby Babes could both try their skills in Europe and, in so doing, earn enough gate-money to purchase the precious but expensive luxury of floodlights for Old Trafford. It proved to be an influential deal.

It was on the return air trip from one of these continental encounters in Belgrade that the Munich disaster destroyed the maturing 'Babes' in February 1958. The artistry of Roger Byrne, Eddie Colman, Billy Whelan, Tommy Taylor and others was lost. Also among the victims was the giant figure of Duncan Edwards. It is persuasively arguable that Duncan Edwards was ripening into the best footballer there has ever been. The usual suspects for that position tend to be attackers, Pelé, Puskas and Maradona among them. The case for Duncan Edwards rests on the perfect calibre of his all-round ability in all aspects of the sport, added to which there are his superb physique, uncanny footballing brain and sane temperament. In cricket, one would have to field Gary Sobers as a near equivalent.

A consequence of the Munich disaster was the encouragement of a national response to the calamity. Again with the aid of television and motorway coach travel, Manchester United began to draw and sustain support from across the land. Supporters, too, began to travel to European venues, for, of course, European cup competitions were played on a two-legged home and away basis. Shortly, there would be the spectacle of British talent - for example, the titanic solidity of John Charles and the goal scoring genius of Denis Law and Jimmy Greaves, both maestros of spiky intuition - journeying to play in Italy. Later, in the late 1970s, the compliment was reversed when, with the signing of the Argentinean stars, Osvaldo Ardiles and Ricky Villa, Tottenham Hotspur presaged the overseas influx of the last decades of the 20th century. The globe contracted further.

Other clubs caught the eye in these first decades after the Second World War. Wolverhampton Wanderers, strictly governed by their manager and ex-captain Stan Cullis, were a fleet-footed band, with the calmness of Billy Wright to organise the defence. Wolves won successive league titles in the late 1950s and the 1960 FA Cup final, not to mention several prestigious floodlit friendlies against major European opposition such as Real Madrid, Spartak Moscow, and most memorably, Ferenc Puskas's Honved. The Tottenham sides of Arthur Rowe and Bill Nicholson, with thoughtful artists such as Danny Blanchflower, indulged their 'push and run', their short ball and very mobile tactics, to genial effect. They achieved the league and cup double in 1960/61. Throughout the 1960s Bill Shankly, superhumanly committed, built the robust Liverpool edifice, one later taken over by the phlegmatic Bob Paisley. They created very hungry, very patient, very persistent and very competent sides, usually with a complete reserve eleven to ensure the consistency never faltered. Whilst restrictive of opposition, almost to the point of being pedestrian, they always had an astute sharp-shooter, such as Kevin Keegan or Kenny Dalglish, to startle the foe. They won an amazing ten league championships between 1976 and 1992 and maintained a superb and unprecedented level of constancy. Newcastle United were a bonny cup-fighting force in the 1950s, as were Manchester City, particularly with the so-called 'Revie Plan' of a deep-lying centre forward. Nottingham Forest, under the idiosyncratic but forceful management of Brian Clough, lifted domestic and European honours; Arsenal, double winners in 1970/71 and Leeds United, under Don Revie, also had moments of glory.

In the event, it was Jock Stein's Glasgow Celtic, composed entirely, to sentimental delight, of Glaswegians or near-Glaswegians, which became the first British winners of the European Cup, when their abandoned assaults toppled the redoubtable defences of Inter Milan, 2-1, in Lisbon in 1967. In 1968 Matt Busby's third and last great eleven, constructed around the imperious dynamism of Bobby Charlton and the sinuous potency of George Best, beat Benfica, fielding the splendid Eusebio, 4-1, at Wembley. Later Nottingham Forest were to win two, a determined Aston Villa one, in 1982, and the formidable Liverpool a splendid five European Cups, while British clubs continued to perform well in the varied European competitions.

All these colourful displays took place against the canvas of an increasing comprehensiveness of European politics. The Treaty of Rome had inaugurated the Common Market in 1957, just after the French journalist Gabriel Hanot and newspaper, *L'Equipe*, had convened the meeting that led to the European club competition being launched. The United Kingdom finally joined the European Union in 1973, but, across continental Europe, there was, of course, already considerable enthusiasm for the concept, an enthusiasm demonstrated through football rivalry.

In the wake of Herbert Chapman and George Allison, it will be noted how managers - Matt Busby, Bill Shankly, Jock Stein and their kith and kin - register in the post-1945 decades just as eminently as the most starry players. There was a recognition that, as on the theatrical stage or concert platform, there is much to be said for a director or conductor who has the license to coerce his players according to his own diktat. The English FA came to believe some parts of this truth and, in 1946, the thoughtful Walter Winterbottom, previously coach to and responsible for a much improved coaching set-up nationally, was appointed manager of the England team. He was, however, constrained by an unwieldy committee structure on the one hand and by suspicious players on the other. He was to reign, a little uneasily, until 1962.

In 1946 England and the other 'home' associations rejoined FIFA and in 1947 a Great British eleven defeated a Rest of Europe team, minus, for a mix of political reasons, Germans, Italians or Russians. A score of 6-1 restored assurance, and, as winner of the 1949/50 Home Championship, England crossed the Rubicon and participated in World Cup football in 1950. English footballers, putting their toes in the waters of international contest, found the temperature no more than tepid. It was not so much that they failed miserably, as that the expectation of the inventors of football was set too high. With the astute Wilf Mannion, the evergreen Stanley Matthews and the adept Tom Finney in their ranks, the English players began their visit to Brazil in 1950 and their first ever World Cup fixture with a 2-0 victory over Chile. There followed the embarrassing and inexplicable loss to the USA by a single goal, then a further loss against Spain, and that was that.

Prior to the 1954 World Cup, England was subjected to the shock treatment of the Hungarian visit to Wembley in 1953. With the irresistible Puskas controlling events, the Hungarians, mobile and cerebral, won 6-3, the first defeat for England by overseas opposition on native soil. Even more so than the discomforts of Brazil in 1950, it brought home, to English football fans and overseers alike, that England had no God-given right to head the world's footballing stakes. Hungary 1953 was football's Suez. A 7-1 whacking by Hungary in Budapest in the lead up to the 1954 World Cup did nothing to dispel the gloom, while, with Nat Lofthouse bravely effective, England did manage to make the World Cup quarter-finals in Switzerland, before falling to the cleverness of Uruguay.

The 1958 World Cup in Sweden was the only one in which all four home countries were represented, but none had much success. England, including Johnny Haynes of Fulham, failed to win their group and were soon out of the tournament. Four years later, in 1962, a stronger combine, featuring the nucleus of the 1966 squad, emerged successfully from the group stages, only to be beaten, unsurprisingly, by Brazil in the quarter-finals. Failure to reach the semi-finals in four outings was not what England had expected.

Alf Ramsey now took over the management of the England team, in preparation for the World Cup on home ground, always apparently a decided advantage. Unsentimental and pragmatic, Ramsey proceeded to build the most efficacious house from the bricks that were available. His 'wingless wonders', as he explained, were of that ilk because England boasted no wingers of reasonable ability. He was sensible enough to put healthy flesh on the powerful spine of Gordon Banks in goal, Bobby Moore, that most authoritative reader of a game, and the bravura of Bobby Charlton. The drama of the final against West Germany is part of national folklore. A late snatched German goal led to extra time, in which the completion of a Geoff Hurst hat-trick precipitated happy scenes of rejoicing at a relieved Wembley and across the nation.

It was the pinnacle of British football history; in fact, over forty years later it remains the pinnacle. There has not been another brush with such proud destiny since, nor have England, let alone any of the other three home associations, won the European national championships, launched in 1960. In a genuine sense, the 1966 World Cup achievement was the last brave huzzah for traditional English professional solidity, playing, where it was most comfortable, in its own backyard, its eleven drawn from eight different teams in a league as yet largely British in breeding, acknowledging its strengths, both physical and mental, yet conscious of its weaknesses. It was an attainment of some magnitude, if assessed within those terms. Competent judges whispered, for instance, that had Hungary or Portugal had goalkeepers in the Gordon Banks class, then they would probably have won the trophy.

A minute cameo is instructive about the Ramsey-induced ambience. At the end of an international match, soon after his dazzling Wembley feat, Geoff Hurst, on leaving the ground, said, 'Cheerio, Mr Ramsey, see you next time'... 'if selected, Geoff,' replied Alf placidly, 'if selected.'

In the Mexico finals of 1970, England fought through to a narrow loss in the quarter-finals, but thereafter there were disappointments. England failed to qualify in 1974 and in 1978 and did not progress to the latter stages in 1982, whilst Scotland and Northern Ireland predictably fared no better in these tournaments. In 1986, back in Mexico, Diego Maradona's two goals, the infamous handled one followed by the famously brilliant one, sent England packing in the quarter-finals. 1990 brought a semi-final appearance in Italy - easily the best showing since 1966, concluding with a lost penalty shoot-out against Germany - ending this quarter century of low attainment on a slightly upbeat note, but, overall, one World Cup, and scarcely even a glimmer of a European Championship, was an impoverished return for football's sometimes self-righteous originators over almost fifty years of international endeavour.

British football had cooked for the world's banqueting table a curate's egg, largely undistinguished at national, but often incisive at club level. This caused some, including one or two at FIFA and UEFA levels, to question the practice and the theory of the UK fielding four national teams, for there was room for the argument that, had the nation-state, like the top English clubs, been bolstered from the celtic fringe, the harvest might have been as fruitful as in the club competitions.

Home Thoughts

Footballers' working conditions had improved in line with the general amelioration of workers' rights and earnings in the post-war world. The clubs had also benefited in 1957 from a £1 million tax rebate and in 1959 from £250,000 annually from the pools firms in return for the use of fixture lists. By 1958 the familiar ring of the maximum wage of £20 a week, with a £17 capping in summer, was agreed, giving the leading players, with bonuses, annual earnings of £1,000, at a time when the average manual worker's income was about £550, a wider gap than had been the norm. There were extra payments also on offer; the bigger clubs might pay parents up to £4,000 for the signature of a promising teenager, but the vexed question of the lack of a minimum wage remained. The indentured contract was a relic of the past and way out of line with the freedom of contract most employees now enjoyed. Not least, as the modern climate proved economically chilly, it was the smaller clubs who were anxious to preserve the status quo, but, in terms of labour relations, it was antediluvian.

It was, politically, a consensual era when the trade union movement in Britain enjoyed respect and power, sometimes, and to its eventual peril, overweeningly so. Not surprisingly, it was the ideal moment for the Professional Footballers' Association to display that mixing of brain and muscle that was currently serving other craft unions advantageously. Jimmy Hill, the ex-Fulham player and manager and pundit-to-be, took a more sophisticated line than his predecessor as PFA Secretary, the pugnacious Jimmy Guthrie. There were two rapid and complementary thrusts. Muscle - the threat of strike action, with the employers capitulating at the brink - and brain - the involvement of the Ministry of Labour - brought about the end of the maximum wage in 1960/61. In 1963 Newcastle United's resolve to keep George Eastham captive at St James' Park was justly interpreted in the High Court as restraint of labour and henceforward professional footballers received the same contractual rights as other workers. The 1964 accord set the stage for the end of century bonanza.

EXPANSION · BRITISH FOOTBALL

Turning to tactics, there was, in the wake of the triumphs of continental and Latin American football, a gradual switch to 4-2-4/4-4-2 formations in British football. In theory, this meant the withdrawal of a forward into midfield and of a wing-half into the last line of defence, as a 'fourth' back. In reality, many clubs had either deployed one inside forward as a playmaker to the rear of the other forwards and/or insisted on one wing-half being more defensively minded than his colleague. In practice, the overall effect depended on whether the general stratagem was geared to attack or defence, and whether the rearguard was cautiously protected or the strikers flagrantly supported.

The common or garden result was flexibility. Particularly with teams like the Russians in the 1966 World Cup, spectators became tuned in to a less rigid pattern. At kick offs, British watchers smiled in wonder as players seemed to be idly waiting in random bunches, rather than taking up the strict placements of yesteryear. Players had to be less specialist and more mobile, with all-out attack sparring with all-out defence, with old-time wingers rushing back to defend and old-time full-backs dashing forward in attack. A traditional winger, such as Stanley Matthews, hardly ever moved back behind the half-way line, except for kick offs, while the conventional full-back would have regarded it as a solecism were he to have been so far from his goalkeeper that he could not converse naturally with him.

The concept of all-round football put an obvious premium on stamina and speed, occasionally to the detriment of other skills, but there was no doubting the need for pace and fitness among players as the century advanced. Of enormous help in this change, and a point that tends to be neglected in analysis, was the introduction of the plasticated, water-proofed ball, the first major alteration in the ball since the leather casing had replaced the pig's bladder. It was almost as fundamental a change. Gone was the old leather 'casie', which, when muddy and heavy, was difficult to propel and perilous to head. With the further assistance of improved and better drained surfaces, it eased ball control and lengthened kicking, speeding the game up immensely. The new ball could be pinged about with gusto. Moreover, it allowed for the change of footwear from near-clogs to near-slippers, another sudden impetus to the tempo of the game. Tactics, health and equipment conspired together to produce a faster and more all-embracing sport.

With Stanley Rous trying to be far-seeing as Secretary of the FA, the amateur game proceeded satisfactorily. The FA promoted coaching schemes, while

Football League club scouting networks became commonplace. In the post-war years, there might be crowds of 90,000 for the Amateur Cup and in the 1970s a wholesome total of 1.5 million amateurs, boys and young men, were regularly enjoying the recreational game. There were 40,000 football clubs by the late 1970s, a notable increase on the 25,000 of the late 1950s, some of it the result of Sunday soccer's popularity. It compared well with the 2,000 rugby union and the 6,500 cricket clubs then in existence.

The Football League still dwelt in the last ditch of reaction. Sunday football and substitutes, and most other bright ideas, were initially rejected, although many were eventually and grudgingly agreed. Pub quiz aficionados may be aware of the name of Derek Clarke of West Bromwich Albion. He became the first-ever FA Cup final substitute in 1968, but, despite the odd incursion, regular desecration of the Sabbath had to await the early 1980s.

Then, quietly but nevertheless profoundly, the last Amateur Cup final was played in 1974. From 1975 all registered players were footballers. Fourteen years after the cricket establishment had rid itself of the outmoded appellations of Gentleman and Player and called everyone 'cricketer', the FA followed suit, bringing to an end the uncomfortable compromises, caricatured by the crumpled notes stuffed clandestinely in the football boot, which had haunted football officialdom for nearly a hundred years.

As the 20th century wore on, the social changes, propelled by the plane, the car and the television set and fuelled by a rising prosperity, magnified. They formed the canvas upon which professional football in Britain was depicted.

First, and after we had 'never had it so good' with Harold Macmillan as Prime Minister, there were the febrile 1960s, nervy, self-conscious and soft-centred. The benchmarks of that feverish decade have only to be listed. Beginning with the '*Lady Chatterley* trial' in 1959 and on past the 1963 Great Train Robbery, the Profumo Affair, involving Christine Keeler and Stephen Ward the same year, to the abolition of theatre censorship in 1968, embracing Premium Bonds, the unshackling of betting, Carnaby Street fashions, Beatlemania and 'Flower Power', as well as suffering the sordid Moors Murders trial of 1965 and the shocking explosion of the system-built Ronan Point tower block in East London, both of them symptoms of urban isolation and despair. The Mrs Grundy outlook - for, truth to tell, the collectivist age had been a censorious and judgemental one - was shattered by libertarian advances, as in women's and gay rights, and in divorce and abortion reforms. These were factored into the Permissive Society, while there was an avid emphasis on consumerism and what J.B. Priestley had presaged in 1973 as the 'admass'.

Celebrities, from varied branches of the entertainment industry, tend to exemplify rather than create cultural canvases. They are social reflectors, not instigators. Where Stanley Matthews had been the homespun and unspoilt hero of the mundane 1930s and 1940s, now arose the footballing Beatle, George Best, coruscatingly if ephemerally brilliant, burning his candle at both ends amid the flashy shallowness of the 1960s and 1970s.

The post-war welfare consensus, predicated on a compound of Keynesian fiscal devices to procure productively full employment and rational educational, medical, housing and allied services, survived until the 1970s. As just one example of the new age, three-fifths of households were owner-occupied and a third council houses, where, in 1914, nine-tenths of housing had been privately rented. The 1973/74 economic crisis, when oil prices were quadrupled, demolished this accord. Economic growth, which had averaged 3% annually, dropped to 1%. The manufacturing core of the nation wilted and faded, while inflation exploded: the retail price index, from its 1962 base of 100, passed the 1,000 mark by 1992.

The political response, channelling the public wish to eschew the dowdy trappings of public ownership and regulation, plumped for a market-led solution that gave full vent to naked individualism. Financially, the monetarist approach, with its tight budgeting and uncontrolled conveyance of capital, proved destabilising. Socially, the 1980s slump, with gross unemployment of approaching 4 million and communal debilitation, proved disastrous. The brutalism of the Thatcher decade, for all its heroic and occasional righteous insistence on the freedom of the discriminating individual, produced what some commentators called 'the hour-glass' society. This had a wealthy upper and a pauperised lower tier (those officially listed as in poverty rose from 5 million to 14 million over this phase) and thus a slimmer middle, in sharp contrast to the pyramidal shape of industrial Britain, with its stolid heart of artisans and clerks.

What Christopher Lasch, about the turn of the century, was to call 'the culture of Narcissism' was worshipped, and respect for the civic ethic further declined. The compounding of self-gratification with economic distress was lethal. Crime soared. There was a 36% increase over the 1980s, with a sour harvest of 15 million annual offences. Crime, in fact, grew 40 times per head of population over the 20th century. There were 791 woundings in 1920; there were over 100,000 in the year 2000. By this time, a third of property crimes were drug-related - there were 300,000 drug addicts in Britain. The late 20th century saw some return to the political unrest and social hooliganism reminiscent of the 18th century.

Therein lies the clue. It is an opportunity to replay Jeffrey Richards's distillation of the 'rough' and 'respectable' elements in society, for, increasingly, as the last century drew on, one witnessed a retrogressive shift in the English national character, with the former 'rough' component once more in the ascendant. As before, the sociological newsprint was not all black and white. There had been football ground disturbances before 1950, just as there were many signs of what George Orwell had called English 'gentleness' after 1950. Nevertheless, the upsurge of a less reverent and even aggressive and xenophobic cadence was very noticeable among the football fraternity, occasionally with a definite right-wing and racist bite. Often it was not so much criminality as what criminologists term 'incivilities', those noisy, over-boisterous, discourteous acts that, when perpetrated by a bunch of hard-drinking youths, may spread dread across a town centre on the Saturday afternoon of a football match.

Both at club and international levels, crowd behaviour, at home and abroad, caused many problems. Three tragic events touched the depths of calamity in the British context. These were the Bradford Stadium fire, with 56 dead, in 1985, a catastrophic sign of the primitive neglect of the nation's football fabric; a youngster being killed at St. Andrew's, home of Birmingham City, when Leeds United fans rampaged, on the same afternoon; and the Hillsborough disaster, with 96 fatalities, an even more calamitous portrayal of how football authority and policing viewed football's paying customers and vice versa. Also in 1985, and with global implications, the Brussels Heysel Stadium tragedy, saw 39 dead and 350 injured. This was the Juventus versus Liverpool European Cup Final, and the Liverpool fans were held to blame for the fatal rioting and assaults that led to the deadly crush. English teams were banned for five years from European competition in consequence, with Liverpool spending a longer period in social quarantine.

The atmosphere and circumstances of the period begat confrontation, with head on clashes between sets of brutally aggressive young fans and heavy-handed policing, some of the scenes all too easily comparable with pictures of the miners and police in seriously strident conflict during the coal industry dispute of 1984. In the 1948/49 season, with 41 million fans in attendance, the police reported only 22 incidents across the entire country. By the 1970s and 1980s as many incidents might have been reported at one match on one afternoon. Eric Dunning, it will be recalled, the thoughtful academic expert on football hooliganism, suggested that 'segmented bonding' was the key, with disaffected youth finding a close mutual loyalty in antagonism to the more 'functional bonding' of society or state. At times, one wondered whether the police force was another such 'segment', as urban centres on Saturdays resembled the cliché township of the movie Western, with the local gunslinger challenged by the visiting hot-shot, and the tough sheriff fastening his gun belt on to deal with both.

The disasters jolted public and politicians. Lord Justice Popplewell's inquiry into the Bradford fire had prompted calls for identity cards and membership schemes for spectators, a plan that won Margaret Thatcher's affection, but it was apparent that the grounds were as much to blame as the spectators. Lord Justice Taylor's interim report of 1989 and his final report of 1990 made wide-ranging recommendations that led to a transformation of football's infrastructure in Britain. Basically, it urged the end of perimeter fencing, a significant element in the Hillsborough disaster, and, more tellingly, the abolition of spectator standing at major grounds.

Football's uncertain economics were as much grounds for this massive change in style and atmosphere as the grave safety issues, although many analysts claim that, without the political impetus driven by tragedy, the football business might have soldiered on without such heroic surgery. With safety and licensing procedures strengthened and in place under the control of the Football Licensing Authority, more money was invested in ground refurbishment in the first four years of the 1990s than in the rest of the 20th century. As an example of the business and safety compromise, an all-seater Wembley reduced the attendance to 70,000, but increased income. Overall, this national refurbishment was an astounding feat. The Victorian construct of British football was overnight imbued with a post-modern, if homogenous and somewhat sterile, look.

Particularly apropos Heysel and Hillsborough, critics were quick to lambast the police and other authorities for their slowness in segregating or otherwise controlling the crowds, either in terms of preventing rank misbehaviour or of stopping the aggressive surges that had come to replace the patient queue of the 1930s and 1940s.

Plainly, such analysis missed the point completely. A football match is an entertainment. Why should the police have to be mustered to ensure peaceful harmony between spectators on grounds and rational conduct as they parade through the streets? During the 1970s and more especially the 1980s, it was well known that there was likely to be violent trouble in and around grounds for many major matches. It is worth recalling that, had these been designated political or similar rallies and processions, the police would have banned them from taking place under existing public order legislation.

Liberal thinkers were right to assert that, if you fence people in, they will behave like captive animals; there was, of course, some truth in the conservative thinkers' view that, if people behave like wild animals, one has to corral them. There was a circular motion of ascending ferocity, rather like an arms race, and with similar consequences.

It was argued earlier that the authorities in the 18th century feared the crowd. They did so with good reason, even if, in turn, they were part of an interaction of violence and counter-violence. The later 19th and early 20th century authorities learned not to fear the crowd. Then the interaction of moderate conduct and mild authority operated in the opposite direction. It was in that environment that football became the nation's main sport of mass spectatorship. After the 1950s, the crowd struck dread once more into the minds of those in authority and, again, it was with good reason, shelving for a moment the role of the ruling orders in that turning, grinding wheel of belligerence.

The governments of the 18th century would never have permitted mass football spectatorship to take root. Had mass football spectatorship been invented after 1950 it would not have been allowed to function. Basically, if crowds cannot assemble and disperse quietly for such and such an occasion, then the event itself, in the interest of the public community at large, is likely to be subject to the severest critique.

We must add another term to the equation that describes the origin and growth of commercialised and professional football. We have identified the demographic, urban and industrial constituents. It is likely that a fourth indispensable facet was the relative quietude of the Victorian crowd. Of course, when the genie was let out of the bottle, the flow of football's magic was unstoppable. Nor, as the next chapter reveals, was the tide receding.

CHAPTER FIFTEEN

EXPANSION; WORLD FOOTBALL TO NEAR THE END OF THE 20TH CENTURY

BRITAIN'S NEW-FOUND interconnections with European and world football serve as an introduction to a generation of happenings in European and Latin American soccer.

UEFA was Europe's attempt to unify the continent's football associations and to form, with a nervous glance across at the bloom of football in South America, a bloc in world football. The unification of television via the EBU, European Broadcasting Union, was probably as big an element in the process, especially with the advent of colour in 1970 and the importation of American practices like slow motion replays and assorted punditry. The sale of television rights was another lesson learned from the USA. In 1960, for the inexpensive sum of £8,000, the famed European final at Hampden Park when Real Madrid routed Eintracht Frankfurt 7-3, was broadcast live to all European countries.

The Continents - Europe

Real Madrid set the standards. They were masterminded by Alfredo Di Stefano of Argentina and Ferenc Puskas, exiled from Hungary, where, after the ruthless crushing of the 1956 uprising and its nasty Stalinist aftermath, the brief ecstatic moment of its inspiring soccer faded. Real Madrid conquered with patrician grace, dominating the European club scene and winning the first five European cups in sequence from 1956. With Benfica, headed by the strong and gifted Eusebio, a child of Mozambique, as a potent Portuguese brew, the Iberian peninsula was a footballing Arcadia for several years. The fascist regimes of

Franco (who died in 1976) and Antonio Salazar (who died in 1968) were beginning to show signs of wear and tear; soon a more liberal dynamism asserted itself and football, too, prospered.

The visits of Real Madrid, Benfica and other European clubs to Britain brought a glamour to British football arenas, the main course after the aperitif of Moscow Dynamo's brief sojourn in 1945. Across the Mediterranean on the Italian peninsula, there was, despite the gaudy riches, the starry importations and the frenzied enthusiasm, not quite the same degree of success, although the two Milan teams and Juventus had their moments of glory. There always seemed to be some trouble, some hint of corruption or scandal, lurking in the background, and Italian football, in those first decades after the Second World War, scarcely lived up to its promise. Still, Italy won the World Cup in 1982, while Napoli, with Maradona, threw down a southern challenge to the northern hegemony focused on AC Milan, owned by the media mogul-cum-politico Silvio Berlusconi, and fielding such talents as Marco van Basten, Paolo Maldini and Ruud Gullit.

A curio of football in the northern reaches of Europe was the late arrival of fully-fledged professionalism, with its legislators clinging stubbornly to an obsolete amateur ethic. Surprisingly, it was 1963 before West Germany created the Bundesliga of sixteen professional clubs, although there had been widespread hidden payments before that. It was established on the cusp of Germany's flourishing and prudently regulated economy, with Bayern Munich, led, all aplomb and aloof command, by Franz Beckenbauer, and Borussia Mönchengladbach. Bayern Munich, having won three consecutive European Cups in the mid 1970s, won six domestic championships in the 1980s.

Holland, so clearly resembling Germany in attitudes and values, also held out through a species of semi-professional compromise until the 1960s, when Ajax, the Amsterdam club with the talented and independent-minded Johan Cruyff its figurehead, charted the trek into full-time salaried football. Sponsored by Philips, the electrical company, PSV Eindhoven gave chase and shared four titles apiece with Ajax in the 1980s. Among the Scandinavian nations, Gothenburg, in Sweden, continued to be the most consistent club, with Rosenborg of Norway giving them a run for their money in the past ten years.

As for France, and in spite of the constant influence its legislators and journalists had on the progress of European and world soccer, the country suffered a lengthy period of ineffectual and peripheral football. It was not until the 1970s, with Saint-Etienne hitting the high spots, that France, urged on by a De Gaullist state that craved national prestige, emerged as a true footballing power, with, in later years, the business-like approach of Bordeaux and Olympique Marseille consolidating that upward swing. Marseille won France's sole European Cup to date in 1993, although the triumph was tainted by the scandal which unfolded after the event regarding owner Bernard Tapie's bribing of opponents Valenciennes in the decisive game in their previous league campaign, which saw them stripped of that title.

After the death of Stalin in 1953, there were some modest relaxations in political stringency and some moderate improvements in material well-being in many of the East European states. Football fed off these advances, with Czechoslovakia, Poland. Yugoslavia and the USSR, and clubs like Sparta Prague, Partizan Belgrade and Dinamo Kiev taking kindly to the opportunities offered by European competitions. For example, the Czechs won the 1976 European championships, beating West Germany on penalties, and Kiev twice won the European Cup-winners' Cup. Russia was not free of stadium disasters, the worst of them the terrible 1982 tragedy when 300 died in a wintry crush at Moscow's Luzhniki ground. In East Germany, football was very heavily controlled and manipulated by the state, with Dynamo Berlin, linked to the national security services, proving unnaturally consistent winners of almost every game they played. A high point for East European - and for Bolshevik-style sport - was in 1986, when Steaua Bucharest beat Barcelona in the European Cup, again on penalties, thereby becoming the first Iron Curtain winners of that prestigious trophy.

America

On the American continent, where governments were often almost as engaged with footballing politics as in Eastern Europe, it was the fluent gifts of Pelé's great Brazilian team that delectably caught the world's imagination. Their superlative capture of the 1970 World Cup in Mexico, a triumph heightened by, for the first time at the world championships, the brassy pigmentation of colour television, was their peak attainment. During the 1980s the Flamengo club also sprang to some prominence in Brazil. Argentina, where the robust Estudiantes de la Plata club were the rigorous front-runners, then came to the fore, hosting and winning the 1978 World Cup. Under the watchful eye of the autocratic General Videla, the Argentineans beat the Dutch in an atmosphere laden with military hauteur and xenophobic hysteria.

The military and despotic regimes of South and Central America during these later decades of the 20th century interacted with football in all kinds of seldom benignant ways, while, in Columbia, for example, where America Cali emerged as the leading team, organised crime as well as high finance appeared to have a stake in the proceedings. Paraguay, where Olimpia won seven titles in the 1980s, also began to move out of the shadows of the larger countries. Mexico remained the chief Central American exponent of the game, but one or two other countries were entering the fray a little more seriously now. El Salvador (1970 and 1982), Honduras (also 1982) and Haiti (1974) were all World Cup finals entrants from CONCACAF, the elaborate acronym of the regional body, but it was, for instance, the Haiti of the despotic Jean Claude Duvalier, not the sweetest of backdrops for wholesome sport.

As for North America, the United States continued valiantly to come to terms with football's marketability, but it always seemed to fall short of promise and expectation. The best moments were in the late 1960s and early 1970s, when nearly a score of sponsored clubs were competing in the North American Soccer League (NASL) with some brio, the pick of them New York Cosmos, strengthened by such veteran artists as Pelé, Beckenbauer, Cruyff and Best. The marvellous Pelé, now at the end of his illustrious and heart-warming career, was the world's record goal-scorer, running up a career total of 1,284 goals, although a meagre three of them are discounted by some statisticians. The salaries of such stars, subsidised by Warner Communications, unbalanced the league, with other teams dropping off as they tried vainly to keep up with New York Cosmos. The NASL dwindled away.

With emotions running at frenzied levels and livelihoods under desperate threat, trouble and chaos were never too far away in Latin American football. A hellish cameo of this condition occurred at Lima's national stadium, when Peru entertained Brazil there in 1964. Fierce crowd reaction to a disputed refereeing decision was met with a harsh police response and, as the spectators stampeded in an antiquated arena, the worst ever football disaster happened. Nearly 500 people died in the crush and many hundreds were injured. It seemed that every negative element in the modern game, from impoverished amenities and boneheaded policing to torridly overwrought nationalism and manic spectator behaviour, conspired to create this catastrophe.

However, just as imperishable a diabolical image was conveyed from Chile, just after the USA-backed Pinochet coup deposed the lawfully elected left-wing government of President Allende in 1973. The national stadium in Santiago was utilised as a prison, a torture chamber and an execution shed for dissidents, but FIFA insensitively insisted the USSR play a World Cup qualifier there, in spite of the Russians' political and - not without a little irony - humanitarian objections. With prisoners still interned and armed soldiery the most numerous observers, Chile scored a hollow goal in the absence of the Soviets and qualified for the World Cup.

It was perhaps the nadir of all those naïve hopes that football and politics should not be mixed.

Asia · Oceania · Africa

While the more established footballing regions experienced these soaring delights and sinking horrors, the genuinely newsworthy story from the post-war decades was the advent of organised football in Asia and Africa. The key to this was the wholesale collapse of European colonialism on these continents. The 'Europeanisation' of the world was gradually being reversed, if only politically, but cultural vestiges, like football, were often retained and employed to new advantage.

Given that much of the imperialism had been British, it was not surprising that football proved to be one of the liveliest of these re-cycled remnants of empire, but, just as the Spanish and Portuguese had followed in English footsteps as almost the whole of the Americas had been de-colonised, there would also be ex-French, Dutch, Belgian and other territories where football would act as a spur to and banner of national independence.

Asia, where the European influence had been less total in administrative and military character than elsewhere, had developed an Asian Football Confederation by 1954, and even China had an embryonic championship by 1951, soon after the Maoist revolution of 1949. China would have to await the death of Mao Zedong in 1976 before really forging ahead football-wise, but the two Koreas, North and South, were willing contenders, with communist North Korea causing a ripple or two in the 1966 World Cup in England. The Indian sub-continent, dedicated to the joys of cricket, was still reluctant to take the soccer plunge too deeply, and Japan was not quite ready for its keen-edged breakthrough towards the end of the century.

It is of incidental interest that, after plentiful political machinations, Australia eventually threw in its hand with the Asian Football Confederation. The Oceania equivalent, set up in 1966, had not proved strong enough to promote the game worthily in international terms and had had only a precarious foothold on the lower slopes of the climb towards the mountainous World Cup summit. Australian soccer was heartened by the influx after 1945 of Balkan, especially Croatian, immigrants, and adopted some urgency in consequence. Australia reached the World Cup finals for the first time in 1974 and New Zealand in 1982.

Oceania's weakness, however, was construed in problematic terms as, from 1986, it was not deemed strong enough to gain a direct qualification place for the World Cup finals, having instead to pit its winner against the lower ranked teams from the South American and Asian conferences. On only one occasion did Oceania's winners win through - in 2006 when Australia defeated Uruguay on penalties.

The position in Africa was more straightforward, if no less daunting. In almost every instance, it was a case of a metropolitan power retreating from direct rule, leaving the native population with the challenge of formulating a series of new states. British servicemen, colonial agents and traders had carried a football, as well as a cricket bat, with them into many of these territories. As in the home country itself, it had been the schools for local boys and the militia and police forces with native recruits that had taken up soccer. On the Cape Coast, as well as Cape Coast Excelsior, initially a schoolboys' team, there were founded a Bolton Wanderers and an Everton, such was the potency of English tutelage. Amid the noise and tumult of post-war struggles for nationhood, Zaire, Nigeria and Ghana emerged as footballing contenders. No other major Western sport had unduly sullied the blank sheet of African leisure and, in practically every case, football was viewed as an instrument of national pride.

South Africa, with its sizeable complement of white settlers, had set the not over-exhausting pace since the Victorian era, and its indigenous people had proved energetic converts. Indeed, the non-racial South African Soccer Federation was quite a vibrant experiment from about 1961, until it inevitably came to grief amid the sorrows and horrors of the Apartheid policy that had been developed since 1948. The self-inflicted wounds of the South African authorities illustrate, once more, the difficulties of a governmental approach that is half scared of football because the lower orders might get uppity, and half pleased because it keeps them peaceful. One might trace this back to those arguments about 'melée' football in old England, but South Africa, unfortunately, tottered to the former extreme in terms of any cross-ethnic games. Despite some not very diplomatic or very humane interventions from European sources, Apartheid South Africa was suspended from membership of FIFA in 1961.

North African football was also on the march. The Egyptians had been the first African nation to enter into global tourney, first in the 1920 Olympics and then in the 1934 World Cup, and they spearheaded the African advance. In 1956 the African confederation (CAP) was established, followed immediately by its first championship in 1957 in the Sudan. There was some movement of players from colonies to Europe. As early as 1938 Labri Ben Barek had left Casablanca for Marseilles and then Atletico Madrid, as well as becoming a French international.

The World

The upshot of this explosion of brand-new nationalism of varied types the world over was a vast augmentation of FIFA membership. This jumped from a pre-war tally of fewer than 100 to 140 by the 1970s. Beginning with Iran in 1945, many African states from north and south of the Sahara, several Asian countries and a few Caribbean nations, now released from colonial rule, flew to FIFA's warm embrace. It was almost as if a FIFA ticket went with every newborn nation-state.

The numbers went on rocketing. FIFA, generally speaking, was open to all comers, perhaps because each entrant meant a possibly pliable vote. The South Americans had worried about European hegemony; now there was a phalanx of members from all corners of the globe that might be a comfort to them. The allocation of FIFA membership to tiny principalities and minute islands, including quite a few not recognised as self-governing countries by the United Nations, began to look a trifle ludicrous. As San Marino, Andorra and the Faroe Islands jostled with larger neighbours in authentic World Cup and European trophy qualifying matches, the notion that Wales or Northern Ireland might be regarded as 'particularist' segments of a bona fide nation looked a little limp. For many critics, this lowering of entry standards, allowing these 'nations' to compete on an equal footing, edged towards the absurd.

The man who presided over FIFA from 1974, the Brazilian businessman Joao Havelange, inherited and luxuriated in this expansion. He replaced Briton Sir Stanley Rous, who had been a prudent and honest, if not inventive, President since 1961. Stanley Rous had, in his turn, replaced Frederick Wall, not the most progressive of officers, as Secretary of the English FA. In these national and international roles, he had initiated several useful practices, like the referee's diagonal line of rule (proposed by English referee Ken Aston), a revised and clear-cut edition of the laws and the red and yellow card system (also proposed by Ken Aston). Politically, however, especially on issues like South Africa (a question that troubled the European overseers of other sports, cricket and rugby union included) and Pinochet's Chile, he had played by the law rather than the spirit of the ideological game. His successor, ambitious and unbothered by too many scruples, grasped the meaning of the rising flood of FIFA membership and observed the tide of football that was surging across a planet now awash with television sets and commercial giants eager to pay for advertising on them.

It was as if Newman Noggs had been substituted by Barnum; the ringmaster for the clerk. FIFA's staff grew in size; so did the World Cup final rounds, with 24 and then 32 nations engaged. The World Cup was FIFA's showpiece and Joao Havelange raised the marketing ante substantially. It was, to some extent, a matter of timing, for, patently, he would have whistled in the wind for funds at an earlier stage, before the televisual and similar commercial building blocks were in place. Coca Cola and Adidas sportswear were among the sponsors, as huge marketing deals were negotiated. Much of this was in place for the 1982 tournament in Spain. It has been estimated that during the Mexico World Cup in 1986, no fewer than a gross total of 10 billion viewers saw that series of televised matches - Italy 1990, and it was 20 billion. With commercial logos on clothing and posters pasted prominently around the grounds as well as with goods and services directly puffed on television, there had never been an advertising bonanza like it.

The admixture of club and national tournaments on a continental and global basis created a complex network of fixtures. The European championships were played every four years, halfway between each World Cup series, while there were two or more club contests in Europe, and both national and club competitions involved qualifying matches, so that the circus of international fixtures was practically non-stop. Other continents and regions had a similar cavalcade of inter-club and national tournaments. There was even a World Club play-off, usually a desultory and sometimes unpleasant affair, between the European and South American champions. All of this made for a highly cosmopolitan pageant of football, strenuously covered, of course, by television cameras, with electronic techniques and clever gimmicks adding all the time to the viewer's entertainment. Critical to these technological miracles was the installation of satellite TV, giving instant access all over the surface of the planet and encouraging, as in the English game, coverage and reportage of every leading match.

Spectators

Football had now come close to achieving saturation in respect of global coverage. The aeroplane ensured that players and teams could be endlessly ferried on the longest of hauls, so that the criss-crossing of national boundaries and oceanic barriers was commonplace. The television guaranteed that as many people as wished to could watch these games from the comfort of their own abode, if not on a bigger set in the local pub or bar, or on an even larger screen in the town square or other open space. The aeroplane had won the geographical war with space and the television had conquered in the battle with human communication.

That martial metaphor is perhaps too loaded. The world game was haunted by an alarming bellicosity. It could have been a carnival. Sometimes it was. There were moments when crowds met in the football stadia of great clubs or in the bars and public areas of great cities and the atmosphere was joyous and colourful. These moments were rarer than they should have been. More commonly, during the closing decades of the century, there was trouble, ranging from the crudity of random misbehaviour to the brink and beyond of outright disaster and death.

The coupling of the politicisation of soccer with the widespread disaffection of urban youth detonated outrage after outrage in the football context. Football's politics operated at two levels, both of them revealing a tribalism of a ferocious character. One was on the club plane. It is possible to trace a confrontational pugnacity from the original 'Derby' games of that town's twin parishes during soccer's pre-history, via the more peaceable rivalries of same city professional clubs, like Sheffield Wednesday and Sheffield United or close neighbours, like Oxford United and Reading. Almost every club managed to uncover a 'derby' rival. The radius of the circle of these pretexts for enmity widened, often regionally, with, in England, something of a north and south divide. In later years, much fuelled by the habit of ample travelling support for the visitors, the clashes became cross-regional or sub-regional, as in the antagonisms surrounding Manchester United, Liverpool and Leeds United.

From about the 1950s and 1960s, England proffered the world yet another footballing model, this time the less attractive commodity of hooliganism, with, frighteningly, the complicit nastiness of organised gangs or 'firms', tooled up for offensive affray. The attachment of violent behaviour to an alleged identity with and loyalty for a football club was, therefore, avowedly political in its expression of localised partisanship. It was copied or spontaneously discovered all over the world, often excused by the very justification offered by, say, opposing sets of more overtly political groups, as in divided Northern Ireland, disintegrated Yugoslavia or strife-strewn Iraq, that the other lot started it.

Naturally enough, this tribal ritualism was transferred upward to the second level of tribal engagement, the ambit of national contest. When foreign teams opposed one's club or national side, the political weighting was laden with a bitter xenophobia and national stereotyping. These, too, became common traits of football spectatorship across the world.

As the character of football crowds was demographically dominated by the more youthful age-groups, with alcohol frequently a predisposing factor, and of youth estranged from the basic values of their host society, the recruitment of these football militias was an undemanding task. Radiating out from London and other English cities to Milan, Berlin, Buenos Aires, Rio and to all points of the compass, autonomous gangs of aggressive fans were on the raucous march.

Dissertations could and have been penned that analyse the specific causes and effects of the scores of examples of this dire phenomenon. Some factions had more direct political, ideological, ethnic or religious links than others and some were more effectively organised and resourced than others. The input may have been thus varied, but the outcome was characterised by and suffered from the lowest common denominator of unpleasantness. If sport was, as George Orwell forewarned, war without the shooting, portions of crowds were keen to provide that missing component with displays of witting hostility. There were, everywhere, feeble protests that the violence was perpetrated by a minority, but, either condoned or unchallenged by the purported majority, these groups, from the 'ultras' of Italy to the 'torcidas' of Brazil, imposed a peculiar and unprepossessing ambience on football grounds and their surrounds all over the world.

The Game

Another, and less threatening, fashion in which there was an abiding sameness about world football was in tactics on the field of play. As with the styling of the possees of fans, there was, superficially, an array of differences, but, in principle, the pattern was very similar everywhere. The ten outfield players were deployed in slightly varying units of attack, midfield and defence, something akin to a 4-2-4 format, but with (as was mentioned apropos the British game) the overwhelming tendency being an enormous elasticity, propelled by the increased mobility and stamina of the players. From the late 1960s, this strategic plasticity was patently assisted by the use of substitutes, initially one and since the late 1980s usually up to three, so much so that the squad, rather than the eleven, was the force with which to be reckoned. Forwards could be added if defeat threatened, or defenders thrown on to protect an advantage.

As with the pseudo-chic self-styling of the blocs of national and club supporters, numerous names and phrases were dreamed up to mark such modifications with rather pretentious titles. They became as beloved of commentators and analysts as they did of managers. There were 'diamond' shapes in mid-field, and 'sweepers', both fore and aft of the mainline defence, lone strikers, with someone lurking in the 'pocket' or 'hole' just behind them, even a 'Christmas Tree' design, numerous foreign language words and phrases, like the defensive 'catenaccio' and the attacking 'libero' and any number of intricate shifts and switches that, of course, might be altered as the game progressed. A complexity was assumed that rivalled much of medieval theology in its hollow and arcane verbosity as the growing media sought to justify its own place in earth's most consuming passion.

Certainly the game had changed from the more definitive positional geometry of the pre-1960s, with the emphasis now more on all-round skills, what in professional cricket are called 'bits and pieces' players. Goalkeepers, especially when passing back to hand was ruled an offence, found themselves acting more as sweepers and kickers, while full-backs evolved into overlapping wing-backs and forwards learned to adopt defensive duties at corners and other set-pieces.

For all that, the essential specialism - the goal-scorer, the raiding winger, the creative or destructive mid-fielder, the robust rear defender - remained; the other responsibilities were add-ons, somewhat like the maths teacher who also offers some elementary physics. Through the often exciting, if occasionally chaotic, melée (to borrow the word employed to describe pre-historic football) the old-fashioned supporter could dimly discern where his ancient heroes would have slipped comfortably into the modern game. It had not been unusual for a demolition expert, like Arsenal's pre-war wing-half Wilf Copping, to have been sighted acting in close contact with the three main defenders, or Arsenal's creative inside-forward, Alex James, assuming a deep-lying and probing role; Eureka! 4-2-4.

The chief difference lay in the speed and movement of the play and in the incredible finesse of the fine tuning, and this latter aspect was mainly the consequence of the massive influence of coaches. With a few rare exceptions, to be discovered in Europe and South America as well as in Britain, the pre-1950 game had belonged more to the players than the trainers and selectors. The positions and the gambits of the game were set and, once on the field, it was up to the players to perform to their best ability at more or less pre-ordained tasks and according to the established script. As football became more coach-orientated, the manoeuvres and ploys certainly increased, invariably in quantity and sporadically in quality.

Curiously, the actual game was less democratic and more monarchic in rule, as the managers dictated events rather than the players, and they did so with increasing firmness. They became all-important, so much so that club and national attainment was judged almost solely by their exploits. It led to theirs becoming a hazardous job. Across the world, their survival rate barely bettered that of an English subaltern in the trenches of the First World War. It was as if the theatre director was busy in the wings each night, stopping or changing the pace of the play, amending the book, shifting the scenery and introducing fresh actors or switching the parts and props of others. Then, abruptly, between performances, he had vanished, and another director had taken his perilous place.

The fundamental effect of all this tactical scheming on the balance of footballing power was not necessarily profound. Brazil and West Germany were dominant. Of the eleven World Cups contested in the forty years between 1950 and 1990, all but one - when Brazil won in 1958 by beating the host nation,

Sweden - was won by a country competing on its own continental soil, a long-range forecast about the joys of home advantage. Brazil, with three wins in this phase, were, certainly, in respect of glamorous theatre, the leading global team, although Uruguay won twice and Argentina once to maintain the wider South American presence. On European terrain, and as well as England's solitary success in 1966, West Germany, with three wins in 1954, 1974 and 1990, showed resilient fortitude and expert application of a remarkable order. Italy, after a long spell in the international doldrums, was, in 1982, the other World Cup winner.

It had been, worldwide, a generation of rapid expansion in the incidence of football and a swift enlargement in the critical nature of football's social and allied effects. It was the preface to the next and most recent decade or so, during which football was to consolidate its global grasp and penetration as a ubiquitous and unprecedented cultural phenomenon.

CHAPTER SIXTEEN

TODAY; BRITISH FOOTBALL IN RECENT TIMES

MONEY BECAME the root of all football. The cut-off date for ultra-modern football in the United Kingdom is not some stupendously edifying historic happening, some bloody revolution, some startling diplomatic coup, but the coming of the Premiership in 1992/93. From a financial stance, this was the elaborate culmination of the long trip from the grudging acknowledgement of professionalism in the 1880s, the preponderant effect of spectatorship and the adoption by football clubs of limited liability status.

Money - The Premier League

This sporting revolution did have its minor political dramas, as the Football Association, in a counter-scenario of the 1880s and the formation of the Football League, conspired with the leading First Division clubs to create a separate alliance outside the Football League's increasingly narrowing clutches. Importantly and instructively, the major item on the agenda was the division of the television spoils, with the senior clubs as anxious to grab the lion's share as the lesser breeds were eager to cling on to what meaty bits they could scrounge.

In an interesting gloss on the ups and downs of the football saga of the Football League's original and intrepid dozen only Aston Villa, Blackburn Rovers, Bolton Wanderers, Derby County and Everton find themselves among the current score of the Premier League, as of 2007/08. The other eight, however, are preserved in various echelons of the Football League, a record salvaged by Accrington Stanley's resumption of senior status in 2006 after 44 years in the frosty cold of non-league football.

Regional distribution had altered over a hundred and twenty years. The twelve apostles of the Football League had been exclusively of Lancashire and midlands, north and central, nativity. Today's twenty disciples of Premier League football hail from a much wider geographical range. The old County Palatine of Lancashire still houses seven Premiership clubs, while the northeast has three and Yorkshire none. The two biggest changes are, first, the reduction of the once prospering midlands to the representation of Aston Villa and newly promoted Birmingham City and Derby, second, the conquest of the south. There are seven southern teams, five of them based in the Greater London area. If anything, the Premiership has a strong southern bias that would have shocked the stolid provincial progenitors of the Football League.

Crucial to an analysis of this fundamental shift in distribution is some recognition, not only of the catchment areas of the southern, but also of the rest of the Premiership clubs. As well as the five teams in the main London region, another, Reading, are well within striking distance, that is, the town is part of the London region apropos transport, employment and other critical socio-economic aspects. Only Portsmouth of the southern clubs could be said to be immediately free from that strong metropolitan influence.

Naturally enough, the configuration of the Premiership alters by a factor of roughly 15% each year, as the buffets of relegation and promotion occur. The 2007/08 exchange of Sheffield United, Watford and Charlton Athletic for Sunderland, Birmingham City and West Bromwich Albion shifted the balance slightly back towards the midlands. That power of the conurbation was becoming more potent as a guide to football pre-eminence throughout the world, as well as in Britain. Indeed, there were tentative feelers from the Clydeside conurbation for tickets to the Premiership ball. Glasgow Rangers and, latterly, Glasgow Celtic continued to dominate Scottish soccer; between them, they had, by 2007, won over ninety of the league championships, leaving the next three best contestants, Aberdeen and the two Edinburgh sides, Heart of Midlothian and Hibernian, trailing with a miserable four apiece.

However, tender Sassenach sentiments prevailed, the loudest wails emanating from the so-called yo-yo clubs, these that found themselves in turbulent ascent and descent between the bottom of the Premier League and the top of what became known as the Championship, and which, for at least a generation, would always be known as the Second Division. Equally aggressive re-branding had transformed the old Third and Fourth Divisions into Leagues One and Two. Such anxiety about extra competition for the envied Premiership places left the senior pairing of Scottish teams in a far from cut-throat arena, a fact used to excuse Scotland's poor showing in both European club and international contest.

Money - The Moneyed Society

Football, like other mainline aspects of the cultural condition, is a reflector of the society in which it exists. Football may not move the mountains of economic or political existence, but its character is in some degree shaped by the weight and pressure of these metaphorical uplands. So, although, in Britain itself, there was no single event external to football that altered its direction, the game was certainly altering in kilter with the economic and fiscal changes at large.

The near obliteration of manufacturing industry in the United Kingdom during the 1980s and early 1990s was to a large extent balanced by the comparable erection of a monumental industry devoted to finance and services. England, a pioneer trading and banking nation, had ever been more than just a manufacturing hub - the start of South American football is just one instance of that effect - but now the scales were weighed down heavily in favour of the banking and commercial elements. It was as if money were the end rather than the means; it was the product rather than merely the system of circulation. In a world hurtling towards a global economy of virtually free markets, yet inclusive of intermediary trading factions, of which the European Community was one, the premium was on finance and services.

The 'big bang' of October 1986, when all restrictions on Stock Exchange practices were lifted, is as near as one may search to discover to a single date to symbolise these changes. The City of London joined ever more fervently into the wild game of international finance, and, adroitly utilising its respected and age-old reputation as a trusty and efficient operator, maintained and enhanced its place as a world financial giant.

In 1984 the hundred chief companies in the FTSE Index were valued in sum at £92 billion. In 2006, and after ten years or so of moderate inflation, the HSBC bank alone is valued at £116bn. That offers a toothsome flavour of the sheer strength of the banking and financial market that overlooks the British economy. The economic expert David Kynaston has written, 'there is a widening discrepancy between the workers' republic of the square mile and the rest of the country.' That dichotomy is well illustrated by income. In the financial year ending April 2006, city executives' pay increases averaged an immense 43%, whereas most workers, in this era of modest inflation, enjoyed rises in single figures. On average, the bosses of the largest hundred city companies were earning £2.9m annually.

Something of a socio-economic apartheid was being built. Contrary to tabloid frenzy over the 'mass affluent', with claims, as extravagant as the city salaries, that 3 million people earned over £100,000 in 2006, only 113,000 people - one in 250 workers or 0.2% of the population - managed to earn that much, while millions remained on wages well below the national average of about £20,000 plus. The city's mean salary was just over £100,000, but that certainly helped to open up a grand canyon of inequality between the richest and the poorest. This obviously demonstrated itself in life-styles, particularly in the crucial field of property, where, with prices ratcheted forever upwards in the prosperous districts, owner occupiers found themselves with estates that made them notional millionaires.

The switch from a manufacturing to a service society revealed itself in basic changes in employment typology. In the early years of the 21st century, those employed in industry plunged to 24% of the work-force, whereas an incredible 75% were in service industries, ranging from retail distribution to leisure. Only 1% of the labour force remained in agriculture, itself transformed by technology; it had been 93% in the 14th century and approaching 20% in 1871, even after the primary industrial revolution. By 2006 there were almost twice as many people working in telephone sales centres as on the land.

There was some restrained amelioration with the end of Margaret Thatcher's harsh ministries and the advent of New Labour. There were some social dividends from the attack on child poverty and the critical impact of the minimum wage, while crime finally halted its long mountainous climb; in the year ending June 2006, there was a 10% fall in the high crime rate, although the prisons were bulging with a record 80,000 inmates. At base, the economy, well-guarded by a prudent Gordon Brown as a long-term Chancellor of the Exchequer, performed with due consistency, so that the supposed impossibility - non-inflationary full employment - was sustained. But Tony Blair was not, nor did he ever pretend to be, a radical reformer. His opponents' pre-1997 claim that, once in power, he would shed the false mask of genteel moderation and become a fiery revolutionary proved groundless. He was a moderniser, sincere and energetic, looking to make sundry improvements, but he never envisaged any fundamental reworking of the foundations of society.

One example of long-term and largely unheeded deterioration was in public transport, a feature of these pages, because, without public transport, the football audience would never have reached anything like its mid 20th century peak. Buses, the grand conveyor of thousands to football matches, were vanishing, outside of London, where the fatal attraction of privatisation had been avoided in favour of publicly controlled tendering schemes. In the other major British urban conurbations, bus passengers had, over twenty years of private enterprise, dwindled by 50%, while fares had risen by 86%.

Occasionally, one witnessed the municipal comeback of the light transit tram, such as Manchester's Metro, but, at base, transport meant the car. 70% of the population now have regular access to a car, although it is justified to mourn the plight of the 30% who do not, and car traffic has risen tenfold from 30 billion miles travelled in 1950 to 300 billion miles in 2000, with 400 billion miles threatened for 2025. Apart from the pollution and 300,000 road accidents annually, 2% of the gross national product is eroded in traffic congestion. Nothing could be further from the position in the first half of the century when approaching a hundred football clubs drew good to excellent crowds to their grounds with the help of a fairly reliable and fairly inexpensive public transport system.

In transport, as in most other elements of the social scene, individualism, in particular individualism plus money, determined outcomes. Thus the cash nexus ruled OK in the UK, as elsewhere. The geographic result was the reversion of economic hegemony to London and its environs. For a few generations, while London had always remained prominent, some of this economic strength had passed to the great manufacturing districts. Before the industrial revolution the provinces beyond a line from the Wash to the Severn estuary had not wielded much sway. Now, especially given its proximity to the newly important European market, linked by the Channel Tunnel, the southeast has reverted to its medieval and early modern eminence. On a long-time chronological graph of British economic muscle, heavy industrialism, and the attendant command of the major manufacturing towns, was beginning to look like a temporary blip.

TODAY - BRITISH FOOTBALL

Money - The Spectators

Football followed the cash flow. As we have observed, the booming London region played host to half a dozen or so Premiership clubs and almost all the others resided in the secondary conurbations. Manchester, the one-time 'cottonopolis' and engineering centre, now kept its prominence by dint of being second only to London as Britain's fiscal, media and advertising nucleus. Population was also significant. Whilst the half a dozen key industrial regions had suffered some overall population loss since World War II, they were, outside of London, the only areas with a sufficient incidence of inhabitants to support the exigencies of an expensive football club.

It is true that, with ease of travel, supporters were prepared to journey longer distances; it was reported that Manchester United, the leading example of a 'national' team in this respect, welcomed 60% of its core support from outside the Manchester area. But this created a double pressure on the lower clubs. Teams in the main residential areas had the benefits of neighbourhood support, plus the glamorous capacity to attract others from further afield, especially as such teams prospered and enjoyed attractive runs in European competitions. Increasingly, lower division teams were, attendance-wise, crushed between these two stones.

On average, the four divisions of English soccer attract something over 16 million customers a year, compared with 40 million in the late 1930s and 1940s. In fact, the 15.4 million of the 1985/86 season was the lowest average attendance for a four division campaign, but in 1994/95 it was a much healthier 22 million. However, the spread is plainly uneven, for half of that number, some 11 million, including 2 million at Old Trafford, attends Premiership fixtures, giving an average gate of 20,000. Normal Saturdays in the 2006/07 season showed the following pattern of attendances. In the Premiership, sponsored by Barclays, the main metropolitan clubs like Chelsea, Spurs and Arsenal gathered in crowds of around 40,000. Manchester United, with a refurbished stadium, was busily breaking Premiership records up around the 76,000 grade, the great majority, an astounding 57,000, being season ticket holders. The two main Merseyside teams were also trading healthily.

Nonetheless, even in the Premier League, the teams outside the mainstream, assessed in population and ability measures, only managed gates of 20,000/25,000, sometimes falling below 20,000. Watford, Reading, Wigan

Athletic and Portsmouth are examples of clubs with all-seater stadia where the capacities are only around such figures, but, in comparison with 1930s and 1940s gates, this was a small customer base. During and after the 2006/07 season several clubs, including some in the Premiership, were reconsidering their prices, either holding steady or reducing the cost, particularly of season tickets. Manchester City, for example, already with debts of £103 million, saw season ticket sales tumble by 20% over the 2006-07 period.

Attendances in the three divisions of the Football League, sponsored by Coca Cola, then tailed away alarmingly. In the Championship, on any Saturday, there were only a handful of gates that crept over the 20,000 mark and often two or three that could not even reach 10,000. In Leagues One and Two, it was now unusual for any attendance to top the 10,000 mark. In League One, maybe half the dozen fixtures each weekend would reach 5000, while, in League Two, perhaps only one or two would attract that number, with two or three frequently dropping under the 2,000 point.

The situation was even worse in the Scottish Leagues. The Glasgow teams had, predictably, big crowds, usually around 40,000 or 50,000, but elsewhere it was woeful, with even the weaker Premier teams playing before derisory numbers of less than 10,000, plummeting to a matter of hundreds in the other three divisions.

Gone were the days of J.B. Priestley's Bruddersford United, when 30,000 was a normal gate for a normal team playing in a normal township. In another simulacrum of the UK at large, the top had soared away and the bottom had shrunk downwards. There had developed a genuine chasm between Manchester United's heaving host and the shivering hundreds at, say, neighbouring Rochdale. A further annotation on this state of affairs was a marginal slackening of the 'derby' temperature. The big Premiership titans, and their supporters, tended to view these rivalries a little more passionately, in that they mattered more in competitive terms, so that the antagonisms among Arsenal, Chelsea, Manchester United and Liverpool began to emulate those between Manchester United and Manchester City or Liverpool and Everton.

By 2007 a noticeable and unusual feature of attendances was the marked absence of great numbers of young people. The youth element that had transfigured the crowds of the preceding generation was now much less well represented. One explanation was that young adults, many of them in employment with poorish pay, had been simply priced out by the expense of tickets. There was something of a return to the more middle-aged profile of the 1920s and 1930s, albeit with decidedly novel female and family additions.

One encouraging and compensatory factor was the continued interest in active participation in football. Despite the dispiriting sale of over 5000 playing fields, usually for profitable building opportunities, between 1987 and 1995, schools football remained prominent, while several major clubs organised youth programmes and academies. Apart from the always rather generalised involvement in walking, gymnastic exercise, swimming and cycling, soccer remains the out and out leader among organised sports. In 2006, 2.9 million reported playing football at least once a month, that period beloved of opinion pollsters. This compared with 1.8 million joggers, 1.4 million golfers, 874,000 tennis lovers, 380,000 cricketers and 163,000 snooker players. They obviously contribute to the 22% of the population that admits to undertaking regular moderate exercise. It betokens an enduring and welcome tie between the playing and watching of football, not least in the respect that one might expect the watching to be better informed as a consequence of the playing.

An intriguing and challenging aspect is the popularity of football among girls and women. Football has now overtaken netball as the most popular female participatory sport, with, according to the Women's Sports Foundation, one in three girls eager to play football. It is claimed that the football-orientated film of 2002, *Bend It Like Beckham*, which contrived to incorporate a happy assault on both ethnic and sexual prejudices, did much to encourage this interest. In 2005, when England hosted the women's European Championships, there were reasonable audiences of 3 million for the BBC's live coverage of England's fixtures. In the 2006/07 season Arsenal Ladies secured no less than four trophies, sometimes watched by sizeable attendances.

It has been something of a revolutionary growth. There were only 80 women's teams affiliated to the FA in 1993 - now there are 8,000, a hundredfold increase in a little over ten years. There are 130,000 registered women players.

The FA has not advanced too far from its stance of 1921, when it judged football as 'unsuitable for females', and there is no woman on the FA Board and only a solitary one on the 90 strong FA Council. The FA has acted to encourage women's football, but it finds - and the prejudice is not exclusively to be found in the FA's offices - the notion of mixed football difficult to accept. It trots out all the old tarnished shibboleths of the sex debate, like the expense of separate changing facilities or differing physiological growth rates. Early in 2006, ten year-old Minnie Crutwell wrote to the Culture Secretary, Tessa Jowell, complaining about her being banned from playing with her chosen team, Balham Blazers, in South London, in spite of her patent skill. Protagonists of mixed soccer argue that, at school age level at least, the criteria should be height, weight and, above all, ability. One wonders how long it will be before women compete with men at professional levels in English football.

Women are also beginning to supply more of the audience for football, a result of all-seater stadia, safer conditions in and around grounds and, most importantly, a proper feminist insistence that males should and must not monopolise the support given this most popular of games.

Money - The Clubs

The 'conurbation' describes the cohesion of several towns, usually around a central city, into an urban complex of high proportions. Conurbations, naturally, occurred where employment and money, as well as people, flourished. The last ten or twenty years has revealed a novel mantra for the successful football club. The game that had won pre-eminence as the child of urbanism and industrialism had changed its parentage. It had become the offspring of the new urban/industrial marriage: conurbation and high finance.

The microscopic replication by the prosperous football club of British society's image was uncannily precise. Money brought success. Success earned money. This was apparent at all points of the football compass, in terms of gate-money, sponsorship and television deals, the marketing of logos, replica kit and the like, and, of course, the remuneration of players and, what became a murky and suspect field, their agents. Not only was London the home of many Premier League teams, the top players emulated the city bosses with regard to their take-home pay.

The opening seasons of the new Premiership were monopolised by Manchester United. With a large national following and an early and astute grasp of global brand marketing - it was said, by the turn of the century, that the Red Devils had a shop in every country, bar Afghanistan - they secured a position as the most financially prospering club in the world. Having floated on the stock exchange in 1991, the club's shares jumped six times in value to £25 by 2001. The Manchester United financial profile demonstrates the way crowds and wealth gravitate to the top. With season tickets averaging £500 each, with corporate seating and hospitality boxes, some fetching close on £50,000 a year, the income from the ground itself is some £80 million annually. In addition, there is TV income, group profit and kit sponsorship, each drawing in around £40 million. The club has a worldwide fan base of 10 million and in the 2005/06 season they generated revenue to the tune of £243 million, although they were toppled from the top perch by Barcelona (£259 million) and Real Madrid (£292 million)

It was, it is, very big business. Five clubs were, in 2007, valued at over £400 million. These were AC Milan (£420 million), Bayern Munich (£427 million), Arsenal (£466 million), Real Madrid (£528 million) and Manchester United (£740 million), the out-and-out winners. Thus they were able to afford a highly competent team. It is rarely as simple as that, and they were fortunate to find in Sir Alex Ferguson something of a Nobel Prize-winner in the chemistry of football teams. Curiously, his background was very similar to those other famed English club managers, Matt Busby and Bill Shankly, in that he was of artisan Caledonian stock and of excellent rather than outstanding personal footballing pedigree. Whatever his somewhat explosive mix of nous and choler, he possessed the knack of renovating teams fluently, where others might build a fine side, but then require time to replace it. He also contrived to amalgamate the products of the Old Trafford youth policy, such as Paul Scholes, David Beckham and Ryan Giggs, with talented incomers like the combatively dedicated Roy Keane, goalkeeping Colossus Peter Schmeichel, and, like some arrogant character who had strayed in from the pages of Alexandre Dumas and *The Three Musketeers*, Eric Cantona.

Manchester United won eight of the first twelve Premiership titles, a hatful of FA and other cups, including an historic treble of league, cup and, excitingly, European Cup in 1998/99. This included a hat-trick of championships, emulating the three previous such endeavours, Huddersfield Town in the 1920s, Arsenal in the 1930s and Liverpool in the 1980s. Apart from a championship for Blackburn Rovers, bankrolled temporarily by the wealthy businessman Jack Walker, there were three titles and an invariably tough challenge from a strong Arsenal contingent, craftily marshalled by its manager, Arsène Wenger, and starring the sublime French striker, Thierry Henry.

Just as the English and Scottish Premierships both seemed destined to be the plaything of two teams, in the mid-2000s Chelsea made it a threesome. Where some British clubs had been heavily financed, often for a short phase, by a rich and interested party, or, like Manchester United and Arsenal, had exploited the PLC device efficiently, the Chelsea effect was unexpectedly innovatory and yet characterised with all the propensities that formed the modern game. The Russian oil mogul, Roman Abramovich, simply bought the club in 2003, paid off its debts and then bought a stack of world-class players for £375 million, including the club record transfer fee of £30 million for the Milan striker, Ukraine's Andrei Shevchenko. He also had the wit to purchase the services of a top-rate manager, for the matter of £5.2 million annually, in the Portuguese master Jose Mourinho, who ensured that his ministry of all the talents would deliver up to expectations, as they did, with two relatively easy Premiership titles in 2005 and 2006. A loss of £140 million that accrued during the 2005/06 season was a mere bagatelle among these proceedings. In all, Chelsea's owner has now spent over half a billion pounds on his footballing fiefdom.

Manchester United mounted a successful counter-offensive for the Premiership in 2006/07. With Cristiano Ronaldo outstanding, and the experienced likes of Ryan Giggs and Paul Scholes in excellent form, they held off a stolid Chelsea challenge with a display of sparkling football. Yet Chelsea were a close second, and they won both the 2007 Carling Cup and the FA Cup. The latter was a cagey, lack-lustre affair against Manchester United, played for the first time at the spankingly new Wembley Stadium, and sealed with a highly competent Didier Drogba goal in extra time. That first 'new Wembley' final offered a tiny cameo of the modern game, illustrating many of its salient points. A thousand policemen patrolled a dull game, between two teams in which fourteen nationalities were represented, watched by 500 million people on television in 160 countries.

Roman Abramovich had benefited from the privatisation of Russian industry during the Boris Yeltsin years of office. He came to own a large share of the oil and gas company, Sibneft, plus holdings in car, airline and aluminium concerns. He was one of those who were close to Yeltsin's inner coterie and who had obtained £50 billion of these national assets, a process involving the cheap purchase of workers' shares and other manipulations. He then sold his holdings for upward of £7 billion and his wealth is estimated to approach £11 billion. To put that in context, the hundred richest Russians are worth more than a quarter of the country's gross national product while the average Russian yearly income is the equivalent of £2,000.

There was considerable unease about this flamboyant proceeding, partly because a bottomless pit of riches created a position unlike the occasional lucky fortune of a transient sugar-daddy or the best efforts of the most competently run limited company. It appeared that Roman Abramovich was prepared to spend, spend, spend, as long as any competitors remained standing in the ring. The discomfort was partly on ethical grounds, with some raised eyebrows over the provenance of the Abramovich fortune. Some of this may have been a trifle hypocritical, as other capitalists involved with football had not always been socially responsible. What was clearly evident was that, in the global economy, football was a product up for sale to the highest bidder and that, in an overtly money economy, the English Premiership title could be legally bought.

It was the ultimate in the lengthy saga of football as a business. Roman Abramovich was the latest, perhaps the last, in an evolutionary trail that began with William Sudell and Preston North End in the 1880s.

Plenty of clubs were habituated to the practice of local tycoons throwing money at them and using them as a kind of rich man's toy, without much thought of profitability. Most football clubs were not solid enterprises, fiscally speaking. It was estimated in the 1990s that, were the banks to apply the stringency to Football League clubs that they did to ordinary businesses, then two-thirds would be closed down and declared insolvent. Indeed, these years were littered with news of clubs passing into administration, to the point where the Football League had to impose points penalties on such clubs, fearful that they were deploying the device as a crafty financial manoeuvre. With Roman Abromovitch, the cult of the expensive toy took on a new meaning.

Of course, there were complaints then as there were now, about how the finer virtues of the game were being distorted by such practices, as fans and commentators alike refused to face the naked truth of the capitalist system, whereby ruthless competition drives out the opposition and corners the market. In 2006 Tesco, with 1,800 stores worldwide, recorded a profit of £2.25 billion, and a turnover that resembled the gross national product of a moderate nation-state. Such triumphs renewed fears of the collapse of independent retailers on the high street, but, of course, just as, say, Marks and Spencer, with its 450 stores and £8.6 billion turnover for the year ending March 2007, had started life as Michael Marks penny bazaar in Leeds, Manchester United and Arsenal had originated in the recreational pastime of a few rail and munitions workers.

PARISH TO PLANET

The capitalist ethic was alive and active. Arsenal and Manchester United, both of whom had fought their way to the fore through years of footballing success backed by astute marketing, had structural troubles. The former had necessarily burdened itself with heavy debts as the club moved from Highbury to the magnificent Emirates Stadium in 2006, while the latter, although making money hand over fist with a refurbished Old Trafford and with aggressive marketing, was now owned by the American Glazer family, a purchase that involved a large built-in debt element at a club which, for years, had famously been the only debt-free senior English club. The Glazer family paid £831 million for Manchester United, of which £272 was their own money and the rest, some £559 million, was borrowed, saddling the club with a current annual interest repayment of £62 million. Martin Edwards, of the family that had backed United for years, made £93 million from selling his shares between 1991 and 2004.

Liverpool lengthily contemplated a refinancing incorporating Saudi Arabian oil funds. Sheik Mohammed bin Rashid al-Maktoun, the oligarch behind the Dubai International Capital company, may have seemed an unusual saviour of the soul of the Kop, but £450 million was quoted as the sum available for a new stadium at Stanley Park and new players. David Moores, of the celebrated 'Littlewoods' family that had invested in both Liverpool and Everton clubs over the decades, stood to make £80 million, just as Ken Bates, having bought Chelsea for a snip in 1982, received £17 million from Roman Abramovich. Perhaps the Liverpudlian contemplation was over-lengthy; the potential Arab funders backed off, accusing the Liverpool board of acting 'dishonourably'. Help was at hand as the American fiscal cavalry came racing to the rescue, in the shape of George Gillett and Tom Hicks, financiers from the USA, with experience of the sports industry and with £470 million stashed in their saddle-bags.

Suddenly, as 2006 drew on and 2007 dawned, several other clubs were contemplating offers. The Jersey-based Belgravia Group were discussing a takeover, at a cost of between £140 million and £240 million, of Newcastle United; and then came news of a counter-bid from the American group, Polygon, and the United Bank of Switzerland. Then, abruptly, the reclusive sports retailing billionaire Mike Ashley bought a 41% stake in the Gallowgate club. Quickly dubbed 'the Geordie Abramovich', he quickly obtained a controlling interest of over 50%.

Manchester City talked of a £70 million takeover with, again, American finance in the frame, but, in the event, it was the deposed Thai Prime Minister, Thaksin Shinawatra, his family under investigation for corruption by the incumbent military government, with whom a deal worth over £100 million was contemplated. Characteristic of the age, the Thaksin fortune comes from that ubiquitous symbol, the mobile phone. Aston Villa also hinted at different funding, even after past chairman, Douglas Ellis had made £24 million from the sale of his shares, chiefly to the American businessman Randy Lerner.

But where big money goes, also attracted is an element of skulduggery. In 2006 West Ham United engaged in the unprecedented transfer of two young Argentinean players, Carlos Tevez and Javier Mascherano, a complicated deal of sell-on clauses involving Media Sports Investments, the front agency for the Iranian oligarch Kia Joorabchian. West Ham was also in the process of being taken over by the Icelandic businessman, Eggert Magnusson, at a price of £85 million, with another well-heeled Icelander, Bjorgolfur Gudmundsson, ready and waiting for his holding company to absorb the Hammers for £105 million. When it was judged that there had been illegalities in the 'third party' control of the Argentine signings, and that Hammers employees had lied to Premier League officials, Magnusson's West Ham were fined £5.5 million by the authorities. The controversy deepend when a disciplinary commission failed to deduct any points - as appeared to some to be the precedent to be followed - and, amid controversy and threats of legal action, the East London club narrowly escaped the relegation that would have been many times as costly as the fine with Sheffield United, despite continuing legal action, suffering that fate.

The news in 2007 of heavy trading in Arsenal shares, with rumours of an interest expressed by the wealthy royal family of Qatar, could be the prelude to a situation where the final top-ranking English-owned Premiership club falls into foreign hands. Further stories of take-over were associated with the American billionaire Stan Kroenke, whose Kroenke Sports Enterprises company own the Colorado Rapids football team, the Denver Nuggets basketball club and the Colorado Avalanche basketball squad. In the spring of 2007 the Arsenal vice-chairman and general footballing politico, David Dein, resigned from his Arsenal directorship, a move suspected by financial commentators as being a stratagem on that Kroenke-linked plan. Senior British football is not just controlled by high finance, but by high finance of a global order, a stream of society that no other sport touches.

Tom Bower, in a gloomy but authoritative analysis, *Broken Dreams; Vanity, Greed and the Souring of British Football*, has properly viewed these takeovers by foreign buyers as of a piece with what he rightly sees a sort of global car boot sale of prize British assets in general. He cites such cases as Pilkington Glass, Rolls Royce, Smith Electronics, Thames Water, and many other concerns rather more integral, in effect, to the everyday basic needs of society than a few football clubs. He calculates that, in 2006 alone, foreign corporations expended the huge sum of £75.5 billion on British assets, and he is very pessimistic about the fundamental effects of such unalterable changes. The more optimistic might argue that globalisation is not only a force not to be denied, but also that the emergent compound, through being more mixed and multicultural, might secure some protection against an undue nationalistic paranoia. However, as cultural icons, like major football clubs, and natural assets, like water, find themselves in the dispassionate hands of faraway financiers, it is not easy to remain over sanguine.

It is the structural as well as the alien nature of the funding that causes disquiet. The movement of private equity into the British economy has unbalanced the relatively orderly process of the public liability company, the trading off of Manchester United being an example. For instance, the Automobile Association was purchased thus privily for £1.75 billion in 2004 and soon cut 3,400 jobs in the dash for profits, while the value of such private deals in 2006 was as high as £22 billion. It has been calculated that companies owned by private equity concerns, their purpose the extraction of rapid gain, employ one in five workers in the British private sector, Sainsbury's and Boots among them. The American private equity group, Blackstone, owns, for example, Madame Tussauds, Café Rouge restaurants and Center Parcs. As Karel Williams, the academic expert in this field, argues, 'the naked self-interest of private equity managers is characteristic of the elites in third world countries.' Once more, the administration of football clubs serves to illustrate what is happening in the wider economy.

For those moguls who are looking for a profitable investment as well as an opulent plaything, television proceeds are a significant attraction. While less than half a million go weekly to watch the English game, millions tune in to watch on television, and that represents a major constituent of the make-up of football. The Premier League have negotiated, as a main broadcasting course, but not the entire meal, with BSkyB and Setana a deal that, from the 2007/08 season, will pump £17 billion into its coffers, at the rate of £550 million each year, that is, roughly £28 million to each club. It is difficult to exaggerate the difference between this and the £36.6 million that will be available to the Football League. It makes the possibility of promotion to the Premiership a succulent proposition, when one club may glean as much from TV takings as the whole of the three-divisional Football League. In 1978 the television companies paid £25,000 to clubs for TV rights. In fact the growth in TV income has been astronomical. The Premier League has doubled the sum for overseas rights, as from 2007, to £900 million annually, the result of English football being watched, such is the global thrall of the game, in over 200 countries, that is almost the whole world.

The total Premiership income for all forms of broadcasting, inclusive of the internet, radio and cable connections, is estimated at £2.7 billion. When the Premiership was inaugurated in 1992/93, TV income was only £60.8 million, and so it remained for five years, while the Football League's three divisions shared a meagre £6 million. The one has grown nine times; the other six times. Of course, there are other financial blessings that come with Premiership membership. It has been calculated that, as well as TV funding, there are extras in gate income, through more customers at higher prices, and in enhanced advertising and sponsorship revenue. The average yearly income for a Premier club from these non-broadcasting sources is £51 million and for a Championship club £16 million. As for prize money, the top Premier club will receive in future £50 million - the bottom club is awarded the consolation prize of £27 million, the most costly wooden spoon ever. To emphasise the distance opening between club and national football, Italy were given £11 million for winning the cherished World Cup, a mere third of the reward of being relegated from the English Premiership to the Championship.

From stadia names and perimeter fencing to replica shirts and shirts with logos that read like a map of world economic geography, every chance is taken to grab extra cash. From Manchester City's Thomas Cook jerseys to the Kyocera electronics label emblazoned on the Reading players' torsos, pounds are being made. The Emirate sponsorship of Arsenal, no less the Spanish property concern Llanera that supports Charlton Athletic, or the partnership of Samsung electronics and Chelsea, or the Chang and Carlsberg breweries that back Everton and Liverpool respectively, point to the multinational style of football sponsorship.

PARISH TO PLANET

Money - The Players

It is a global economy in players and coaches too. British clubs have scoured the earth for footballers. The European Community's freedom of labour restrictions eased the conveyance of players across national boundaries, while, for suitably qualified players, work permits could be arranged. The Bosman Ruling by the European Court in 1995, despite some stalling by the football authorities, oiled the wheels even more juicily. It did so in two ways. First, it insisted that the agreements struck by UEFA about restricting the number of non-nationals in club sides was in contravention of European Community labour regulations. Second, it affirmed that, once out of contract, players could move freely and without the need for transfer fees. This loaded the dice even more in favour of the professional footballer, now is as far removed from the wage-slave of the previous generation as Michael Jackson from Uncle Remus.

The odd foreigner, a South African or a German or an Argentinian, had, in previous generations, appeared like an exotic bloom in the English country garden of the Football League, just as British émigrés to Italy or the Americas had been viewed as alien, if usually welcome, figures. Now the smallest clubs bragged of their foreign players, revealing them to their awed supporters as talismanic characters.

The *Guardian's* David McKie has waxed, with mischievous lyricism, on the strange delights of Ishmael Demontagnac, albeit London-born, turning out for prosaic Walsall, alongside men qualified to play for Portugal, Australia, Grenada and Trinidad and Tobago. He claimed that, as of the 2006/07 season, Leyton Orient had signed players from Nigeria, Angola and the Congo; Tranmere Rovers had registered emigrants from Utrecht, Kinshasa and the Seychelles, while Brentford placed faith in Olafur-Ingi Skulason of Iceland. Even below the prestigious ranks of the Football League, he uncovered a Woking team-sheet which included Jalai, Sole, Sankah, Berquez and El-Salahi, with Lambu and Oyedele among the subs. Of course, the rhapsodic poetry of today's programmes, as opposed to the humdrum names of yesterday's elevens, relates to a more multiracial society, as well as to the invasion of non-British stars.

It might be observed, parenthetically, that overseas players had, subject to limitations, become a standard component of every first-class county cricket team, while the legerdemain with passports, especially involving the European

Community, permitted an influx of, in reality, foreign born cricketers, rather as Ireland contrived to conjure up all manner of filial attachments to solve the national football team selection posers; Kevin Pietersen and Graeme Hick being the two most obivous examples.

Taking the long view, this was the termination of a lengthy process of de-localisation. In the days of football's antiquity, it was usual for players to have been born or have dwelt in close proximity to the club, and, it may be remembered, the FA, apropos its famous cup, had initially attempted to enforce a residential clause in the rules about player eligibility. There were groans of disapproval in the local press when the 'professors' arrived from Scotland and Wales, with neighbourhood hopefuls dropped in consequence, not only because they were paid, but more because they were immigrants. Thereafter, English clubs, while preferring to pick locally born talent, spread the net widely over the kingdom. Similarly in Scotland, bile was likely to be poured on the 'Anglo-Scots' - those from north of the border playing for clubs south of the border - who were believed by Scottish fans to be the ruination of the national team.

In the last twenty or so years, first Europe, then South America, then, latterly, North America, Australia, Africa and Asia, indeed, the whole world, became the nursery for the Premiership and the Football League. On occasion, teams like Arsenal and Chelsea have fielded elevens without one of that number being eligible to play for England. In addition, from the national side, in the not so palmy days of Sven-Göran Eriksson, to the handful of non-British managers in the Premiership, the same applies to many of the coaches. At those times when dates are set aside for international matches, the training grounds of the top clubs are deserted as their staffs air taxi to the four corners of the globe to represent their manifold countries. In 1966/67 there had been ten overseas players registered in the entire Football League; in 1992/93 there were eleven in the Premier League; in 1998/99, the Premiership figure alone was an amazing 166, the equivalent of fifteen teams, with three-quarters of them hailing from the European Community.

The Premier League, then, is distinctly global in character in terms of ownership, marketing, management and player recruitment.

Two comments are in order. Firstly, the purpose of a spectator-driven sport is entertainment, and, for most, that means some balance of success and style, with an emphasis on the former. It is the spectators who provide the continuity of community identity and the players are their transient representatives. Naturally, there might be a tendency to prefer someone from off the neighbouring streets to a much-travelled Portuguese or Brazilian - but only if their effectiveness is equal. What successful football clubs have had to do since the inauguration of the Football League is to supply a team for - rather than of - the locale. Hard cash is changing hands and spectators demand value for money in the shape of glowing success. Few Chelsea fans, not least after a pronounced dearth of trophies, complain about the ethics of their club's fiscal foundation. 'Relax and enjoy it' is the text for the day.

What is patently observable, in both the higher ranges of cricket and football, is that spectators are acutely sensitive to the disposition and attitude of overseas performers. Better the Argentinean who gives his all for the cause than the local lad who can't be bothered. Spectators very much cherish and prize team loyalty of that kind, a phenomenon equally noticeable in county cricket.

Secondly, the combination of plenty of money and plenty of choice of foreign stars has resulted in top Premiership teams with large and powerful squads. British club football is very strong at present. It is frequently said that the English Premier League is the most vigorously contested tournament of its kind in the world. Admittedly, this is often said by indigenous commentators - supporters of Spain's La Liga might have a case to make, but the Premiership is undoubtedly a top-quality competition. It is certainly true that the divide between national and club prowess has never been wider in England. While the club teams have not been found wanting, the national team has not glittered. Apart from a fourth place in the 1990 World Cup in Italy and a semi-final spot in the 1996 European Championship, staged in England, they did little, and, along with the other three 'home' nations, failed to qualify at all for the 1990 World Cup finals in the United States.

One might be tempted to draw an architectural lesson by way of analogy, as between the fluent way in which clubs like Manchester United and Arsenal refurbished or rebuilt their arenas and the shambles that characterised the FA's dismal attempt to re-create Wembley Stadium. However imposing this edifice might be for the few games that will be staged there, and however one might point to the excellence of the Cardiff Millennium Stadium and a number of well-appointed English grounds, for national and club requirements, nothing could excuse the mess into which the scheme deteriorated. This fixed price contract of £466 million came to engage the client, the Wembley National

Stadium Limited, a wholly owned subsidiary of the FA, and the Australian builders, Multiplex, in a major wrangle over design and allied matters. The project dragged on into its fifth year, dating from the demolition of the old Wembley, as Multiplex demanded compensation of £150 million, blaming WNSL for most of its £186 million losses on the deal. It was the spring of 2007 before the gleaming new stadium, at a gross cost of £780 million, with its world record for one building of 2,618 lavatories, was eventually ready for use.

There was another vivid illustration of this cleft between nation and club in 2006, where, after England had drooped to a drab and disappointing low in the World Cup finals in Germany, no fewer than four Premiership sides, Chelsea, Liverpool, Arsenal and Manchester United, plus Glasgow Celtic from the Scottish Premiership, qualified for the sixteen places in the final stages of the 2006/07 European Club Championship. In fact, three English clubs would eventually be semi-finalists, but the eventual winners were AC Milan, who emerged from the clouds of disgrace swirling around the Italian football scandals to defeat Liverpool in the final at Athens. Liverpool, although rarely competing vigorously in the Premiership, sustained their well-deserved repute as bonny European Cup fighters, having won that tournament for the fifth time in 2005. They had rallied valorously in Istanbul in 2005 to pull back a three goal advantage established by AC Milan.

It is apparent that the influx of foreign players, no less the assistance of the best Irish, Scottish and Welsh footballers, must have much to do with that national/club imbalance. And a not dissimilar condition occurs in Spain, with its glamorous-cum-grim tradition of multi-starring club teams and underachieving national elevens. One way of stating the case dramatically is to suggest that nine times out of ten (for football has its inspiriting moments of anti-form upsets) Chelsea, Manchester United or Arsenal, of the current Premiership, would normally beat England, especially if any English heroes played for their club. Probably, the 1966 England World Cup eleven would normally have defeated the top teams of the mid-1960s.

There is an understandable anxiety in some circles that this influx of foreign players should be curtailed so that the national team might be succoured more competently. There is a tendency to assume that the nation's interest should always come before the club's, but that is rather a facile presumption. The regular weekly diet of club football absorbs the emotional and social being of thousands of people. The clubs have a responsibility to give value for money and build the best side they can. At the risk of some heresy, they do not exist primarily as recruiting officers for the national team, and one might suspect that many keen supporters actually and actively find more pleasure in the success of their club than sorrow in the failure of their nation. Loyalty is double-sided. Adherence to the club may spill over into parochialism; adherence to the country might spill over into xenophobia.

Whatever the philosophic niceties, the players are well rewarded for their labours. The most overt and easily comprehended piece of the plutocratic jigsaw of English football is the player's pay. Cutting to the mustard, Barclays Bank published these figures on sporting salaries in 2006. County cricketers earned, on average, an annual £43,000. Even in the humdrum ranks of county cricket, there are inequalities. Surrey players averaged between £51,000 and £60,000, while Glamorgan's stars had to be content with £32,000, while, with sponsorships, there are exceptions, such as Andrew Flintoff, who, on the back of his rip-roaring 2005 Ashes antics, earned an estimated £1 million to £1.5 million. Senior rugby union players did better, with £60,000, but life in soccer was sweeter. The average yearly wages for League Two players was £49,000; for League One players £63,000 and for Championship players £195,000. The average salary in the Premier League was £665,000. A telling tale of inequity also existed here: goalkeepers averaged £500,000 and strikers £800,000.

Another source puts the Premier League average, with all earnings, including sponsorships, and before tax, at £884,000, a pleasing matter of £17,000 a week, and, over a fourteen year career, an income of over £12 million. Even that awesome average hides the real wealth of the top earners, such as Frank Lampard of Chelsea and Steven Gerrard of Liverpool, whose total earnings, with endorsements, are estimated at £5.2 million a year. David Beckham, while playing abroad with Real Madrid, had a yearly income calculated to be £25 million, inclusive of £17 million from advertising and other contracts. The majority of Premiership players must already be among Britain's 376,000 paper millionaires.

The close link between the wages of professional footballers and cricketers had thus been well and truly disconnected. There was an amusing cameo in the Manchester press in the late 1990s, when Roy Keane of Manchester United and Andrew Flintoff, the Lancashire all-rounder, were both demanding salaries of £50,000. The one was for the week; the other was for the season. The footballer negotiated £52,000 and the cricketer £32,000. The Manchester United,

Everton and England utility player Phil Neville, deemed by experts to be one of the most outstanding schoolboy cricketing prospects ever, was offered much the same, about £1,500/2,000, for a week as for a summer at the adjacent Old Traffords, when he turned professional as a teenager. Sir Alex Ferguson commented that, when the youngster asked him whether he should concentrate on football or cricket, 'he thought he was taking the piss'.

In the same light, it is worth noting how the English Premier clubs have much more clout apropos the national football authorities than the first-class cricket counties do in relation to the cricketing powers-that-be. The counties are so much in hock financially to the English and Welsh Cricket Board that they have to agree to central contracting, which means that members of the England squad barely ever play for their counties, leaving a position where an aspiring county might shrewdly seek to recruit an eleven of very good players, none of them, that is, excellent enough to be spirited away into the national maw. In football, the clubs hold the reins for they hold the purse strings. The notion, for example, that an international match might be played on the same day as a Premiership fixture has long since fallen into oblivion.

It is safe to presume that, had the same conditions prevailed for them, the well-known footballer/cricketers of the past, such as Denis and Leslie Compton or Willie Watson, would never have lifted a cricket bat in anger. The same goes for that promising soccer winger, Wally Hammond, the splendid England batsman and captain, who told John Arlott that he concentrated on cricket rather than football in the 1930s, because he would be able to afford a tiny car and even a small house. When all the saloon-bar arguments are made about the shortcomings of English cricket, the crucial one is the counter-attraction of the salaries in football for those youngsters with a sporting flair and the mental stamina to match.

It is otiose to state that footballers and, indeed, cricketers, had extended what had hitherto been a slight advantage apropos the income of the average manual worker. With an annual median average of £23,000 pay for all income bands, footballers are now streets ahead. In 1966, when England won the World Cup, the average footballer earned about five times the national average; now it is twenty-five times that norm.

Johnny Haynes of Fulham had been heralded as the first £100 per week footballer all those years before; in 1970 Manchester United's Lou Macari was the top football earner, with £300 per week, whilst Andrei Shevchenko and

Michael Ballack, both of Chelsea, now apparently hold that honour, with over £120,000 a week. Allowing for inflation, Lou Macari's wage would now be roughly £2,100 a week.

Of course, the wages were but the baseline of their income, for the more famed players benefited richly from advertising and sponsorship deals. In the year 2007 the top earners in the Premiership were Michael Ballack and the populist hero Wayne Rooney from Manchester United, who both earned £8.7 million and Thierry Henry with £8.2 million. John Terry of Chelsea and Steven Gerrard came next in this plutocratic parade wit £7.1 million each, but Ronaldo (AC Milan; £11.7million), David Beckham (Real Madrid; £14.8 million) and Ronaldinho (Barcelona; £15.2 million) were the world leaders.

For all that, possibly the critical tendency in English football is not so much the horizontal comparison with other sportsmen and the work-force at large, but the vertical contrast from top to bottom of the football construct. The relative wealth, attendances, commercial opportunities and, ultimately, players' income of the Premier League clubs compared with those of the Football League clubs is outrageously extravagant. Even within the Premiership, there are obvious sets of opulently rich as opposed to simply very rich clubs.

In football, as in society, there is gross inequality. Once again, football mirrors its host community. There is talk of social exclusion. It is lamentably true that several million Britons do not have the financial wherewithal to mix normally with the rest of the population and enjoy what passes for life's ordinary pleasures. But there is another form of social exclusion. There is a column of people so preposterously wealthy that they lead a life-style which, at the other end of the monetary gamut, excludes them from everyday social intercourse.

Secluded in excessive mansions behind exacting security defences, conveyed privately in monstrous vehicles, entertained in luxurious and cloistered clubs and resorts, they are withdrawn into an entirely inaccessible cult of pretentious and evanescent celebrity and ostentatious affluence. This group includes several leading footballers. Interestingly, it is argued that, because of the metropolitan effect in this respect, there is a reluctance by incoming players to gravitate away from London and a couple of other conurbations towards less fashionable cities, because of the siren calls of this type of life-style.

If one were to draw a cultural graph linking the British football heroes of successive generations in the personages of Billy Meredith, Stanley Matthews, George Best and David Beckham (all of them wingers of one sort or another) then the changes of emphasis would be social rather than sporting. One line might trace the route from a more localised icon, via a comprehensively national one, past one irrevocably bonded with the youthful music and fashion of transatlantic chic, to one with global 'celebrity' manifestations. Another line would, of course, show a colossal ballooning in income, complete with massive earnings from marketing and sponsorship.

A third line might construe changes in social class, especially in respect of income, and aspiration. Billy Meredith and Stanley Matthews were comfortably off, relatively well-to-do working class heroes; George Best was a trendy, middle class idol, pushing towards substantial prosperity; David Beckham finds himself among the upper class plutocracy, the new aristocracy, not of fortuitous birth, but of sheer unadulterated wealth; the king of conspicuous consumption. He is an example of the social exclusion of celebrity.

A corollary of that cultural voyage has been an increase in the social distance between the adored and the adoring. Before the 1960s the gods were not so remote. Now they are as lofty and aloof as the 1930s Hollywood stars or the Bourbon monarchy of the 17th and 18th centuries.

The author's first sight of Stan Matthews was of him testing a dodgy knee prior to a wartime game at Maine Road, Manchester. He was wearing his RAF uniform, with his tunic off, his grey braces strapped across his blue shirt, and his service trousers tucked into his football socks. (It is said that his father, Jack Matthews, 'the fighting barber' of Stoke, never asked his son how his football match had gone; 'he never asks me', said Jack, 'how many haircuts I've done'; there spoke the voice of genuine professionalism).

The author's last sight of David Beckham was, by chance, on his birthday, as he trotted hurriedly, accompanied by his celebrity wife, across St Mark's Square, Venice, on his way to a select celebration party, bodyguarded, but chased by paparazzi and harried by an ever growing legion of tourists of all nationalities, snapping their cameras like automatic weapons, knocking over tables and chairs in the alfresco cafes, as they scrambled, amid mounting hullabaloo, to bear witness.

It would take a lateral surge of imagination to envisage those two great players in the alternate positions.

CHAPTER SEVENTEEN

TODAY; WORLD FOOTBALL IN RECENT TIMES

OF GENERAL import to world history, and with some influence on football history, the defining happening of the recent past was the emphatic drawing aside of the Iron Curtain and the liberation of a large tract of Eastern Europe from Soviet dominion. The Fall of the Berlin Wall in 1989 symbolises the whole epic tale.

The thrust of this release was, perhaps unfortunately, and as the Abramovich 'Chelski' story exemplifies, most extreme in respect of its economic indicators. Where a more temperate liberal model, on Scandinavian lines, might have been more advantageous, or had the ideals of economic liberalism and political openness, the 'perestroika' and the 'glasnost' initiated by Mikhail Gorbachov, been more enthusiastically supported, the outcome may have been more humane. The tilt after 1985 from a static, suspicious and bureaucratic police-state to a blatant free-for-all was too excessive. The wholly free market solutions pressed upon the former Soviet possessions were quite severe and abrasive. It was to leave many citizens wondering if they were much better off than under the old, oppressive regime, as health and other social indices showed telling ravages.

The World - Democratic Capitalism

There were a number of ramifications, some of them affecting international football. The collapse of the Soviet empire led to a string of new nation-states, either former Soviet republics, fifteen in number, like the Ukraine, or arising from the splintering of states, such as the former Yugoslavia and Czechoslovakia. These obviously swelled the bulging FIFA ranks. It has to be said that, apart from isolated spots of endeavour, or of individual talent, the freeing of Eastern Europe from Moscow's control did not lead quickly to any burgeoning of football authority. The polities, old and new, were insufficiently sized, and sometimes subject to civil disorder, if not outright internecine warfare, or the economies were inadequately resourced to uphold either club or national teams in the era of affluent football.

The more overriding repercussion was the self-casting of the USA in the role of planetary policeman. The cold war clash of the super-states, the United States of America versus the Union of Soviet Socialist Republics, had ended in the comprehensive rout of the latter. With the USSR split into its component parts, there was only China, lurking in the oriental wings and accelerating its industrial progress with immense dash, which looked a likely, and later, competitor. For example, the Chinese were building power stations by the score, and also 48 new airports, making, by 2010, a total of 190, for its 1.2 billion people. They planned to buy a hundred planes and train a thousand pilots every year.

The role of world cop was lustily played by the United States - where, incidentally, there are over 10,000 airports and but a quarter of China's population - inclusive of martial forays into the Middle East. The Middle East, that eternal cauldron for the world's stormy brews of feuding and hostility, was still the salient region.

At worst, this was characterised by the desperate and distorted extremities of Western and Eastern civilisations. The military pomp of neo-conservative Christianity; the blindly suicidal terrorism of Islamic zealotry - these were the inhuman extremes that gave an almost medieval air to events as grotesque as the aerial attacks on New York and other American targets in 2001. Murderous hostilities raged in Afghanistan, in Iraq and where Israel and Palestine continued to clash with harsh fanaticism.

In spite of these terrible troubles, some commentators saw the world as a safe and ubiquitous bastion of restrained capitalism. In 1989 Francis Fukuyama published his celebrated text *The End of History*. It proclaimed that, having temporarily stalled at the red lights of so-called Communism, the bus of historical progress had arrived at its terminus, with every state arrayed in the livery of democratic capitalism, 'the only viable alternative of technically advanced societies'. Capitalism created the wealth and democratic institutions safeguarded the citizenry from too outrageous a consequence, by way of public services. For Francis Fukuyama, the problem posed to the west in the middle east, whilst not negligible, is the last, despairing fling of the old order - 'rearguard actions from societies whose traditional existence is indeed threatened by modernisation' - as the system of corporate mercantile states is consolidated for ever.

It is an apocalyptic account of history, as millennial as that of Christian apologists, like St Augustine, of the German philosopher G.W.R. Hegel, something perhaps of Francis Fukuyama's mentor, or of Karl Marx himself. The cruel and parlous events that have occurred among the debris of old Yugoslavia, or in African states such as Rwanda, remind one that ethnic and religious facets may need to be entered into the analysis. Nonetheless, it is a useful indicator of the world's political condition and the effect of this on the world's football. In 1998 a survey was prepared of the world's 191 nation-states. It suggested that 88 of them, representing two-fifths of the global population, enjoyed free civil and economic liberties, compared with 44 out of 144 countries in 1970. Another 53, with a quarter of the population (34 in 1970) had partial freedoms and a weak rule of law, while the remaining 50, with a third of the population (67 in 1970), had no basic rights or freedoms. In fact, 117 polities are electoral democracies, but, in some cases, they are hedged in by oppressive regulation. However, democracy has been on the rampageous march. Given a mark out of ten, the average democratic score by country has advanced from 0.9 in 1800 to 3.6 in 1900 to 5 in 2000.

On the credit side, it is right to acknowledge that in South America, where, in 2006, the death of General Pinochet, the extreme right-wing Chilean dictator, and the passing from power of Fidel Castro, the extreme left-wing Cuban autocrat, personified a shift to governments of pragmatic and constructive progressivism, more in keeping with the criteria of human rights and needs. One might hope that such increased stability and humaneness should augur well for football, as well as much else, in that often embattled and volatile region.

Of particular interest to the football analyst is the continuing diversity of nations, a phenomenon already noted. The Balkanisation of many regions has become confused and fragmentary. In 1914 there were only 59 independent states, and, with a world population of 1.8 billion, they averaged 22 million in number of subjects. By 1995 this had risen to 191, yet, with a much higher population globally then of 5.5 billion, this average had only grown to 28 million. 87 of these states are less than 5 million, 58 are less than 2.5 million and 35 are less than 0.5 million in population. Half the countries of the world have smaller populations than Manchester; Iceland, with 270,000, is the same size as Leicester. It continues to raise doubts about the viability, inter alia, of national and club football in many nations.

Of more pressing impact is economic inequality. The reality of a global economy cannot be gainsaid. In 1980 the global bond market was valued at $4 trillion; it now stands at $40 trillion, with a half of this located in the USA. This is more than the capitalisation of all the world's individual stock markets and national GDPs. With electronic wizardry having quickened the pace towards the global village, already reduced to small proportion by air travel and television, these are inequalities that may not be easily dismissed, even by neo-realists, as being far removed from the sight and mind of the developed nations. The inequities are enormous. It is said that the world's three richest billionaires hold more assets than the poorest countries to a sum of 600 million in population and that the total income of the richest fifth of the world's population is 75 times more than that of the poorest fifth.

Transport has justly been a consistent feature of this ongoing analysis - and transport offers another illustration of global inequalities. Road accidents are now, according to the expert George Monbiot, 'the most neglected public health issue'. 1.2 million people are killed and 50 million injured on the world's roads every year, a figure comparable with the ravages of malaria or tuberculosis. 'The poor get hurt much more than the rich', with 85% of these casualties living in the developing countries. Indeed, the economic cost of mayhem on the thoroughfares of Third World nations is between $65 and $100 billion, much the same as foreign aid to these areas. By 2020 it is estimated that road accidents will have decreased by 28% in rich countries and increased by 83% in poor ones.

Just as Britain has its very wealthy and its very impoverished people, so do most other countries. In addition, there exists this raft of inequalities from very rich to very poor nations. No change there, then, might be the rejoinder, but, of course, the interdependence of the world's nations has been intensified by modern technology and commercial practices. In the briefest and most general terms, one finds approaching 200 nations, each competing valiantly in the global market-place to keep its economic head high, while endeavouring, at the same time, to sustain some civil and social security for its citizens, should the commercial buffets be too strong. And practically every one of them has a football league and a national football team.

How have these national and club sides, outside the United Kingdom, fared over the last twenty years?

The World - The Ubiquity of Football

It is estimated that there are 60,000 full-time professional footballers in the world today. They play in leagues in many of the 207 nations and statelets that comprise FIFA's membership. All but three late candidates - Comoros, East Timor and Bhutan - entered for the 2006 World Cup in Germany, and the World Cup is a competition that now takes almost as long as the intervening four year periods to negotiate, so convoluted are its many and varied qualifying rounds. It has been a magical growth of football's beanstalk from the 20 FIFA members of 1912, to say nothing of the 68 of 1950.

Beyond just the professional game, it is calculated that there are some 320,000 football clubs in the world, two-thirds of them in Europe, with scarcely a district that does not boast a properly registered football side. Of course, most clubs run several teams. It is suggested that there are actually 1.5 million teams on the planet. The best educated guess at the number of regular players might be 250 million. That is close to being the equivalent of the population of the United States of America (270 million). There is even, under the title of FIFpro a global players' union.

It adds up to FIFA, presided over from 1998 by the Swiss lawyer and Havelange protégé Sepp Blatter, being big business now. FIFA's income from television rights for and sponsorship of the 2006 World Cup tournament was £1.4 billion, whilst its general annual income touches on £400 million. Much is disbursed in promoting football on a worldwide basis and organising tournaments.

The 2006 World Cup was watched on television in 189 countries. Apart from the direct funds from television and sponsorship, it has been calculated that the event sparks off all manner of consumerist expenditure all over the globe, as those interested buy drinks or national favours or otherwise spend their money. It was calculated that the World Cup generated £1.25 billion of such spending in the UK and no less than £4 billion in Japan. Areas without a direct interest in the tournament, such as China, Thailand,

Bolivia, Bangladesh and West Bengal, enjoyed increased football-orientated marketing activity.

Although it may be some time before American soccer viewers reach the total of nearly 100,000 million estimated to watch the Super Bowl, the almost 50 million strong Hispanic proportion of the USA's population have become the flag wavers for watching soccer in the United States. Possibly there will be a burgeoning of interest with the coming of David Beckham in 2007 to the Los Angeles Galaxy club, on a five year contract and a crusade to lift soccer from being a sport primarily enjoyed by women and youngsters, 20 million of whom are said to be regular participants. It is an expensive promotion. Beckham's deal was estimated to be worth £128 million, a matter of £25.6 million a year, or almost £1,400 an hour for a normal working week, something in advance of the minimum wage in Britain.

Ronaldinho's £15 million a year had made him the highest paid of the world's footballers until this coup, although both are still behind one or two specialist individual sports personalities like Tiger Woods (£50 million) and, until lately, Michael Schumacher (£41 million). The Anglo-Saxon galactico's salary will be funded mainly by the owner of LA Galaxy, the billionaire Philip Anschutz, who also owns that other somewhat ambivalently regarded English institution, the Millennium Dome.

Moreover, American corporations were not backward in forking out from £40 million to £60 million each for a piece of the World Cup action. Mastercard, Yahoo, McDonald's, Coca Cola, Gillette and Budweiser were all engaged in this frenzy of advertising on a planetary scale. Oxfam and other agencies have been quick to point to yet another illustration of the gross inequalities that shame the world, in football, as in most matters. Nike paid about £8 million a year to the Brazilian national side, whereas their workers in Asia subsist on as little as £2.50 a day, and Adidas workers in Indonesia earn no more than 30p an hour.

These corporate investments are major contributions to football's currently enormous commercial market. Europe, predictably, holds the most expensive stall in that market. Its yearly turnover is a colossal £7.8 billion. Over half this revenue is generated by the five main European leagues. The French 'Ligue' (£500 million), the Spanish La Liga (£700 million), the Italian Serie A (£800 million) and the German Bundesliga (£900m) are major earners, with the English Premier League lording it over the others with an income of £1.3

billion. It is fascinating to note that the next most prosperous league after the big five is the English Championship, logging in on £306 million.

Tritons and minnows abound throughout Europe as in Britain. This was exacerbated in 1992 when the European Champions League rather ominously replaced the old European Cup. The traditional European knock-out format was exchanged for one that began with a qualifying stage that favoured the elite, for the top clubs were seeded. UEFA then, from 1997, allowed more than one entrant from the four superior leagues, a reward for their seeming supremacy in these contests. Clubs from smaller countries have done badly ever since. Only Dynamo Kiev, from Eastern Europe, has reached as far as the semi-final since these changes, while Sweden, which furnished three finalists in the late 1970s and 1980s, has also rather disappeared from view.

This seeming bias has been challenged by the new UEFA president, the old French star, Michel Platini. He has promised a Poujadiste crusade on behalf of the little man, that is, the smaller European countries and statelets. His proposal that the bigger nations, England, Spain, Germany and Italy, should yield up one of their Champions League places has already fluttered the larger dovecotes of European football. He has also called for the disbandment of the elite G14 group and their abandonment of their lawsuits claiming compensation for players injured on international duty, among whom Newcastle United's Michael Owen has been a prime example, his having suffered a long-term injury early in the 2006 World Cup finals. Michel Platini is promoting a new body, the Professional Football Strategy Council, as a forum for the airing of these and other such grievances.

Michel Platini may discover, like the Poujade-led small shopkeepers of France or, for that matter, tiny nations turning to the United Nations for succour, that, like supermarkets and super-powers, the wealthy football clubs, in alliance with the wealthy television companies, will continue to prosper.

There may be a contributing reason, aside from the gerrymandering of the draw. Over these same years, the elitist teams have also, as in England, attracted the best players. The range of standards and skills across Europe is probably wider now than it has ever been.

Television again rears its glittering head. The TV chiefs want the top clubs on show, because they draw the large audiences. It is said that when Manchester United are on the telly, 3.5 million viewers tune in, whereas, for other teams, the figures are considerably less, and the same principle is true throughout

Europe, where 97 out of a hundred people out of a hundred have access to colour television. When Porto of Portugal won the Champions League in 2004, the club's take was just over £13 million, while Manchester United, who did not contrive to make it beyond the last sixteen, earned £19 million from the same competition. In 2005 Liverpool, the victors, earned £38 million.

It is noteworthy that these games themselves have a televisual penetration second only to the World Cup. They are watched in 200 countries across the world, another pressing reason why the TV bosses are anxious for the best-known teams to be represented. In 2005/06 UEFA earned almost £400 million in television rights. £250 million went to the 32 qualifying teams, with the remainder deployed in administration and in trying to help tend the grassroots of soccer in some of the smaller nations. In that connection, UEFA has shown a catholic spirit in its geopolitical approach. As well as welcoming into the fold the fragmented components of Yugoslavia and old Soviet republics, it has bestowed its blessings on Israel and, among other areas with Asian roots, the former USSR republic of Kazakhstan, maybe with one eye on being sympathetic and the other on an extra wedge of votes at FIFA assemblies.

G14 is the somewhat John le Carré title given to the cabal of Europe's richest eighteen clubs. They act as a pressure group and have recently issued a document, *Vision Europe*, explicitly arguing the case for their enduring supremacy. When Arsenal, one of the G14 clubs, was knocked out of the contest at an early stage in 2005, manager Arsène Wenger was honest enough to claim that 'you can't afford to have big clubs who invest so much money going out in the last sixteen'. There is an argument that the best rather than the most representative clubs should compete for the European club championship.

Purists may argue in support of Michel Platini for fairness, for straightforward knock-out formulae and more equitable distribution of television funds, but purists are not often stakeholders. It is the natural tendency of commercial operators to protect and enhance their product. The rich European clubs are involved in substantial investment, not least in what many would perceive as the over-extravagant salaries of their recruits. In Spain, Germany and, in particular, Italy, the proportion of turnover expended on players' salaries is, ludicrously, over 80%, beyond which little explanation is required as to why football clubs are precarious and not often profitable businesses.

The possibility that much might be lost during ninety minutes of whimsy relating to the pluck and derring-do of some smaller outfit is thus commercially unacceptable to the senior clubs. Hence the proclivity of G14 to form a corner in the market. At a lower level and in a different sport, the clubs in the English rugby union premiership have also tabled their anxiety about the effect of relegation, given the outlay necessary to establish a leading club. The English football Premiership operates a system of so-called 'parachute' payments for dropouts, and these have softened the landing back into the Championship, but they are, of course, emollient rather than curative in character.

Even within the upper tiers of continental European football, there is room for controversy over financing. Karl-Heinz Rummenigge, the Bayern Munich chairman, has complained about the excessive funding of Chelsea's team and suggests that no German team will appear in a European final over the next ten years. He believes that the English, Italian and Spanish leagues have now monopolised the European game. The example he used was of the German club Werder Bremen, with its £24 million profit in 2006 all reinvested in the team, and the gigantic losses of Chelsea, met by Roman Abramovich. He pointed out that, during the recent season, Bremen had received £15 million from television rights and Barcelona £90 million. That said, the German Bundesliga received £240 million in annual television receipts in the first years of the 21st century, where, in 1990, the take had been only £16 million.

There is tension between UEFA, the umbrella for as many as the 52 leagues of its large membership, and G14. It is, unsurprisingly, a monetary tension. In the 2005/06 season, 32 clubs fought out the Champions League and raised £288 million in so doing. The difficulty lies in devising an equation that satisfies both the chief generators of the cash flow, namely, the G14 clubs, and, at the other extreme, the remainder who play no part in the competition. The uneasy solution has been to pay more to, for instance, England, where most TV money is earned, whilst saving a few crumbs, about £120,000, for the likes of Luxembourg, San Marino and Wales, countries without representatives in the Champions League.

Spectators are customers rather than, as in the beginning, members. Spain still preserves some of this sense of popular ownership. For example, the mighty Barcelona, stationed at its grand arena, the Nou Camp, has 140,000 members or socios, and, under the presidency of the reforming lawyer Joan Laporta, has somehow combined the integrity of the membership club with the pragmatism of selling the brand and signing the stars. It is reported that Roman Abramovich had glanced lasciviously at both Barcelona and Real Madrid, only to find that, as members' clubs, they were not so commercially available. In Britain, it is only among some smaller teams, such as Lincoln City and Chesterfield, that supporters' trusts have made some headway in the running of clubs.

The future of the shape of European football depends substantially on the outcome of the precarious balancing act of selfish ambition and altruistic co-operation. It is something of a truism to add that this, of course, includes the United Kingdom. British football is inextricably linked with the rest of Europe in complex ways that would have been hard to predict in the 1950s. There is little insularity now. There are, in Britain, many players, coaches and competitions that are European, so much so that it becomes much more difficult than earlier in this text to separate the two and analyse them autonomously. The English Premiership squads are now drawn from upward of sixty nations.

The World · The Nations' Football · Europe

If one traces the contribution of individual European countries to football in the modern era of market-led democracies, one finds an uneven range. At face value, the extremes appear to have suffered most and succeeded least. To the right, politically speaking, the offspring of the former USSR were now, with wry topsy-turvydom, the most outermost apropos the freedom of the market. To the left, there were the nations of Scandinavia, the Low Countries, France and, to a lesser degree, Germany, where social market solutions had remained comprehensive and sometimes heavy-handed, and where there was some disdain for what was contemptuously dismissed as the Anglo-American or even Anglo-Saxon privatising answer.

Football in the former Iron Curtain states went into virtual meltdown. The industrial and institutional basis for its main existence at club level vanished overnight. Clubs disappeared, stadia were abandoned and players, if they were gifted enough, made tracks for foreign parts. Sometimes nouveau riche businessmen intervened, spurred on by greed or images of social cachet. Occasionally there were survivors. The Czech Republic, perhaps attaining a more favourable social balance than its old comrades-in-arms of the Warsaw

Pact, boasted the skills of Sparta Prague, oft times winners of the Czech senior league. In Russia, Spartak Moscow forged ahead as the leaders of most Russian championships, and, like Sparta Prague, thereby found in European competition tasty pickings to keep body and soul together. Dynamo Kiev, helped by strong commercial links, was the pick of the Ukrainian clubs.

Nevertheless, the bold decision was taken by UEFA in 2007 to locate the 2012 European National Championship in Poland and the Ukraine, with the final to be played in Kiev. The 2008 finals are to be played in Austria and Switzerland, while the 2004 tournament was extremely successfully held in Portugal. There has been some adverse comment about the staging of such prestigious tournaments in smaller and less fashionable footballing areas. Italy had made a strong bid for the 2012 finals, but it was believed that the continuing violence among Italian followers, plus the previous summer's revelations about match-fixing which had disgraced a number of clubs resulting in points deduction and the relegation of Juventus from Serie A, had thwarted that submission. On the other hand, the acceptance of the Polish/Ukrainian tender spoke of a willingness to spread the good times of football further eastwards in Europe.

At the other end of the scale from the old Iron Curtain states, Denmark, having won Euro 92 as outsiders, fell away, while Sweden, with its deep football roots, could only muster a semi-final appearance in the 1994 World Cup to keep up appearances. Feyenoord won the UEFA Cup in 2002 and PSV Eindhoven, funded by Philips Electrics, occasionally shone, whilst Holland did well in the 1998 World Cup and in Euro 2000, but the heady days of Johan Cruyff were, in reality, no more.

In France and Germany, as in Denmark and Holland, the resistance to commercial ownership or backing lasted longer than elsewhere. Although Marseille and Monaco enjoyed occasional momentary ventures into the sun, until, for instance, the investment of Canal Plus, the media company, in Paris Saint-Germain, French club football was, by comparison with England or Italy, seriously under-financed, so much so that almost all the national eleven played outside France. Their impressive victory in the 1998 World Cup in Paris was, however, a further catalyst for improved national recognition of football.

Germany, too, had to wait some time for the switch to commercial support as opposed to forms of state aggrandisement. Nor had Germany benefited at all from the unification that brought the lost sheep of East Germany back into the pan-Germanic fold, in that the footballing lambs were thin and wan, with the likes of Dynamo Dresden collapsing in the manner of other East European teams. The Bundesliga was transformed by the incursion of big business. VFl Wolfsburg suddenly became a team of renown, courtesy of the Volkswagen label, and Bayer Chemicals sponsored Bayer of Leverkusen, another relative newcomer to the feast of European football. Bayern Munich, managed by Ottmar Hitzfeld, won the European Champion's League in 2001 and, needless to say, its successful staging of the 2006 World Cup further encouraged German football. Even more advantageous was the £1.2 million offered to the Bundesliga by Canal Plus for television rights over a three year period.

In the socio-economic middle, a recuperating Britain, Italy and Spain had, by accident or design, fallen on a more amicable balance of the private market and its public oversight. Real Madrid and Barcelona rarely failed to please and ever kept the Spanish flag flying high above football's citadel, while, in Italy, AC Milan, coached by the insightful Fabio Capello, and the Juventus of Pavel Nedved and Zinedine Zidane customarily did well. Parma and Inter Milan, boosted by the oil monies of Massimo Moratti, also performed at a high standard, and Lazio won the Champion's League in 2000. Sergio Cragno, in a precedent for the Abramovich phenomenon, invested £100 million in Lazio, where Sven-Göran Eriksson made his later to be somewhat tarnished name.

With the marked exception of oil-rich Norway, many of these nation-states, whether lurching to left or right or hovering uncertainly in the centre of the political divide, were cursed with some of the questions and responses that had bedevilled British society in the 1970s and 1980s. For example, unemployment, whether caused by stagnating, bureaucratically bound regulos or running uncontrollably wild in the wake of the lack of public protection, was frequently rife. It was, as had been the case in the United Kingdom, youth who seemed to be the worst and were certainly the most vociferous victims. That was one primary cause - copycat imitation was probably another - that led to an outbreak of often organised football hooliganism across the continent.

While there was a relative calmness on the British scene, the Italian 'Ultras', regimented around the big Italian clubs, were, not surprisingly, still in vogue, but their Francophile equivalent next turned up at Paris Saint-Germain, while there was news of AIK Stockholm's 'Black Army' in supposedly peaceful, neutral Sweden and the vicious Feyenoord/Ajax confrontation, avowedly anti- and pro-Jewish, in purportedly placid Holland. In Eastern European countries, like

Poland, and also in Turkey, there was fan violence, unpleasantly streaked with anti-Semitism and abrasive racism. Every nation seemed to have a minority to hate, such as the Kurds in Turkey, and football was too easy a vehicle for such overt detestation.

For all the nastiness of these gangs of football hooligans, stretching to all points of the European compass, the excessive political and ethnic response of the Red Star Belgrade 'Delije' or Tigers touched the nadir of football-related violence. Under the influence of former president Slobodan Milosevic, many of them were recruited as active participants among the ranks of murderous Serbian paramilitaries. Of all football's spectators' connections with political, ethnic and religious unrest, this was perhaps the most directly shaming.

As for the clubs, the whiff of corruption that had ever cast a noisome miasma over professional football from its earliest days remained. There were rumours and rather indecisive inquiries in England over the nefarious influence of players' agents and 'bungs', a deceptively euphemistic slang term for bribes, to avaricious managers. The long-standing suspicions over the importuning of referees and other improprieties in Italian football came to a head with a set of severe judgements on some Serie A clubs in 2006, while, in the general collapse of institutional existence in the Warsaw Pact states, there was considerable corruption in football as in every walk of life. One result of the planetary coherence of the Internet, as other sports, such as cricket, were to find, was a stupendous extension in gambling. In country after country, there would be inquiries into the criminal tampering with betting on football. What must be urged is that it was a change in volume; the actual crime of interfering with the orderly outcome of a football match for felonious motives had a long history.

Indeed, a capitalist football system was the natural heir to the sins of the parent capitalist organism. The ups and downs of adventurous free enterprise were exemplified by the mini-crash caused by the failure of the digital television venture of 2002. Clubs across Europe that had spent such money in advance of actually receiving it caught a cold, Leeds and Borussia Dortmund among the more notable victims. In Greece, where Olympiakos and Panathanaikos emerged as the leading teams, the economic construct of football imploded into near financial ruin, overshadowed with strong hints of fraud and sleaze.

In Portugal, which, like the Republic of Ireland, enjoyed an economic boom consequent on European Community membership, an excellent European

Championship was organised in 2004, when Greece unexpectedly beat the home side in the final. Amid cries and accusations of corruption and match-fixing, Benfica took a financial tumble, leaving Porto as the prime Portuguese team. Turkey, too, with its general will to turn to the west, had moments of glory. Its professional leagues dated only from 1959, but, in Galatasaray and Fenerbahce, they fielded useful clubs sides in the European competitions. All this was clouded over with tales of match-fixing and rigged betting on a widely criminal organised scale and by crowd violence,

Over against these atrocity tales of corruption and aggression, there was good news. Global football led to a cosmopolitanism that indirectly celebrated the integrity of the human family. Although there were insular sighs over the dearth of local talent, most fans readily accepted the inclusion of a foreign endowment. South Americans in Italy; Africans in Belgium, this was now the norm, and there were, as in Britain, a growing number of local-born players with ethnic roots other than those of the indigenous populations. The French national eleven was a splendid example, with their captain Zinedine Zidane himself of North African Berber origins, Patrick Vieira with Senegalese roots, and goalkeeper Fabien Barthez with Spanish blood.

It reflected the growing incidence of multiculturalism in Europe and, in particular, in its capital cities, with, for instance, a third of the Brussels population estimated to be non-Belgian. Over a tenth of the European labour force, in the early years of the 21st century, had been born abroad, that is, in a country other than the one where employment had been found. Although it spurred on racist resentment and the manipulative operations of neo-fascist political parties across Europe, there was a welcome counter-flow of acceptance in which football, among other sports, played a rational part. It was calculated that, in the early 2000s, there were 500 footballers of South American extraction and as many as 1,000 of African origins playing in European football, and it was a total that was destined to rise.

The presence of the mainline multicultural incidence in the capital cities is a reminder of the 'London effect', that is, the practical takeover of major football by the conurbation or mega-city. It is true that capital cities possibly played a more outstanding role in football outside of Britain in the early days, but the European preponderance of big city football has proved unstoppable. The capital city is normally, as with London, not only the administrative, but the financial, advertising and media centre, with the conduits available for the major funding of football clubs, as well as with a populace large enough to marshal support for such clubs. In many European countries now there are one or often two clubs, based in the capital city, that dominate the national league, and often with the aid of overseas players. From Glasgow to Athens, that is the key.

On the negative side, the manufacturing areas that were once the source and basis of professional soccer are less influential. Apart from the loss of effectiveness of and support for some of the football clubs in Britain's traditional industrial districts, the German Ruhr, that once potent manufacturing region, has witnessed, like some other similar areas, a decline in its footballing might. As in the European economy as a whole, a colourful display of services, especially those connected with finance, had replaced the harder tack of solid manufacturing.

Football in these hopefully civilised climes attracted to its turnstiles a more middle class clientele, with corporate hospitality and the use of private boxes a notable feature, while the macho image of football was also moderated by the flowing tide of feminine influence. In 1957 an unofficial European Championship for women had been attempted and in 1969 an International Federation was formed. Semi-professional leagues were started in Italy, England and in some of the Scandinavian countries, while there was an admittedly precarious effort at a fully professional competition in the United States. International competition became the norm and the breakthrough of television coverage was achieved.

Just as important was the growth of the number of women watching football. For over a century, anecdotal evidence suggested that the attendance of women and girls at professional matches in Europe rarely, if ever, rose above 10%, and usually it was even more negligible than that. As in England, the changes in both the typology of stadia and in approach to sexual equity led to a minor social revolution that saw this normatively doubled to over 20%, with, at some of the more prestigious matches, an unprecedented 50% of women. Needless to say, in the much wider congregation of viewers gathered around millions of TV sets, the proportion of women is well above that 20% pointer.

All in all, and in spite of the downside that must never be ignored, there are millions of Europeans getting an awful lot of fun out of football. Although football clubs may fail to make much money, they certainly gladden hearts. Some of J.B. Priestley's mantra of 'art and conflict', as portrayed by

Bruddersford United, continues to inspire many people and provide them with weekly injections of passion, unfulfilled or otherwise. It is difficult to overestimate the cultural impact of football in Europe. The scholar, Noam Chomsky, marvelled at the intellectual grasp of football demonstrated by persons of apparently limited education and intelligence, claiming that it testified to the academic potential of the human race.

Certainly, it affects great numbers. Every national or club victory in a major competition is greeted with massive outbreaks of affectionate and usually peaceful celebration. When France won the 1998 World Cup, a million supporters packed the Champs-Elysees in delighted parade. As with several similar assemblies in other European capitals to rejoice over football victories, it was said to be the largest host to gather in Paris since the liberation celebrations at the end of World War II.

A further illustration is the fashion in which the television focus on football is energetically backed by newsprint, internet blogging, radio phone-ins, specialist magazines, fanzines and a dozen other samples of audio-visual and literary exposition. The press, from tabloid to broadsheet, devotes acres of space and gallons of printers' ink to the doings of football clubs and the antics of football players. Politicians and religious leaders may only look on with envy, pausing only to find a foothold on this runaway bandwagon of footballing interest.

In his major text on world football, David Goldblatt provides an incisively amusing account of the activities of the soccer-crazed Greeks. He describes how, apart from a multitude of ordinary newspapers supplying an unending delivery of supplements and pull-outs, there are nine dailies dedicated to sport, principally football. Almost 5% of Greece's GDP is invested in betting on football of every conceivable brand: 'Two channels spent the whole of Saturday and Sunday broadcasting updates on the Scottish Second Division and the third round of the Norwegian Cup.'

Nor is there much hope for those believing that religion might bring some spiritual balm to football. There was, for example, a disputatious end to the 2007 Clericus competition for priests and seminarians, the final of which, played in the shadow of St Peter's Basilica, Rome, was marred by ill-tempered rancour. The Pontifical Lateran University players accused the Redemptoris Mater College striker of diving to gain what turned out to be the decisive penalty. Blue cards, used to send offenders, not inappropriately, to the sin bin for a purgative few minutes, were flourished in all directions, as fans of 'the Vatican's Milan' chanted exultantly in Latin.

What penetration! Europe was football mad.

The World - The Nations' Football - The Rest of the World

Football was part of the Europeanisation of the world. The gradual conquest of the planet by a form of Mercantilism, with, at best, a creative tension between classical economic liberalism and the counterbalance of democratic rights, was now near complete. Europe, not least through the zealous lead, for the child is father to the man, of its most remarkable creation, the United States of America, had forged the template for this worldwide pattern. Its social and cultural attributes, its McDonalds and its pop stars, were the necessary underpinnings of this development. Its chief recreational device was football, pressed, first as a cheerful pastime, next as an urban entertainment, then, last as a televisual spectacle with a live audience. Football was, by the end of the 20th century, the premier sport not only in Europe but on every other continent as well.

Global football follows the European pattern as European football followed the British fashion. There was the national league and cup competition, with victory usually leading to a continental tournament. There was even the frequent continuance of that age-old British, then later European (Olympiakos and Panathinaikos in Athens, for example) curio of the rival pairing of clubs in the same city. These stretched from the well-established pairings of several cities in South America to Soweto's Orlando Pirates and Kaiser Chiefs in South Africa. During the 1990s the British practice of three points for a win and one for a draw became commonplace, with FIFA's blessing, and there was a wholesale tightening of discipline in regard of tackling from behind and the attempted outlawing of the oxymoronic 'professional foul' when defenders, including the goalkeeper, illegally prevented a certain goal. In a further effort to speed the game up, the goalkeeper was no longer permitted to handle the ball when it was passed back to him, although it often resulted in the ball being hoofed into the grandstand.

These were all essays, everywhere ruled by the yellow and red card device, to promote more attacking football, as befitted a worldwide spectator sport. As a symbol of this ubiquitous regime, the selection of South Africa in 2010 as the first African site for the World Cup heralded the acceptance of a complete circle of the competition being played in sequence in each of the six major confederation areas. Every one of the world's mainstream regions henceforward would host the World Cup on a regular basis.

Two areas were still not as fully converted as the rest. The United States, while running a World Cup competition in 1994 and with a try-again attitude to a professional football alliance of which Robert the Bruce would have been proud, still regarded baseball with greater favour, although the arrival of the Beckham circus in the summer of 2007 will provide its sternest test yet as the worlds of professional sport and celebrity collide, Hollywood-style.

Soccer, however, had developed quite a cachet appeal among suburban mums and dads and, in fact, showed signs of finding favour among women. 7 million American women are said to be playing football, compared with less than half a million in Germany, something of a female football stronghold, and the USA women's teams have done well in the women's international tournaments. The NASL was resurrected in 1994, with thirteen teams in the Major League. Salaries are capped for all but one player in each of these squads, suggesting those touring variety shows in Britain where a bravura mainline star commands most of the time on stage and most of the profits off stage, with just a handful of puny artists in sparse support. Beckham will undertake that singular role at Los Angeles Galaxy.

On the sub-continent, football flourished but sparsely, although the NFL, a professional league, was founded in India in 1996, but cricket still sustained its attractive and peculiar appeal to the masses in the old Raj. Yet even in the USA and in India, football was played and was watched on TV. It is a relative calculation. Hereabouts was the least interest expressed, rather than no interest at all.

If democratically restrained capitalism was the crucial politico-economic factor and global warming the alarming ecological factor, the determining social factor for the condition of this new world was demographic. In Europe and throughout the world, the population just keeps on rising. When the FA was founded in London in 1863 the world's population had touched a billion for the first time. In 1950, when England first competed in the World Cup, it had grown to 2.5 billion. In 1992, when the Premier League was formed, it had more than doubled to 5.3 billion. When the World Cup was contested in 2006, it was 6.5 billion - and when it is next contested in 2010, the total will be over

7 billion. That represents a sevenfold growth over the course of the history of organised football.

The mathematics are simple enough. Every year 131 million babies, the equivalent of the population of Japan, are born. Every year 57 million people die, the equivalent of the population of Ethiopia. Result; a net profit of 74 million global inhabitants, the equivalent of the population of Vietnam. Microcosmically, there are 249 births and 108 deaths a minute, so that the world's population rises by 141 every 60 seconds.

The traditional debates in Europe and North America about the relation of the demographic explosion to industrial expansion, and which was chicken and which was egg, have rather been confounded on a global basis by the sheer pace of the acceleration in population. It has tended to overwhelm or even bypass industrial advance in some regions, although the technology of improved medical and welfare care has largely contributed to the vast decline in infant mortality, which is the constant element in any explanation of such population growth.

Assuredly, industry has extended into many areas, including the application of industrial techniques to agriculture on a wide basis, but there are also locales where population has jumped without the benefit of the industrial crutch. What is more transparently evident is the expansion of urban life. In summary, in the half century since the end of the Second World War population density has climbed from 20 to 50 per square kilogram. This has resulted in a change almost exactly the same as that which occurred in Britain during the reign of Queen Victoria and in almost exactly the same number of years. In 1945, 71 out of a hundred people on earth lived in rural circumstances and 29 in urban habitats. Now the ratio is almost 40 rural and 60 urban, a shift from three-tenths to three-fifths in town dwellers.

The phenomenon of the conurbation or mega-city was quick to emerge. On every continent there are examples. Mexico City; Cairo; Jakarta; Seoul; Buenos Aires; Manila and Tokyo are non-European capital cities with populations in excess of 10 million, some of them reaching 15 million. If one counts in the regional population dependent on the focal city, the totals are, of course, much larger, with Sao Paulo or Mexico City weighing in at 25 million denizens and Buenos Aires or Rio de Janeiro at 18 million. These are the cities that act as the financial and administrative centres for regions and for nation-states and where much of the commercial and manufacturing activity is located. These include many of the Asian sweatshops that produce the majority, not without some irony, of the material for world football in the shape of shirts, balls and all the rest of the essential items. These are the cities where football is often played and watched to the uttermost, just as in Europe.

Several of the latest developments have been in Asia, where professional leagues like Japan's J-League and South Korea's Super, later, K-League have been formed over the last ten or twenty years in many countries and where the addition of five ex-Soviet Asian republics has swelled the band of the large Asian Football Confederation. The AFC, especially under the guidance of the accomplished administrator Peter Vellapan has been very competent, modernising, for example, the AFC Cup which, in 2004, was played in China, something of a political leap forward in the region.

Few will need reminding that the world's conurbations are the loci for many of the world's problems. The curses as well as the benedictions of urbanised existence fell on the fresh conurbations, as if they followed the example of the earlier European cities that had themselves been roughly modelled on British industrial moulds. For all the variegated pigmentation of differing cultural flavours, struggling to live in a mega-city was the fundamental influence. Many cities suffered underemployment and appalling social problems, resulting in crime, drug and alcohol abuse and mindless violence, especially within disaffected youth. These could occasionally brew up into something wholly more unpalatable and destabilising; organised gang warfare, sometimes accompanied by shootings and stabbings, and often met with over-excited and brutal policing, much of it associated with football.

There were the 'barras bravas' of Argentina; the 'torcidas' of Brazil, and, in some cases, such aggressive bands attempted to intimidate the management of the clubs they supported and which had cultivated their affection and lent them support, an instructive example of the clubs in question being hoist with their own petard. There were kidnappings in Latin America, an unwonted mark of the celebrity value of footballers, while, infamously, after Columbia's enforced retreat from the 1994 World Cup, its players were abused and one of their number, Andres Escobar, was shot dead. In 1985 in Beijing there was an ugly riot when Hong Kong defeated the Chinese team, whilst even Japan suffered from the aggressive capers of the Crazy Cats, the hooligans attached to Urawa Red Diamonds.

Soccer's spectatordom is identified, with one or two prominent instances, the world over with violence and misbehaviour. The 2006 World Cup in

Germany required the deployment of over 100,000 police officers. Entertainment should not require that degree of protection.

There was the feature of inhospitable and perilous stadia, which, often as a consequence of furious rioting, led to the kind of disasters that had soured British and European football. Rioting at the 1991 Soweto 'derby' match, Kaiser Chiefs versus Orlando Pirates, caused the death of 40 and injuries to 50 others. When the same teams met at Ellis Park, Johannesburg, in 2001, 43 died when crowds left outside invaded the ground. There was a terrible incident in Ghana in 2001, when Accra's Hearts of Oak met Kumasi's Asante Kotoko. In that volatile human cocktail of crowd violence, police harshness, including the heavy use of tear gas, and locked gates, 126 were killed. In 1994 the clash of Zambia and Sudan in a World Cup qualifier led to a stampede in which nine died and 78 were injured - and Zambia has also followed the unhappy European precedent of the air accident, with, as with the European examples, accusing fingers ready to point blame; in 1993 the Zambian team was completely wiped out on a doomed flight to play Senegal.

And that is just a few sad choices from an unsavoury list of tragedies related to football matches in many countries across the planet.

There was incessant gambling, which inevitably led to charges of match fixing, while there were other forms of corruption, as, for instance, when politicians tried to utilise the game for their own perverse ends. Soccer was very adaptable as a political football. Here there was Uday, son of Saddam Hussain, running a despicable and brutal football regime in Iraq for his own vicious purposes. There the young people, including the young women, of Iran found in football a rallying standard around which to combat the extreme religious conservatism of their elders. Here was the princely and opulent control of the Saudi Arabian national side, twice winners of the Asia Cup and occasional visitors to the World Cup. There were the struggles of Senegal or Cote d'Ivoire to progress in World Cup competition, despite impoverished economies.

As for the more straightforward business of fixing matches to make money is concerned, Asia supplied many examples. Japan and South Korea, who jointly hosted the 2002 World Cup with some panache, and also China have suffered from such scandals, while the sabotage of English floodlighting around the turn of the century, in an attempt to rig score-lines, emanated from Indonesia and Malaysia. It would be difficult to imagine a more malignant or odder example of football's worldwide incidence than the deliberate disruption of power in 1997 at West Ham's Upton Park for an innocuous looking midweek match against Crystal Palace planned by an oriental gambling syndicate.

South African football bounced back with some vim after 1992. The end of Apartheid and the advent of Nelson Mandela was the obvious catalyst; in 1995 Orlando Pirates won the African club tournament and the following year South Africa won the African nations' trophy and, in 1998, qualified for the World Cup. Yet - shades of the gambling scandals in white-dominated South African cricket - South African football was troubled with corruption and allied predicaments. In the last ten years, FIFA has been forced, at one time or another, to suspend Guinea, Gambia, Tanzania, Cameroon, Kenya and Sierra Leone for forms of malpractice.

No region of footballing note has been free of hooliganism, disasters or, in the wake of rampant gambling, match-fixing scandal or other forms of corruption. When one recalls the gambling on horse racing, boxing, 'pedestrianism' and cricket in 18th century England, one is entitled to believe that organised sport and gambling are inexorably wedded.

But when all the horrors of football have thus been catalogued, one must return to its beneficial survival in locales of depressing turmoil. It is astonishing to read of football in war-torn Iraq or amidst the civil strife of Columbia. David Goldblatt movingly describes the 'great rotting shanty town' of Mathare, Nairobi, a site of endemic poverty, where the Mathare Youth Sports Association has organised a hundred leagues embracing a thousand teams, including, very significantly, 200 girls' sides, and where the team at the top of this enormous pyramid, Mathare United, has won the Kenyan Cup three times. It is, undoubtedly, a truism, but, like every other human agency, football may be a force for evil or good.

The clubs themselves continued to require the support of business, were they to compete at the higher levels. By the onset of the 21st century, there was an abandonment of dictatorial regimens in many parts of Africa and elsewhere, as in South America, in favour of more democratically inclined governments. This, one hopes, will shortly lead to a more secure backdrop for football in particular and society in general in these areas. One immediate effect was the disappearance of many clubs backed by the state apparatus, a cheerful development already witnessed in Eastern Europe. Even in China, where, predictably, the army and state industries had been the promoters, there has been a turn to more benign local government, as had previously happened in

Spain and Germany and other parts of Europe. The players in Jia A, the top Chinese league, now wear logos and enjoy relatively inflated salaries.

A mix of local government agencies and big business sponsor the mainstream clubs of Japan and South Korea. Occidental stars, of the likes of Gary Lineker, have graced the Japanese footballing stage, where clubs such as Kashima Antlers, managed at one time by Arsène Wenger, or Tokyo Verdy, with its strong fan base, enjoy corporate support. It is evidently well nigh impossible for a senior club anywhere in the world to survive in a monetary vacuum, relying merely on the goodwill of its local fans.

The World - The Multi-culture of Football

A worrying aspect was the vanishing supporter in many parts of the world. Outside the capital cities of Latin America, the gates at many provincial games had reached a derisory low Although the proportions of blame varied from place to place, a mix of unwelcoming and risk-strewn stadia, the menace of aggressive mob behaviour, impoverished economies leaving people unable to afford the entrance fee, and the contrary blandishment of television were the chief causes of the desertion of the grounds. Except for some clubs and some games, audiences around the world were not as high as one might have expected, a trend noticeable, in the same random vein, in other spectator sports.

Of course, this lack of immediate support was compensated for a thousand-fold by the increasing volume of the television audience, plus all the trappings of newsprint, radio, internet and other outlets for information, gossip, speculation and discussion about the game. One of the most globally intriguing facets of the new countenance of football was the interest shown in clubs and players at a distance, with millions - 50 million, it was estimated in the case of Manchester United - across the world seeking to fasten their ribbons to football clubs and their stars in far-off climes, usually in Europe or South America.

In counterpoise to sedentary fans with dynamic ambitions, local players aspired to be upwardly mobile, migrating - as we have noted already through the European lens - principally to Europe for professional contracts. With often indifferent prospects facing players in their own backyards, the promise of a ride on the European gravy train proved very enticing. In Africa especially the emphasis on youth development had a legitimate and proper eye on this possibility. The football construct was aimed at producing skilled players for the markets abroad as an alternative to the brain drain based on the other extremity. The South American clubs, too, found themselves forced to pick this option, with transfer receipts from Europe becoming a major part of their revenue.

In spite of the logistics problems, national coaches were not too aggrieved to have their charges playing in the upper tiers of the European leagues, where the standards were usually higher than in their parochial environs. Provided the hosting clubs were reasonably obliging with the release of players, it boded well for the progress of the national team. From Finland to Bulgaria, these players from the new worlds of Africa, Asia and America are duly welcomed into practically every European nation-state. The whole of this process was personified in 1995, when George Weah, the agile Liberian star with AC Milan, was voted World Player of the Year.

By the early seasons of the present century, it was estimated that as many as 2,000 non-Europeans were playing as professionals in the several European leagues, the largest number being African, but with a huge allocation of Latin Americans, and then smaller packages of players from a wide range of countries in Asia, Oceania and North America. On the positive front, it could be decently regarded as payback time. The British and their European disciples had taken the truth to the peoples of the world; now gifted neophytes from the four corners of the globe were returning to the founts of football and adding to the pleasures of the original faithful.

Another multicultural step forward was taken with the playing of international matches on neutral soil, to take account of the vast number of overseas players playing in Europe, especially in the English leagues. Many contemporary readers, no less than those from a by-gone age, would have been astonished to scan the fixtures in London for Wednesday 6 February 2007 and to find included: Australia v Denmark, at Queen's Park Rangers' Loftus Road; Brazil v Portugal, at Arsenal's Emirates Stadium; Ghana v Nigeria, at Brentford's Griffin Park, and Greece v South Korea, at Fulham's Craven Cottage. 110,000 tickets were sold for the four games, while the TV coverage was substantial. 100 million Africans were estimated to have watched the Ghana/Nigeria contest, while the Brazil/Portugal fixture was screened throughout Europe. Millions in the southern hemisphere tuned in at 6.30 am on Wednesday morning to view Australia's adventures. The coaches were delighted. The players were not weighed down or, worse, unable to make the trip, because of the excessive travel. Such is the polyglot mixture of soccer that it was simpler and more effective to bring the fixture to the players.

For those committed to the quest of happy multiculturalism, there was much over which to rejoice. Celebrities from foreign nations might make admirable role models for indigenous populations, perhaps more so than the native prototype, although it must be added that, in many examples, the competition was none too brisk. Whatever else, they destroyed archetypical myths of long standing in European football circles and among European football crowds. It soon became apparent, for example, that the Nordic and Anglo-Saxon races had no monopoly on tough, uncompromising defenders and these were to be found anywhere in the world. Although racism remained a nasty quandary for the football authorities in many parts of the world, it was difficult for fans to withstand the talents that a purportedly alien player might bring to the fortunes of their own club.

In all this vast compass of activity, television was the predominating cultural feature. By the end of the 20th century, television had inveigled itself into almost every community, with Africa the last continent to succumb to the lure of the flickering screen. It may, by American standards, have been a trifle primitive in parts of Africa, with sets scrambled together and run off all sorts of improvised electrical resources, a situation reminiscent of the old cat's whisker days of early wireless in England, but television, nevertheless. One guess is that there are a billion households with television sets in the world, as well as large screen public outlets, the thousands of sets in hotel rooms, and the screens available in myriad bars, cafes and pubs of all descriptions across the planet. It is a sci-fi image of fantasy, a technological feat that H.G. Wells or Jules Verne might have predicted, whereby, through the vehicle of the satellite modus operandi, everyone may look at the same picture at once. It is also an image that, in more dystopian mood, either George Orwell or Aldous Huxley might have envisaged

Certainly, to combine the imagery of that latter pairing, the *Big Brother* watching you in this *Brave New World* was likely to be a purveyor of football. The television service that did not supply a diet of football was, by the end of the 20th century, rare indeed. Where football was a long established and regular aspect of national life, the TV companies, as in South America and parts of Asia and Oceania, paid reasonable sums that were, as in Europe, of value, often of indispensable value, to the football clubs. Africa, last in the queue, had, as yet, found relatively small funding for its football teams, but a minor part of that was down to newness, as well as, in major part, the depressed nature of the continent's general economy. The more sprightly Asian economies are peopled by millions of football fanatics. When South Korea progressed well in the 2002 World Cup there were 2,000 screens hoisted across the nation, with an estimated crowd of a million in Seoul alone to watch the fun. When Chinese players, such as Li Tei, appeared for Everton in the English Premiership, it is said that 150 million of his countrymen and women watched him on the flickering box. For the 2006 World Cup it was estimated that half of the TV audience was Asian.

Television, with the visceral probing of slow-motion replays, not only added thereby to the fascination of analysis, but to the identification of brutal behaviour on the field, and, through close circuit systems, off the field. At best, the presentation was extremely entertaining, even if there was some vexation about the peculiar timings of matches to coincide with TV schedules. In an earlier chapter, the effect of spectatorship on football methodology was examined, in respect, for instance, of touchlines, and, as the television viewer became the key customer and the television company the key client, there were analogies.

Extra time, replays and, in particular, golden goal play-outs are anathema to the telly scheduler, while the 'away goal' premium in two-tie contests is frowned upon as lacking direct lucidity. Conversely, the penalty shoot-out, with its quick, built-in drama, with individuals feted or branded for a moment's action, makes for excellent television. For the football stickler, its artificiality and negation of football's team-ethic is abhorrent. A preferable and logical solution for settling a drawn cup match might be the count of corners, for they do usually signify the degree of pressure exerted by each team, but that might be regarded as too cerebral for the guardians of the public's television fare.

As in Britain and among its European brethren, the 21st century tale of football throughout the world is, at its upper levels, largely about money - and much of that money has television connections. While politicians and governments still hold some sway over soccer, the influence is more covert and less malign, with football as a privatised entertainment industry being more the norm. It is also about masses of people, cramped into huge urban confines, finding recreational solace in a doubly vicarious fashion. They may not play and they do not attend - but they observe on the television. It is a form of mass electronic voyeurism. At the same time, it is fair to protest that many young people play as well as watch, with the watching, as from the beginnings of football, inspiring the playing, not least when there might seem to be the smidgeon of an opportunity to make a living from football. One in every 250 human beings plays football regularly, a very agreeable degree of active participation.

The Game - Changes In Football

Football itself has not changed radically over the last ten or twenty years. One of the by-products of the restless migration of players, the ceaseless round of club and national competitions and the endless screening of innumerable matches has been a sameness about the patterns of play all over the planet. Football is brisk, bustling and pliable. Although the incessant tinkering with tactics continues non-stop, the basic strategy of the four man (or woman) defence, four or five across the mid-field and one or two strikers is standard. The emphasis, as in Europe, remains on elasticity, with, either for an entire game or during parts of a match, players retreating into protective positions or filing forward in wholesale attack.

Coaching and training is now intense everywhere, often down to lower leagues in most countries. This has proved to be something of a leveller. Although the best resourced teams will usually win over time, and thereby conquer over the lengthy stretch of a league programme, the prevailing high levels of fitness among closely regimented players, especially in defensive prudence and ball possession, may allow teams to hang on for longish periods. Stamina and strategy, plus concentration, permit many clubs to offer sterling battle against all-comers. This is a slight counterweight to the monopolistic authority of a small number of national and club teams within national, continental and world competitions.

Peter Hartland - who astutely tipped Italy as the Germany 2006 winners - has elaborately completed many tallies of how nations and clubs have performed over time. This does tend to confirm the control established by the few over the many. There have been eighteen World Cup tournaments, and, although half a dozen or so newer nations have progressed to the last eightsome reel, top level football is 'confined within a continent and a half'. Only seven nations have won the World Cup. These are Brazil, with five victories; Italy, with four wins; Germany, with three; Argentina and Uruguay, albeit a generation or so ago, each with two, and France and England with one. Brazil alone, it should be reiterated, has travelled victoriously from its own continent, to Sweden in 1958 and Japan/South Korea in 2002, as well as the half-way house of the United States in 1994.

Europe and Latin America, of course, had the impetus of a start. The miracle has been the velocity of the rush at which practically every other world power has endeavoured to catch up with the front runners. South Africa 2010 may be too soon for a team outside the two chief regions to emerge victorious, but another twelve years might see a surprise or two.

In any event, the fact that there have been only seven winners, three of them taking twelve of the eighteen spoils on offer, suggests, self-evidently enough, that it is certain nations, as much as certain regions, that catch the eye. Germany has also won the European national championships three times out of a dozen tourneys, leaving two to France, and a single trophy to just seven others, namely USSR, Spain, Netherlands, Czechoslovakia, Italy, Denmark and Greece. Although the Copa America, established in 1917, is now less prestigious than the World Cup qualifying competition, it also demonstrates the dominance of two or three top dogs, with Uruguay (11), Argentina (10) and Brazil (7) contributing a sum of 28 out of a possible 34 titles.

Club competitions, vividly distorted by foreign transfers, provide a much more varied pattern. In the European Cup/Champions League rankings 1956-2004, Real Madrid easily lead the way with nine pennants out of 49 opportunities, with AC Milan, on six, the runner up. Bayern Munich, Ajax and Liverpool, each with four, follow next, as of 2004, with another sixteen having won once or twice. Peter Hartland supplies the interesting register of club-by-nation success, which shows that Spanish and Italian clubs have won the title ten times each, 1956-2004, with English teams next with nine cup victories, followed by German and Dutch clubs with six. In all, ten European nations have provided European club champions.

In Latin America, the equivalent competition, the Copa Libertadores, presents something of the same pattern, using the similar 1960-2004 rankings. Independiente of Argentina (7), Penarol of Uruguay (5) and Boca Juniors of Brazil (5) have taken seventeen of the 45 laurels on offer, with a further seventeen clubs having won the title once, twice or thrice. The national distribution of club titles, in a region where foreign transfers have not been such a feature, is even more concentrated than in Europe. Not surprisingly, Argentina (20), Brazil (11) and Uruguay (8) have swept the board, leaving only six to the also rans of Columbia, Paraguay and Chile.

At the very top of the pyramid, a few nations and a few clubs thus monopolise the richest of the competitive pickings. However, the prediction might be that, as China, or Japan or South Africa or the United States or Australia or South Korea, for one reason or another, overhaul the giants among football's founding fathers, then the balance of power might alter. Certainly, the incidence of football, with a professional league in the majority of nation-states, would argue for such an outcome.

The reverse conjecture might arise from an awareness of the minuteness of the global village. In so far as television is to be the arbiter and medium of the professional game, there are signs that people may opt to watch and support the best rather than the most local, especially if local boys are making good among the best. Those who scoff, for example, at Manchester United finding fans outside the Greater Manchester area - 'cockney reds' is one contemptuous appellation - may then find that their range of abuse might have to encompass thousands from much farther afield among the townships of Singapore and Hong Kong and all points of the compass. Another intriguing example is the proxy excitement shown for Brazilian football in West Bengal.

In the small world of today, one might find fans anywhere as well as football everywhere.

CHAPTER EIGHTEEN

FOOTBALL;
THE GLOBAL CULT

THUS WE ARRIVE, full circle, at our starting point in chapter one, with the World Cup Final of 9 July 2006 in Berlin, when nearly half the world's population watched Italy's penalty shoot-out victory. It was only 134 years since, on 16 March 1872, the occasion of football's first-ever showpiece match, the first FA Cup Final, had attracted about 2,000 spectators.

Football and its Formative Factors

It was suggested, in that introductory chapter, that 5% of the humans that had ever lived were thereby involved in watching the Italians defeat the French in Berlin, by far the largest number of people ever engaged simultaneously in a single activity in the history of the world, outstripping anything a political, religious or other cultural creed, belief or interest could possibly muster for one event. That is the astounding measure of football's conquest of the hearts and minds of the world's population.

The key factors are demographic and electronic, in the sense of many people having access to many television sets. The demographic feature may require some exegesis.

The calculation that five out of every hundred people that have ever lived is based on a demonstration that the human species suddenly moved, in maritime terms, from dead slow to full steam ahead, with repercussions for football, as for all other social matters.

For all but a century or two of human life over some half a million years, the population has been woefully tiny. It has been calculated that a small family unit of gatherers and hunters would have required some twenty square miles of propitious land to survive. About 10,000/8,000 BC, when the Neolithic Revolution ushered in the first primitive agriculture, with the domestication of animals and the cultivation of crops, the total world population was no more than 5 million to 10 million, much the size of one major city, such as Washington DC, today. As agrarian practices were adopted over many areas of the world, population expanded, and then with the commercialisation of the economy and the spread of urban habits, it grew more rapidly. With the impact of industrialised economies, the growth became exponential. Thus, during one per cent of man's life span on earth, his numbers have suddenly inflated by no less than 700 times.

This is why the overall number of human births, conservatively estimated by demographers at 60 billion, seems so small, given that there are 6.5 billion alive now. Simply, over 10% of the people who have ever lived are alive at this moment - and half of them watched the 2006 World Cup Final. As with many species, it is sorrowfully true that many of those 60 billion persons suffered but brief sojourns on earth, with possibly a majority dying in infancy. The problem of manoeuvring babies through their first year and then through the first five years of life is usually the key to population growth and, in this connection, industrial technology and scientific know-how has frequently proved to be a prerequisite of the forward march of population.

The linkage of the demographic explosion with urbanism is direct and self-evident. Throughout this text, the close correlation of urbanisation with football has been underlined, with especial reference to the extension worldwide of professional, spectator-orientated football. The industrial town or city, later the conurbation, often with major financial concerns, has been demonstrated as the home of professional football. For a number of reasons, association football has emerged as by far the most apposite spectator sport for urban man and, increasingly, urban woman. The corollary to that argument is to press the point that, had the global population remained at lowish levels, football might not have been the most appropriate of recreations for the majority. A leading image of professional football is the slightly claustrophobic one of a congested stadium, tightly confined by urban housing and other buildings. Completely different conditions might have led, naturally enough, to completely different leisure provision.

Another motif of this study has been that other palpable factor of transport. The conveyance of performers and spectators has been to the forefront of this scrutiny, again for the most obvious of reasons. The technical apparatus of the railway, the motorised vehicle, the steamboat and, emphatically, the aeroplane has been urged as an essential precondition of football's conquest of the planet. Without air travel, the entire fabric of continental and global competition would, of course, be impossible on its present scale.

But that was not to be enough. Mahomet and the mountain: football had to be taken to the people as well as people being taken to the football. For football to be a genuine cult, its priesthood of athletic strikers and stalwart defenders available to all, it needed the genius of television to articulate its delights pictorially into every household. This was the ultimate stage in communication; the transportation of football matches into people's living rooms and kitchens. In turn, television was to supply football with a major proportion of its revenue; by the beginning of the 21st century, TV monies constituted 30% of Arsenal's income and even at Manchester United, with its large fan base and global market, the figure was 10%.

In 1926, on the back of much arduous and previous research, John Logie Baird produced what has been called the first 'true television', when he contrived the electrical transmission of moving 30 line pictures, in half tones, at the rate of ten per second. By the 1930s there was an embryonic television service in the London area, although it had to await the end of the Second World War before it became authentically national in scope. In 1938 Georges Valensin, the French inventor, began the experiment that led to the exciting breakthrough of colour television in 1967, by which time over 90% of British households had television sets. The development of satellite television completed the comprehensive system by which pictures could be delivered to every part of the world at once and it became possible for a live event, such as the World Cup Final, to be seen everywhere.

Acceleration is the constant. The growth of population; the expansion of industry and town-life; the development and spread of transport; the invention and increasing range of organised football; the discovery and circulation of television - each process speeded up ever more frenetically, each one interacting with the other elements in an upwardly twisting, escalating spiral.

If one were to personify these developments toward a planet satiated with football, one might do worse than hail the joint efforts of Charles William Alcock and John Logie Baird and adore them as the genuine founders of the faith.

The adaptability of football to television is the ultimate mark of its genuine degree of accessibility to the human consciousness. In truth, some individual games, played out on a smaller stage, like boxing or tennis, are, at first sight, more amenable to the small screen. It has been said that, had snooker not been invented, colour television would have enforced its creation, so snugly does it fit Logie Baird's box of delights. However, soccer does not have too much of a difficulty, especially in an age of multiple cameras, and the play may be followed very easily.

Other sports are covered with great efficiency on television, but several have drawbacks. Rugby Union, despite its late acceptance that, in a spectator sport, it is pleasing for onlookers to see the ball occasionally, is a little too elaborate, in rules and in scoring, for real popularity. Golf suffers from the disbenefit that hurts it as an ordinary spectator sport; it is not easy to follow the overall pattern of competitive play at any one time or from any one vantage point. Cricket gains from the close-up view of the initiatory action, but loses from the sheer dimensions of its setting; you see the ball struck, but you cannot know who, if anybody, lies in wait. Horse and motor racing, and other circuitous sports, although quite popular, can be equally hard to watch in any meaningful context. Some of the individual games, like tennis or badminton, can become a trifle static and stately and even predictable...and so on. They are enjoyable and, for the aficionados, they are addictive and gripping, but, in all conscience, they are not the material by which 3 billion watchers might be lured.

Football, on television, retains its age-old virtues. It is almost ridiculously simple. Its earlier codifiers should be congratulated for their pristine wisdom. Apart from the always vexed question of offside, it is usually clearly apparent what is going on and who is doing what. The dimensions of the pitch, its vivid markings, the lucid definition of teams by uniform apparel, the marvellously unfussy and trouble-free fact that there is only one way of scoring, that this score means 'one' and that it is not too common an occurrence, as, say, in basketball, but remains special and glorious - these, and umpteen other factors make football so impressively unadorned. The time element is important. 90 minutes, with an interval to visit the lavatory and make a cup of tea or whatever might be the foreign equivalents of those insular traditions, is exactly right. Compared with the absurd brevity (to the non-athletically predisposed mind) of, say, the hundred yards sprint and the equine flat race or the preposterously lengthy travail (to the non-cricketing intellect) of the five days Test match, an hour and a half is ideal. Fascinatingly, it is very close to the two hours of the old-style variety theatre bill or 1940s cinema show - and they both had an interval, too.

It is unpretentious enough to have been the participatory game of choice of many who watch, for, unlike many sports, it is flexible enough to be played in small groups and with little or no equipment beyond a ball. As well as the 250 million amateur footballers on the planet in regular competition, there may be as many again playing soccer in a more desultory and sporadic fashion. It is sufficiently gladiatorial to command attention, and, in that a team game has its own special allure, it lends itself possibly better to the screen than any other combined sporting enterprise. Although the dual battles of boxing, wrestling or the racket games may be riveting, the twosome may become a little tedious, save, of course, to the soul of the true believer. Somehow the football eleven, usually more widely extended than the stern military lines of the rugby codes and able to communicate by the long kicked pass rather than by the short thrown rugby pass, offers an intelligible composition for the TV screen. By and large, it provides sufficient variety of personnel without becoming too clustered.

All in all, the more one analyses football, the more one comes to marvel at the wit and perception of its founders, that they could have produced a game that, in much the same construct as when it began, is now part of a worldwide television extravaganza.

A negative illustration of the quintessential minimalism of football is its lack of eloquent commentators. That is something of a begged question, but it is arguable that, compared with the appropriately expressive and articulate presenters and analysts of cricket, golf and other popular games, those concerned with soccer have been and are somewhat banal and trite. They may be cheerful and anorakish or they may offer solemn remarks about trivial technical bits and pieces, but they rarely stretch the imagination with lyricism or the intellect with insight. Much the same applies to sports literature, where cricket, especially, but also golf and boxing and one or two other sports, have evoked writing of some majesty and class, where football, an occasional imperious exception apart, has signally failed so to do. Recently, the England manager, discussing his team's future prospects on BBC television, declared, 'we need goal scorers; you win football matches by scoring goals.' It was heartfelt but not profound.

Lest one be tempted to find the broadcasters, pundits and authors culpable of frailer gifts, the point must be promptly and firmly made that all this is because there is little to say or explain or elaborate in respect of football. Its plainness leaves precious little room for exposition or even description. It may be, in turn, balletic, dramatic, brutal, invigorating or bathetic, but it is never obscure. There is often nothing to add. The interviews with players and the comments of experts are so cliché-ridden and stale that they rarely rise above the norm of a friendly discussion between a few mates in the pub after the match. The opposite case of cricket is instructive. The chief attraction of cricket is its very complexity. Cricket lovers may engage in a wide range of what to others might be tedious intellectual exercises, statistical, historical, geographical, meteorological, literary, as well as enjoying the dissection of a convoluted series of technical actions. Every ball may be the subject of a prolonged inquest.

For all its straightforward appeal, football may, of course, collapse as a global diversion. Assuredly, were television suddenly to withdraw its fees, it would suffer inward breakdown. Some dolefully recall the example of ten pin bowling, which, in the early days of television in the late 1950s, received enormous coverage. Then, abruptly, it all but vanished from the screens. The counterargument is that football is so much more firmly rooted in so many areas that this is unlikely on a worldwide scale, even although there might be minor failures of heart and confidence in football from time to time in this or that region.

In 2007 the UK based television company GTV launched a relatively affordable - £17 a month - package for subscribers in Africa. Broadcasting from the suburban calm of Gerrards Cross in Buckinghamshire, its central selling point is a weekly dose of eight English Premiership and six Italian Serie A matches, twenty one hours of soccer in all. There are already 46 million colour television owners in the region, with the numbers expanding at 10% a year, and their interest in top-class European football is immense. It would be difficult to dismiss world football as a transient craze or fad.

Football and Population

Whither football...what will happen next to the global game? It is seductively tempting to gaze into the crystal ball. Nonetheless, the salutary anecdote may be related of the clairvoyant's kiosk - 'cross my palm with silver; your future revealed' - on a windswept seaside promenade. It was locked and barred and it bore the legend: 'closed owing to unforeseen circumstances'. Unforeseen circumstances do have a habit of catching out the most percipient of historians, as they attempt to trace from the past what might happen in the future. Ecological disaster; nuclear warfare; virulent pandemic; social unrest - perhaps generated by what analysts call the 'new instability risks' of, by 2035, 60% of the world's population living, many of them inadequately housed and fed, in urban surrounds. As Noel Coward was apt to warble, 'there is bad news just around the corner'.

In the context of an analysis that has focused on urban living, it may be salutary to recall the counterintuitive fact that the number of horses in Britain increased rather than reduced because of the industrial revolution, especially in connection with railway freight, such as coal. With a horse population of over 2 million in 1871, the numbers peaked at 3.3 million in 1901, with over half of them working in the towns. During the 1914-1918 war the heaviest cumulative weight of any one article shipped into France from England was not, as might be supposed, ordnance, but fodder for the horses. With each horse generating four tons of droppings annually, a social historian in 1900 calculated that, were horses to grow in numbers at the same rate as in the last few decades, London would be six feet deep in horse manure by 1940. The metropolis was saved from that odorous fate by the arrival of the motorcar.

In the face of such uncertainty, the best that one might offer by way of half-hearted prophecy is to examine the entrails of recent happenings and wonder aloud what might occur should progress continue unabated in the same directions. One might sensibly inspect the question contextually, rather than look narrowly at the game of football itself, for the socio-economic preconditions for football are of paramount import. The three key elements seem to have been, firstly, population, its size and typology, and, secondly, communication, critically now the usage of television, as well as, thirdly, the evolution of the construct of football itself, set, as it must be, against a global political backdrop.

The academic health warning must be reiterated. Population could be decimated by Malthusian factors, like epidemics, like the numbers of people overwhelming the sources of food and water, or like the frequent deadly onset, some of which has already been witnessed in the Balkans and parts of Africa, of what military sources term 'inter-communal conflict'. Television might suddenly be replaced by an unanticipated invention that offers the world a different pleasure through a different mode. 3.2 billion people might abruptly suffer from a surfeit of football and find 'play' in another exercise or diversion...

Population may be the safest gamble of that threesome. The highly competent Yorkshire county cricket team of the 1930s toured North America and were taken to see the Niagara Falls. Stolid and dour, they watched, unmoved, as the excitable guide waxed lyrical about how many thousands of gallons of water a minute cascaded over that mighty brink. Muttered one sombre Tyke, 'well, there's nowt to stop it'. His laconic explanation applies to world population. In just eighteen more years, that is, in 2025, the demographic estimate suggests that there will be a global population of 8.2 billion, something over a 30% growth in that very brief spell. It is estimated that, over this period, the population of sub-Saharan Africa will increase by 80% and that of the Middle East by 132%. One consequence will be a huge conglomeration of the world's younger people in the developing world, with some experts putting the figure as 87% of those under 25 living in these less developed areas. The equivalent of today's world population may watch the 2024 World Cup on television.

What is also fairly certain, even if only because so many people must necessarily crowd more intensely together, is the continuing saga of urbanism, with the conurbation or mega-city ranking high in any analysis such as this. Nearly two-thirds of the world's population will be living in towns and cities by 2025. Jericho, one of the earliest sites to be excavated, dated 9,000 years ago, was a settlement of about 3,000 souls, spread over some ten acres. Urbanisation has raced on subsequently. One or two gloomier prophets have hinted darkly that this is anti-Darwinian, in that humans are adapting the environment rather than the converse. The less pessimistic biologists counter this with the brighter opinion that modern humans building cities are no different from stone age hunters making dwellings from caves or skins, or, for that matter, birds constructing nests. Needs must, where nature provideth.

As well as, in some part because of, expanding population, there is internal migration globally. The kind of country-to-town resettlement that characterised the industrialisation of Britain is sustained almost everywhere. China is the leading example of this today, emerging, from an impoverished start a quarter of a century ago, to become a $2 trillion industrial economy. During the Maoist epoch alone, there was a thirteen-fold increase in industry. Every year 8.5 million Chinese peasants are relocated in cities. Britain has five conurbations of over a million inhabitants; China has 90. The largest is Chongqing, currently a name of cultural anonymity but likely to be much heard of in time, for it is already the world's largest municipality. Chongqing has a population of 31 million, more than Peru, Malaysia or Iraq. Its inner core city has 10 million residents, and, just as during the British industrial revolution when the town populaces grew faster than the nation at large, it is predicted that by 2020 that 10 million will be 20 million, with the whole unit pushing 60 million.

As an example of the essential warning note, the farsighted economist Will Hutton, has voiced pessimistic tones about the Chinese economy, describing it as 'Leninist corporatism'. He views China as a vast centralised state, dominated by the ruling political party, and with no 'public sphere', as with representative government, the press and other facets of the western democracies, to moderate the excesses. The result, he concludes, is waste, instability, corruption and - average income is less than £1,000 a year - continuing poverty often in shanty town circumstances, conditions that could have tragic consequences, political as well as economic.

Notwithstanding such caution, if history goes on repeating itself, those great communes - and, self-evidently, there are others across the world - will require 'play', either actively or more passively, as spectators, and football is well placed to fill that vacuum in hundreds of new and growing cities throughout the world. Unlike ancient Jericho, all those Chinese cities will have a few professional football teams, now or before long, with several possibly hosting their own leagues.

China was home of tsu chu or, in loose translation, 'kick the leather ball', a game apparently played in the Han Dynasty two hundred years before the birth of Jesus in the Christian calendar, and a final example of ancient 'play' with a kicking element that serves as a vague precursor to modern football. Over 2,000 years later, in 2004, a professional league, the China Super League, with a variable number of around fifteen teams, was established. Shandong Luneng won the 2006 title. Apart from qualifying for the 2002 World Cup, the national side had not yet lit many fireworks, but one or two individual players - Sun Jihai at Manchester City and Zheng Zhi at Charlton Athletic - have made some impression in Europe. Their presence has led, as elsewhere in Asia and Africa, to a lively interest in European football. Perhaps even more interesting is the speed of advance of the women's game in China. The national side was the losing team in the finals of both the 1996 Olympics and the 1999 World Cup.

The switchback of global football is being played out in China. Chinese players are migrating to Europe; European clubs, such as Manchester United, Juventus and Real Madrid, have targeted this huge host of people and its apparently booming economy. The most ambitious project involves the entrepreneurs of Chelsea, who are also eager, in the quest for world football dominion, financial and sporting, to make inroads into the Indian and American markets. Through the major Chinese internet portal of Sina, they aim to touch the spirits and pockets of 100 million Chinese fans - the website launch featured Ashley Cole 'speaking Mandarin with a cockney accent', according to one press account. Tours and grassroots coaching are among back-up plans.

China, then, is the latest of the big potential customers to enter the trading mart of global football, as well as an area where football is increasingly popular as a participative and professional sport. It is scarcely a surprising prediction, for it rides on the back of the many basic, if somewhat optimistic, forecasts about economic and social advance in that vast country, but it is probable that China will win a football World Cup within 30 years. Perhaps a woman or two will, by then, have figured in the World Cup finals.

Football and Television

In respect of television, the immediate and likely prospect is for more and better sets and receptivity. All the electronic accessories of mobile phones, computers, video, Sky plus boxes and DVD players are available to supply ever more access to football games and news, to say nothing of the boost to gambling - destined to remain a decided element in football's story - provided by electronic communication. TV sets may become bigger, perhaps with some three-dimensional aspect, and also smaller for highly personalised viewing, while the menu of interactive and other facilities will doubtless improve to even more sophisticated levels of technical artistry. It is surmised that by 2035 there might well be an implantable 'information chip, wired directly to the brain, that could obviously include the latest score from Old Trafford or Chongquing.

The tale of football spreading from the parish pump to the global satellite is naturally one of transportation, of both players and spectators, by rail, by road, by steamship and by flight. While flying times will continue to shorten and airports to proliferate, there is a natural arrest to the speed of travel. We have noted how a pre-industrial society was practically pedestrian in character and how the railways conquered that limitation - but a limit always remains. Flight, for instance, could make possible a weekly Europe-wide league, but a planetary league on a weekly basis is still not quite feasible, bearing in mind the need for recuperation and training. Satellite television has magically turned that premise on its head by instantaneous transmission of games. Basically, there is no temporal boundary to the games one might watch.

The probability is that the rugged power of television companies will erode any remaining stoppages, for example, apropos matches played at the same time as the rest of a league programme. Extended highlights of all Premiership matches are already retrospectively available on Saturday evenings. Most British senior professional matches are, in any event, recorded and soon available. Holidaymakers in European resorts may stroll from bar to bar until they find the one showing their chosen club performing. Furthermore, in that Premiership matches are televised live for foreign consumption, enterprising clubs and pubs have quickly devised technical means of bootlegging games directly on to their screens. The current staggering of a round of Premiership fixtures, often over three days, may develop, until it is possible to see them all as they happen, as well as the situation now, where the unshown games all become available soon after the event.

A 17th century proverb opined that 'sport is sweetest where there be no spectators'. In the 21st century, that opinion may be severely tested. South American gates and many in Europe are low; British spectators, outside of the Premier League are well below previous standards, and there have been some concerns expressed about lower attendances even in that august company. Some African professional leagues offer free entrance, so lacking in briskness are the turnstiles. Yet the African countries are facing an unprecedented marketing assault by satellite television companies, offering inexpensive deals, including a massive input of British and European football, in the run up to the World Cup being competed for in South Africa in 2010. Other sports are facing the same dilemma of good television coverage and bad spectatorship.

It is a blasphemous whisper, but, to add a modern word to another ancient adage, 'the (television) spectator sees most of the game'. It is less expensive, it is more comfortable, it evades the woes of travel, the refreshments are usually tastier, there is less anxiety about crowd violence, the information flow, plus interviews and analysis, is more competent, and, above all, what with endless replays, slow motion reprises and varying camera angles, it offers a more comprehensive observation of the game.

The question might rather be: why should anyone go to the bother of attending a game in person? The direct answers undoubtedly refer to the social and cultural bonhomie, the dramatic sense of 'having been there' and the sheer team loyalty of being present at exciting and meaningful events and, in many cases, devoting a substantial amount of time, money and nervous energy in the commitment. Thus the faithful will queue overnight to line the processional route of, say, a royal funeral, exchanging a brief glance in person for the more synthetic but fuller coverage of TV. It is likely that factor will be sustained in the future, even if to a decreased extent.

It was earlier suggested that the origins of professional football as a draw for spectators were fortunate to fall in an epoch when British crowds were, on the whole, self-controlling, otherwise the authorities might have jibbed at the very concept. Afterwards and elsewhere, it was, of course, too late to alter the direction of circumstances. The brilliance of television does provide the option of playing games behind closed doors, and thereby dodging any hazard of crowd misbehaviour in or around the ground. As we have observed, many clubs around the world are finding this has started to happen unwittingly.

The safety strategies imposed on football grounds in Britain and in other parts of the world, especially in regard of all-seater stadia and more intense stewarding, has halted much of the violent conduct, although it does not follow that the neighbourhoods around football grounds have similarly benefited. Higher prices and the extensive use of pre-booking, season ticket and debenture facilities, plus a shift towards a more middle class and less male dominated audience, have also contributed to a less menacing air on many grounds. There is a sense in which several English Premier League arenas are hermetically sealed venues, with the less biddable fans sifted out. Some supporters mourn the loss of the standing terraces, just as some people claim the Second World War was, despite the killing, the happiest time of their lives, and the platitudinous wail is of lack of 'atmosphere'. It is still, sorrowfully, deemed essential to house opposing fans in separate areas, but, overall, crowd troubles, at least in Britain, are not as dire as once they were.

THE GLOBAL CULT

There was something of a portent in the early months of 2007, in that, in Italy, following extreme crowd troubles, including the killing of a police officer, Filippo Raciti, in Catania, Sicily. As John Foot's valuable book on Italian football, *Calcio*, makes clear, violence is no stranger to the relationship, sometimes financial, of clubs to militant-minded fan groups. Grounds are mainly municipally owned, leaving some undue dispersal of responsibility as to their very rudimentary maintenance and ineffective security. The Italian government, having temporarily halted the whole Italian sporting programme, finally moved to control the menace, threatening 'spectator-free football' unless the clubs could supervise matters more satisfactorily. Brutal policing of the Manchester United and Roma Champions' League quarter final at the Olympic Stadium in Rome in the spring of 2007 and knife attacks by the notorious 'Ultras' suggested that much remained to be done.

Could football cope with empty stadia at the highest level and rely solely on television coverage? Would footballers wilt without the encouragement of the crowd? These are all pointers to what appears to be occurring in terms of football's television coverage. The relatively few who go to matches, compared with the millions who follow events on the screen, are fast becoming part of the show. But the completely spectator-less game would actually be problematic for TV producers. Football is following the paradigm of the music hall, later the variety theatre, that, in Britain, developed at much the same time and for many of the same reasons as professional sport. Television virtually destroyed the variety theatre in the 1950s and early 1960s, but, when it came to supply something close to a light theatrical experience, it frequently found an audience was obligatory for atmospheric purposes.

Shows were thus 'recorded before a live audience' (few contemplated the alternative sort of audience). They were heard and also seen, often having been encouraged by a 'warm-up' merchant, reacting, approving, laughing and clapping, conducted by studio floor managers, taking on the role of Judas goats for the outside watchers, wrapping around them the comfortable embrace of being included in the genial revelry. On occasion, they would be costumed, as in the long-running BBC old-time music hall series *The Good Old Days* or deployed almost as extras, as in BBC's *Top of the Pops*, with teenagers, suitably accoutred, dancing and cavorting to the hits.

The apparel and ritual of the football crowd has already become part of the pageant. The wearing of replica kit or other fancy dress, the face-painting and hair-dyeing, the chants and songs, the tribal rites of rivalship between opposing bands of supporters, the camera captures these and inducts the observer at home into the wider camaraderie of the exercise. Favours, such as posters, scarves or other adornments, are freely distributed to crowds that they might rise in decorative unison to greet their heroes. When this is reproduced at national level, as in the 2006 World Cup, the pageantry of the spectators sometimes bids fair to transcend the not infrequently dreary football itself.

Increasingly, in the future, the actual spectator will probably become more and more akin to the carefully overseen studio audience for the television variety spectacular. Football will be fundamentally a televisual entertainment.

Football and...Football

Whether, in the light of such demographic and electronic challenges, the football itself will change is a matter for conjecture even more speculative than predicting how population or television might behave.

The all-inclusive planetary incidence of football is very pronounced, not only in the widespread playing of the game, but also in the multiethnic constituency of the players. The prominence of club football, with little or no limitation on narrow racial or political boundaries, has led to an exciting cosmopolitan mix. Often derided as the destroyer of local talent and communal affiliation, it does provide the world with at least a simulacrum of tolerant international togetherness. From veteran Europeans playing in Asia to youthful Asians playing in Europe, it lends colour to the theatre of football. Didier Drogba of Chelsea and the Ivory Coast, Michael Essien of Ghana and Chelsea and Samuel Eto'o of Barcelona are currently outstanding examples of Africans assisting their adopted European clubs in great achievements.

As many 'live' crowds diminish and fans gather around the screens to watch the world's finest, the lowlier clubs concentrate more on cultivating nurseries for their loftier brethren, just as working men's clubs, comedy stores and other small venues offered something of a training ground for entertainers, anxious to break into television, after the collapse of the variety theatre circuit in the 1950s. The lower divisions of the professional leagues always included that shot in their revenue-generating locker, but now the application is worldwide. The bigger clubs in the stronger leagues enjoy special arrangements with smaller clubs in weaker leagues, often in other countries, such as Manchester United's link with Royal Antwerp in the Belgian competition, where young players are dispatched on extended loan. On balance, the emphasis remains on Europe, and, within Europe, in its three strongest leagues, with South American and African clubs extremely dependent on European largesse in return for their talented products.

The capitalist ethic rules world football, as it does amid most areas of the global economy, along with, another feature of modern liberal democracy, some input in some regions from local government. It is often said that football clubs do not behave in a business-like manner and that, through maladministration, they do and may come to commercial grief. It is true that football clubs become embroiled with personal, political, communal and cultural ambitions and illusions that, in any self-respecting trading company, would be neutral considerations. It is forgivable to fall into the delusion that, red of claw, all other commercial initiative is unencumbered by such baggage. Right-wing media and other political propagandists try to persuade the gullible that private enterprise is ever more efficient than public engagement. Yet plenty of businesses fail for strictly non-commercial reasons and, in any event, it is in the nature of the capitalist exercise for some to go under and for others to rise and conquer.

So is it and will it be with football clubs. Some will do well and others will founder. They are part of the gigantic service industry. In basic effect, they are subcontracted to the television companies to provide entertainment and, if they do not come up to scratch, either singly or severally, they will crash. The professional football club is in the same position as the pop group. It tours its country, if it is lucky, its continent, hopeful of attracting crowds, building up its reputation, and desperate to earn a breakthrough into major television. Its sponsors and other backers share that hope, keen to see their logos emblazoned on the team shirts, and the advertisements rolling around the inner walling of the stadium, sparkling on millions of telly screens. Similarly the league and cup competitions, and even the very TV programmes that present the football matches, are heavily sponsored.

For the successful players, the rewards are very similar to those of other television stars, with outrageously high salaries paid at the top of the tree. The leading players are treated like pop idols, certain members of the royal family, soap stars and the rest of the celebrity circus. When an appeal has to be made - the lost child, nurses' pay, knifes in street fighting, to cite three recent examples

- the famous footballer, to his credit, is recruited, rather than the prince or the film star. Football, its scandals and highlights, are front page news all over the world. It is a whirling flurry of vulgar opulence, tricked out with gossip and tell-tales, and there is not a scrap of deference, which is no bad thing, nor scarcely a scrap of privacy, which is less acceptable.

Television has already had its effects, for good and ill, on football. Are there more changes in store for the game? There has been talk of avoiding the nullity of the draw, even in league matches, with the melodrama of the penalty shoot-out, although wiser counsels may remind that an honest draw, like a gripping play that ends with the outcome left hanging in the air, may provide a satisfying spectacle. One possibility is that, under the pressure of high fitness levels and the amazing stamina of today's players, the screen may become too cluttered - occasionally, at a corner kick late on, everyone, including the attacking goalkeeper, except for the actual kicker is cramped into the penalty area, not a pretty nor a distinguishable sight. Teams of nine might make for easier viewing, and yet the ancient tradition of eleven, mooted by some sporting antiquarians to have misty origins among the foggy marshes and woodlands of Anglo-Saxon times, is a powerful one.

That conservatism may stem the occasional desire to enlarge the goal. The delicious legend has it that, in the 1860s, a member of one of those seminal old boys' teams sprang to touch the ceiling in one of those central London hotels, where such formative meetings were held, and thereby provided an agreed height for the goals. It is a moot point whether a sublime one-nil thriller or an error-strewn six-all fiasco makes for better entertainment, but, should more goals be required in an epoch of Brobdingnagian goalkeepers, gigantic enough to frighten Jonathan Swift's Gulliver, then the size of the goals may be reviewed.

Those swarming set-pieces mask an alarming amount of wrestling and arm-tugging that mars the game. A referee, at any corner, might conceivably blow his whistle and indiscriminately award a penalty or a free kick to the defence on any such occasion, so grotesquely illegal is the scramble. Because it is committed en masse, it is difficult to control, but it is a vexatious issue, among others, including the nastily inflicted damage to an opponent, the feigned injury, the simulated foul and the harrying of referees. What, from the viewpoint of this scrutiny, is not clear is whether the effect of television - offering an overt image of wrongdoing - is a force for good in this regard, or a force for bad - in that TV presenters may believe that an evil edge sharpens the drama.

THE GLOBAL CULT

A less controversial alteration might be in a simplification of field markings. The six yard box seems now to have little purpose beyond providing a mark for goal kicks, and they could be taken, logically enough, from the goal-line, perhaps from where the ball crossed the line. There may be reasons, in a reversion to the 1890s practice, to extend the penalty area to the touchlines, while, if this were accomplished, it might make sense to limit offside to those areas. So long as the ten yard/nine metre distance rule is enforced, the centre circle and the penalty area arc could be judged redundant, all in an effort to clarify the playing area for spectators both present at the game or sitting cosily in their own homes. In short, the game could be made even simpler.

Another sci-fi possibility that has been mooted is the electronically controlled markings, critically the goal line, to arbitrate more precisely on hair's breadth's decisions. The referral of decisions to television judgement has also been mooted and is already standard practice in cricket and the rugby codes. Here the constant television worry over timing might comfort both the conservative, who feels the referee and his assistants should be left to make human judgements within a human contest, and the sports-lover who detests the longueurs of technocratic decision-making within a fast-moving game. In fact, the truth behind why television or similar technology has not been brought into action lies in the simple fact that no foolproof system has yet been developed which would adequately serve FIFA's purpose of keeping the game ostensibly the same at all levels, from Wembley to Hackney Marshes.

While Wimbledon uses the Hawkeye system (developed first by TV production company Sunset + Vine for Channel 4's cricket coverage in 1999 from the technology which guided RAF missiles to their targets) on only its show courts, and, using wizardry, a high speed processor and a selection of cameras dotted about the court to predict the precise landing point of the ball, football prefers the more prosaic, all-encompassing, and ultimately purer fairness of the human eye.

The game of football itself has not changed much, relative to the vast alterations in the context in which it is played, another example of its simple construction. As with other sports, modern commentators rather agitatedly and maybe superficially claim that today's players are superior. More than dreamy nostalgia prompts one to query this finding, at least to the point of assuring that like and like are being compared. There is a tendency, when these *Star Trek* beamings up through time are imagined, to relocate the old player, complete with his heavy boots and a heavy leather ball on a heavy muddy pitch. The more realistic image is of such players, still with their precious ball skills, their diligent mental concentration and commitment, their abundant confidence and, above all, their shrewd readership of the game of yore, but, having benefited from up-to-date training and dietary techniques, clad in modern boots, pinging the light plasticated ball about a well-drained surface, and with the distinct advantage of more rigorous discipline in respect of charging and tackling. And, of course, while in this *Dr Who* mode of time-transference, one must also envisage today's stars locked in combat of that olden style. A tolerant decision might be that both would do well in either environment, according to their individual lights, and that, in this most straightforward and uncomplicated of diversions, great players would and will be great players...similarly with mediocre ones.

These are all speculative thoughts. Less speculative, for they are matters already being debated, might be changes in international and club football. It is likely that the four year interval between World Cups will remain, for it would be perilous, yet tempting in terms of short-term financial gain, to lower the value by over-presentation, while there is also the standard series of continental trophies to be fought over and won across the world, staggered accordingly. The argument over the status of the tiny principalities will continue and both the continental and global tournaments may have to be reordered to take account of such anomalies.

The more dramatic reforms may come about in club football. The prospects of an Atlantic League for the top teams of the smaller north European nations, or of the two outstanding Scottish clubs finding a place in the English Premiership, have already been mentioned, whilst the concept of a European club league appears to be inbuilt into 'the Champions League' concept of the current major European club competition. This might take the form of the senior clubs, principally, one assumes, the G14 confrères, establishing a full-scale league format, maybe with the top four playing out a knock-out tourney at the season's end. Financially, it could prove most lucrative. If this happened, there would be the usual barney about membership and whether there would be promotion and relegation, against the prudent voice urging the commercial sanity of evading such dreadful hazards and rather feather-bedding the top teams within their own autonomous unit. Whatever the outcome the driving factor will be financial rather than sporting.

THE GLOBAL CULT

Were that to occur, with a club regularly engaged in European outings, home and away, of, say, 30 or more fixtures, the question arises as to whether such a princely outfit would then field a reserve side in the national senior league. The deployment by some top clubs of fringe squad players in cup tournaments in England lends some semblance of credibility to that possibility. It would certainly bring credence to the old jibing riddle about which are the best two teams in Manchester: answer - Manchester United and Manchester United Reserves.

Even more likely, for the precedent has been created in Spain and Italy, although not presently in operation in England, is a Premier League reserve side playing in the Football League Championship or Leagues I and II. For example, Castilla is the Real Madrid reserve eleven playing in a lower league. Jose Mourino, the Chelsea manager and Rafael Benitez, the Liverpool manager, have asked for this to be considered in English football. With large and gifted troupes of artists, they find the sketchy motivation and desultory air of reserve football unwholesome as an arena for encouraging such talent, and would prefer their second strings to face more testing conditions.

In days gone by, the old Central League and London Combination, the homes of Football League reserve elevens, were of a good standard, with the level of football above that of much of the lower Football League divisions and with, at the larger clubs, crowds sometimes of over 15,000. The advent of squad management, rotation of players, and, of course, the use of substitutes tended to dilute the potency of reserve football. It became more the province of up and coming youth players, plus a sort of convalescent home for players returning from injury. Often reserve team football, once enjoyed as a chance to observe the progress of fledglings, has been relegated to strange times and frequently played away from the main club stadium, where the need to keep the turf sacrosanct for the gladiators' next television appearance is paramount.

Incidentally, the English football authorities were extraordinarily and short-sightedly harsh on clubs, like Luton Town, who experimented in the 1980s with all-weather pitches. They were by no means perfect, leading to unnatural bounce and specific injuries, but the response might have been to perfect them, rather than to abandon the idea. As a communal facility, with dozens of youngsters enjoying the thrill of playing on a Football League pitch, and as a money-raising amenity, with lots of concerts, festivals and other sporting shows presented, the artificial pitches had some social mileage in them.

Were the authorities to become more flexible, could one envisage a parallel evolution whereby the likes of Chelsea, Arsenal and Manchester United ran three competitive sides, a super-team in Europe, a Premiership team, and a third team in the English Championship, League One or League Two? With the proviso that no two teams could play in the same competition, because of the effect that might have on the promotion and relegation battles, the logistics would not be unduly difficult to maintain.

It should be emphasised that these guesses are not listed as some kind of authorial wish-list of what urgently needs to be done to improve football and save it from sinking into turpitude and disfavour. It is much more humble than that. It is a navigational essay in studying where and how the currents are running and what erosive and other changes might be effected. Indeed, had historians 50, 100 or 150 years ago tried to foresee what would happen in the football stakes, their prophecies would have probably been overwhelmed by the pace and diversity of events.

Few would deny that the easiest of predictions might be those that suggest there will be no end to insidiously foul play, crowd violence, match-fixing, corruption of all kinds, excessive and sometimes improper gambling, scandals broadcast across the press and media, political intrigue and intervention and all the other sins which have marred football.

Maybe football success in its all-encompassing, all-consuming domination of the thoughts, words and deeds of the vast majority of the living beings on planet earth is that it merely mimics the human condition. It is not wholly good, certainly, but it is not wholly bad. It is right to worry over the evils. It is wrong not to celebrate the good things. Football continues to provide the essential 'play', both energetically active and more vicariously passive, for millions of the citizens of our planet. There are recreational players, professional players, spectators, readers and listeners and, above all, viewers on television. They love the game.

According to Sophocles, Ulysses, that constant personification of fallible humanity, said to his companion, 'but it is a pleasant thing to get the prize of victory; be daring - we shall show ourselves honest another time'. All those millions of fans could empathise with that temporising position. It is likely that for many years they will, despite the tawdry aspects, continue to yearn for 'the prize of victory' that so gladdens the heart and lightens the burden.

THE GLOBAL CULT

Examining England's calamitous loss of the Ashes in Australia over the winter of 2006/07, the distinguished Australian cricket writer Gideon Haigh defined his nation's future cricket prospects in the wry phrase of the retired baseball player Dan Quisenberry. His ironic statement also serves as the canniest prediction of what will probably happen to football. 'I have seen the future - and it's much like the present, only longer.' 150 years on, 'the Simplest Game' of a few ex-public schoolboys has become, and will almost certainly remain for many decades, the planet's premier pastime.

INDEX

INDEX

INDEX

INDEX

INDEX